Programs
That Work

////////////////////////

Programs

////////////////////////

MODELS AND METHODS
FOR WRITING ACROSS
THE CURRICULUM

That Work

/ /

Edited by

TOBY FULWILER, *University of Vermont*

and ART YOUNG, *Clemson University*

BOYNTON/COOK PUBLISHERS

HEINEMANN / PORTSMOUTH, NH

Boynton/Cook Publishers
A Division of
Heinemann Educational Books, Inc.
70 Court Street, Portsmouth, NH 03801
Offices and agents throughout the world

Library of Congress Cataloging-in-Publication Data
Programs that work : models and methods for writing across the
  curriculum / edited by Toby Fulwiler and Art Young.
    p.   cm.
  Bibliography: p.
  ISBN 0-86709-248-3
  1. English language—Rhetoric—Study and teaching.
  2. Interdisciplinary approach in education.   I. Fulwiler, Toby,
  1942–   . II. Young, Art, 1943–
  PE1404.P67   1990
  808′.042′071173—dc20   89–15430
                                                                            CIP

Printed in the United States of America.
94 93 92 91 90 9 8 7 6 5 4 3 2 1

For
Laura, Ann, Megan, Molly,
Anna, Sarah, and Kelsey

Contents

Introduction

Toby Fulwiler
Art Young

Writing-across-the-curriculum programs originated in the mid-1970s at American colleges and universities as a response to a perceived deficiency in student writing and thinking abilities. While the term "writing across the curriculum" (WAC) is fairly recent, the problem it addresses is basic: the relationship among language, learning, and institutions of education. As a consequence, the general movement to establish comprehensive "writing and learning" programs at colleges of all kinds and in all parts of the country has gotten stronger each year: 35 percent of all colleges and universities report having writing-across-the-curriculum programs, according to a recent estimate by the Association of Departments of English (*ADE Bulletin*, Fall 1986).

The movement to treat writing more seriously in all disciplines has caught on nationwide because it addresses simultaneously a number of problematic issues in undergraduate education: For students, writing-across-the-curriculum programs promote general literacy, critical thinking, improved writing, and active learning. For faculty, the programs address issues such as disciplinary isolation, teacher training, curricular coherence, writing skills, midcareer burnout, and institutional morale. These points—in various combinations—have been made in many articles over the last ten years, as can be seen in the carefully annotated bibliography C.W. Griffin has prepared for this volume.

Some writing-across-the-curriculum programs have made real changes in the nature of undergraduate education, while others have made minor changes and still others have foundered after promising beginnings. It seems fairly clear to us that no single model of writing across the curriculum will work for all colleges and universities. In talking to dozens of people who plan, administer, and assess these comprehensive writing programs at small colleges and large universities alike, we found—as you might expect—both points of commonality and points of difference. For example, most institutions (1) articulate remarkably similar program goals: to improve student writing and

1

learning in all content areas of the curriculum; (2) base their programs on a common core of language theorists, most often including some mix of James Britton, Don Murray, Janet Emig, and Peter Elbow; and (3) promote similar process-oriented composition pedagogy. At the same time, we found less consensus on issues such as the nature and scope of faculty training programs; which curricular structures best insure that program goals are met; and sources of new or continued funding.

To date few mechanisms have been available for disseminating information about WAC programs in a systematic and comprehensive manner. At present, information is generally shared in three ways: (1) by reading professional English journals such as *College English, College Composition and Communication, Writing Program Administrator*, and *Association of Departments of English Bulletin*; (2) by attending conferences such as the National Council of Teachers of English and/or the Conference on College Composition and Communication—where individual programs and special-interest sessions are conducted; and (3) by inviting writing consultants to campus to introduce program ideas or conduct workshops. The limitations are obvious: only English teachers read the English journals; only those who can afford it—primarily English teachers—attend the English conferences; and the consultants are few, busy, and fairly expensive. In addition, unless one has a long-term planning grant, it is difficult to schedule extensive planning time among interdisciplinary teams of teachers amidst the hectic routine of campus life.

FREQUENT QUESTIONS

In planning this book, we felt the need to address—concretely and specifically—the frequent and recurrent questions asked by administrators and developers of writing-across-the-curriculum programs. After more than a decade of programmatic activity, we know what many of the questions and problems are. The following questions are typical, if not comprehensive:

Should writing be required in the curriculum?
  Some institutions have conducted long-term faculty development programs related to writing, but have instituted no curricular requirements. Other institutions have voted in place strong curricular requirements (e.g., writing-intensive courses, proficiency examinations) for all students. *Related questions*: In the long run, do all programs need to be curricular? Are there noncurricular models that will achieve the same effect? What is to prevent the curricular models from becoming mechanistic? What have we learned so far from these different approaches?

What kind of writing should the curriculum require?

These are among the more common curricular requirements for writing: (*a*) writing assessments, (*b*) proficiency examinations, (*c*) writing-intensive courses, (*d*) first-year seminars, (*e*) first-year composition courses, (*f*) upper-division writing courses, (*g*) senior seminars, and (*h*) discipline-specific writing instruction. *Related questions*: Which of these work best in which situations? Is some combination of these requirements more desirable than others for particular institutions? Have some of these options produced undesirable effects? And if so, what are they and how can they be avoided?

What faculty training models have proved most effective?

Most WAC programs are teacher-centered, premised on the belief that permanent faculty are the route to stable institutional change. Some programs have offered multiweek summer seminars funded by soft money. Other institutions have conducted semester- or year-long faculty seminars, meeting weekly or monthly—often with released time for participants. Other programs, financed entirely with internal funds, have run one- or two-day intensive workshops at the beginning, middle, or end of semesters. Sometimes faculty training workshops are residential (including overnight accommodations), but more often they are not. And some programs focus most of their instructional energies on graduate students—who, in fact, may do most of the undergraduate instruction. *Related questions*: Do all of these work equally well? What models seem to have the most staying power? How many practical ideas do workshop veterans actually implement in their classes after they leave the safe and inspirational domain of the workshop itself? After one year? After two? After three?

Does WAC also work in secondary, middle, and elementary schools? If so, how do college programs articulate with them?

In order for writing-across-the-curriculum programs to be successful at the college level, some people argue that the ideas should be planted much earlier, before students reach college. Consequently, some colleges actively sponsor training programs for teachers in all disciplines and grade levels. *Related questions*: How well do the ideas promoted at the college level translate to other grade levels? What is a good design for college–school cooperation in writing across the curriculum? Can such cooperation work both ways? If so, how?

What are the goals and objectives of successful WAC programs?

Some programs set out primarily to improve student writing, others to improve student learning—yet in the long run most programs try to do both. *Related questions*: Are the premises of the different programs compatible? Do programs vary in fundamental ways if they operate on different assumptions? Which language theorists support which premises? If one wants to find out about program premises, which books are essential reading?

What are the characteristics of second-generation programs?

Many programs have started with lots of enthusiasm and support only to find both of these elements in short supply later on. Still other programs seem to be flourishing after five or more years. *Related questions*: What mechanisms keep faculty involved over a long period of time? What strategies for self-renewal have been discovered by the more successful programs? How are introductory workshops followed up?

What is the role of the English department in WAC programs?

Most programs have been started by instructors based in the English department. Yet some successful programs have been deliberately located outside the English department. *Related questions*: Are there any successful programs which entirely bypass the English department? Under what circumstances is this desirable? If the English department helped initiate the program, what should its role be two or three years down the line? What are the professional incentives to induce nonwriting specialists to become involved in administering WAC programs? Are there any?

What kind of influence do WAC programs have on the total undergraduate curriculum?

It is sometimes claimed that increased use of writing throughout the curriculum makes learning more active and student-centered (and we are among those who claim this). But it is also apparent that many factors—including student and faculty morale, faculty salaries, pressure to publish, teaching load, class size, student SAT scores, and the like—influence the total undergraduate curriculum. What claims can we make for writing's influence? *Related questions*: What does the research say about the role of writing in creating an active student-centered curriculum? At some schools writing has been linked to other educational programs such as general studies, honors, and core curricula: how successful are such linkages and how do we know?

How are programs funded?

The initial WAC programs were developed at small, medium, and large institutions alike, and were supported by a variety of public and private funding agencies. For example, Beaver College, a small private liberal arts college in Pennsylvania, was supported by the National Endowment for the Humanities (NEH); George Mason University, a large state university, is supported by funds from the state of Virginia; Michigan Technological University, an engineering school, was supported by a grant from General Motors; the University of Michigan, a major research university, was supported by the Mellon Foundation; the University of Vermont is supported exclusively with internal funds. *Related questions*: To what extent have institutions picked up the cost of interdisciplinary writing programs after grant money has run out? How costly do such writing programs need to be? What are the arguments which persuade institutions to operate entirely with internal funds? How do such models work?

How can WAC programs be evaluated?

Attempts to measure the effect of cross-disciplinary writing programs don't seem to have been very successful. For example, those who have claimed that programs improve student writing ability in a fixed period, say three years, have been (to our knowledge) unable to support that claim. What is the problem? Have programs been ineffectual? Or has it been the instruments used to measure them? Are the lines of influence too diverse to measure? Is the training of faculty the best way to affect the writing or learning of students?

These questions are illustrative, not exhaustive, and are fairly typical of those asked after writing-across-the-curriculum programs have been launched, for no comprehensive models existed for such programs until quite recently. As institutions formulated, modified, and experimented with the shape of WAC programs, questions such as these occurred over and over, though the means of answering them remained elusive.

ABOUT THIS BOOK

We have assembled this book, in large part, to allow readers to browse through a real range of program possibilities finally collected together in one sourcebook and to make their own comparisons and contrasts. For one reason or another, however, not every type of program or institution is represented in this collection. Nor are these the *only* or necessarily the *best* programs in the country. There are easily a dozen other programs we are aware of—and probably more of which we are unaware—that deserve featured space in a book like this. However, we went with our best guesses and most available contacts at the time.

In inviting people to write chapters for us, we asked that they include certain common information: (1) the nature and mission of their particular institution, (2) the history and development of their program, (3) how they were funded, (4) how their program is organized, and (5) what problems they faced and continue to face. We also asked that each chapter be cowritten or collaborated upon by interdisciplinary teams of writers so that this would not be simply a tale told by English teachers. In this book you will find frank firsthand accounts of how these ideas work in practice, from as many disciplinary perspectives as possible.

AN OVERVIEW OF THE CHAPTERS

The first chapter describes Georgetown University's program in writing across the curriculum, a program anchored in the idea that writing helps us develop and then express our "way of being in the world of the mind." In describing their program, Slevin, Fort, and O'Connor make a useful distinction between "writing across the curriculum" and "writing within the disciplines"— suggesting that a comprehensive program must address both activities. This chapter describes writing programs aimed at both faculty and graduate students and concludes with specific sample assignments in biology, environmental zoology, sociology, and theology.

In Chapter 2, the UCLA authors focus on the politics of running a writing program at a large research university where undergraduate teaching clearly takes a backseat to research and scholarship. Kiniry, Strenski, and Rose raise thoughtful questions about the role of teaching with writing in an institution where the full-time faculty view their primary teaching role as disseminating knowledge to their students—not generating knowledge with them. Along the way they describe well the plight of the fully credentialed instructor who teaches writing from a nontenure track position, concluding with the observation that the writing program may well be the "university's gadfly and conscience."

Chapter 3 describes the program at the University of Vermont, which has involved several hundred faculty in a dozen writing workshops during its first five years in operation. Dickerson, Fulwiler, and Steffens describe the program's impact in five distinct ways: (1) as generating faculty community, (2) as a pedagogy project, (3) as an introduction to ideas associated with writing-as-learning, (4) as an attempt to improve undergraduate writing, and (5) as an influence on faculty writing. The chapter includes many voices besides those of the coauthors, including a botanist, librarian, mathematician, chemist, German teacher, and business professor. It concludes by describing ten problems the program has yet to solve.

In Chapter 4, the many authors of the chapter on Prince George's Community College provide a close look at a writing-to-learn program in a large institution (36,000 students at 130 locations!) which serves a diverse student body. Most of their students are part-time, older than twenty-one, and come from a variety of ethnic backgrounds. Teachers of psychology, philosophy, and mathematics discuss how writing across the curriculum changed both their own lives and those of their students. Among the strategies they describe are "linked courses," "peer review," and "storytelling."

Williams and Colomb describe in Chapter 5 "The Little Red Schoolhouse," a program they designed to teach writing to juniors, seniors, and graduate students at the University of Chicago. They base their approach on the lessons learned helping doctors, lawyers, and other professionals improve their jargon-riddled writing. In addition, they supply useful insights into the nature of learning that characterize novices and experts in any field, explaining carefully why good writers in one discipline are seldom good writers in another.

In Chapter 6, the eight coauthors from California State University at Chico describe how interdisciplinary faculty leadership creates common purpose in a university writing program. Wedded to the idea that "writing is a means of learning and communicating disciplinary knowledge" for faculty and students alike, Chico has developed a multifaceted writing program that includes a junior-year competency test, writing-intensive courses, student publication projects, and faculty development workshops.

In the mid-1970s, Beaver College became one of the first and most prominent sites for the new movement called writing across the curriculum. Chapter 7 describes the history of this ground-breaking program in terms of an ongoing "conversation" across campus. Much of the conversation described in this chapter focuses on psychology, biology, and English. In addition, the authors explain the way that writing reform at Beaver eventually led to substantial curricular reform.

Chapter 8 features Michigan Technological University, another early successful program still alive and well on the shores of Lake Superior. Flynn and Jones point out that the early years of the Tech program focused on writing and learning techniques especially useful to teachers in the traditional liberal arts curriculum—but perceived as less useful by teachers of more technical subjects. They emphasize their recent and substantial efforts to tailor writing-across-the-curriculum strategies to the particular needs of engineering and science instructors.

Robert Morris, a small private business college in Pittsburgh, is featured in Chapter 9. Sipple and Stenberg describe the origins and special purpose of their program and provide a detailed explanation of how writing has completely changed the nature of one exemplary course in cost accounting. This chapter concludes with a careful look at how "protocol analysis" supplied useful data with which to evaluate the success of their program.

A junior-level writing requirement is the keystone of the University of Massachusetts writing program described in Chapter 10. All juniors at the

Amherst campus must complete a writing component designed and staffed by faculty in their major department. The authors provide a lucid overview of the whole program, with detailed descriptions of how this requirement works in anthropology, physics, and business.

The George Mason writing program flourishes at a large state university in Virginia that is getting even larger. Chapter 11 provides a detailed look at an extensive faculty development program specifically focused on the faculty who teach in a general education program described by the authors as "interdisciplinary and language-intensive." The chapter examines the effect of increased attention to writing in the areas of mathematics, sociology, history, and the fine arts.

The Minnesota Writing Project is the subject of Chapter 12. This multi-campus enterprise is modeled after the National Writing Project, the enormously successful program aimed at improving the teaching of writing in the elementary and secondary levels. Tandy and Smith describe both the early heady successes of this seven-campus endeavor as well as the later frustrations caused by political and budgetary problems that threatened to shorten the scope and life of the project.

The University of Michigan created the English Composition Board in 1978, establishing writing across the curriculum for the first time at a large research university. In Chapter 13, Hamp-Lyons and McKenna tell the story of the development of the comprehensive junior–senior-year writing requirement and provide a close look at two writing-intensive courses—a twenty-student class in linguistics and a hundred-student class in biology. In addition, they provide a useful discussion of "centralized control" in a program enlisting the efforts of many separate departments.

Chapter 14 describes the comprehensive and complex Baltimore Area Consortium for Writing Across the Curriculum (BACWAC). Walvoord and her many associates do not so much conclude the book as suggest additional opportunities for any college program that has not yet created links to other colleges and schools in its neighborhood. Since 1980 this Consortium has been serving more than twenty institutions of higher education and virtually all schools in the Baltimore area. The chapter ends with a description of the benefits of collaboration for four individual schools within the consortium—a state university, a private college, a community college, and a high school.

A selected and carefully annotated bibliography by C. W. Griffin closes the volume. Griffin's bibliography will be especially useful for program developers and administrators who want to pursue current information on a movement that involves both faculty development and curricular reform.

/ / / / / / / / / / *Chapter* 1

Georgetown University

James Slevin, Keith Fort, and Patricia E. O'Connor

> *The way students write reflects the way they think, their fundamental relation to what they are studying, the function and meaning of language in their lives. Their writing is their primary way of being in the world of the mind.*

Institution:	*Georgetown University*
Institutional Size—Students (FTES):	11,900
Institutional Size—Faculty (FTEF):	1,600
Student/Faculty Ratio:	8:1
Highest Degree Granted—	
Institution:	Ph.D.
Highest Degree Granted—English	
Department:	M.A.
Public or Private Institution:	Private

Institutional Mission: an urban, private university committed to the liberal arts, undergraduate education, and graduate programs in selected fields. A selective institution (13,500 applicants for 1,200 places), but committed to affirmative action, with a minority student population of approximately 18 percent.

For more information on the program described in this chapter, contact: James F. Slevin, Department of English, Georgetown University, Washington, D.C. 20057.

Having graduate programs in almost all fields, Georgetown University nevertheless retains—as it has for nearly two hundred years—a strong commitment to excellent undergraduate education. The goal of liberal learning is the basis for the undergraduate curriculum. It is in accord with this goal, not just as a preliminary "service" to it but as its center, that our university-wide writing program has formed its conception of writing. Such a conception informs both our general education courses and our various disciplinary concentrations.

Georgetown has an undergraduate enrollment of approximately 5,000 students, with 375 full-time faculty, all of whom teach undergraduates and nearly all of whom regularly teach first-year and second-year students. While we have as resources fine graduate students who serve as teaching assistants, they are genuinely *assistants*, because all courses are taught by regular faculty members. This institutional policy locates a "research faculty" very much within the undergraduate curriculum, which means among other things (some more important than this, to be sure) that a university-wide writing program has to locate itself fully within the professional life of scholar-teachers who are balancing several demands on their intellectual life: publication, graduate teaching, undergraduate seminars for majors, and general courses for almost anyone who elects to enroll. In any given semester this might mean that a history scholar, for example, can be working on her own professional projects, directing dissertations, conducting a small undergraduate seminar for seniors, and teaching a relatively large introductory course. Writing is obviously essential to all these activities, but not exactly in the same way to each, and the various "ways" writing is essential are not always easy to sort out. Writing may seem "natural" to each, but like much in nature, while it may be predictable it remains mysterious. It was to scrutinize such mystery and to unsettle what we all too easily take for granted as "natural," that the writing program began its work with the Georgetown faculty almost ten years ago. The aims of our program at that time remain essentially our aims now.

THEORETICAL FOUNDATIONS OF THE PROGRAM

Because full-time faculty teach our courses, our program focuses on faculty development, and it begins by addressing certain fundamental attitudes that faculty members generally bring to the question of "student writing." The problem here, we believe, is essentially philosophical, having to do with the relationship between writing and thinking and the place of writing within those intellectual communities we call "academic disciplines." Most university teachers—at Georgetown and elsewhere—do seem to have a generally held "philosophy of composition" that, while not always consistent, serves as a model for the way in which student writing is perceived. The center of this philosophy is a belief that the kind of writing that can be taught is a pragmatic tool for the expression of ideas. Within such a view, writing is not, in itself, fully appreciated as having the kind of importance for the shaping of values that content does. A student's intellectual being is seen as dependent only on *what* she knows, as if *how* she knows it (the way of thinking that becomes the way she writes, the way of writing that so profoundly influences the way she thinks) were a problem different in kind.

In the eyes of many teachers, the ultimate goal for student writing is to make the writing, to some extent, "unimportant." What teachers want in "good" writing is unobtrusive, transparent prose that does not get in the way of their perception of the truths being written about. The attitude they have toward student writing is much like an attitude that parents adopt toward their children. They "rear" writing that they hope will be correct, good-mannered, quiet, and that will do its chores efficiently and accurately. Bad writing is like a badly behaved child who demands parental time for his discipline and training. It is perhaps fair to say that student writing most often receives attention when it is bad.

Fundamental to this view is the separability of "writing" from content and the assumption that there is "neutral" prose. Such an attitude is common, perhaps a defining characteristic of most academics' views of writing. But, when we view writing in this way, we apprentice our students to mediocrity and fail to promote those powers of reflection, wit, humanity, and persuasion that are, presumably, among the values to which a university is committed.

The form and purpose of student papers have a meaning. Writing is, in itself, value-laden and is not a neutral means for the expression of content. The way students write reflects the way they think, their fundamental relation to what they are studying, the function and meaning of language in their lives. Their writing is their primary way of being in the world of the mind.

Our view of writing, then, is related to Georgetown's declared philosophy of education, one that is centered on the commitment to the inherent value of active participation in an educational community. We take it that the notion of a *curriculum*, developed to meet the needs of *learners*, is centered on university programs of study, while the notion of a *discipline* is centered on a shared way of knowing the world and communicating and debating that knowledge. With regard to the teaching of writing, then, we distinguish between the concept of writing across the curriculum and the concept of writing within disciplines. In the former, writing across the curriculum, we look for general practices, common procedures for teaching writing that will work in all sorts of courses; so our attention here will be on generalizations about the writing process, learning, and cognitive growth. The latter concept of writing within disciplines begins with a different question: When a political scientist, or historian, or philosopher discusses the writing she studies and teaches (e.g., the texts of Locke and Hume) and the scholarly and student writing that intends to say something convincing about those texts, what does she mean by *writing*? While the answers to this question may be many, the premises behind it are supported by some of the best current research in rhetorical and cultural theory. Our notion of "writing within a discipline" embraces both the student writing submitted and the writing studied by student and teacher together. When we talk about "writing" in philosophy, we mean not only student papers on Locke or on the epistemological issues Locke raises and addresses, but also *Locke's* writing and the writing of those who study Locke.

A discipline is characterized not simply by its object of inquiry but by principles governing how propositions about that object can properly elicit interest and assent, can legitimately induce in other members of this community the conviction that a particular idea is not only true but also important to know. To master a particular discipline is in part to understand how statements of truth can genuinely inform one another or be made persuasive. How one effects comprehension, concern, and assent—that is, the study of writing and rhetoric—is thus a central question in all disciplines. Raising such a question underscores the notion that to know a discipline is to know, through attention to writing, how one forms the truth, makes it understood and persuasive, and thereby contributes to the collaborative study undertaken by the community of scholars and writers who constitute that discipline.

Within this framework, the scholarly endeavors of our faculty are not an obstacle to good teaching but a major resource, because the process of writing is at the center of their active participation in their disciplines. SCHOLARS TEACHING WRITING: if a slogan is helpful, that would be ours. Often when scholars are asked to become teachers of writing, they do so with a tacit understanding that for the time being they must put their own scholarly interests and commitments aside in favor of teaching. We believe that, rather than putting them aside, they should make them central and use them to guide their students as emerging writers within an educational community. Then, rather than seeing their scholarship as relevant only to the *content* of their courses, teachers would see that the activity of their scholarly work is directly relevant to the way they can talk to students about writing. They can draw upon their own scholarly activity and writing processes as resources in their work with student writing.

Within such a conception of scholarship and teaching in an educational community, the place of writing is altered. We give more attention to the academic and human values implied by certain writing assignments, and we encourage students, as part of their efforts to master the material of the discipline, to explore the values inherent in the way we ask them to write about that material. We spend time discussing the relationship between writing (the writing in the assigned texts and the writing prepared by students) and what it means to become members of that discipline's intellectual community. By its nature, all such writing serves a function not only in the student's learning but as an activity essential to the advancement of knowledge within the disciplines and within the larger educational community. Our program is designed to help faculty to understand this conception of writing more fully, to examine its implications, and to give such an understanding its rightful place in the study of traditional disciplines.

GOVERNANCE, STRUCTURE, AND GOALS OF THE WRITING PROGRAM

The Georgetown writing program came into being in what we take to be a somewhat unusual way. It began early enough so that it was not the brainstorm of some administrator who had somehow heard about WAC and decided that every campus needed one. Ironically, it emerged out of a program with high school teachers. This "articulation program," funded by the National Endowment for the Humanities (NEH), brought together eight or ten Georgetown faculty from different disciplines with high school teachers from different subject areas to explore how writing could be integrated in the curriculum of local schools (especially the District of Columbia's public school system). Early in that program, the desirability of offering similar opportunities to Georgetown faculty became obvious, and a group of faculty undertook to explore with our colleagues how that might best be done. This exploration took almost two years, involving extensive interviews and surveys, with follow-up meetings to examine particular proposals. In short, the program was from the beginning envisioned and shaped entirely by the Georgetown faculty. The administration has been, throughout this process, responsive in the best sense—appreciative and supportive. Support began with funding for a full year, with encouragement to seek outside support to supplement the university's commitment. NEH generously funded this program for our second through fourth years, so that in its formative stages we had sufficient funds to establish a permanent program. During that period, we were able to work with over one hundred of the regular full-time faculty, reaching twenty-seven different departments in all five undergraduate schools. Upon this foundation the program now continues, entirely supported by the university. It also remains entirely a faculty project.

The program is guided by a University Writing Committee, made up of faculty from across the campus. Permanent members of this committee are now former participants in the program along with the chair of the English department, the Writing Program's codirectors, the director of the Writing Center, and the program coordinator. The committee's responsibility is to monitor all aspects of the program, recommend changes, develop new ideas, and submit an annual report to the provost. In general, this committee is responsible for coordinating the writing instruction provided throughout the university, from introductory courses for first-year students to advanced seminars for graduate students. Its main function is to guide and evaluate the work of the program's three major components: (1) faculty development, including symposia and workshops available to all faculty members; (2) the training program for graduate teaching assistants; and (3) the special program for English department faculty. (These three components are discussed at greater length in the following sections.)

Specific authority for the planning and daily administration of the Writing Program rests with the codirectors. They are appointed by the provost, in consultation with chair of the English department, the college dean, and the Writing Committee. Since the directors have generally come from the English department, the budget is processed there—a choice made by the Writing Committee, which judged that such an arrangement was more likely to secure permanent funding and retain control of the program in the hands of the full-time faculty who directed and participated in it. Specific responsibility for budgets, scheduling, and a host of related administrative duties falls to the program coordinator, a full-time position shared with the English department.

FACULTY DEVELOPMENT PROGRAMS

Faculty Symposia on the Teaching of Writing

At the heart of the program is the faculty symposium offered each spring, usually in May just before graduation. It is worth noting that we sponsor several kinds of symposia in addition to this one. Most are shorter versions of this (two days rather than a week) but designed essentially to achieve the same basic aims. It is the longer symposium, however, that best illustrates the sort of faculty development we have undertaken.

During the period when the program was funded by NEH, we sponsored a two-week session attended by twenty-five faculty members representing almost as many departments. Having worked with well over one hundred colleagues, we have begun to reduce the size of this introductory symposium in order to offer different kinds of follow-up workshops and meetings for those who have already been through the symposium. So we now work with anywhere from twelve to fifteen faculty, and we have limited the length of the symposium to one week.

Each participant currently receives a stipend of four hundred dollars for participating in this symposium, which is an intensive study of up-to-date theories of rhetoric and composition and their application to writing in all disciplines. These discussions are open-ended, giving all participants a chance to explore different ways of approaching and solving shared problems. We open our symposium with the admittedly impossible task of looking at writing in our society as a whole, then we consider writing at Georgetown in the lives of both faculty and students. For the first few sessions, participants are asked to think about writing as a way of learning, writing as a political act, the philosophical implications of the forms of writing we teach, and (to relate these issues to a particular poststructuralist intellectual movement) modern academic writing and its relation to feminism. In this context, we examine the way writing assignments, forms, processes, and audiences differ among the various disciplines represented by participants. We then devote a full session to bashing the English department (one of the codirectors is its frequently bashed chair), asking what the English department now does or doesn't do to prepare students for writing across the university.

The next set of sessions is concerned with Georgetown students as writers, exploring the background students have when they come to us, along with the usual and even the unusual problems they face. All of these sessions are attended (and some of them are led) by Georgetown undergraduates, usually tutors in the Writing Center who can look at student writing from both sides of the conference desk. Within this framework, we also discuss ways of working with underprepared students and students whose first language is not English.

We then turn to the issue of creating effective assignments, asking all participants to bring samples of topics they have used and addressing such questions as these: What makes a particular assignment ''work''? What kinds of assignments don't work? What are the relative merits of different kinds of papers and examinations (including length, frequency, etc.)? We also relate this concern with assignments to a more fundamental concern with the audience for student writing, addressing the faculty's generally unquestioned assumptions that almost all academic writing is for the teacher. We also attend to some of the standard concerns of writing pedagogy: the uses of prewriting, nongraded writing, peer review, and collaborative work to improve student writing and to form a community of inquirers. We encourage participants to consider the process of their own writing and the communities they form through writing in relation to what they ask students to do. Here, as at other times during the symposium, several former participants join us to discuss the classroom strategies they have found most effective.

The final phase of the symposium concerns the creation of a sequence of writing assignments and a plan for a writing-intensive course. We ask participants to prepare or revise several short writing assignments or a single longer assignment that they will be using in their writing-intensive course next year. We suggest that it might be preferable to try these in the first two or three assignments of the semester, since doing them will allow participants to explain the purposes of writing in the course, to give some directions on format and methods, and to introduce students to a few of their own main concerns about writing and its relation to learning and thinking. We encourage them to try to incorporate in these assignments such techniques as peer review, guiding students through the process of writing, specifying and diversifying audiences, encouraging revisions, and so on.

These writing-intensive courses are not required of our students, since our aim is rather to encourage faculty to reconsider how they integrate student writing in all their courses, not just special ones. And "writing intensive" will mean different things in different fields. But, to establish some common ground, we ask participants to think of such a course as including conscious attention to how learning in a discipline is enhanced by writing and to place some emphasis on good writing as being of value in itself. A writing-intensive course, then, need not require more writing, but rather a shift from regarding writing as a mere tool toward seeing it as an integral and valued part of the discipline. Through this exercise, we hope that participants will be able to identify the various purposes that student writing can serve in the study of their discipline, explaining to students the aims and pedagogical emphases of the course. Since the audience for these assignments is the students they will teach, we commission the three or four undergraduates who have worked with the symposium to read and comment on these pieces, a "role-reversal" of both symbolic and practical importance.

Follow-up Activities

During the following academic year, while participants are teaching a writing-intensive course, we meet regularly to discuss further the issues raised during the summer. These follow-up activities, scheduled and conducted by the symposium's codirectors, are important because the application of what participants learn during the summer requires continued discussion and guidance. After they have taught the course, the teachers submit formal evaluations to the Writing Committee, which then uses them to guide the creation of other writing-intensive courses throughout the university.

In addition to individual and small-group meetings, we also sponsor workshops to which all former participants are invited. We usually try to identify particular concerns that are widely shared, and then gear the session toward an open discussion rather than a highly directed presentation. Recently, for example, we conducted two such sessions. The first followed from our concern with the audiences and forms of academic writing, and the difficulties students face when encountering unfamiliar disciplinary requirements. Our aim here was to help individual faculty create statements about the intellectual methods, genres, conventions, and style considered appropriate to different disciplines. A sample selection, "To My Students," by Timothy Wickham-Crowley of Georgetown's sociology department (reprinted later in this chapter) illustrates the sort of thing that can emerge from sessions like this. The second follow-up workshop this past year focused on the interests of the many linguists and foreign-language faculty who have participated in the program (roughly 20 percent of the total). They became interested in some of the theoretical as well as practical issues of learning to write a second language, whether it be foreign students working in English or American students working in one of our foreign-language courses. During this workshop we developed a proposal for an international conference devoted to these questions, and a committee of former participants have continued this planning.

TRAINING PROGRAM FOR TEACHING ASSISTANTS

As mentioned above, Georgetown expects all courses to be taught by full-time faculty, so that no courses are actually taught by teaching assistants. But, in our larger lecture classes, the professor usually has little opportunity to offer extensive personal advice to individual students—except in the form of comments on drafts or completed papers. Georgetown TAs, who meet with the students in discussion sessions to go over course lectures and assigned readings, and who hold special office hours for these small groups of students, are in a good position to offer the kind of personal attention that seems essential to improving a student's writing. With effectively prepared TAs, then, even large lecture courses can function as writing-intensive courses. The professor can now confidently require that papers be submitted in stages that reflect the process of scholarly research and composition—that is, in a series of submissions beginning with prewriting and notes, then a rough draft, then a more complete draft, and finally the finished paper. At each stage, the student receives from the TA the kind of guidance that improves not only his writing but his learning.

To assure that such guidance is of the highest quality, the Writing Program provides TAs with special training in the teaching of writing. Each week, TAs from five different disciplines meet in small, discipline-specific groups with one of the Writing Program staff to apply readings to specific examples in the disciplines and to formulate methods for bringing writing, reading, and speaking experiences in to the conferences and discussion sessions held by all the other teaching assistants in the various disciplines. Additional full-day meetings for the participating TAs occur twice each semester; they are designed to share experiences unique to the various disciplines and to find common approaches to teaching writing. For their participation, TAs receive a modest stipend in addition to the university's fellowship award. Our major goal throughout each year-long program is the "raising of consciousness" by helping the TAs to explain to their students that learning to write means learning how to discover ideas and communicate them effectively and persuasively. While this training program cannot duplicate entirely the objectives of the faculty symposia and workshops, it nevertheless addresses the same basic issues. Ultimately, it provides yet another way of helping undergraduates to see the profound connection between learning to write and entering fully into the educational community of each particular discipline.

SPECIAL PROGRAM FOR ENGLISH DEPARTMENT FACULTY

At Georgetown, no matter how successful our efforts to encourage and improve the teaching of writing in all disciplines, it is in our English courses that students receive their primary training in writing. We endorse, rather than lament, this fact; and we want to make such writing instruction the best it can be. For this reason, we have devised a special program designed specifically to assist a faculty who, while committed to the teaching of writing, have been trained primarily as teachers and scholars of literature. This program, involving high school teachers *as colleagues* in this attempt to learn what should be done, is in some ways unprecedented.

In 1980, Georgetown's primary writing course was called "Expository Writing"; it was *staffed* by (generally) unwilling faculty who taught it every three or four years, out of a sense of duty; and, it was *taken* by (generally) unwilling students who enrolled because they were required to do so (as the result of a placement examination). Beginning in 1984, with the help of the NEH grant, the department started to change both the nature and "status" of this course by involving full-time faculty in both its planning and its teaching. With the help of Writing Center Associates (high school teachers enrolled in our graduate program) and through weekly staff meetings for those teaching it, faculty members taught the course with greater enthusiasm and commitment, developed through their exposure to current theories of rhetoric and composition. In 1987, at the suggestion of these faculty, Expository Writing was upgraded to the status of all our other freshman courses and was renamed the Writing Workshop. Student interest is now high—in fact, it is always the first course to fill in both the fall and spring semesters (and this without the coercion of the placement exam, which has recently been dropped completely).

The Georgetown teachers in the program are selected from among those scholar-teachers of literature who have not regularly taught writing courses but who have an interest in expanding their knowledge of how to teach writing. Each year, four different members of the English department participate. As more and more faculty members have been prepared to teach these courses effectively, the department has been able to offer more sections on writing at the freshman, intermediate, and advanced levels. The place of writing in our literature courses has been dramatically altered, becoming more integral not just to the study of particular texts but also to the way these texts—the writing itself—can be conceived.

DESCRIPTIONS OF SAMPLE COURSES

Given our assumption that the aims and forms of writing differ among the various disciplines, generalizations about writing-intensive courses and about the program's effect on the curriculum can be made only with caution. As the following descriptions make clear, we have encouraged individual participants to use the symposium primarily to build on their *strengths* as teachers; that, rather than some conformity to guidelines, has been our main goal in redefining the place of student writing at Georgetown and in promoting curricular and pedagogical change. It is in accord with that aim—of making it possible for faculty to rethink what they are doing and build on their successes—that the following documents in fact have come into being. Longer versions of all of these pieces first appeared in *Developing Writing*, the Writing Program's newsletter, published quarterly and distributed to every faculty member. The purpose of this publication is simply to make the work of program participants available to all faculty—for their consideration. This is as close as we want to come to telling people what they "ought" to do.

If forced to generalize, we would suggest that the program's most productive and permanent changes have occurred in these areas of our colleagues' use of writing in their courses: (1) developing ways to motivate students to care about their writing—as writers care; (2) clarifying the relationship between learning and thinking in a given field and within the discursive conventions of that field; (3) developing in students a more sophisticated sense of writing as collaborative and intertextual; and (4) empowering students to take control of their writing by questioning how it serves their own knowledge and the knowledge of those to whom it might be addressed.

Writing in the Sciences: An Example from Biology

Douglas Eagles is among the most distinguished scientists and teachers at Georgetown. He has always had great success in his classroom, and students recognize and appreciate the rigor with which he approaches their assignments. But he enrolled in the writing program symposium because he felt a gap between the writing students did for him and his own work as a scholar. What is innovative for Eagles in the course described here is his willingness to reduce the amount of student writing in order to focus more on the quality of what gets produced and on the audience, aims, and process of scientific writing, which depends regularly on collaboration. His own revised, writing-intensive course manages to bring writing itself successfully into the foreground as an essential part of science, so that students may come to see that their own work, like the scientist's, is as much a matter of rhetoric as of laboratory investigation.

/ / / / / / /   *Writing in Environmental Zoology*
Douglas Eagles

Environmental Zoology is an advanced undergraduate biology course, focusing on the range of physiological adaptations which animals employ in meeting the stresses of their environments (e.g., heat, desiccation, cold, etc.). There are two lectures and one four-hour lab each week. In the laboratory, students design and conduct well-controlled physiological experiments (some including small animal surgery) and prepare well-organized and well-written scientific reports.

Since communication with one's peers is a central part of the scientific enterprise, I decided to reduce the number of laboratory reports so that the students could devote their efforts to producing reports of high quality. An important part of that goal is met by giving students formal responsibility for reading and making constructive comments upon the efforts of their colleagues, thus going through the process most scientists employ in preparing their work for publication. These efforts elevate the laboratory report to a level approaching that of published scientific literature.

The goal of this exercise was to get the students to take writing seriously and to make it a more visible part of the overall process of doing science. My hope was that they would see this as more of a "real life" experience than most course laboratory efforts, which have generally been viewed as merely college exercises. Although more work was required for each exercise s/he prepared or evaluated, there was a significant reduction in the number of reports each person had to write. The point was to place more emphasis on quality and thought and less on "just filling in the blanks." Finally, I hoped to make the students aware that they were writing for the audience that would judge their work for the rest of their careers: their peers.

Laboratory exercises were to be written using the standard five-part organization characteristic of most modern scientific journal articles. This format consists of the following sections: Introduction, Materials and Methods, Results, Discussion, and References Cited. I provided students with full descriptions of the aims and discourse conventions of each section.

Students were organized into self-selected groups of three and, in the first laboratory, assigned titles of *Organizer, Experimenter*, and *Reader*. During the semester, students rotated through these positions on a weekly schedule and in an orderly, consistent manner. The Organizer was the person who prepared most extensively for the lab, organized the group's activities, and wrote the lab report. The Experimenter did most of the "hands on" work during the experiment.

The Reader then had two tasks for the next week—to prepare for the upcoming lab as its organizer and to read the lab report. In reading the lab report, the Reader was expected to (*a*) correct every overt error (typos, spelling, grammar, etc.) on the report; (*b*) list the difficulties he or she had reading it (figures, wording, arguments, conclusions); (*c*) list the strengths of the report ("good introduction" *because*, etc.); (*d*) write a list of suggestions for improvement; (*e*) keep these points in mind for writing his own report during the following week; and (*f*) submit the report and his appended comments. The author of the report was invited to make his own remarks, including an evaluation of the helpfulness of the Reader's comments and suggestions. Within this system, then, students not only wrote reports but regularly reflected on that writing, serving as "peer reviewers" not only in the sense that composition theory uses the term but also in the way that scientists regularly serve their colleagues.

In general, I was quite pleased with the way the students responded to this effort and with results it produced. One of the biggest obstacles, however, was getting the students to write for their peers; they knew very well who was grading the paper and so they wrote what they thought would please that person. During the latter part of the semester they seemed more inclined to write to their "colleagues," probably because most of them were receiving the same sorts of comments (and they certainly talk among themselves) and possibly because they finally realized that I meant it when I suggested that they might want to have others read their reports and make suggestions that they would use in their final submission. Some apparently feared that that was cheating, even though I had indicated that it was an acceptable practice in this course—as it is in the scientific community.

In any case, I intend to continue with this format, with one addition. At the beginning of each lab, after we have received the first reports, we will have a brief "round table" discussion on the good and bad points of the group of reports, without indicating whose report is under discussion. The purpose of this discussion will be to get the students to relax a bit, to realize that they share many of the same problems, and to approach the task of writing as one which merits just as much attention as the experimental work.

Writing in the Social Sciences: An Example from Sociology

Timothy Wickham-Crowley has only recently completed his Ph.D. at Cornell and now teaches in the Department of Sociology at Georgetown. He partici-pated in the most recent writing symposium because he wanted to work out for his students, and in some ways for himself, a sense of the distinctive features of writing in his field. So he concentrated on preparing a statement for his students, generalizing about the characteristics of sociological thinking and then relating these characteristics to the discursive forms in which they are embedded and by which such thinking is made possible. These are not so much guidelines as concise meditations, addressed to his students, on such issues as the nature of sociology, the role of the researcher's personal values in sociological inquiry, and the place of theory and methodology in particular sociological investigations. He then derives from these meditations a series of suggestions and admonitions about the form and style of students' writing, raising important questions—much discussed and quite vexing, particularly in sociology—about the proper balance of a specialized vocabulary suitable to disciplined thought and a more accessible style that can make that analysis available to readers.

/ / / / / / / /   **To My Students: Writing Guidelines for Students in Sociology**

Timothy Wickham-Crowley

Students are often unfamiliar with sociology and with the work of sociolo-gists, the former only one social science among many at the modern university. A hidden theme of *any* course in the university is the attempt to get students to think, argue, and write in the manner appropriate to the discipline they study. Sociology is no exception. Some of the points that follow apply to all the social sciences—anthropology, political science, psychology, economics, demography—while others focus much more narrowly on sociology as a distinctive kind of intellectual enterprise.

How Do Sociologists Approach the Study of Social Life?

1. Society is *organized* both in peoples' thoughts and in their behavior (that is, both in culture and in social organization). Social life is neither random nor chaotic. We therefore try to detect, measure, and even explain those *patterns*. Your mission, therefore (should you decide to accept it), is to participate in such intellectual adventures, to push back the chaotic appearance of day-to-day life in search of underlying regularities.

2. Social life is not reducible to psychological states: if we as human beings

have a singular psychic substructure, why do societies vary so greatly in their social patterns? Hence, individualistic psychology can make at best only modest contributions to our understanding of *social* patterns.

3. We cannot view all sociology simply as studies of the behavior of *individuals*, or *micro*-level studies. Sociology often takes as its topic the study of larger organizations, even entire societies, whose patterns are produced through *interaction* among social "units": among individuals, among small groups, among classes and races, among organizations (e.g., war and diplomacy). Such patterns of interaction produce *social structure*, whose nature in turn affects individual behavior. These latter topics display sociology in its other "hat" as a *macro*-level discipline.

4. *How* do sociologists study their chosen topics? Max Weber described our mandate as one of "*value-freedom*." Does this mean we have no values, no hopes, no fears, that we're emotionless robots? No, and indeed our values may well dictate the topics we choose to study. For example, I have chosen the study of revolutions and economic development because, with the potential exception of nuclear war, I believe these phenomena have had the most profound effects on human lives in the modern era, and I wish to understand the contributions they make (or do not) to human misery and welfare. Weber argued that we should adopt the (value-laden) stance of choosing to treat social life (including social values) as "given," rather than as "good" or "bad." One may hate or fear homosexuality, capitalism, slavery, political violence, concentration camps, or totalitarianism. Yet widespread hopes and fears about them have not precluded the objective description, analysis, and casual study of change in each of those areas of life. Our mandate, then, is to treat all social life simply as *there*, rather than good or bad, and to describe and explain it to the best of our modern abilities. We can even apply this stance to the study of values themselves (cf. R. Williams, *American Society*)!

5. Toward these ends, sociologists attempt to apply careful, often highly sophisticated *research methods* to their chosen topic, and to try to produce *theories* or explanations of the varied outcomes they study, whether they be revolutions (or their absence), crime rates (and their variation across groups and nations), or varying rates of illness among people in different social groups or situations.

How All This Relates to the Way You Should Write

1. Since sociology is about *general propositions*, not unusual cases, our attention as sociological writers should be firmly on the general. We are concerned about typical patterns of the American middle-class family, not your personal biography therein. Therefore try not to get bogged down in unnecessary detail. Telling examples are fine—they often drive the general point home—but do not confuse single examples with "proof." In our writing, therefore,

we should *state* those general propositions, as theories and hypotheses, and then *consider the available evidence*—whether we or others generate it—to see whether it tends to *support or disconfirm* such propositions.

2. Nonetheless, *marked exceptions* to those patterns (*anomalies*, or exceptions to the rule) often merit our special attention, and hence a portion of our prose. Yes, many (most?) children of poor, black families later remain poor as adults. Yet some succeed. Reginald Clark has studied those latter cases closely, and found that they come from family backgrounds different from those of their peers who "inherit" their parents' poverty. Anomalies give us pause in our rush to generalize, and often force us to *clarify our concepts*, or invent new ones, which can adequately account for both the pattern and the anomalies. Perhaps poverty itself is not a "vicious cycle," but the de-emphasis on literacy skills in poor households: those families, rich and poor, who emphasize reading skills can pass on more "cultural capital" to their children, which better prepares them to succeed in school and beyond.

3. Sociological writing therefore should always force *confrontations between theory and evidence*, to see if theory tends to be supported, supported only in qualified or reconceptualized form, or disconfirmed.

4. Does this mean you should write like professional sociologists? Given the typical prose in the *American Sociological Review*, I certainly hope not. No, instead pay attention to (most of) the mandates laid down by classic guides such as Strunk and White's *Elements of Style*. If you must imitate sociologists' prose, consider economic stylists, such as George C. Homans or C. Wright Mills; or more elegant writers, such as Robert K. Merton or Robert Nisbet; or those who combine elements of both, such as Peter L. Berger and Barrington Moore, Jr.

5. When writing your sociological pieces, believe that you have something important to say, for *I* believe that you do. If that is true, then you must consider your audience as well, and try to communicate with them in your clearest, most comfortable prose.

Writing in the Humanities: An Example from Theology

James Thomasson is a professor in the theology department, where he has taught since 1967. Over the years, he had developed a teaching style that emphasized process, and he decided to participate in the writing symposium because he sensed a possible connection between his own pedagogy and our program's process approach to writing. The writing-intensive course he developed builds on his own theories by incorporating writing more centrally in the kinds of reflection and critical analysis expected of students. Through this use of student writing Thomasson successfully connects formerly discreet activities into a powerful sequence that, with its reliance on such techniques as peer review and collaborative writing, resembles the Freirean mode of instruction so clearly aligned with his own aims as a teacher. The students' final project reflects a new awareness of how Thomasson's own theory of "processive learning" can find an enabling institutional form in the carefully sequenced writing process required for the course's final, synthesizing essay.

/ / / / / / / / *Writing in Theology: The Problem of God*
James Thomasson

Rationale: The "problem" of God is "man." Whether or not god or gods exist, from the earlier expressions of human culture "man" has expressed *belief in* or *the sense of presence of* some reality transcendent of his own being and somehow responsible for it.

In this course the student-learner is asked to join me, a teacher-learner, in an educational adventure. Two specific presuppositions are woven into the fabric of the course: (*a*) that learning is a lifelong process, triggered by a sense of wonder or the pain of alienation, threatened by radical uncertainty, renewed by the joy of discovery, and urged onward by desire to know the self and its world; (*b*) that processive learning is liberating to consciousness because it challenges established "worlds" of meaning, truth, and value and dares to engage the present and dream the future as creative acts. In short, learning is an adventure of critical consciousness.

Methods: The course highly prizes extensive reading and reflection and intensive writing. Students will read varied and important writings drawn from several disciplines, just as the "problem of God" cuts across many disciplines. Critical reading and reflection are necessary for discerning the various dimensions of this problem. At the same time, the ability to think critically cannot be separated from the concern for forming one's thought with clarity, precision, vitality, and creativity. Therefore, the course will promote intensive writing in the service of effective discussion. The presupposition here is that good writing assists good thinking in becoming good conversation.

Format: There are two lecture sessions each week, with the class divided into discussion groups for the third hour. Each discussion group is divided further into writing teams of four to five members. During the course of the semester students are responsible for *five* writing assignments (see below), three to be written independently, two to be the result of collaborative writing by the writing team.

Discussion groups will focus primarily on the relation of the readings to the issues covered in class. Students are encouraged to write a critical analysis and evaluation of the reading to serve as the grounding for participation in the discussion.

Writing Assignment for Discussion Groups: Students will prepare a two-page critical analysis and evaluation of the reading for sessions indicated on the reading schedule. Emphasis will be on a critical evaluation of the author's position in light of the student's own position or in relation to existential experiences the student can articulate or other authors' positions with which the student is familiar. Within the writing team students will read and critique each other's essays, writing helpful comments where appropriate.

Three of the five papers will be rewritten by the student to take into account the peer review by members of the writing team. Each student is responsible for submitting (*a*) the initial draft, (*b*) critical comments by other team members, and (*c*) the final draft of the critical essay.

On two of the five final essays the writing team will produce a single integrative essay resulting from the labor of all team members. The team's writing exercise will comprise individual essays and commentaries leading to the final collaborative essay.

Processive Final Examination: Two weeks before the end of the semester each student will submit a three- or four-page essay expressing his/her own resolution of the "problem" of God. This will be a working draft to be commented on and returned. One week before the end of the term each student will present a three- or four-page critical, synthetic evaluation of the "problem" as seen from the points of view of the various authors of the course readings. This, too, will be commented on and returned. Finally, students will produce an essay in which they articulate their own position from the correlative points of view of the readings.

CONCLUDING REMARKS

These three sample courses illustrate some of the basic strengths of our program—foremost among them, we think, our commitment to the integrity and independence of individual faculty and our confidence that, by increasing their concern with student writing, making student writing a central concern of the course, individual teachers can only improve what they already do best. Like many others at Georgetown, these teachers have developed ways to bring writing into the foreground as an aspect of the discipline they teach, to encourage effective writing processes, and to specify how the writing will serve and be served by the thinking that students are asked to do. In addition, these and other faculty have begun to specify the writing's aims and audience, to describe and explain conventional forms, to engage students in collaboration with one another, and to clarify their expectations and the standards that will be used in evaluation.

Of course, not all participants find *all* these changes compatible with their aims as a teacher; but nearly all are willing to consider change, and most have altered their pedagogy in beneficial ways. This general receptivity makes all the more puzzling one area where success has not been so easy: our colleagues' tendency to discount the importance of (to use the current formula for a complex and important function of student writing) "writing as a way of learning." This, one of the major principles of most writing-across-the-curriculum programs, simply has not taken hold here at Georgetown, despite the fact that faculty express strong interest in the idea and support of its basic aims—at least during the pastoral harmony of our symposia and workshops. Something seems to happen between May and September, and we are, quite frankly, not sure what that is.

We try to rationalize our failure with a number of stock answers, among them this one: if our students are already motivated and prepared to succeed (and they are), then they seem to learn "naturally" and do not need encouragement or training in producing discovery drafts or exploratory journals. Of course, this characterization, even if true, is hardly pertinent, since students rarely engage as fully as they could in the kind of preliminary inquiry and critical investigation that can so enhance their writing. Our faculty, if pressed, would surely acknowledge that.

Perhaps a more basic explanation has to do with what members of a research faculty assume about the aims of their courses and discourses. In the three samples above, faculty members see writing in dynamic terms, but the "explorations" and "discoveries" that interest them are historical and collective—occurring among readers and writers in a public forum. In each of the courses, the process that interests faculty most is what follows from writing, not what precedes it, not the individual writer struggling to construct a meaning through writing. What matters, for example, is the exchange among the biology students, or effective persuasion in the sociology class, or the collaboration in the theology class. This priority is consistent with what our colleagues seem to value in their own work, for to them the excitement of writing is publication and participation in the disciplined exchange that publication makes possible. For them, writing means responding to prior writing and inviting others to respond in kind. They all too often simply take for granted what goes into making their own writing powerful in just this way.

Perhaps the Writing Program does too little to challenge what our colleagues take for granted. From our theoretical perspective, every discipline is essentially historical, and its history is a history of discourse that responds and leads to other discourse. The questions we tend to emphasize for students, then, are these: How do they learn to read so that they can enter this history, join this dialogue? How do they learn to situate themselves, through their own writing, within the central, debated issues in their field? In other words, how do they learn to write so that their writing elicits other writing, thereby joining the historical dialogue? The major advantage of this theoretical perspective is that it enables a writing program to embrace the whole life of the university and to conceive of it in terms of writing, which is thereby placed at the *center* of the university's goals.

But it is clear that this view takes too much for granted, and that ways must be found to help faculty, and in turn their students, recognize the important relationship between writing and learning. Fortunately, as our Writing Program enters a more mature phase, no longer needing to justify itself but rather confident of the goodwill and support of the institution, we find ourselves in a position to work again with former participants. That is, having reached about one-third of the faculty, we are able now to divide our attention between the interests of those who have yet to participate and the pressure we feel from former participants who want to continue their discussions of writing. As we return to the latter, we can try to raise in more substantial ways our consideration of how they produce texts—with particular attention to how their reading is itself "productive." This conception of reading seems consistent with our larger theoretical framework and useful in rethinking how writing—as process and as metaphor for critical reading—enables knowing and all that follows from a knowledge that is worth sharing and debating.

We need to address directly, then, the nature of analytical reading and interpretation, again with the same sensitivity to disciplinary distinctions and their different conventions for constituting and questioning the meaning of a "text." To attend so directly to reading may seem to threaten the focus of a "writing" program, but this is less likely if the texts studied (interpreted and criticized) are seen as writing and if student papers are among the texts studied. When reading is seen as producing writing, it can also be seen as produced by writing. These subtle, intricately related productions are what has been and can be meant by "learning," in the ancient, still to be recovered understanding of that most important word.

REFERENCE

Freire, Paulo. *Pedagogy of the Oppressed*. New York: Herder & Herder, 1970.

/ / / / / / / / /   *Chapter 2*

UCLA

Malcolm Kiniry, Ellen Strenski, and Mike Rose

> *Perhaps that is the true function of a cross-curricular writing program: to be the university's gadfly and conscience.*

Institution: University of California at Los Angeles
Institutional Size—Students (FTES):   34,400
Institutional Size—Faculty (FTEF):   2,400
Student/Faculty Ratio: 14:1
Highest Degree Granted—
  Institution: Ph.D.
Highest Degree Granted—English
  Department: Ph.D.
Public or Private Institution: Public

Institutional Mission: an urban, public university; only the top 12 percent of high school graduating class eligible for admission; one-third of students are ethnic minorities. Consistently ranked among the top half-dozen research universities in the nation, it is one of the largest university-based research institutes in the world.

For more information on the program described in this chapter, contact: Ellen Strenski, UCLA Writing Programs, University of California, Los Angeles, CA 90024.

Two quotations can frame the predicament of writing across the curriculum at a state-funded research university like UCLA. The first is the opening sentence of *The Research Universities and Their Patrons* (Rosenzweig, 1982: 1):

> A research university is one whose mores and practices make it clear that enlarging and disseminating knowledge are equally important activities and that each is done better when both are done in the same place by the same people.

The second, a local echo, is taken from UCLA's current *General Catalog*, which announces the administration's perception of what it means to call UCLA "one of the outstanding 'research universities' in the country." The catalog copy explains:

> It means that the same faculty members teach both undergraduate and graduate courses and that these instructors create knowledge as well as transmit it. They spend a major portion of their time engaged in research in libraries and laboratories and out in the field.

Superficially, such declarations seem unimpeachable: our teachers, nationally acclaimed in their fields, are not above undergraduate teaching. But the phrasing of both statements betrays an attitude toward student learning with damaging overtones for student writing. Professors "enlarge" and "create" when they publish professionally; when they teach, they "disseminate" and "transmit." We can call this the "broadcasting metaphor" for university teaching—students are seen as passive receptors on a one-way channel. But if "enlarging" and "creating" include not only additions to the aggregate pool of human knowledge but also intellectual growth aroused in students, the communication needs to be at least two-way. Writing—assigning it and responding to it, drafting and revising it—is, of course, the best medium for such communication. Research universities, however, are just not structured to reward scholars for spending time assigning and responding to student writing. At UCLA, as in other research-based universities, many undergraduate courses don't assign writing, and when it is assigned, it is more often used as an evaluative tool rather than a pedagogical one. This attitude isn't universal—there are many individuals and some departments that make thoughtful use of student writing—but it is systemic and common. It is part of the climate within which a writing program with cross-curricular interests must try to move. Encouraged in some quarters (but always somewhat against the university grain), "UCLA Writing Programs" has had a significant but qualified influence upon the UCLA campus.

THE DEVELOPMENT OF UCLA WRITING PROGRAMS

UCLA Writing Programs came into being during 1979–80, from a convergence of circumstances. One was a growing unrest with the quality of writing across the university. Another was a campus conference on undergraduate education, which formalized that feeling by calling for a more concerted effort to deal with student writing. More crucial than either of these, however, was a backlog of students unable to enroll in the freshman composition course required of them by the university. During the late 1970s, a dwindling number of graduate students, together with the sustained popularity of the English major, created a demand for more composition teachers. Seizing the opportunity, Richard A. Lanham of UCLA's English department, buttressed by the institutional support of Executive Vice-Chancellor William D. Schaeffer, who had recently returned from his tenure as MLA executive secretary, sought and received funding to create a new program. The program was incorporated into the existing composition section but was expected to develop new writing courses as well. It was conceived as semiautonomous, reporting directly to the dean of humanities but dependent upon the English department's Executive Committee for hiring decisions. Lanham was appointed the first director of Writing Programs and became simultaneously vice-chair for composition on the English department's Executive Committee.

Backed with the financial go-ahead, Lanham spent the remainder of 1979–80, with a staff of six, surveying the perceived writing needs of other campus departments and recruiting faculty. By the fall of 1980, over thirty lecturers had been hired to staff Writing Programs and a reorganized Composition Section (Lanham, 1983: 169; See References at end of chapter). This arrangement did not deprive teaching assistants of jobs, but it did radically shift the proportions of lecturers and TAs in the composition classes. Lecturers were hired as temporary faculty, on one-year contracts renewable up to four years. Although lectureship positions, technically called "Visiting Lectureships," were a well-established convention at UCLA (most departments employ a few lecturers, usually to staff large introductory courses), there was no precedent for a program composed entirely of lecturers. To make these positions attractive to new Ph.D.s and ABDs, Writing Programs was able to offer an attractive starting salary, a reasonable teaching load, and the promise of professional enhancement. New faculty were encouraged in various ways to make their freshman courses cross-curricular, and they were offered the chance to develop relations with other departments through two new types of adjuncted writing workshops (Lanham, 1983: 160ff.). Writing Intensive English (English 100W) was offered as a two credit course attached to a specific course in another discipline, and was to be taken by a portion of the students in that base course. A Writing Component was also offered as a workshop conducted by a writing consultant within the base course, and took up several of its class hours—an infusion of writing pedagogy.

In the years that followed new structures emerged and others shifted. Carol P. Hartzog became acting director of Writing Programs, and Richard Lanham moved to the new position of executive director. Various advanced, upper-division writing courses were developed, some of which remained undifferentiated while others became specialized (pre-law, pre-health care, pre-business, etc.). Components dwindled in popularity and eventually disappeared. The Intensives courses (English 100W), increasingly popular with both students and faculty, burgeoned, though not without pedagogical problems. As Writing Programs faculty developed more expertise with individual disciplines, teaching strategies shifted. The early 100Ws, for example, had emphasized revising strategies and style to a degree perceived as helpful; in later courses Writing Programs lecturers began to intervene more directly in writing decisions involving substance, genre, and perspective.

Conditions of employment also began to shift slightly for lecturers. Under the representation of the American Federation of Teachers at the statewide level, the four-year limit on lectureships was rescinded in favor of a six-year limit; then the six-year limit itself gave way to a new possibility. After six years of employment and after undergoing a stringent review, some lecturers can now qualify for renewable three-year contracts. In 1987 seventeen of the forty-five lectureships were occupied by people with sixth-year status, while a maximum of only eight three-year contracts were being granted to Writing Programs by the university's central administration. Writing Programs currently faces its largest turnover of personnel since its creation. The departure of nine or more of the veteran faculty, combined with the usual attrition along with the extra attrition of those apprehensive about their own approaching sixth year, meant that the program was faced with a potential turnover of some 50 percent of its faculty in 1988–89.

UCLA WRITING COURSES AND REQUIREMENTS

As do all the University of California campuses, UCLA requires its entering freshmen to take a placement examination. About 40 percent are first held for remedial writing instruction; the others go directly to Freshman Composition. Unlike the other UC campuses, however, UCLA requires only one quarter of this required freshman composition instruction; other University of California campuses require two quarters (e.g., UC Santa Barbara) or even two semesters (e.g., UC Berkeley). UCLA has no exit writing-proficiency exam, nor are there any other general campus writing requirements (such as a junior-year composition course) although specific departments and programs do have their own writing requirements, and all undergraduate courses in UCLA

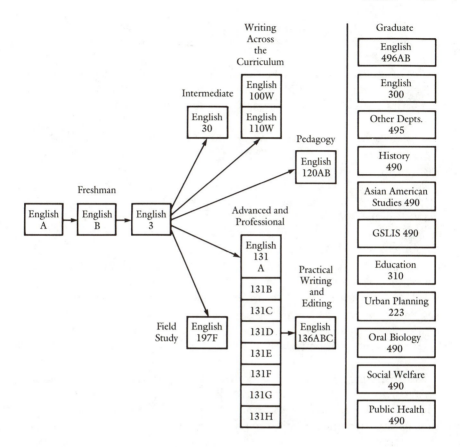

Figure 2–1
Prerequisite Path for Writing Programs Courses

Writing Programs are required by some major or program. Almost all courses in Writing Programs are cross-curricular in nature; their purpose is to prepare students to fulfill the demands of the writing tasks they face in their other courses or in their professions after they graduate. Figure 2–1 illustrates the range and relationship of courses taught by UCLA Writing Programs.

English A A noncredit basic writing course introducing students to academic reading and writing.

English B A noncredit basic writing course consolidating instruction in the conventions of academic writing.

English 3 Freshman composition course focusing on sophisticated strategies of academic writing, especially analysis and argument.
Includes a research component taught by college librarians.

English 30   Intermediate course built upon challenging books (not anthologies) in the natural and social sciences. Includes a research project related to students' majors.

English 100W   A two-credit (half-course) writing workshop paired with selected courses outside the English department wherein students work on improving the specific skills they need for success with writing assignments in the paired course.

English 110W   A four-credit course otherwise identical to English 100W.

English 120   A writing course stressing language issues of special interest to prospective school teachers.

English 131   A series of advanced writing courses tailored to various professions or fields: business, pre-health care, pre-law, journalism/communications, fine arts, science and technology, and literature.

English 136   A series of advanced courses in practical writing and editing for students intending to enter the publishing profession.

English 495   A two-course series for teaching assistants on theories, methods, and issues of writing pedagogy.

Graduate Courses in Other Departments   As indicated on the figure, Writing Programs lecturers teach a variety of writing courses in other departments and professional schools. These courses aim to help students write up their research for publication as well as to revise papers related to their graduate study.

Worth noting, as well, are two affirmative-action programs with strong cross-curricular emphases. The Freshman Summer Program offers underprepared and economically disadvantaged students (most are minority students) the opportunity to adjust to the college environment by taking a pair of courses during the summer before their freshman year. Students take a basic writing course along with a course from another discipline (recent offerings have included courses in computer science, geography, history, political science, and psychology). The program's administrators, instructors, teaching assistants, and tutors meet frequently to coordinate assignments and discuss pedagogy—a collaborative arrangement made possible by the program's self-contained hiring structure.

The Freshman Preparatory Program is also designed to help underprepared students, mostly minorities, to meet the demands of writing across the curriculum. This program enables students to move through the sequence of composition courses during the regular academic year under the guidance of the same instructor—and supported by extra class-time, tutorial assistance and instruction in word processing. These sequenced courses, culminating in English 3, are not attached to courses in other disciplines, but most are decidedly cross-curricular, introducing students to the discourse of science and social science as well as to literature. One instructor has experimented with a sequence designed to complement social science courses, and another has constructed a sequence of writing courses with a biological emphasis for apprehensive would-be premed students.

THEORETICAL/PHILOSOPHICAL FOUNDATIONS

UCLA Writing Programs has been informed from its earliest days by a coherent pedagogical philosophy. The following curricular principles— developed for our freshman courses—also apply, with a few modifications, to our upper-division and graduate courses. They represent our approach to teaching composition and inform the spirit if not the letter of all our courses. Note that they promote cross-curricularity and force a melding of process pedagogy with a concern for proficient academic performance.

1. Writing must be taught as a vital process that aids the storing, structuring, discovering, and re-visioning of information for self and others, a process central to our attempts to make sense of the world.

2. University students must learn to write the kind of discourse that is central to academic inquiry.

3. When possible, writing assignments should be built on the kinds of materials students encounter at the university. This approach will contribute to the interpretive skills students must have and, as well, provide an introduction to thinking and writing across the disciplines.

4. The most efficient writing curriculum is one in which classes build sequentially on one another as do specific writing assignments within each class.

5. Grammar and mechanics should not be taught in isolation. Rather, this instruction should be woven into the writing students do, provided through indirect methods like stylistic imitation, or offered individually in conferences and tutorials.

6. Composition instructors must encourage their students to try new words, syntactical patterns, and new rhetorical devices; a dogged insistence on correctness can stifle linguistic exploration.

7. Motivation and intelligence ought to be expected of university-level students. Writing curricula, then, should challenge the student, even in a "basic" course, for high expectations contribute to high performance.

8. Stylistic and rhetorical issues should be the concern of all levels of composition courses.

9. Instruction in writing must include instruction in reading.

Since these principles—and no specific prescribed texts, topics, or approaches—are what shape the program, individual instructors have a great deal of freedom in constructing their courses. They are encouraged to make informed choices as a result of continual dialogue, reappraisals, and readjustments. The expectations of such ongoing pedagogical self-critiques are established at the initial job interviews, carried on through a fairly lengthy faculty orientation, and extended through classroom visitations and informal staff seminars. This system of freedom within constraints has helped to establish coherence while promoting creativity and self-determination. Administratively, this structure requires ongoing negotiation, but it allows for a fluidity of dialogue and invention that keeps the program vital.

SAMPLE COURSES

Let us describe in more detail three of these courses, stressing their cross-curricular orientation. After each general description, we offer an example of how a particular instructor has interpreted the course.

English 3 ("English Composition, Rhetoric, and Language")

English 3, the required freshman composition course, as George Gadda, assistant director for Freshman Writing, has described it,

> focuses on sophisticated strategies of academic writing, most notably analysis and argument, and involves students in the practice of research that serves that writing. Academic writing itself becomes, increasingly, an object of investigation as students learn how conventions of reasoning and writing vary across disciplines.

In English 3, students are asked to write a minimum of five papers (from three to five pages), at least one of which must draw on independent research.

Within this general framework, approaches to English 3 vary widely according to the preferences of instructors. Nearly all require drafts and revisions. Most make use of peer editing groups. Many range widely across the curriculum. Some stay closer to the traditional literature course, though usually with readings selected around a central theme. A number of instructors favor the "great ideas" approach exemplified in texts such as Lee Jacobus's *A World of Ideas* or *The Course of Ideas* by Jeanne Gunner and Ed Frankel of Writing Programs. Others prefer to structure their courses topically and with mostly contemporary readings, employing readers such as Laurence Behrens and Leonard Rosen's *Writing and Reading Across the Curriculum* or *Making Connections Across the Curriculum*, a reader constructed from the theme-centered courses of ten Writing Programs' lecturers (e.g., "The Urban Experience," "The Nature of Learning," "The Nuclear Predicament"). Still other instructors have developed their own theme-centered courses and have compiled their own sets of readings, printed according to proper copyrighting procedures by UCLA's Academic Publishing Service. (Some sample themes: "Freedom and Control," "Darwinian Thinking," "Perspectives on Los Angeles," "Ways of Seeing."

Example: An English 3 With A Literature Emphasis. While it is misleading to offer any single version of English 3 as representative, Dr. Cheryl Giuliano's theme-centered English 3 course illustrates one that stays within the spirit of the cross-curricular guidelines while confining itself to literary texts, in this case fiction.

This particular English 3 was taught within the Freshman Preparatory Program described above and thus had the advantage of building upon the previous quarter's curriculum. In the prior course students had been asked to explore the theme of "Individual Conscience vs. Authority" in readings that included the "Obedience to Authority" chapter in Behrens and Rosen, Peter Elbow's *Writing Without Teachers*, Thoreau's "On the Duty of Civil Disobedience," and *A Clockwork Orange* by Anthony Burgess. Drawing upon the students' experience with the earlier course, and particularly with *A Clockwork Orange*, Dr. Giuliano's English 3 addressed the theme of "Alternative Languages." Particularly apt in a class of underprepared students who are faced with problems of adapting to academic language, the course presented a sequence of novels—*Riddley Walker, The Color Purple*, and *Huckleberry Finn*—which require the acquisition of unusual languages on the part of the reader. The process by which students work through these texts, says Giuliano, "models imitations they will perform later in adopting academic discourse." The students' progressively nuanced experiences with the imaginative use of language in these books also help to break down the stifling misapplications of "right" and "wrong" language that they may have brought with them to the classroom. "Accepting alternative language systems in an academic setting sets the tone for honoring all forms of English, academic and nonacademic." The topics for assigned papers are sequenced so as to get students to explore with increasing complexity their own choices as writers.

English 30 ("Intermediate Exposition")

Many students who complete the composition requirement, either at UCLA or through transfer courses, still need lower-division instruction in writing. This is a common university problem, and even when advanced courses are offered—as they are at UCLA—they tend to be too advanced. English 30, designed and first offered in 1984, has become a popular and valuable option for students who find themselves in this uneasy situation between freshman composition and advanced exposition. English 30 builds upon challenging readings that represent the types of full texts students will encounter in specific academic fields. At the same time, by means of a sustained research topic, it introduces them to the research tools and strategies they will need within these fields.

This research project can take several different forms besides the traditional term paper. Depending on the individual student's interests and major, it usually lies somewhere between an argumentative essay and a state-of-the-art report. For example, a humanities major might choose to write an argumentative essay organized around a strong thesis having to do with, say, the ethics of genetic engineering; an engineering student, on the other hand, might want to document and then prepare a thoroughgoing update on developments in robotics or CAD/CAM (Computer Assisted Design/Computer Assisted Manufacturing).

English 30's built-in comparative approach to academic disciplines necessarily (through book-length readings and assignments) requires students to draw on information in the natural and social sciences in addition to the humanities. If fiction is assigned, then it is used to demonstrate ways the humanities can represent knowledge, not to teach techniques of literary analysis. The success of English 30 in meeting its goals may be measured by the steadily growing number of students who take it and by the the number of lecturers who ask to teach it.

Example: English 30 With a Social Science Emphasis. Dr. Bruce Beiderwell has designed an English 30 course around *The Mismeasure of Man* by Stephen Jay Gould and *An Essay on the Principles of Population* by Thomas Malthus. He chose these texts because of the range of possibilities they introduce. Not only does each raise important issues of its own, but they play off each other in many interesting ways, illustrating how quasi-scientific information can be exploited in a variety of disciplinary contexts to promote particular economic, social, political, and other interests. The two texts also embody and illustrate a variety of topics, conjectures, methods, styles, uses of evidence, tones, implicit explanatory models, and tacit assumptions. Beiderwell uses these readings for analysis, for stylistic emulation, for critiques, for summaries—indeed, the whole range of composition-class activities. From methodological and conceptual issues raised by Gould or Malthus, students generate topics for their own research paper projects, as related to their own majors. For example, applying appropriate explanatory models from course readings (e.g., Gould's analysis of the cultural determination of scientific and other beliefs, or Malthus's analysis of the effect of competitive demand on finite resources), students have written research reports on such different topics as new methods of countering soil erosion, the conflict between Jefferson's racial ideology and his democratic ideals, the impact of political change on the changing perception of beauty in twentieth-century Persian culture, and the influence of psychology on the growing use of indeterminate sentencing in California courts.

English 100W ("Intensive Writing")

English 100W is a two-unit writing course (that is, half a regular course) offered in conjunction with a course in another discipline. All 100Ws work with the writing assignments of the base course and stress organizational strategies, analytical thinking, and revising techniques. The base courses have been paired with twenty-eight different departments (e.g., biology, chemistry, computer science, folklore, history, political science, military science, sociology, women's studies, etc.). We offer a disproportionate number of 100Ws attached to sociology courses because it is a graduation requirement for sociology majors. Our experience teaching these courses is reflected in *A Guide to Writing Sociology Papers*, with coauthors from both Writing Programs and the Department of Sociology.

The internal dynamics of the 100Ws have varied considerably in relation to their base courses. The most important variables include the amount of writing assigned in the base course, the timing of those assignments, whether supplementary assignments seem necessary or helpful, working relations of the writing teacher with professors and TAs of the base course, the extent to which the two courses share the same standards for good writing, and the rhetorical range customary within the discipline itself. The best 100Ws have achieved reciprocally close relations with their base courses; these relations, however, are by no means fixed but are matters for continual negotiation.

Example: An English 100W attached to Biology 5L. Biology 5L ("Organismic and Environmental Biology") is an introductory laboratory course in which students have their first experiences writing lab reports. The 5L/100W attachment has existed for several years, and during that time both courses have been modified under each other's influence. Biology 5L has become more sensitive to writing pedagogy: the three major lab reports increase in difficulty as students gain familiarity with the form; typed drafts are required for two of the three reports; TAs are encouraged to respond carefully to these drafts, but without simply becoming an editorial service; and students are given additional short assignments throughout the quarter that help them to refine their appreciation of how good reports work. In addition, the course introduces students to the biomedical library, and the three main reports make increasing demands in using research literature.

For its part, the English 100W has grown more committed to working within laboratory conventions and to paying precise attention to the logic and details of particular experiments. Where early versions of the course worked primarily at a stylistic level—for example, on matters of conciseness, syntax, and word choice—more recent versions have helped students to think through more fundamental questions about the construction of hypotheses, the presentation of evidence, and the development of fully interpretive *discussion* sections. Like the base course itself, the 100W now builds in sophistication as the course progresses. Early classes are apt to focus on conciseness, coherence, diction or on the many matters of format which seem so alien to students encountering research reports for the first time. As the course goes on, the emphasis shifts toward decisions about context, evidence, logic, and likelihood; and the teacher-student relationship becomes more individualized as different students run up against very different problems.

Thus, in its current form the 100W attached to Biology 5L calls for a close knowledge of students' experiments. It also requires a willingness to make judgments about scientific quality and a somewhat aggressive resistance to the bifurcated expectations students often bring to the two courses ("You'll be grading us for style and the biology teachers for content, right?"). One of the functions of the 100W has become to draw into the open for discussion certain decisions which might otherwise rest unexamined. None of this would be possible, of course, unless Biology 5L itself were conceived, not as some kind of scientific cookbook course emphasizing experimental procedures, but as a course in experimental thinking.

The Future of Writing Across the Curriculum at UCLA

The future of writing across the curriculum as an emphasis for learning at UCLA depends upon the complicated business of university politics. First, there is the problematic position of Writing Programs itself. As a nondepartment without tenured standing, it depends for its continuity and mission upon the favorable disposition of the English department and the university administration. How the university interprets its new contractual relation to lecturers will do much to determine whether the possibility of relatively secure employment encourages ABDs and new Ph.D.s to pursue cross-curricular expertise, or whether the Writing Programs lectureships become merely temporary way stations for those who have not yet landed the tenure-track literary jobs they are after.

While it's hard to imagine Writing Programs disappearing altogether, it is possible to imagine its role shrinking to the traditional Guardian of English, the enforcer of minimal writing standards. It's also possible that Writing Programs can hold its ground as a program promoting intellectual inquiry through courses that speak to the concerns of departments across the campus. It's even conceivable that Writing Programs might play a larger role—for instance, through the development of an upper-division writing requirement tailored to specific majors (something like our present English 30).

Also important to the health of writing across the curriculum at UCLA will be the preservation of an interdisciplinary emphasis in its freshman composition classes. At present, this emphasis is by no means a settled accomplishment, but something for continual negotiation. Composition instructors at all levels of freshman English are free (within the guidelines of the curricular principles) to choose their own texts and develop their own writing assignments, and thus there is no imposed cross-curricular agenda. The selection of texts and creation of assignments with cross-curricular benefits are matters of individual judgment and collective propagandizing. Writing Programs lecturers as a group are by no means united on how far across the curriculum composition classes should be trying to reach. More crucially, the English department teaching assistants who now staff approximately half of the composition courses tend, understandably, toward more conventionally literary interpretations and approaches in those courses. They are encouraged to move in cross-curricular directions through their TA training, including the mandatory pedagogy course described above. Some graduate students are also hired each year by the Freshman Summer Program, where they get intense cross-curricular experience. Despite such influences, however, it's still possible to teach composition at UCLA without feeling a strong motive for cross-curricular teaching. It's an issue that needs perennial reopening and airing.

More broadly, the future of cross-curricular writing at UCLA depends on attitudes toward writing from various departments across campus. A part of Writing Programs' mission has been to promote more writing—and more thoughtful uses of writing—in a variety of departments. The contact has been successful in many ways, but the strongest connections of course have been with departments and individuals already committed to writing. There are still many departments and many instructors who either do not assign writing at all, or who use it exclusively as an evaluative tool rather than a pedagogical one. It's still possible in some majors—not only in the hard sciences but also in fields like economics—for students to avoid any serious engagement with writing. Sophomores often find themselves with their most intense college writing experiences behind them in their freshman composition classes. The widespread faculty indifference toward undergraduate writing seems to have ebbed significantly in the 1980s, however. Further, the university's newly restructured general education requirements should help; departments have been urged to include more writing assignments in their introductory courses. But these guidelines are more advisory than binding. Departments such as history, which are already committed to giving good writing prominence in their courses, take the guidelines most seriously. It remains to be seen how valued writing becomes in the introductory courses of most other departments.

Also, each department's commitment to assigning writing can only be as strong as its own graduate students' interpretation of how to respond to that writing. Undergraduates at UCLA can expect a very good deal of what they write to be evaluated by teaching assistants, but TAs in departments other than English are rarely trained in how to work with student writers. Even where conscientious, their comments are all too often either just editorial in nature or intellectually dismissive. Writing Programs lecturers have worked in ad hoc ways with the TAs of various courses, such as English 100W, where they have come in contact with them, and Writing Programs is in the process of trying to institutionalize a more formal role in TA training. The issue, at bottom, is financial. TAs need to be remunerated for the extra time a real commitment to student writing demands, and departments need to make the rewards for that commitment palpable.

More broadly still, stress on cross-curricular writing will depend not only on making the teaching of writing urgent on campus, but also on making it imperative in the schools. The realization that writing serves a multiplicity of purposes in college (not to mention in work and life) needs to be recognized and communicated as forcefully as possible, especially to high schools, which are even more rigid than universities and often tend to behave as though writing is a skill that is solely the domain of English departments (Applebee, 1981). In this regard, UCLA has a well-developed program—the Center for Academic Interinstitutional Programs—for making university resources available to high school teachers, particularly those in the Los Angeles School District. Through this Center, Writing Programs lecturers have played a significant role in making contact with local high school teachers, including some from subject areas other than English. This influence needs to be sustained and extended.

Finally, the success of cross-curricular writing at UCLA, as elsewhere, depends upon the willingness of its participants to use writing to address real social issues in a truly interdisciplinary spirit. The opposition to writing across the curriculum in this sense is specialization—entrenched, proprietary, and premature specialization. But at its best, writing across the curriculum isn't just a buzzword meaning "lots of writing in lots of places." It's an endorsement of the belief that writing—as a means of synthesis, analysis, and influence—is one of the most powerful instruments we have for making sense of the world. So valued, writing across the curriculum encourages students to think critically, in shifting contexts, about their own lives and about the institutions which shape their experience, including the university itself. It's far from clear that a state-funded, research-oriented university is in the business of supporting such a critical endeavor. Carol P. Hartzog, former director of UCLA Writing Programs, has pointed out that writing programs "bring into question our common understanding of academic structures and procedures, our very notion of academic legitimacy" (1986:71). Perhaps that is the true function of a cross-curricular writing program: to be the university's gadfly and conscience.

REFERENCES

Applebee, Arthur N. *Writing in the Secondary School: English and the Content Areas.* Urbana, IL: NCTE, 1981.

Hartzog, Carol P. *Composition and the Academy: A Study of Writing Program Administration.* New York: Modern Language Association, 1986.

Lanham, Richard A. "Composition, Literature, and the Core Curriculum: The UCLA Writing Programs." In *Literacy and the Survival of Humanism.* New Haven, CT: Yale University Press, 1983.

Richlin-Klonsky, Judith and Ellen Strenski, *A Guide to Writing Sociology Papers.* New York: St. Martins, 1986.

Rosenzweig, Robert M. *The Research Universities and Their Patrons.* Berkeley, Los Angeles, London: University of California Press, 1982.

The University of Vermont

Mary Jane Dickerson, Toby Fulwiler, and Henry Steffens

> *The more students write about something, the better they
> learn it; the better they learn something, the more active they
> are in discussing and writing more about it; and the more
> active they become as classroom learners, the more active they
> become in the intellectual life of the campus community.*

Institution	University of Vermont
Institutional Size—Students (FTES):	11,100
Institutional Size—Faculty (FTEF):	870
Student/Faculty Ratio:	13:1
Highest Degree Granted— Institution:	Ph.D.
Highest Degree Granted—English Department:	M.A.
Public or Private Institution:	Public

Institutional Mission: primarily the liberal arts with a strong
emphasis on teaching and scholarship. Called a ''Public
Ivy'' with highly selective enrollment for 50 percent out-of-
state students admitted and moderately selective for 50 percent in-state students admitted.

For more information on the program described in this
chapter, contact: Toby Fulwiler, Department of English,
University of Vermont, Burlington, VT 05405.

> What I needed from this workshop is a way, or ways, to help my students to write well, and to help me to incorporate writing into the thinking and learning process in science. To me, to write well is to think clearly, and to think clearly, you need to write things down. The two are interconnected. In a nutshell, this workshop has brought those ideas forward in my mind, crystallized them, and provided me with some concrete examples of how to implement writing in my courses. This is the best thing that I have done at UVM to improve my awareness of teaching. In a few months, I will tell you if the ideas work.

These words, written as an anonymous evaluation at the conclusion of a Faculty Writing Workshop, describe what continues to be the most important feature of writing across the curriculum at the University of Vermont—an engaged faculty. Instructors go away from our two-day workshops full of good feelings, enthusiasm about teaching, a renewed interest in their own writing, and, of course, with some ideas about ways to implement more writing into the courses they teach. Perhaps even more important, however, is the sense of community they discover at the workshops. Now, after six years, writing across the curriculum at the University of Vermont has many authors and speaks through many voices. This chapter is our attempt to capture these several dimensions of the Vermont program.

THE FACULTY WRITING PROJECT

Vermont's Faculty Writing Project formally began in February 1984, in a two-day workshop at the EconoLodge Conference Center two miles from campus—just far enough away from mailboxes, telephones, students, and committees to allow full concentration on the role of writing in the UVM curriculum. Mary Jane Dickerson and Toby Fulwiler co-led a group of thirty faculty members from sixteen disciplines for two eight-hour days. The Vermont workshops followed the Michigan Tech experiential model, covering topics such as (1) the role of writing in learning, (2) making good writing assignments, (3) evaluating student papers, (4) developing audience awareness, and (5) examining the relationship of writing to reading, speaking, and listening.

Word-of-mouth evaluations judged the workshop successful enough to make easy recruiting for a subsequent May workshop. Further workshops were then offered to new groups of faculty on a regular basis in August,

January, and sometimes May, from 1984 to 1989. Follow-up workshops were offered periodically during the academic year to former participants who wanted to continue to explore further questions.

Assumptions

The Vermont program is based on a set of assumptions about language and learning derived from the work of James Britton and his colleagues at the University of London (1975), as well as the work of American theorists Janet Emig (1977), Peter Elbow (1973), Ken Macrorie (1970), James Moffett (1968), and Donald Murray (1968). We might articulate these assumptions as follows:

1. Language—verbal, mathematical, visual, etc.—is central to thinking as we know it; written language is central to disciplined thinking; writing is central to teaching and learning in all disciplines.

2. The more students write about something, the better they learn it; the better they learn something, the more active they are in discussing and writing more about it; and the more active they become as classroom learners, the more active they become in the intellectual life of the campus community.

3. Writing is a complex intellectual process for students and professors alike; instructors who understand this will assign and evaluate writing with greater sensitivity and receive better learning and writing in the bargain.

4. Writing, revising, and editing improve the quality of ideas, information, and expression in any piece of writing; students and faculty can learn techniques to help them do these activities effectively and efficiently.

Scope and Dimension

From the beginning, we tried to develop a program that followed a consistent set of beliefs with voluntary participation and frequent and regular points of entry. A brief overview of the program from 1984 to 1989 looks like this:

1. *Introductory faculty workshops*: Two to three workshops per year have been offered to introduce UVM instructors to new ideas for teaching with writing in all disciplines.

2. *Follow-up workshops*: Workshops and seminars have been scheduled throughout the academic year for writing workshop veterans to (*a*) explore new ideas and research, (*b*) share successes and solve problems, and (*c*) work on manuscripts and conference proposals.

3. *Graduate student training*: Workshops and seminars have been offered annually to introduce graduate students in all disciplines to strategies and problems related to writing and teaching.

4. *Consultation with faculty*: Assistance has been provided on a limited basis to individual instructors who have sought help designing assignments or assessing student papers.

5. *Consultation with departments*: Assistance has been provided to selected departments for discussions about developing and monitoring writing requirements for majors.

6. *Consultation with colleges*: As this book goes to press, the College of Arts and Sciences is formulating a comprehensive writing requirement whose shape and substance is informed by our project.

7. *Research and assessment*: UVM has become an active laboratory in which to study the implementation of ideas associated with "language and learning across the curriculum." The results of these studies will continue to be presented at national conferences and published in professional journals.

8. *Coordination with existing writing programs*: The Faculty Writing Project provides support and/or training for faculty who teach first-year and advanced writing courses as well as the several writing-intensive courses developed by specific departments.

9. *Coordination with the Writing Center*: The Writing Project supports and helps publicize the services to both students and faculty of the Writing Center.

10. *Articulation with Vermont K–12 education*: The Writing Project has developed programs to support writing-across-the-curriculum activities in all grade levels in Vermont's public and private schools.

Funding

To date all the funding for the Writing Project has been internal, patched together by a loosely coordinated set of contributions: the director of the Writing Project has received from one to two courses of released time from his three-course teaching load by the provost's office; the associate director has received one-third released time by the English department to direct the first-year writing program; workshop coleaders are provided with modest honoraria ($150 per day) for helping out; the operating budget—$1,500 per two-day workshop (mostly for food)—has come from Arts and Sciences and other professional development funds.

While it would help our program to bring in soft money to provide released time for more research and evaluation projects, internal funding guarantees an internal commitment that is unlikely to disappear so long as the program delivers what it is supposed to deliver. Let's look at what that is.

In preparing a report about our Faculty Writing Project for the provost, who was new to the University of Vermont in the fall of 1987, we found ourselves pointing out the multidimensional benefits of the Project—benefits that we found to go far beyond just requiring more writing from undergraduates. Indeed, most of this chapter is organized around these five benefits: (1) an increased sense of faculty community, (2) new ideas about student-centered pedagogy, (3) an introduction to the principles of "writing to learn," (4) an extension of activities related to "learning to write," and (5) more interest in faculty scholarship and publication, especially of a collaborative nature.

PROGRAM RESULTS

A Community of Scholars

> I found the experience of meeting with a multidiscipline group of faculty members to be very positive. This is the first time I have been with a cross section of the University faculty when we shared ideas about *teaching* as opposed to research issues, administrative issues, parking issues, benefit packages, computer use, etc., etc., etc.
>
> *Anonymous, January 1986*

It has become common campus knowledge by now that the writing workshops promote dialogue among faculty who don't normally interact with each other. In fact, the workshops are really the only regular game in town for interdisciplinary faculty discussions of ideas related to teaching, writing, and learning. As the anonymous teacher above points out, workshop participants have begun to recognize how little time—except for the odd hallway or lunch conversation—we spend discussing and sharing information and ideas concerning the craft of teaching and our intellectual interaction with students through the courses we teach. Along with the rediscovery of writing to learn for ourselves and our students is the recovery of some of that initial joy of encouraging others to share the body of knowledge that excites us.

Because faculty spend two days together talking and writing, they are more likely to collaborate on both pedagogical and scholarly projects after the workshop is over—but more about this later. We also believe that this esprit de corps spills over into the classroom as workshop veterans at UVM now are more likely to know about other courses their students are taking.

The communal activities that we can trace to the writing workshops include: (*a*) coteaching of several regular UVM courses in the English and education departments; (*b*) the coteaching of courses offered through Continuing Education as an in-service for Vermont school teachers; (*c*) the development of an ongoing (1985 to the present writing) interdisciplinary Institute on Thinking and Writing for Vermont school teachers; (*d*) publication projects for coauthored books and articles (see Appendix at the end of this chapter); (*e*) collaborative presentations at regional and national conferences; (*f*) curricular proposals for UVM colleges and departments; (*g*) joint consultations and presentations invited by other colleges and universities; (*h*) a collaborative assessment project investigating the prevalence of writing-related activities on the UVM campus; and (*i*) the coauthoring of several grant proposals (results so far unsuccessful).

Student-centered Teaching

The Faculty Writing Project begins with faculty because most college and university teachers receive similar preparation for teaching—none at all. Most enter the classroom with only the pedagogical model of their major professor and mentor in mind and do as he or she did: lecture, administer exams, assign occasional reports and papers, grade. When this process fails to achieve satisfactory results, faculty have few other models on which to rely, few other sources for ideas to help them modify and improve their teaching and their students' learning. Both teachers and students find themselves caught in the web of past practices and experiences without knowing how to make learning mutually rewarding.

The faculty writing workshops have opened the forum for pedagogical discussion and change. By the end of the two-day workshops, after talking in small groups, writing in personal journals, and reflecting on their own writing and teaching practices, participating faculty realize that writing across the curriculum encourages significant changes in attitude toward both the subject matter taught in the classroom and student learners who sit in that classroom.

As a result, teachers recognize that they are not the only ones responsible for the material covered in the course, but that they can share that responsibility with their students. If students come to be regarded as responsible learners and active partners in the learning process, however, the old methods of short-answer or objective quizzes and tests (designed only for grading) denigrate and demean this new responsibility and active involvement. At this recognition, the real excitement begins.

All of the workshop sessions use and model informal writing (writing to learn) as the basis for writing activities during the sessions; we ask participants to write regularly throughout the two days in personal notebooks (we call them journals) to help them learn and log their way through the workshop and to model how they might be used in actual classroom settings. We will commonly begin a session with some fast writing (freewriting) about a topic we want to discuss ("What makes writing hard?") and ask participants to share with a neighbor, then as a whole group we make a cumulative list of difficulties. Other times we will conclude a session with similar writing ("Write about one insight you had this morning") to be picked up again after lunch, perhaps with volunteers reading passages to the whole group. In this way we are able to introduce an active pedagogical model to participants and, at the same time, demonstrate exactly how it might be used to stimulate focused discussion at the beginning of class in any subject.

When teachers return to their classrooms, many report having devised original and successful ways to make the journal serve their students' learning processes and to go from this informal writing toward having their students do more formal writing as well, making use of some of the pedagogical methods that encourage writing as a process involving real readers and their responses.

Michael Strauss, professor of chemistry, has described some of his innovative pedagogy in an article coauthored with Fulwiler on using informal writing to learn chemistry (Strauss and Fulwiler, 1987). Here is a more recent description of some of the things Professor Strauss is trying to accomplish through writing in his classes:

> The writing workshops have helped me change the way I teach chemistry. Lectures are still a major part of the way I teach, but once students have begun to familiarize themselves with the material, writing in a notebook/ journal begins. Students are encouraged to use carbon paper to make a copy of the questions and insights they wish to share with the instructor and with the class as a whole. The student keeps the copy and hands in the original anonymously.
>
> I make overhead transparencies of the students' questions and project these to the class at the next meeting. As the course proceeds, these notebook writings become the focus for the lecture hour, especially during the week before examinations when there are extensive queries and requests for clarification. This student writing is discussed in detail and becomes the centerpiece for many minilectures which deal with specific queries of relevance. I use an overhead projector pen to mark directly on student copy to elaborate where errors occur and to show how the material can be clarified. Students' thoughts and ideas are highlighted during this process and I always deal with them in a positive fashion.
>
> The lecture hour begins to evolve from the students themselves and the responsibility for engaging with content shifts to their reading and problem solving. The lecture hour becomes a time where guided reinterpretation and more critical thinking begin to occur within the students' minds. The course content gets displayed through their own writing—in their own symbolism and language—and they become more completely involved.

What interests us here is that the focus in Professor Strauss's chemistry course never strays from the subject itself, but student writing has been brought into the pedagogical framework, thereby enhancing, we believe, the potential for learning to take place.

Biology professor Joan Herbers modified Strauss's question box to suit her own purposes, with good results:

> This past fall I taught our large freshman biology course for the first time and used Mike Strauss's question-box technique; I am so enthusiastic about its merits in large lecture courses that Mike and I are planning to coauthor a paper on it.
>
> Several other faculty in my department have attended the workshops, and there are variable levels of enthusiasm for writing across the curriculum. Nonetheless, I sense that we all agree it *can* be a useful tool; the question that remains unresolved in some colleagues' minds is whether the time it takes from formal lecture is worth it; I have no doubts that it is.

Professors Strauss and Herbers have presented their work to other UVM faculty at follow-up workshops and are currently collaborating on an article about teaching large science classes through the question-box technique.

Because the workshops introduce writing-to-learn pedagogy the first day and model it extensively over the two days, it is not surprising to find these techniques being most widely adopted by workshop veterans. In the next section we focus more closely on writing to learn.

Writing To Learn

> Now that I have been exposed to *many* other ways of using the written language—beware, students, here I come—we are going to have fun!
>
> *Anonymous, January 1985*

The idea that consistently strikes participating faculty as newest, most useful, and highly adaptable to any teaching subject or situation is the concept of writing to learn. Most of the Vermont instructors know quite a bit about using language to evaluate and measure their students, but few have consciously thought much about the other more positive roles language plays in the learning process. As we explained above, the whole first day of our workshop introduces the concept of writing to learn through a variety of informal writing activities. We don't believe teachers are very likely to adopt anything new unless they have personal experience trying it out: consequently we ask participants to do a fair amount of freewriting and journal writing themselves the first day of the workshop, before we even say anything about making and responding to more formal writing (the second day's workshop agenda).

In addition to promoting journals and freewriting, the workshops also introduce—but do not necessarily model—the following writing-to-learn techniques:

1. Writing to pose and solve problems (including listing, mapping, and role-playing, which can be done in students' notebooks, journals, or on scraps of paper).

2. Letters between students and teacher or students and students, a technique which implies an equality between writer and reader (and not an evaluative relationship).

3. Expressive papers—short (one or two pages), one-draft writings in which students express opinions on course matters, but which the instructor grades in quantitative ways (simply passing in the assignment results in credit).

4. Revision activities, which are done after the initial draft of a paper is done but before the fine-tuning begins (because much of the learning actually occurs at this stage in the writing).

5. Class notebooks, which are too often mere copybooks, but which could become more interesting if instructors consciously asked for more exploration or speculation or problem solving to be included (and provided some class time for this).

Here again, we think the best description of these techniques in practice comes from workshop veterans. Botanist David Barrington uses writing-to-learn techniques in more selective ways with his botany majors:

> I have used writing in the classes in a very different way from before: I am using expressive [informal] writing in lab, where students are assigned writings in their lab notebooks designed to move them toward organizing their thoughts on a problem and doing what they can to solve it. Also, when I assign term projects, lab notebooks have served as journals where students can develop the ideas and methods for the projects.
> If there are any problems with expressive writing—some people are simply not writers, don't want or need to write to work out problems—these people are being cheated when I invest as much time as I do in reading and commenting on writings in classes. I have personally worked toward having several options, including writing, open in my classes so that different orientations are served.

Math professor Karen Larson also uses more writing in "Geometry for Elementary Education Majors":

> In the geometry course, the students wrote journal entries for each class-meeting based on a homework question or problems. . . .The journals were collected about every three weeks, and I had a separate commentary (with a copy for my records), so I could see how they improved on the basis of my suggestions. I did give a grade and feel it was the only way students would have stayed motivated and disciplined in keeping the journal. It was appropriate to grade because it included homework problems and their reworking of problems they had not understood initially. The journal helped students get more focus in a lab-oriented course that was different from most math courses they had ever had.

About another mathematics course, Karen writes:

> The "Finite Mathematics" course is a conglomerate of abilities, back-
> grounds, and degrees of motivation. Many would avoid math altogether. (It
> is the noncalculus alternative to fulfill the Arts College math requirement.) I
> am experimenting this semester with the journal on a volunteer basis. . . . I
> am having periodic appointments with each student doing a journal, rather
> than collecting them and responding to them as a group.

Learning to Write

Of course, the reason that most faculty attend the workshops in the first place
is to get help assigning and evaluating their students' more formal writing.
They are tired of complaining about poorly researched term papers, weak
critical essays, unfocused lab reports, and a host of general problems including
misspellings, incorrect punctuation, and inadequate documentation.

At the workshop, usually on the second day, we examine various strategies
for improving students' formal writing, including peer critique groups, editing partners, multiple-draft papers, short (rather than long) papers, and
sequenced assignments. Many teachers try these ideas out and find, as composition teachers have found for some time now, that these strategies can make
a big difference.

Again we hear from some of the instructors:

> I attended the workshop some three years ago and have incorporated writing
> into three courses I've offered. In upper-level courses, the writing compo-
> nent consists of term papers with peer review; this works very well; the
> students like reading others' work and especially appreciate getting feedback
> on their own writing. [Joan Herbers]
>
> I also assigned research papers in this course, and the quality of the final
> papers was greatly improved by having the following initial stages: (*a*) topic
> proposal, (*b*) first draft, (*c*) peer review, (*d*) final draft. Students benefited
> from reading what others had chosen as topics and also took their own topics
> more seriously because their peers were going to read and make suggestions.
> [Karen Larson]

Our approach to the writing-across-the-curriculum concept emphasizes the
writing that faculty are least familiar with—the informal and expressive; as a
result, we spend proportionately less time on the expository (informational)
writing with which they are already familiar. However, we are careful to point
out the relationship between the two, especially noting that it's hard to get
improved *writing* without first (or simultaneously) getting improved *learning*.
It simply cannot happen the other way around.

Faculty Writing

> I'd forgotten how much fun writing can be!
>
> *Anonymous May 1984*

Our experience suggests that faculty who themselves write are more interested in the workshop ideas and stick with them longer. As a result we now devote a substantial amount of time and energy to encouraging faculty to write and to share their writing with each other and with others in their own disciplines.[4]

Ron Savitt, a professor of business, well published in marketing, describes the effect of the writing workshop in his own poetic way:

> I now keep lots of journals, enough to annoy the cats Sarah and Ann, but not enough to get in the way of my own interests. My scholarly writing has improved greatly, and the writing, rewriting, thinking, and rethinking has moved me from the search for "what is" to the completion of "what should be."

Dennis Mahoney, a member of the German department, describes the workshop influence this way:

> As for my own writing, it may be coincidental and just a matter of my becoming more self-confident as my expertise grows, but I do think I have experienced less in the way of "writer's cramp" since that first workshop back in the spring of 1986. One of the key chapters in my book on the novels in the Age of Goethe, which I had been sweating about immediately prior to the workshop, ended up being written quickly and easily and is one of my favorite sections in that soon-to-appear book.

In addition to several single and coauthored articles written for professional journals, we describe below some of the more unusual and collaborative book projects that have found their way into print:

1. *Writer's Guides.* As a result of attending a writing workshop in 1984, Arthur Biddle planned, edited, and coauthored a series of short books, *Writer's Guides*, to introduce writing to students in specific disciplines. He arranged for each book to be cowritten by a content teacher and an English teacher. The idea for this series came from faculty collaboration begun at the writing workshops. The *Writer's Guide* series is currently in production at D.C. Heath (see Appendix).

2. *The Journal Book.* After attending workshops in 1984 and 1985 and subsequently trying out journals in their various classes, five UVM professors wrote chapters for *The Journal Book* (Boynton/Cook, 1987), edited by Toby Fulwiler, which explored the role of writing in their particular disciplines: Jane Ambrose on "Music Journals"; Mary Jane Dickerson on "Journals in the Writing Class"; Karen Wiley Sandler on

"Journals in the French Class"; Henry Steffens on "History Journals"; and Richard Sweterlisch on "Folklore Journals."

3. *Writing, Reading, and the Study of Literature.* Another project that grew out of workshop collaboration involved eleven faculty members in the English department, who decided to put their knowledge of reading and writing together in a multiauthored book, *Writing, Reading, and the Study of Literature* (Random House, 1989). This project developed among faculty members who (*a*) teach literature and (*b*) have attended a writing workshop. Coeditors Biddle and Fulwiler met with the group for a full year, each author sharing his or her chapter with the rest of the group workshop-style and receiving friendly critical suggestions for revision. (An article describing the collaborative process by which the book was written is scheduled to appear in the *ADE Bulletin*.)

4. *In the works*: At present, two separate teams of Vermont faculty, one within the English department and one across the disciplines, are collaboratively composing textbook anthologies for use in composition and literature classes. A third group is collecting manuscripts for a professional book examining the nature and development of one's academic writing voice.

PROGRAM EXTENSIONS

The Writing Center

At Vermont the Writing Center is part of the Learning Cooperative, which is centrally housed in the dormitories and the place where students go for academic support services of all kinds, including tutoring in reading, mathematics, and study skills.

Susan Dinitz, director of the Writing Center, explains the business of our center this way:

> The Writing Center and the writing-across-the-curriculum program at UVM began at about the same time and with a similar underlying assumption: that the more students are engaged in active rather than passive learning, the better they will learn. The faculty writing workshops show teachers how writing turns students into active learners. The Writing Center provides support to those professors attempting to incorporate more writing into their courses. And through its trained peer tutors, the Writing Center provides an environment which encourages and models active learning.

Susan commonly leads sessions about peer tutoring at the faculty workshops, first dividing the group into pairs, then asking them to role-play "tutor and tutee" about a sample piece of writing. In this way she is able to demonstrate firsthand the most common Writing Center activity and, at the same time, to give professors from a variety of disciplines actual experience and guidance in conferencing techniques.

The University Libraries

Staff from many areas of the university take part in the writing workshops so that they can better serve the students now being introduced to writing-across-the-curriculum practices. For this chapter, Nancy Crane and Maura Saul, reference librarians at the Baily/Howe Library, wrote the following:

> Programs such as the Faculty Writing Project, as well as recent technological and curricular innovations, have resulted in a reexamination of research instructional techniques. . . . Most reference librarians have attended writing workshops, and have begun to discover ways to collaborate with faculty from many disciplines who are experimenting with new kinds of writing assignments, many of which require students to use library resources for satisfactory completion of their work.
>
> As librarians work with teaching faculty, the range of research or library assignments has changed. It is no longer just the traditional research paper for which the library is useful. Students writing speeches, debates, argumentative or persuasive essays, newspaper articles, annotated bibliographies, collaborative writing projects and in-class presentations, and even course journals are asked to look for information outside themselves in order to support their assertions and ideas.
>
> In classroom sessions, librarians have begun to emphasize overall research strategies and the research process, in addition to focusing on specific courses, thus encouraging students to view information-finding, as well as writing, as a process that can be applied to questions outside of a particular class. In some cases, students have documented their research experience in a research log: here they write about the information-seeking process, working through research problems and questions as they arise and reacting to individuals and other information sources.
>
> Because of the interest generated by UVM's new computerized information technologies, and by the writing-across-the-curriculum program, librarians at the University of Vermont are planning a Research Across the Curriculum (RAC) session that will bring faculty up-to-date on research and research writing possibilities. Modeled on the Faculty Writing Project, RAC will formally support and enhance efforts of those committed to the Writing-Across-the-Curriculum Program. Just as writing across the curriculum has engendered a university-wide commitment to clear and effective student writing and to the writing-to-learn concept, the intent of Research Across the Curriculum is to foster skills that facilitate information retrieval, evaluation, and synthesis in conjunction with effective written or oral communication.

Graduate Student Workshops

Soon after the faculty workshops began, the Graduate School asked us if we could provide a similar experience for graduate students who were teaching assistants. We have developed a two-day workshop, held each January, that especially addresses the concerns of graduate teaching fellows and is conducted just down the hall from the faculty workshop. The second January (1986) we invited one of the English graduate students to help coconduct the workshop—a tradition we have continued since that highly successful experience.

Patricia Ferreira, an English graduate student, coconducted two of these workshops while also struggling to complete her own master's thesis. Here is her report of the experience:

> For the second year in a row, I assisted one of my professors in the UVM English department with a writing workshop for graduate students only. Within two eight-hour days we attacked such problems as the importance of writing, revision, evaluation, and editing in both your own work and that of your students.
>
> Ironically, this year the focus of my presentation was "Breaking the Writer's Block." Along with such roundtable suggestions as taking an extensive trip to an unknown Pacific island, cleaning the oven, and washing the dog, the most common solution offered was "simply begin." Even if you're writing garbage or copying notes, your brain shifts into gear, and most people find, before they know it, they're rearranging paragraphs, chopping dead wood, and replacing jargon with meaningful active prose.
>
> There is strength in numbers. Realizing that there are other graduate students, like myself, suffering from a paradoxic last-semester malaise and the fear of finally finishing, also helped boost my courage to "simply begin." Equally, listening to my own encouragement to my peers reinforced my own self-confidence that I too could do "it"—write. After our two-day session, I found myself locked in the English department's computer room on weekends, working on my thesis and walking home afterwards to think about what I'd written.

Institute on Thinking and Writing, K–12

Soon after the Faculty Writing Project began, we began to receive requests from local public school teachers and administrators to allow them to be guest participants in our workshops—which we did gladly. We also realized, however, that we should develop a model or course especially for the K–12 teachers in the state. As a result, several of us who met and worked together at the writing workshops put together a summer institute in 1985 for one intensive week to introduce and discuss ideas related to writing, thinking, and interdisciplinary learning. It proved successful and we have taught that course each summer since then, using four or five faculty from the disciplines of history, education, chemistry, psychology, and English.

At this writing, plans are underway to offer this interdisciplinary institute on an annual basis for graduate credit during the school year.

PROBLEMS

We consider the Vermont program successful, but never as good as it could be. What looks good on paper—numbers of workshops, numbers of participants, types of activities—is one thing; what is actually happening in the curriculum and classroom is something else. Here are ten problems we are attempting to solve:

1. *What should be required?* At present there are no curricular requirements for writing in our largest college, Arts and Sciences—a condition which may change in the near future. We have supported the cautious approach to requirements, believing that when and if writing becomes required in some way in the Vermont curriculum, it will be voted in by an informed faculty. We are also suspicious of so-called "writing-intensive" courses, preferring the idealistic retort: "So what course shouldn't be writing intensive?" In other words, we hope to infuse the entire curriculum with writing in the same way it is infused with reading. But we are not sure our noncurricular approach will work: without curricular requirements, the whole movement could wither and die. We don't think it will, but we see the danger.

2. *Mixed messages.* All the forces in the university, from department to college and university level, conspire to make research and publication more important than teaching. No matter what we say or do, our program asks instructors to think and do more about their teaching than the university rewards them for. And though we promote the workshops in part by suggesting that faculty will learn how to assign and assess student writing more effectively and efficiently, etc., thoughtful teaching does take more time—time away from something else.

3. *Home base.* For the English department this program is a mixed blessing: some members have embraced the workshop ideas about writing as compatible with the mission of English departments while others would prefer that the subject of writing in general, and the workshops in particular, simply go away. Every single member of the English department has a literary degree; the serious treatment accorded composition and rhetoric at the university level remains a bewilderment to

many; the idea of hiring someone with a Ph.D. in composition to help administer and assess the university-wide program is still impossible and would fail if put to departmental vote. At the same time, the existing leadership and the operating budget are housed here.

4. *Too many students/Too many classes*. At Vermont, like so many other public institutions, too many classes are too large to do interesting things with writing: Journals, peer writing groups, and multiple draft papers in political science, psychology, and sociology classes of a hundred to two hundred? Chemistry, physics, and biology classes of two to four hundred? And for many faculty, three-course teaching loads are the rule. Where is the time to hone one's teaching to come from?

5. *Follow-up*. The introductory workshops are wonderfully successful and achieve all that could be hoped for in a two-day retreat-like setting. But we have had no similar success in conducting advanced workshops, which we commonly advertise as one-, two-, or three-hour affairs during fall and spring semester. Instructors are too busy teaching or researching or meeting or whatever to find time to attend these sessions. Our best meetings occur two months or so after an introductory workshop with just the members of that workshop—and then a 60 percent turnout is considered good. Our semesters at Vermont are too jammed up for anything resembling methodical faculty development to occur.

6. *Follow-through*. Joan Herbers writes the following about her experiments-in-progress with writing in a variety of science courses:

> In a summer field course I taught at the Rocky Mountain Biological Laboratory, I used the journal technique to focus class discussions, to encourage students to think about class material, and to get them to write down their observations on natural processes. This worked middling well; since it was my first experience with journal writing, I probably did not give the students enough direction nor did I keep on top of them sufficiently.

Joan's description of her uncertainty about using journals is mirrored by instructor after instructor, who may try things out, have "middling" success, and next year maybe abandon them.

7. *Journal overkill*. "Do you know how many classes I'm keeping a journal for!" This has become a comment too often overheard at the student union or in the library or sometimes blurted out in class. However, we seldom hear complaints of overkill about quizzes, exams, or term papers. The problem seems to arise for two reasons—first, students do not perceive journals to be traditional academic assignments; and second, when instructors use journals in a tentative or additive way in classes, students do not perceive them as central to the real business of learning in the course.

8. *But does it work?* Evaluation and assessment are tough. To evaluate *student* writing and learning when the program itself focuses on *faculty* writing and teaching causes all sorts of problems. The treatment process is too far removed from the client product. And even if it could be demonstrated that students at Vermont were either writing better or learning better since the program began, could such improvement be credited to the Faculty Writing Project? Probably not. So by what justification does the program continue to exist?

9. *Who pays for it?* Now in its sixth year, the Vermont program is still funded on a year-to-year basis, often with somebody's leftover budget. Everybody says nice things about it in public, but in private nobody quite knows whose program it is or should be: the English department started it and Professor Virginia Clark, chair of the department, deserves special credit for making sure the funding does indeed come from somewhere, but the program serves the whole university. Arts and Sciences funds half of it, but two-thirds of the faculty served by it are outside Arts and Sciences. And so on. Each year we seek a more permanent source of internal funding, but so far we haven't found it.

10. *The Big Bang.* This program is ever expanding and enlarging so that it becomes increasingly difficult to keep track with existing resources of all that is or should be happening. At this writing, no one really knows what the universe of writing across the curriculum will look like five, ten, and fifteen years from now. To our knowledge, no program has yet fully accomplished what it is capable of doing—*transforming* an entire college (let alone university!)—into an active language-intensive learning community. When our deans and provosts ask us, ''What's next?''—we really don't know. We haven't been there yet.

NOTES

1. By August 1989 fifteen two-day workshops had been conducted for well over three hundred UVM faculty and staff, both full- and part-time. Additional guest participants at these introductory workshops have included faculty from other colleges and universities, teachers from public and private secondary schools, and a sprinkling of our own students, both graduates and undergraduates. Workshop co-leaders have included Arthur Biddle, Mary Jane Dickerson, Toby Fulwiler, Anthony Magistrale, and Robyn Warhol from English; Mary McNeil from education; Henry Steffens from history; and Michael Strauss from chemistry.

2. Ten workshops and a variety of individual consultations to explore further aspects of writing were held for faculty who had attended one of the introductory workshops. Topics for these workshops included ''Assigning Writing in Large Classes,'' ''Journals Revisited,'' ''Response and Evaluation,'' ''Research in Student Writing,'' as well as just general sessions with faculty to discuss what had worked and what hadn't since the workshops began.

3. In 1985, after the first year of the Faculty Writing Project, the graduate school asked if we would run a series of workshops designed especially for graduate students, whose needs are somewhat different from faculty. From 1985 to 1988, five two-day workshops each January have been conducted exclusively for another one hundred graduate students and teaching fellows from all disciplines (co-conducted by Patricia Ferreira, Magistrale, Warhol, Strauss, and English department TAs). In addition, a "teaching workshop" for fifty-five graduate students in the sciences—conducted in September 1987 by Professors Lynn Bond (psychology), Barry Doolin (geology), and Strauss (chemistry)—was directly inspired by the Faculty Writing Project. (All of these workshops were funded independently by the Graduate School.)

4. While we did not design the workshops to directly address participants' own writing, we quickly discovered that many professors welcomed the opportunity to study more closely their own writing habits, processes, and problems. Consequently, we organized one- and two-day retreat sessions for faculty to work on their own writing. Four such workshops were held between 1985 and 1989.

Appendix

PUBLICATIONS FROM THE FACULTY WRITING PROJECT

Articles. The following articles have been written since the beginning of the Faculty Writing Project:

Fulwiler, Toby. "Writing Across the Curriculum: Implications for Teaching Literature." *Association of Departments of English Bulletin* (Winter 1987), 35–40.

———. "Writing and the Alternative Curriculum." *Illinois Association of Teachers of English Bulletin* (Fall 1986), 7–13.

———. "Writing is Everybody's Business." *National Forum*, the Phi Kappa Phi journal (Fall 1985), 21–24.

———. "How Well Does Writing Across the Curriculum Work?" *College English* 46, no. 2 (Feb. 1984), 113–125.

Magistrale, Anthony. "Writing Across the Curriculum: From Theory to Implementation," *Journal of Teaching Writing* 5, no. 1 (Winter 1985), 151–157.

Steffens, Henry. "Collaborative Learning in a History Seminar. *The History Teacher* (forthcoming).

———. "Designing History Writing Assignments for Student Success." *The Social Studies* 80, no. 2 (March–April 1989), 59–64.

———. "Students Writing to Learn." OAH Council of Chairs Newsletter, June 1988, 11–14.

Strauss, Michael, and Toby Fulwiler. "Interactive Writing and the Teaching of Chemistry." *Journal of College Science Teaching* (Feb. 1987), 256–262.

———. "Writing to Learn in Large Lecture Classes: The Economics of Engagement." *Journal of College Science Teaching* (forthcoming).

Books. The following books have been published since the beginning of the Faculty
Writing Project:

Bean, Daniel, and Arthur Biddle. *Writer's Guide: Life Sciences.* New York: D.C. Heath,
    1987.
Biddle, Arthur, and Toby Fulwiler, eds. *Writing, Reading, and the Study of Literature.*
    New York: Random House, 1989.
Bond, Lynn, and Anthony Magistrale. *Writer's Guide: Psychology.* New York: D.C.
    Heath, 1987.
Fulwiler, Toby. *College Writing.* Glenview, IL: Scott Foresman, 1988.
_____. *Teaching with Writing.* Portsmouth, NH: Boynton/Cook, 1987.
_____, ed. *The Journal Book.* Portsmouth, NH: Boynton/Cook, 1987.
Fulwiler, Toby, and Art Young, eds. *Writing Across the Disciplines: Research into Practice.*
    Portsmouth, NH: Boynton/Cook, 1986.
Holland, Kenneth, and Arthur Biddle. *Writer's Guide: Political Science.* New York:
    D.C. Heath, 1987.
Steffens, Henry, and Mary Jane Dickerson. *Writer's Guide: History.* New York: D.C.
    Heath, 1987.

REFERENCES

Britton, James, and others. *The Development of Writing Abilities 11-18.* London:
    Macmillan Education, Ltd. 1975.
Elbow, Peter. *Writing Without Teachers.* New York: Oxford University Press, 1973.
Emig, Janet. "Writing as a Mode of Learning." *College Composition and Communica-
    tion.* 28, no. 2 (May 1977), 122–128.
Macrorie, Ken. *Writing To Be Read.* Portsmouth, NH: Boynton/Cook, 1984.
Moffett, James. *Teaching the Universe of Discourse.* Portsmouth, NH: Boynton/Cook,
    1983.
Murray, Donald. *A Writer Teaches Writing.* Boston: Houghton Mifflin, 1968.

/ / / / / / / / / Chapter *4*

Prince George's Community College

Joyce Magnotto with LeRoy Badger, William Blanchard, Catherine Cant, Clyde Ebenreck, Thomas Garrah, Christine McMahon, William Peirce, and Mary Helen Spear

> *In addition to better papers, we now have better test scores and higher success rates in our courses.*

Institution:	*Prince George's Community College*
Institutional Size—Students (FTES):	8,870
Institutional Size—Faculty (FTEF):	420
Student/Faculty Ratio:	21:1
Highest Degree Granted—	
Institution:	A.A.
Highest Degree Granted—English	
Department:	A.A.
Public or Private Institution:	Public

Institutional Mission: to address the educational and employment needs of the people of Prince George's County, Maryland. An open admissions institution that offers two-year Arts and Sciences programs, Technical and Career Education programs, and Certificate programs at over one hundred locations in the county.

For more information on the program described in this chapter, contact: Joyce N. Magnotto, Department of English, Prince George's Community College, Largo, MD 20772–2199

Community college teaching is a challenge. Classes often contain a heterogeneous mixture of well- and ill-prepared students, good and poor readers, experienced and inexperienced writers. Students may be enrolled in degree or certificate programs, transfer or technical curricula, credit or noncredit options. Full-time faculty teach fifteen hours a semester, which means five classes and three or more preparations; part-time instructors are even busier, with full-time jobs elsewhere. At Prince George's Community College, we developed our writing-across-the-curriculum program in response to these challenges and in the spirit of the college's special mission: to provide higher education to all students regardless of their diverse cultural and academic backgrounds. Our WAC program focuses on effective instructional strategies, with an emphasis on writing to learn.

In the thirty years since the founding of Prince George's Community College in 1958, enrollment has increased from 150 students meeting at a local high school to 36,000 students meeting on a 150-acre main campus and at 130 satellite locations. Approximately 13,000 of these students are registered for credit while the others take noncredit and community services classes.

"Diverse" is the best word for our 17,500 credit-seeking students:

34% are under 21; 20% are over 35

52% are white, 42 black, 4% Asian, 2% Hispanic

42% attend only at night

78% are freshmen

61% are female

72% are part-time students

Many of us who teach at Prince George's actively search for classroom methodologies that make traditional college courses more accessible for our nontraditional learners. Thus, it was natural for William Peirce, a professor in the composition department, to become intrigued by journal articles describing WAC programs at four-year schools and to consider aspects of WAC that might work at a community college. Writing to learn seemed to hold the most promise.

FIRST STEPS

In 1981, Peirce convened a committee to discuss WAC theory and to develop a WAC program for Prince George's. Committee members read articles, attended workshops at local and national conferences, and enrolled in courses offered by the Baltimore Area Consortium on Writing Across the Curriculum (See Chapter 14). We focused on the following issues: how to engage the faculty in attending to student writing, how to publicize WAC to full- and part-time faculty, how to coax a budget-stretched administration into funding non-revenue-producing ideas.

Our first strategy was to talk to as many administrators and faculty as possible. After a presentation to the associate deans, we spoke at department meetings and conducted a survey of student writing problems. More than 100 of the 197 faculty who completed the survey signed their names to Item 7 (see Appendix A at the end of this chapter):

> I am interested in helping with the writing-across-the-curriculum project (perhaps by discussing it further, supplying samples of writing assignments or student writing, or generally keeping in touch); please contact me.

Another strategy was a WAC preview session. We invited faculty to join us for refreshments while we introduced the theoretical framework for writing to learn in the content areas, described WAC programs at four-year institutions, and recommended a program tailored for Prince George's. We also provided practical examples of assignments that an instructor need not grade (or even read), and reassured faculty that using writing as a tool for learning would not turn them into English teachers.

Despite these careful explanations, some teachers thought that students who were asked to do expressive writing would write about their Saturday nights. Some teachers resented WAC's intrusion into their turf. One professor called the composition department to ask why English teachers didn't give tests or exams. Proposing change does have a way of making the proposer a lightning rod for other people's frustrations!

The WAC Committee also began a newsletter that: *(a)* restated the writing-to-learn theme, *(b)* gave examples of low-effort writing activities (such as writing about the day's topic in the first or last five minutes of a class period), *(c)* invited faculty to brown-bag lunches, *(d)* listed addresses where faculty might write for guides prepared at other colleges (such as the one written by Andrew Moss and Carol Holder of California State Polytechnic University at Pomona), *(e)* carried news of the rejection of our grant application and the substitution of a more modest backup proposal, and *(f)* in general kept the WAC flame burning until the following fall.

WAC OFFICIALLY BEGINS

In the fall of 1983, the WAC program became part of the college's operating budget. With $1,200 in funding and released time for Joyce Magnotto to direct the program, we held our first official WAC event during Professional Development Week (a presemester series of meetings). Elaine Maimon presented the keynote speech, and Christopher Thaiss led a two-day workshop. Both Maimon and Thaiss encouraged faculty to see writing activities—class journals, freewriting, draft exchanges—as ways for students to speculate about ideas. These sessions and all that followed were voluntary. None carried a stipend, but all included lunch or light refreshments.

Since that auspicious beginning, workshops have covered topics from assignment design to nonsexist language. One of the most popular sessions was presented by Michael Marcuse from the University of Maryland, who made a return visit at faculty request. He discussed handling the paper load, sequencing assignments, writing instructions to take one's audience into account, responding first to *what* students write and then to *how* they write it. At other sessions Barbara Walvoord and Virginia Gazzam from the Baltimore Area Consortium for Writing Across the Curriculum explained how to deal with term papers in the natural sciences and how to turn ineffectual assignments into successful ones. Jeanne Fahnestock introduced "definition archives" as a writing-to-learn project applicable in any discipline. Teacher-consultants from the National Capital Area Writing Project gave discipline-specific presentations. William Peirce kept us up-to-date on the writing/thinking connection. One session with a different twist was led by an accountant, an auditor, and a writer/editor from the U.S. General Accounting Office. They confirmed the importance of writing in the workplace.

Our overall goal for these workshops has been to help the faculty improve student writing. Faculty comments on workshop evaluations reveal what they like:

"An excellent teaser and reminder of what we should be doing in classes."

"I picked up a few new ideas—but mostly I had that delightful experience of Moliere's character—that of recognizing that I have been speaking prose all my life. Thanks."

"This was such a rich, informative workshop that I will need time (months? years?) to digest, synthesize, reflect upon and apply what I have been exposed to. Thank you!"

"I feel that the exchange of ideas between departments is very valuable."

"I enjoy hearing views on writing from people I have known across campus for a long time."

"[The workshop] was much better than I had anticipated. I appreciated the theory and specifics."

"I was motivated enough to go home on Monday and think and work on my plans."

Comments also reveal what faculty do not like. The following evaluations followed a session that turned into a lecture:

"I expected to write more. It was good but not a workshop."

"I expected a hands-on workshop with participants actively involved."

"I liked the earlier workshops better because we got to practice WAC, not just listen to lectures."

Changes in the Classroom

Inspired by WAC workshops, many faculty at Prince George's have increased the writing component of their courses. Jennie Thompson gives her math students several algebraic expressions and asks them to supply a verbal problem in complete sentences that leads to each expression. Thompson realizes that in writing out procedures for solving word problems, students become more confident and capable. Robert Spear asks students in his computer science courses to put into their own words a computer function which he has lectured on during the previous session. Spear discovered that such writing increases student comprehension of difficult material. Some faculty teaching telecredit courses ask students to write one-page summaries of the programs and to discuss how the material applies to their lives.

In the next few pages, Mary Helen Spear from the psychology department, Clyde Ebenreck from the philosophy department, and Catherine Cant from the mathematics department explain in their own words how writing across the curriculum has changed their teaching.

/ / / / / / / /   *Writing in Psychology*

Mary Helen Spear

Most introductory psychology classes only require that students pass a number of short, multiple-choice tests and a comprehensive, multiple-choice final. Over the past several years, I have observed that many students who receive A's, B's, and C's in these introductory classes have a superficial and sometimes shaky grasp of the material. This is especially obvious when students are asked to write essays that require them to *apply* their knowledge or to make up a skit demonstrating a concept or theory. Because of my participation in faculty development activities such as writing across the curriculum and whole-brain learning workshops, I have begun to employ other techniques for both teaching and testing—techniques that engage the students at a deeper level.

One project is linking a general psychology class with a freshman composition class. In 1984, Christine McMahon, from English Studies, and I both received some released time to plan these classes. At the same time, I decided to demand more writing in all my classes. I saw no reason, in linked or unlinked sections, to be satisfied with the minimal requirements and superficial learning that I had perceived was a result of the exclusive use of "multiple guess" tests.

Students in the linked classes keep a journal as part of the English requirement, but I also encourage them to summarize the psychology reading assignments in that journal. I include short-answer questions on all the exams and designate two exams as essay exams. I provide the class with a sample essay question and with sample student essays from previous semesters as well as with a sample essay I have written. The English instructor reviews techniques for writing essay exams, and students prepare practice answers in the English class. The first essay exam requires a straightforward description of a topic such as operant conditioning. The second essay exam, which is given toward the end of the semester, is a persuasive essay.

I tell the class that in grading these essays I consider their introductions, conclusions, definitions of terms, organization, and accuracy. I do not mention sentence structure, punctuation, or spelling—and these have not been glaringly deficient. The samples from previous semesters make it obvious to students that three or four sentences or a short paragraph is not an acceptable length. One reason I discontinued giving essay exams twelve years ago was that I was disgusted with the students' perception that three to four sentences were acceptable. It was Joyce Magnotto, my current partner from English Studies, who told me that I should give sample answers to show the students what I want.

We are now assigning two short research papers—both linked to the psychology class. Again, paralleling the essay approach, the first paper is a fairly straightforward summary of material while the second paper requires the student to take a position and defend it using outside sources. For example, we have students agree or disagree with Bruno Bettelheim's Freudian interpretation of various fairy tales (from his book *The Uses of Enchantment*). We select a different fairy tale from semester to semester and distribute sample papers from previous semesters.

Over the last few semesters, the students' reactions to and problems with both the essay exams and the Bettelheim paper have changed. Initially the students were intimidated by the assignments, and many of their papers and essays were not very good. In addition, they nearly pestered the English teacher to death with their pleadings and worries about the Bettelheim paper. As one student told me the first semester we tried this: "I've written research papers since sixth grade, but I've never had to think before." My English

Studies partner thought that maybe the assignment *was* too difficult (both Bettelheim's concepts and writing level are a challenge to the majority of our students). I wasn't sure, but she was dealing with most of their worries as they tried writing first drafts. In subsequent semesters we have had more success by spending one day with a class discussion (not a lecture) on Bettelheim's ideas. This seems to relieve much of the class anxiety and has generated some fascinating discussions. Younger students are frequently convinced Hansel and Gretel's *real* mother could not have sent them off into the woods—it had to have been a stepmother. The older students (since this is a community college with a wide age-range) are outraged by these views since many of them are stepparents. They feel that the younger students are perpetuating a stereotype. The discussions have been lively.

At this time, things progress much more smoothly as we now have confidence in the students, and they can see sample work from former students. Finally, since writing assignments are being given in many other courses on campus, our writing assignments no longer seem unusual.

I enjoy "linked" teaching. I have come to expect more and get more from the students. I have also learned from working with my English department partners to be very specific about my expectations and to show the students sample answers. I have been encouraged by the results.

A Note About Linked Courses from William Peirce. Arranging linked courses can be a nuisance for the department chairperson. The class schedule goes to the printer ten months before the courses start, so decisions about who will teach the linked courses must be made long before other teaching schedules are assigned. The Registration Office has to request from the Computer Center a computer program to ensure that students enrolling in one course also enroll in the other—and that no one else does. Additionally, for the psychology department there is a risk that the English prerequisites will prevent the psychology course from attracting enough students. Flyers publicizing the courses have to be designed, printed, distributed to counselors and faculty advisors. All these problems are solvable and certainly worth the effort, but one often wishes these obstacles weren't there.

/ / / / / / / / **Writing in Philosophy**
Clyde Ebenreck

A few years ago, I made most writing assignments without much thought as to what the students were learning by the process: writing was the sign of how students had mastered the wonderful things that I conveyed to them. In my philosophical tower, one learned first and then wrote—I had little sense that writing itself was a method of learning.

In time, I recognized that the students were not integrating the ideas and notions that they learned in class into their lives. I wanted to find ways to bring philosophy and their lives closer together. The papers seemed to be the sticking point. Although assignments were focused on getting students to reveal their thoughts about the issues raised in the course, classes were too large and too numerous to assign and grade as much writing as seemed needed. I was nagged by the question, what was the real value of a grade and its impact on learning? My answer seemed to be negative. The grade hindered learning by telling students that it wasn't safe to explore an idea that might be "wrong" or might not work out the way they had hoped it would. Further, the grade asserted that an authority figure had the power to determine the value of their thinking—and philosophy is, at its heart, antiauthoritarian.

Then, in 1983, I attended my first writing-across-the-curriculum workshop. During those few hours a breakthrough occurred: not all writing needed to be graded! Students would not only still write without a grade, but they would also learn. Through this and subsequent workshops, I saw writing itself as a process of learning and not just a delayed report of learning. Below are some changes I made as a result of these sessions:

Journals. First I shifted class journals from graded to ungraded. I had asked students in the past to enter their written assignments into a journal which I would collect every two weeks and grade on a normal scale of A–F. Now the journals were collected with just the fact of their completion noted. The students could not pass the course without having done the journals, but the journals themselves would not be graded. One immediate result was that the legibility of the writing decreased—words were crossed out and written over or more frequently misspelled. Some students took the opportunity to develop their ideas at great length; others did no more than the absolute minimum. These problems have been gradually resolved into something approaching the normal distribution of talents and interests in the classes. Students seem to react in several ways to the ungraded assignment. Some feel cheated that this work will not add to their grade. Others put in the minimal amount of time they can (and at the last minute) to create the entries before the journal is collected. Yet, most find that their minds work more freely when they can seriously explore ideas that are not guaranteed safe in advance.

Freewriting. A second WAC tactic that I have added to my classes has been freewriting. I have been impressed with its success in getting slow discussions moving and in letting students explore an idea without the pressure of having to raise it in class before their teacher or peers. For example, a combination of guided imagery on feeling oneself chained and then released plus freewriting on how the liberation occurred set the stage for a discussion of the reality of freedom in John Stuart Mill's essay *On Liberty*. Another example: freewriting on what it would be like to exist without a body led to a discussion of the mind-body problem in René Descartes' *Meditations on First Philosophy*. I have found that issues involving personal moral decisions often appear in the exploratory freewritings. Students have shared with me decisions that involved leaving a wounded comrade in the heat of a firefight, aborting a mixed-race child, and reporting a duplicate paycheck from a county agency. They have said that those issues would not have been shared with the class (and I suspect there were a good number of other serious issues not shared with me either).

Peer review. The third major addition to my classes has been the extensive use of peer review for the graded work of the semester. I have found that asking students to review each other's papers not only strengthens the papers under review, but also improves the work of the reviewers on their next assignment or draft. In one of my introductory courses, I have the students do three drafts of a comprehensive examination of the structure and meaning of their lives. To preserve their privacy, I ask them to choose pseudonyms to use for their written assignments. (Only at the end of the course do I know which student has written which paper.) Their submitted papers are then distributed to the class and each reviewer adds observations, comments, and suggestions to the essays. By the end of the semester the final work that the student hands in has been evaluated three times by me and once by three of his or her peers. All the students have praised the review process not only because it showed them where they were lacking in clarity or support for a position, but also because it allowed them to see the work of others and sharpen their own perceptions. I have this assignment structured in such a way that additional material needs to be incorporated into each new draft.

Additional practices. By combining in-class ungraded writing with guided imagery, small-group discussions, and storytelling (I believe that the stories we tell reveal much more about our basic perceptions of reality than the dissertations we write), I find that my classes learn more about their own vision of reality and are thus able to understand and evaluate alternate visions from the long tradition of human thought. For example, in an ethics class I have asked small groups of students to write myths to reflect the fear of the "alien" or to deal with the bases of pornography. These exercises in group writing not only produced better myths than individual writers would have been likely to produce, but also the exercises helped shape the class into a learning community rather than a competitive arena.

Efforts to change my teaching style have been greatly assisted by the fact that all of my colleagues in the philosophy department use various notions from writing across the curriculum in both the basic and advanced courses: ungraded journals to review the material; peer reviews to improve the structure and content of the assigned, graded papers; end-of-class summaries or questions raised by the material (ungraded, but necessary for the grade of the semester). These changes in the philosophy department are enhanced by the increasing number of our fellow teachers across campus using similar methods and by the mutual support offered in the periodic workshops conducted by the WAC Committee.

/ / / / / / / /   ***Science and Mathematics***
Catherine Cant

Mathematics professors have not historically assigned much writing except in classes where a paper was obviously appropriate: statistics courses and math courses for elementary education and liberal arts majors. Poor writing in those courses inspired the professors who teach them to be among the first in the math department to attend WAC workshops. We who went to learn how to improve our students' papers were also introduced to the concept of writing to learn. (In addition to better papers, we now have better test scores and higher success rates in our courses.)

Math and science courses at Prince George's are successfully completed (D or better) by only 50 percent of those enrolled; some entry-level courses have much lower success rates. The faculty and administration have initiated a number of programs to improve retention, including free tutoring and personalized letters to students who need help. As part of this effort several science professors and over half of our full-time mathematics faculty have attended at least one WAC workshop, and writing is regularly being used to help improve success rates.

Business math. After several WAC workshops and a five-week summer institute sponsored by the National Capital Area Writing Project, I introduced a series of writing assignments in a business math class with a particularly poor history of student success. There are ten assignments, one for each chapter. They vary in length, audience, style, and purpose, exposing students to increasing challenges in writing. Acting on a suggestion by one of our workshop presenters (Dr. Michael Marcuse of the University of Maryland), I attempt in each assignment to make students focus on an important aspect of the chapter. I also follow Dr. Marcuse's advice on reducing plagiarism by making most assignments too personalized to be copied. For example:

1. Find an advertisement or invoice that mentions terms and/or freight charges. Use the information to invent a word problem for the final exam.

2. Find a current magazine or newspaper article that discusses a particular company's stock and/or bonds. Use it to write a letter to a potential

buyer, including such computations as current yield and profit or loss at the time of a sale.

The first time I made these assignments an integral part of the course, 70 percent of the students passed compared with under 50 percent for the same course without the writing. In my spring 1987 semester, among all students who completed all writing assignments, not one failed the course.

Statistics. I have always required my statistics students to write papers, but unguided writing assignments were very disheartening. I felt compelled to correct grammar and spelling—but before WAC, I had not looked at papers in the early stages of production. I had used essay questions on tests, but I hadn't encouraged students to write for their own benefit. Now a WAC convert, I use writing-to-learn activities throughout the course. For example, in preparation for a paper on hypothesis-testing, students write critiques of poor examples of statistical inference; then they practice writing questions for a survey or experiment; then they write me brief notes about their intended projects. They also bring drafts of their papers to class for peer review. They are encouraged to read one another's papers for content and clarity, and to point out, but not correct, problems in grammar and spelling. A "semifinal" draft then comes to me for comment, and each paper is briefly presented to the class. The student can accept a grade at that point or submit another draft if my comments suggest it.

This process takes very little class time and produces better papers. It also seems to improve test scores, since students have to put concepts into their own words as well as numbers into formulas. An unexpected fringe benefit is a reduction of the infamous "math anxiety," especially when writing begins the first day of class.

Essays and essay exams. Most math professors begin each semester by asking students about their math background. WAC has inspired many to replace filling out forms with writing a brief essay. In this way the student can describe math courses taken and also any problems or anxieties. Another short writing activity for the first day might be: "Write what first comes to mind when you hear the word *calculus* [or *algebra* or *statistics*]." This often encourages students to confess openly the panic with which they greet math. They are relieved to discover they're not alone. Student comments from course evaluations illustrate the reaction to writing activities:

"I was intensely petrified of this course but Mrs. Cant has changed my attitude toward statistics."

"The writing projects made the problems *real*."

"Writing assignments were extremely helpful in understanding concepts."

"Projects were the most useful part of the homework."

Essay questions are also helpful in reducing anxiety. "Discuss how . . ." instead of "Prove that . . ." somehow seems less intimidating. Prior to the WAC program, only three or four math classes used essay test questions, and science professors had almost given them up in frustration at students' inability to respond in complete sentences. Now that students are *practicing* for essay exams, with graded and ungraded writing assignments shared in class, the essay questions are returning. An added benefit to science classes is the improvement in lab reports. Professors who don't want to and who don't feel qualified to correct writing problems can send students to the Writing Center for help with lab reports and other writing assignments. It is wonderful to feel comfortable in demanding acceptable writing without having to "teach writing."

THE PROGRAM DESIGN AT PRINCE GEORGE'S

WAC originated in our English division, where it received funding and encouragement for several years. In 1987, WAC moved to Instructional Support Services—a new area with its own coordinator, budget, and clerical staff. Since WAC began at Prince George's, the administration has supported the program while entrusting the faculty with its design and implementation. With this ongoing support, we have been able to attract a large number of participants. So far, more than 120 instructors (48 percent of the full-time faculty) have attended at least one workshop. Many faculty have attended several workshops.

The WAC Director. At Prince George's the WAC director receives six hours of released time out of a fifteen-hour teaching load per semester. Joyce Magnotto currently holds the position. Her responsibilities include: (*a*) arranging and presenting WAC events (design, publicity, recruitment, follow-up); (*b*) serving as liaison with area schools and organizations such as the National Capital Area Writing Project and the Baltimore Area Consortium; (*c*) managing paperwork (budgets, yearly proposals, correspondence); (*d*) consulting with individual faculty; (*e*) editing a WAC newsletter; (*f*) keeping abreast of developments in the field; and (*g*) publicizing the program on and off campus.

The WAC Committee. Prince George's WAC Committee is composed of her duties and to provide creative program ideas as well as vital feedback from around the college. One of our early tasks was to establish program goals and to write a rationale statement (see Appendix B at the end of this chapter). The committee also determines and evaluates the content of WAC workshops, encourages colleagues to attend WAC events, and provides follow-up support. Each committee member brings to WAC his or her special talents. For example, Mary Stevenson and Hisako Calhoon have promoted discussions of writing between the English and nursing faculty. Tom Garrah lends his cable television expertise and takes minutes at our meetings. Joanne Jefferys' faithful attendance and enthusiasm keep us motivated. Others keep us informed about curricular changes and general education requirements. The WAC Committee is the heart of our program.

Budget. In addition to released time for the director, the WAC program receives funding of approximately $1,800 per year for workshops, association dues, library acquisitions, and publicity.

Beyond Writing to Learn

Writing to learn has been the main focus at Prince George's because it offers practical ways to increase and improve student writing without unduly burdening faculty who must teach five classes per semester. Of course, writing to learn isn't our only focus.

The Writing Center. At Prince George's, WAC paved the way for a writing center by educating the faculty about process theory, by creating a demand for a center that would help students complete newly designed writing assignments, and by providing a pool from which to recruit faculty tutors for the center. Following extensive research, Christine McMahon, a member of our WAC Committee, designed and developed our Writing Center, which opened in the spring of 1987. The center is staffed entirely by faculty tutors, who offer students assistance with writing assignments from any course across the curriculum. Only faculty who participate in WAC activities are invited to apply for positions as Writing Center tutors. So far, faculty tutors have come from English, biology, business and management, foreign languages, philosophy, and psychology.

Each faculty tutor meets with individual students five hours a week (ten half-hour appointments) and participates in a one-hour training meeting each week. These activities replace one three-credit course of the regular teaching load. The weekly training meetings function as a kind of advanced seminar in WAC. The tutors study the demands of writing assignments in various disciplines, discuss process theory, view tutoring videos, and learn how to use the center's computer software. Because of this training, each of the tutors is capable of assisting with assignments from any discipline.

Faculty Writers. As a way of fostering faculty writing, the WAC program sponsors "Writing for Pleasure and Profit," a series of brown-bag lunches at which faculty discuss their current writing projects. For example, Marianne Strong from English Studies has regaled us about her romance and mystery novels, while Bruce Dudley from the history department has reported on his book chronicling ten years of the Cleveland Indians, and David Russell from mathematics has outlined the negotiations involved in textbook publication. At these sessions faculty receive encouragement to begin or to return to writing projects that they thought they didn't have the time or energy to pursue. As a result, the number of faculty writers at Prince George's continues to grow.

Collaborative Workshops. The WAC spirit spins off in other directions as well. The Writing Center staff and WAC Committee are now cosponsoring student workshops on report writing and on taking essay examinations. We hold sessions for faculty who are writing tenure applications, and we have cosponsored a workshop on "Gender Issues in Writing" with the Committee on Integrating Scholarship on Women into the Curriculum.

A Look Ahead

Those of us on the WAC Committee at Prince George's hope to expand and improve the program over the next few years; but in order to do so, we must meet several challenges.

Challenges. Obviously, not all faculty participate in WAC activities, and not all attempts to incorporate writing are successful. Of critical importance are the more than four hundred part-time faculty whose other commitments make it difficult for them to attend WAC workshops—yet these faculty teach almost half our students. Another problem is the absence of upper-division students or graduate assistants to serve as readers in large sections. A third issue involves certain technical curricula. Often faculty in these curricula depend heavily on lectures and multiple-choice testing because they must cover extensive amounts of material to prepare students for licensing examinations. And a final issue concerns part-time students who take courses out of sequence, enrolling in a sophomore history course, for instance, without taking freshman composition first. This situation can be frustrating for both the student and teacher when a writing assignment is part of the sophomore course.

The Future. The WAC Committee is always planning ahead. At a recent collaborative session, we discussed several ideas. One was more individual consultation with faculty needing assistance in implementing writing. We also want to try departmental approaches such as with nursing. We plan to feature the work of a faculty writer in a special column in future issues of our newsletter. We also hope to invite faculty from nearby high schools and transfer institutions to a workshop. We might design a composition course linked with a technology course to foster some connections valuable to both areas. We could arrange a workshop for part-time faculty and offer it in the evening or on a Saturday morning. We could survey the faculty as we did in

1982 and compare the results. Perhaps a new survey would show widespread agreement with a statement made by Clyde Ebenreck from the philosophy department: "Today it is not so necessary to overcome student resistance to writing; students have been exposed to writing across the campus."

When Prince George's Community College was founded in 1958 as an innovative approach to higher education, traditional classroom methodologies were often the norm. In recent years, faculty have been reexamining classroom practices and looking for more effective ways to teach our diverse student population. Many of us have learned that the techniques covered in WAC workshops are not enough. (Consider how many workshops faculty attend over the years only to return to comfortable old habits on Monday morning.) The crucial difference seems to be that faculty who write with each other in a supportive atmosphere learn not only about the WAC topic of the moment, but also about learning itself: learning occurs in a collaborative context, and writing is a good way to learn. The intellectual and social rewards of writing are powerful. In classroom terms, this leads to innovative practices: placing students at the center of their own learning, shifting to participatory methods, and valuing student diversity. At Prince George's Community College, writing across the curriculum is helping a faculty committed to undergraduate education share what we know across disciplines and educate one another as well as our students.

Appendix A

FACULTY SURVEY: STUDENT WRITING

Department _____

1. Do students need to use writing skills in your courses?
   ☐ yes   ☐ no   ☐ not applicable

2. Is poor student writing a problem in your courses?
   ☐ yes   ☐ no   ☐ not applicable

3. Have you changed or eliminated writing assignments or test questions because of poor student writing?
   ☐ yes   ☐ no   ☐ not applicable

4. What kinds of exams or major tests do you give? Circle all that apply.
   a. Objective questions or fill-in-the-blank short answers
   b. Combination of objective questions and essay
   c. In-class essay
   d. Take-home essay

    e. Problems to solve that require very little writing
    f. Problems to solve that require at least a paragraph of explanation
    g. Other (specify) _____

5. What kind of writing assignments do you give? Circle all that apply.
    a. None
    b. Technical or lab reports
    c. Out-of-class essays
    d. In-class essays
    e. Journals, logs, notebooks
    f. Reports of reading (abstracts, summaries)
    g. Research papers or research projects
    h. Other (specify) _____

6. Please tell us how frequently you encounter the following common writing problems:

		Rarely	Sometimes	Very Frequently
a. Grammar, punctuation, spelling	NA	1	2	3
b. Incorrect format	NA	1	2	3
c. Inadequate understanding of the content	NA	1	2	3
d. Insufficient supporting details	NA	1	2	3
e. Disorganization	NA	1	2	3
f. Poor quality of thought or logic	NA	1	2	3
g. Incoherence	NA	1	2	3
h. Other _____				

7. I am interested in helping with the writing-across-the-curriculum project (perhaps by discussing it further, supplying samples of writing assignments or student writing, or generally keeping in touch); please contact me.

        Signed _____ Ext. _____

Appendix B

RATIONALE FOR WRITING ACROSS THE CURRICULUM AT PRINCE GEORGE'S COMMUNITY COLLEGE

The writing-across-the-curriculum program at Prince George's Community College is based on the following ideas about writing:

1. Writing is a process, somewhat different for each person, but usually including the stages of thinking, content gathering, planning, drafting, revising, editing, and proofreading.

2. Writing is a basic literacy skill. Its mastery as a tool for learning and for communicating is critical to a student's success in all areas of study, not just in English classes.

3. Writing is valuable for teaching and for learning. Students who write about mathematical concepts or philosophical theories often learn the material more thoroughly and retain it longer than if they had only read or discussed the material without writing about it.

4. Students learn about their own writing processes and become more skilled at writing through practice. Not all practice writing needs to be or should be graded. Class journals, freewriting (writing to see what one thinks), lists, and rough drafts are examples of writing which does not have to be graded.

5. Assignments that guide and support students—in gathering ideas, composing drafts, revising after receiving reader response, and polishing final copies—promote better finished products.

6. Professionals in different fields follow different writing conventions, so students should be exposed to and asked to practice the types of writing used in the fields they are studying.

Because of its concurrence with the ideas listed above, the writing-across-the-curriculum committee is working toward the following goals:

1. Providing frequent professional development opportunities that allow faculty to examine the usefulness of many kinds of writing in their disciplines.

2. Increasing the across-the-college network of faculty who show their students that writing is important—first by writing themselves and second by requiring writing of the types and quality that students will need to practice if they are to become successful in a particular field.

3. Improving the support system for faculty who accept their share of the responsibility for student literacy. This system shall include such things as a writing center, consultancies, opportunities for informal faculty discussion of writing, studies of additional ways of improving writing, and a newsletter.

The overall aim of the writing-across-the-curriculum program, therefore, is to promote the development of writing ability across the college because writing is valuable in all disciplines.

The University of Chicago

Joseph M. Williams and Gregory G. Colomb

> *Those new to a knowledge community often exhibit some characteristic patterns of learning behavior, patterns that teachers can learn to anticipate.*

Institution:	*University of Chicago*
Institutional Size—Students (FTES):	9,000
Institutional Size—Faculty (FTEF):	1,150
Student/Faculty Ratio:	8:1
Highest Degree Granted— Institution:	Ph.D.
Highest Degree Granted—English Department:	Ph.D.
Public or Private Institution:	Private

Institutional Mission: the liberal arts and academic/scholarly preparation.

For more information on the program described in this chapter, contact: Joseph M. Williams, Department of English, University of Chicago, Chicago, IL 60657.

As the term is usually understood, there is no "writing problem" at the University of Chicago. The class of '91 has an average VSAT of about 625; the graduate and professional schools are, if anything, more selective. This is not to say that all students write well, or that faculty do not complain about writing at predictable points: in the first quarter of the freshman core courses, in the second year of core courses, in the first few courses in the majors, in the first year of graduate and professional schools. But the faculty feels no sense of crisis, probably because more than 80 percent of our students go on to graduate and professional school, where they seem to succeed. Seven years ago, this same sanguine view accounted for the state of the writing "program." It consisted of a few untrained graduate students sitting in a small office waiting for first-year students to drop by. Few did.

Since that time, the university's Writing Programs have grown quite substantially. At their center is "the Little Red Schoolhouse," a.k.a. Advanced Professional and Academic Writing, a course that combines large lectures and small seminars. Originally intended for juniors and seniors, the Schoolhouse now enrolls as many graduate, professional, and postdoctoral students as undergraduates. In 1987–88, the Schoolhouse will enroll over 150 undergraduates (two-thirds from the social sciences and hard sciences, fewer than 15 percent from the Department of English); without budgetary restrictions on the number of graduate students to teach the small seminars, we could triple enrollment. At the graduate and professional level, the Schoolhouse now enrolls about ninety from the graduate business school; about fifty from the humanities, social sciences, and physical sciences; a few professional students from the School of Social Services Administration; and a small contingent of postdoctoral fellows from the Center for Medical and Clinical Ethics.

Three years ago, graduate students with experience teaching in the Schoolhouse began to be used in other programs. They now assist in teaching writing in the first-year Humanities Core, where most of the faculty are assistant professors and above from all quarters of the Humanities Collegiate Division. Few of those faculty are especially experienced, much less trained, much much less interested in teaching writing; so as an inducement to teach in the Core, senior faculty are now offered these "Writing Interns."

There are other Schoolhouse spin-offs: graduate-student writing tutors in the dormitories and the library, Saturday courses in professional writing for graduate students from all fields, a future seminar for postdoctoral students in the biological sciences. The writing component has been significantly expanded in an upper-class course taken by about one-third of all undergraduates—Art 101. Schoolhouse faculty have led seminars for several groups of colleagues: those teaching writing in the Law School and in the Humanities and Social Sciences Core. They also put on a program for about 150 returning alumnae every year and will probably be doing the same for alumnae from the Graduate School of Business. Most of this growth has come largely outside the Department of English, principally among juniors, seniors, graduate, and professional students—students who might be expected to have the fewest writing problems because they have already succeeded in their program of studies.

The Writing Programs have grown in this way, largely because the writing faculty was able to persuade the university administration that in fact there was a "writing problem," not just at the University of Chicago but in the world at large—in academe, in the professions, in government. This problem is not defined by an inability of students to make their sentences parse or to spell and punctuate at some minimal level of freshman competence. Rather, it was to be found first in the turgid, abstract language that defines the most mature, hyperliterate writing of our culture, the kind of discourse that advanced students regularly confront and increasingly emulate as the model of successful professional prose.

This first problem finds its roots in the deeper inability of even good writers to point beyond such slogans as "be clear, be direct," in order to explain to others what counts as good writing and how to produce it—or at least to explain how to revise mature turgidity into mature clarity. This inability to articulate what it means to write well, much less how to revise well, only perpetuates the first problem. Those teachers, editors, supervisors who are responsible for the writing of others are too often unable to explain and so to achieve their standards for simple, direct, open communication. These are the hidden writing problems that institutions with no obvious writing problem consistently fail to address, because they are least likely to recognize it. It is these two hidden problems that the Writing Programs set out to address.

First, the writing faculty developed a line of research that suggested a simple and coherent curriculum. The faculty then developed a theory of teaching writing that graduate students from all areas of the university, with no training or experience, were able to master and apply successfully to teaching undergraduates. Finally, the faculty were able to demonstrate to the university that this curriculum and pedagogy not only helped its own undergraduates, but prepared its graduate students—regardless of field—to become successful teachers of undergraduates elsewhere. (Another benefit was unexpected: as the graduate students taught undergraduates how to write, they themselves began to write substantially better.)

The full story of the Chicago program—call it remedial English for the advantaged student—begins with The Little Red Schoolhouse.

THE LITTLE RED SCHOOLHOUSE

Some Organizational History. We founded the Schoolhouse about seven years ago using much the same program we had developed for private consulting with the federal government, professional groups, law firms, etc. As consultants, we dealt with mature writers who nevertheless had problems with their style and organization. More significantly, we dealt with professionals who supervised others with these problems but who could not effectively help their charges to write better. After devising ways to address such problems, we realized that what we had learned was relevant to working not with freshmen perhaps, but certainly with advanced undergraduates. (At that time we also had no particular insights about what to do with first-year students, at least nothing significantly different from what had been done since the time of Hutchins.)

To create the program, we had to convince the college to come up with enough money to support a seminar component of the course. We had come to realize how important it was to have participants in our programs talk explicitly with one another about what they were learning, so we incorporated small groups in the Schoolhouse. On Thursday, a professor lectures on transdisciplinary aspects of writing to the assembled upperclass, graduate, and professional students. After the lecture, the class breaks into groups of seven or eight to discuss with a lector either their own writing or materials based on the lecture. On Tuesday the lectors meet with the small groups to discuss the papers written over the weekend and circulated to the group on Monday.

We invite graduate students from all areas of the university to apply, and we ordinarily receive about one hundred. The largest single group of applicants is from English, but the majority come from other areas—political science, sociology, linguistics, philosophy, history, art, anthropology, etc. Selection is blind: applicants submit anonymous writing samples and anonymously mark up a sample student paper. Only after the applications have been independently evaluated twice do we know whom we have selected. This blind process regularly yields about one-third from the Department of English, two-thirds from other departments, with about half of those from the social sciences, an outcome that precisely meets our needs. (As we shall describe below, it is also a process that has insulated us from certain political pressures within the Department of English.) Lectors who work with undergraduates are trained in a ten-week seminar; senior lectors who work with graduate and postdoctoral sections have at least two years experience before they take on advanced students.

The Rhetorical Pitch. It was not easy to get funds to support the first group of lectors. The original budget—under $15,000—would be pocket money in a large university, but in a small one like the University of Chicago (at that time, only about 2,800 undergraduates) the sum was substantial, particularly when few faculty were seized by any sense of crisis. Our argument went like this: If the university believes that it provides an education worth the price (now, the third or fourth highest undergraduate tuition in the country), then it ought to do more than teach students to write competently. If the university thinks it trains students to think especially well in their fields, then it ought to teach them to write especially well. Since most Chicago undergraduates will go on to graduate and professional school, their prose will (if our recruiting propaganda is true) carry special weight. Our students will write the articles, books, reports, memos that we expect to help set the standard for the writing in their fields. We in the Schoolhouse claimed we knew not only what counted as effective writing in the professions, in government, etc., but also how to teach it and how to teach our graduate students to teach it.

There was a second half to the argument. If our students do go on to write those books, articles, monographs, memos that distinguish them, then they will eventually become responsible for the writing of others: they will become the teachers, the dissertation directors, the journal editors, the managers who will have to pass on the writing of those they supervise. To do that job well, they must do more than model good writing, more than distinguish good writing from bad. They must also be able to articulate the difference between good and bad writing, to explain the basis for their judgments, and then to explain how to turn bad writing into good. The coda to the argument was the value the teaching experience would have for the graduate students from departments other than English. Not only would they learn to teach writing but they would, in the act of teaching writing to others, improve their own writing.

It was an argument received at first with some skepticism, but over the last few years with increasing enthusiasm—enthusiasm based on feedback from our alumnae, on the reports of the graduate students who teach in the Schoolhouse, on the experience of faculty in other departments. When the graduate students teaching in the program report to their home departments that they are able to teach writing—and when they show that in the process they have learned to write better themselves—they become the best evidence for our argument.

The Theoretical Basis. The curriculum and pedagogy rested on a theory of discourse developed through our experience working with professional groups around the country. The problems that face writers at this advanced level are, in one way, wholly different from the problems that face first-year students. Very little of what we then believed could be done in freshman composition was relevant to the problems of mature writers. A standard line in the first Schoolhouse lecture is,

> "You probably don't write as badly as this:
> 'Such multi-variate strategies may be of more use in understanding the genetic factors which play a role in the vulnerability to such conditions

> than strategies based on the assumption that the presence or absence of pathology is dependent on a major gene or on strategies involving the study of a single biological variable.'
>
> But if you are smart, work hard, and go on to graduate school, you probably will."

It is a timely joke because at this point in their academic careers, most upperclass students are just beginning to encounter the professional prose of their field in the journals and monographs that so often display such prose at its worst. This experience leads many to doubt their ability to understand the complexities of their field. When they realize that often the problem is not with them but with the prose they have to decipher, they experience a sense of liberation that makes them better students.

We largely ignored much of the current wisdom about teaching writing, wisdom directed chiefly at first-year students: the need to help them with their "processes" before they got anything down on paper, to assist them to "invent" their material or to find their "authentic voices," to cajole them into engaging with some arbitrarily selected subject matter. We assumed that just as professionals are able to draw on their own expertise and experience for the substance of their writing, so were our juniors and seniors. We assumed that if there was a problem with "voice," it originated with the reader's perception of that voice, not with the writer's finding or losing it. Since these issues were never raised by the advanced writers with whom we worked, we concentrated on those matters of style and structure that seemed most relevant to the writing of attorneys, judges, physicians, federal officials, and so on—those elements of discourse that we claim cut across all genres, and that control the way readers respond to text. As for the conventions in particular fields, we matched graduate students with undergraduates in corresponding majors: a graduate student in history with seven undergraduate history majors. This allowed the graduate students to draw on their own growing expertise both in their fields and in those principles that define good prose in all fields.

Because the Schoolhouse is the source of all other graduate student teaching, it constitutes not only the Programs' training center, but their conceptual center as well. The Schoolhouse is where the Writing Programs articulate their teaching both downward toward the first- and second-year courses and upward toward the graduate and professional schools. It also provides the entry-level training for the graduate student instructors who make the rest of the program go, the platform from which we present the most comprehensive exposition of the theory of style and structure that now informs all phases of the Writing Programs.

Undergraduates who have succeeded have overcome two hurdles. First, they have mastered the skills required in the common core—not only writing in the different areas (humanities, social, physical, and biological science), but also their characteristic forms of reasoning and arguing. The students have, in short, been socialized into the general academic community. Second, and more importantly, these students are also being socialized into the discipline of their majors. This is not to say that all third- and fourth-year students, or even graduate students, are yet full members of a disciplinary community. But they have become apprentices, able to participate in ways that those more fully socialized can recognize. Thus these students understand the academic community, are casually acquainted with a few subcommunities, and have gained some local knowledge of one disciplinary community. Engaged in a discipline enough to see how it works, these students are not yet *professionally* engaged (with all the rigidity *that* can bring). This is an opportune moment for students to begin to appreciate their situation with respect to both their own discipline and others, and so to become aware of the linguistic aspects of their efforts to join an academic and professional community. So the program of the Schoolhouse is calculated to help students understand writing in both the expanse of disciplinary variety and the narrows of local disciplinary convention.

The Curriculum. The first focus of the Schoolhouse is on the grammar that governs all academic and professional texts. We begin with a grammar of style that we assert characterizes "reader-friendly" prose in all fields. As seriously as we take the stylistic differences from discipline to discipline, we also believe that there is a universal grammar of style underlying professional texts in all disciplines, a grammar that transcends the syntactic grammar found in most handbooks (Williams, 1988). The second half of the ten-week course emphasizes matters of structure, again based on a discourse grammar (Colomb and Williams, 1986). In the small groups, students analyze one another's texts, specifically using Schoolhouse language to explain why they respond to those texts as they do and suggesting ways to revise texts they find unclear, disorganized, confused, unconvincing, etc. To this degree, the course teaches students not only to write well but also to analyze texts theoretically and then to articulate the results of that analysis in ways that are courteous and helpful to others.

We believe that once a writer can recognize how a text may mislead (or help) a reader, she can revise in light of her own intentions and in light of the way readers predictably read. This does not mean catering to the reader by saying what the reader wants to hear, but rather anticipating the structural and stylistic signals that the reader looks for to make sense of a text. We expect that within a few weeks this "reader-based, text-based" approach becomes a "process/revision" approach, that the analytical process becomes *pro*spective and informs the process of drafting.

The second focus of the Schoolhouse is on the particulars of local disciplines, an issue addressed chiefly in the small tutorial groups, where students work closely with one who is already an initiate within the disciplinary community and with other apprentices like themselves. The students refine their knowledge of the conventions of the discipline, articulating features accepted as tacit knowledge by those socialized into that community of disclosure. They also practice what may be one of the most important abilities of the socialized professional, the ability to write clearly and intelligibly to those who do not share their professional expertise and to explain to others not only how to do it, but why it is important to do so. Students learn which features of their disciplinary practice are local conventions (and so can be dropped when the situation demands) and which features may be constitutive of the discipline.

To this end, early assignments in the Schoolhouse begin with rewriting some typically foggy scholarly prose, followed by a straightforward summary of a longer article, followed by an exposition of some difficult concept in the field for an intelligent outsider who has to understand the concept (e.g., the putative reader might be a senator who has to converse with an expert appearing before a Congressional committee). From that point on, the writing may move in a variety of directions, including working on a longer paper in conjunction with another course, or pursuing some independently conceived project.

One final aspect of the role of grammar and the disciplines in the pedagogy of the Schoolhouse permeates all aspects of the program. It goes to the heart of how we understand the purpose of education at an institution dedicated to a liberal education. Traditionally, the goals of a liberal education are articulated in terms both of personal development of the individual and of the social responsibility of the citizen. This traditional liberal education wants to create a community of widely literate individuals able to understand and to participate in arenas of social and intellectual debate. We address one part of this objective by insisting that our students learn to communicate to this more general community of citizens, and that they do so without either compromising what they know or condescending to those who do not share that knowledge.

But there is the other responsibility for which we hope our students will be prepared, one perhaps even more important to the good health of a commonweal of educated citizens. Persons with the kind of responsibilities we hope for our students—teachers, scholars, editors, managers—must be in a position to evaluate, criticize, and if necessary to change the standards they have learned to articulate and defend. In this exercise of critical intelligence, they need even more the ability to understand and to articulate the nature of their practice and of its rationale, to see their practice as one of many, and to say explicitly and clearly how and why it ought to be otherwise. Grammar, even in the larger sense it comes to have in the Schoolhouse, may be the least part of that kind of critical intelligence. But such a grammar is, we believe, crucial to its successful exercise.

Evaluation. Student response to the program has been overwhelmingly favorable; the Schoolhouse has become the most popular course in the college. For us, the critical question on the course evaluation is "What would you say to a friend who asked you for advice about taking LRS?" The most frequent responses are represented by these answers:

From juniors and seniors: "Take it; be prepared to sacrifice the next ten Sunday nights." "It's not quite as bad as rumor has it—but if you're lazy, stay away. If you can handle it—take it!" "Take the class. Admittedly you will work your butt off and admittedly you will postpone your social life for ten weeks, but what you get from the class is definitely worth it."

From graduate students: "If you are a grad student take it in the summer—if you take it during the academic year, do not take a full load of courses. It is an excellent course." "Be prepared to do a lot of work and sacrifice your weekends." "I have already recommended this course to other graduate students in Behav[ioral] Sci[ences]/Biol[ogical] Sci[ences]."

From MBA students: "Although it seems like a lot of money to pay for a writing class [the current cost per course per student in the Graduate School of Business is $1,350], it is worth the price." "Take it. It's been one of the most useful and enjoyable courses (at the G[raduate] S[chool of] B[usiness])." "No matter how good you think you write, LRS will improve your writing."

From postdoctoral students: "[The Schoolhouse] helped me improve my writing skills in three key areas: to think before I write, to think while I write and to think after I write, not easy for doctors to do." "[The Schoolhouse] represents the ultimate triumph of form over content. Although I say this tongue-in-cheek, the system of higher education, particularly of professional education, truly pays less than adequate attention to the process of intellectual discourse. . . . I have seen my own writing improve over the course of the quarter, and for this, I am grateful."

WRITING INTERNS IN CORE HUMANITIES

First-year students are not mature writers. But as we began to see past the local conventions that make the writing of doctors, lawyers, judges, etc. seem mature and professional, we began to see similarities between those mature writers and "immature" writers, similarities that became especially prominent at points of transition in an academic and professional career—first-year students, students new to a field of concentration, new graduate and professional students, new attorneys, new judges.

This was a fortunate insight, because as the Schoolhouse grew, it generated increasing numbers of graduate students who were able to teach writing, but who had no continuing job—we insisted on turning over all of the graduate student teaching staff every year. Once we recognized that the graduate students could address problems of first-year students at a level appropriate to them, we suggested to the college administration that one way to attract more senior faculty to the first-year core—a chronic problem in a college that claims it does not use graduate students as faculty—would be to provide them with writing assistants. It agreed.

The writing assistants, or interns, read and comment on student papers, run small groups, meet with students individually, teach an occasional class, and so on. They have substantial influence on a faculty not particularly trained in or interested in teaching writing, because they have a view toward writing based on substantial experience teaching it to upperclass students, experience that gives them a cachet graduate assistants ordinarily do not have. The interns have been able to communicate an expertise about writing and teaching that particularly impresses faculty from departments other than English, and, often against their expectations, even faculty in the Department of English.

The writing component of the Humanities Core resembles the LRS model. Students meet in classes taught by regular faculty to discuss the readings, then every two or three weeks meet in small tutorial groups led by the graduate student intern. In the tutorial groups, students read one another's papers and discuss them in ways that try to account for why those papers seem clear and persuasive or confused and disorganized, what their point is or why they seem to have no point or no argument to support the point. Again, the tutorial groups emphasize not only how to analyze and revise one's own papers and then to extend those insights into the process of drafting the next paper, but also how to articulate that analysis in specific, useful terms. Those abilities could not be developed if the students saw only their own papers and heard, or read, only the responses of a teacher. When one student can see how six or seven other students have attacked the same problem, that student expands her experience with solving problems and widens her range of options.

The small groups typically begin with a structural analysis by searching for the Point Sentence of a paper. This is the sentence *expressed on the page* (not the general idea in the student's mind) that captures the reason for the paper, that makes the major claim of the paper. Students learn to ask, Where is the Point? Why is it *there*? If the Point Sentence is not at the end of the introduction, is it at the end of the whole and does the end of the introduction set up a way of getting to the Point at the end? Or is that Point at the end simply discovered in the act of writing? What kind of Point is it? What concepts does the introduction promise to develop? What words in the rest of the paper explicitly or indirectly stem from the words in the Point Sentence? Then repeat the process for individual paragraphs, along with stylistic analyses. (For details, see Colomb and Williams, 1986.) From there, students look at the paper from a viewpoint based on Toulmin's layout of argument (Toulmin, Rieke, and Janik, 1979): what's the claim, what's the evidence, what lets you connect that evidence to that claim, what would prove you wrong?

Interns must participate in a three-day seminar before classes begin in the fall quarter. In that seminar, our principal objective is to persuade them that they cannot attend to the same issues in the writing of freshmen that they attended to in the writing of advanced students. Rather than dealing at the outset with matters of turgid style (what we do in the Schoolhouse), they must first address questions of point and argument: "What point do you think you are making here? Show me where it is. Why do you think that? Show me where you have shown us why you think that."

A few English department faculty find the Schoolhouse philosophy too formalistic for the first-year class. But in practice that usually becomes an issue only when the interns are dealing with the very first papers in the fall quarter: not yet comfortable criticizing the substance of a textual critique, new interns fall back on the Schoolhouse analysis of style and form that they know so well. (We now try to warn new interns and prepare them to respond more flexibly.) Otherwise, the faculty response has been overwhelmingly favorable:

From a faculty member in Romance languages: "The fall quarter of 1987 marked the second term of collaboration . . . with L. . . . I am pleased to report that my impressions of his talents as teacher and tutor in the art of writing are even more favorable now than they were before. . . . He was especially talented at exploiting examples of different kinds of writing and bringing them to bear on difficulties which the students themselves had felt. . . . For me, this was an impressive feat, having witnessed other, less successful attempts at teaching the basic skills of composition."

From a faculty member in the Humanities Collegiate Division: "C has been far more than a writing intern. . . . For the students she has been like a second teacher, but one unencumbered by the trappings of authority—students speak to C freely, seeking consultations and advice about their writing problems, their thinking problems, or just plain any problems. . . . On [the matter of commenting on papers] C has been my guide. The summary with which she typically begins her typewritten page(s) of comments has become a model for me. She has the uncanny ability to get right to the center of a difficulty, but her comments are always balanced—she manages to show what is wrong as connected with what might be right. Hence, she criticizes as she encourages."

From a faculty member in Slavic languages: "What astonished and impressed me was the significant, marked improvement in those students who entered the course with poor writing skills (primarily at the paragraph level and higher: problems in organization and argumentation). I frankly had become accustomed in all my years of teaching to seeing good students learn and get better, and bad students fall further behind. Not in this case! The improvement in writing was spectacular. Whatever system P uses (I believe it's the Little Red Schoolhouse system), it really works in his hands."

ART 101

Two years ago, this first-year intern program expanded to include the second-year art requirement and, briefly, a music requirement (the music faculty found the idea of actually *teaching* writing so exotic that, after trying it once, they suspended their participation until they could digest the idea). Because Art 101 is part of the core curriculum, about a third of all undergraduates enroll in the course. In the remote and middle past, the art faculty have complained that second-year students wrote so badly that they could not require any extended writing. They attributed this problem variously to the first-year core's failure to teach writing, to the fact that over the summer students "forgot" how to write, to a lack of continued practice in writing in the college. As a result, the art faculty was reluctant to increase the time they devoted to writing. In addition, they argued that they also had to "cover" a substantial amount of material in a single quarter, and—no surprise—they were not teachers of writing and so did not feel competent, much less motivated, to teach it.

The problems of time and competence were overcome by providing the art faculty with writing interns who were art graduate students trained in the Schoolhouse. The interns began by meeting with students in small groups to go over preliminary drafts of papers, particularly with an eye toward showing them how serious students of art appropriately talk about art. (It is, for example, usually inappropriate in analyzing a work of art to assert, "The painting reminds me of my uncle's farm" or "It would clash with my sofa.") By reading one another's papers, students saw a variety of approaches—appropriate and inappropriate—to a form of discourse at first alien to almost all of them.

More significantly, the interns and the faculty began to be more explicit about what counted for them as appropriate and inappropriate discourse about art. To that end, the faculty instructors and the interns were persuaded to model both kinds of behavior *impromptu*. In practice, both the intern and the instructor bring in a slide of a work of art. One projects the slide up on a screen and the other, with no preparation, verbally composes two papers out loud. The first is intended as a typically inappropriate analysis of the work; the second a paper that falls within the boundaries of what counts as appropriate discourse in the community of art criticism. Once the students and the faculty understand the "game-playing" quality of this exercise, they all become more willing to take risks in their spontaneous analyses. Moreover, students are able to watch an expert do what they in turn are asked to do, with all the uncertainties, false starts, backtracking to correct themselves, and so on that all professionals indulge in private, but rarely display in public.

The interns devised a number of other writing exercises. They have asked the students to keep an "analytic sketchbook" (a slightly fancier name than "journal" or "diary") in which students lay the informal groundwork for papers to follow. They ask students to write postcards describing a work of art, with the objective of teaching them to boil down their observations to a very short space. They ask students to write objective descriptions of a work of art preparatory to writing an analysis of it. This exercise anticipates one of the two predictable responses to a request to "analyze" a work of art. The first, private impressionism, has been modeled by the instructors and ruled out as inappropriate. The second, summary, is explicitly assigned, allowing students to do what many will do anyway so that they can then be moved on toward analysis.

As a result of this program of writing instruction, the art faculty claims to have seen not only a dramatic improvement in the writing of their students, but a dramatic improvement in the ability of students to *think* about art in complex ways. And in class evaluations, students agree. Now the senior art faculty, like the first-year humanities faculty, resist teaching Art 101 unless they have an intern to assist them (even though there are not enough art interns to go around).

From the director of undergraduate studies in Art History: "Writing interns have become an essential and integral part of the teaching of Art 101, the art department's core course in the humanities. From the first day of class, these interns work along with the faculty member to focus students' thinking about articulating their visual responses to works of art. . . . We have found the inclusion of writing interns has dramatically increased the effectiveness of Art 101. All too often the undergraduate, inexperienced in critical thinking about his or her visual environment, expects works of art to be easily apprehended. He or she "sees" the object, "names" it, and has the feeling that it is understood. Students quickly learn that even naming or describing objects is more complicated than they initially thought, and that through the process of articulating what they see, they begin to see more. Writing is an essential part of this articulation. . . . By focusing on these complex issues both together in class, and separately with the intern, the student is able to isolate his or her problems—in conceptualization or in writing—and develop a deeper critical understanding of works of art more quickly in a short ten-week quarter than would be possible if faced with these problems together, and without the close supervision of the writing [intern]."

A PEDAGOGICAL/PHILOSOPHICAL OVERVIEW

Some Preliminaries. As the the Writing Programs grew out of the Schoolhouse, we began to put in place (1) a coherent theory of discourse underlying the writing instruction, (2) pedagogical strategies both for presenting the theory in usable language and for putting that language into practice, and (3) a group of trained and experienced graduate students ready to serve as instructors in a variety of classes. What we didn't have was a coherent account of how the kinds of individual programs we had developed might comprise a pedagogical whole.

Most college and university writing programs are driven "bottom up." Since first-year students by and large don't write very well, the faculty blames the high schools and institutes a first-year writing course, often with remedial and advanced sections. But second-, third-, and fourth-year students often don't write very well either. So, many writing faculties extend their activities upward into upperclass courses, and in the best programs they influence faculty in other departments to include more writing activities in their courses, to give specific courses in disciplinary writing, etc.

The Writing Programs at the University of Chicago have developed differently. They have been driven "top down." We established the Schoolhouse as a result of our work with organizations in the professional world. That initial program attracted interest from the professional schools, increasing the opportunities for graduate students to teach. Those trained graduate students filtered down into the first year of the curriculum, taking with them the philosophy and methods originally designed for mature writers—particularly the emphases on articulating the basis of their judgments as readers, on explaining the specific sources of perceived problems, and on making specific suggestions for revision.

While the *theory of discourse* underlying that common language for talking about writing was "top-down" by design, constructing a holistic hierarchy of discourse structures where lower-level structures are explained in terms of higher-level ones (see Colomb and Williams, 1987; Colomb and Turner, 1988), the *pedagogical structure* of the programs was top-down at first by dint of circumstance. However, in all the activities of the programs we began to find pedagogical problems recurring and to see some useful generalizations. We have since developed and incorporated into the program a body of thinking and research concerning the generic differences between expert and novice thinking. In that work can be found a metaphor for conceiving the structure of a multilevel writing program, a metaphor that we think holds the key to a coherent view of top-down pedagogy.

Two Metaphors for Learning

Progress as Linear Movement. Metaphors influence not only how we think about experience, but how we deal with it. We speak of anger, for example, with images of liquids boiling inside sealed containers: "I was so boiling mad that I blew my lid. After I let off steam, though, I felt better" (Johnson, 1987). Had circumstances been different, our culture might have adopted the metaphor of the machine: "I was so racing mad that I was already running too high for my specs, so I knew I had to lower my rpms or burn out my bearings. After I cooled the system down, I operated better." Under our presiding metaphorical frame, we often encourage—or at least condone—the expression of anger because we consider its "release" therapeutic; under another metaphorical system, we might consider the expression of anger damaging because it could lead to systemic breakdown.

The metaphors we use to describe learning, particularly skills such as reading, writing, and thinking, are metaphors of natural development and growth. When we develop normally, we grow "up." As we grow "up," we also "progress" left to right along a time scale (controlled by the tacit metaphor of reaching a "goal"). So we visually graph development from low to high and progress from a starting point on the lower left to a goal on the upper right. We picture normal growth as a curve (or stairstep, if we think growth has stages), from lower left to higher right. We typically combine this growth metaphor with construction metaphors: We have to "lay a solid foundation" and then "reinforce" what we learn so that we both "maintain" what we have learned and "build" on it toward mastery.

These metaphors of linear development and building up come so naturally to us that we become particularly receptive to theories of learning expressible through them. So it is not surprising that administrators and teachers, particularly those who teach "generic" skills such as reading, writing, and thinking, should be attracted to the work of developmentalists such as Jean Piaget (Inhelder and Piaget, 1958), William Perry (1968), Lawrence Kohlberg (1984), and others whose models of development would seem to impose order on the more puzzling patterns of student behavior.

For Piaget, developing children move from concrete operational thinking to formal operational thinking, not smoothly, but in ways that let us account for their early cognitive limitations not by IQ or diligence, but by a qualitative structure of mind. Young children are not yet able to manipulate the abstractions derived from sets of sets; they are not able to juggle multiple hypotheticals, think probabilistically, etc. To put it crudely, younger children are incapable of thinking abstractly, a cognitive constraint Piagetians explain not by intelligence or cultural background, but by genetic epistemology.

Perry found a roughly similar pattern of development in the social/academic development of Harvard undergraduates: In their academic careers, students often appeared in his office at a stage he calls "dualistic"—the stage at which students simply want to know who the authorities are and what they know. When students "progress," they move to what he called the "multiple/ relative" stage, that stage where students believe that since there are no final authorities and no final answers, then "everyone's opinion must be equally good." Perry claimed that the dualist stage regularly precedes the multiple/ relative stage, and that these are followed by stages in which the student is increasingly able to handle ambiguities, to appreciate the legitimacy of different conclusions drawn from different premises, to understand the importance of the process of reasoning as opposed to its outcome, etc.

Kohlberg laid out a sequence of moral reasoning that begins at the stage of preconventional moral reasoning involving immediate, concrete approval and disapproval; then moves up to conventional moral reasoning governed by socially established values and peer pressure; and culminates in postconventional moral reasoning, that stage where the mature moral reasoner comes to recognize that local systems in particular societies rest not on rules that govern, but on universal moral principles that guide. Again, this is movement from the concrete to the abstract.

All three of these models describe a pattern of cognitive growth that begins with the immediate, concrete, rule-governed here and now, and that develops to more abstract, hypothetical forms of reasoning guided by principles. To be sure, these models differ profoundly, in ways our reductive description ignores. But to put it in a way that is not deceptively reductive, they describe a movement from relatively "lower-level" concreteness to relatively "higher-order" abstraction.

Like all models that reflect tacit metaphors, however, these models have consequences. One is that "regression" is bad. A student who does not continue to perform at a level "reached" earlier has "fallen back" to a "lower" level of performance. And whoever taught the student at that "lower level"—teaching writing is a paradigm case—did not do the job right. The student failed to learn the "bas(e)ics."

It is a metaphoric scheme that motivates us to abuse those who taught our students before they reach us. In the case of writing, teachers of first-year college students criticize the high schools; teachers of upper-class students criticize teachers of first-year composition; teachers in professional and graduate schools criticize the colleges; and professional organizations such as law firms and businesses criticize the whole educational system. A skill such as writing, the story goes, should follow a model of steady, linear development from lower-left to upper-right. When our students do not write as we expect, we feel empowered by our metaphors to decide that our predecessors must have failed to raise them to the level we think they should have achieved. A related consequence is that entire curricula are constructed to "raise" the student to achieve objectifiable levels of performance. If students are identifiably dualists when they enter the system, they should be measurably closer to being multiple relativists at the end of the first semester. That kind of thinking produces a system of testing that reductively categorizes students according to their cognitive/moral/social/academic development.

But the most problematical consequences come when we rely on these linear models to make policy decisions about education. Such decisions may be costly, because evidence suggests that these models may not entirely comport with reality. The evidence comes from three directions. First, some reports increasingly suggest that children who test at the concrete operational level of thinking can be induced to behave in ways that characterize formal operational thinking (Bryant, 1983). By manipulating the form of the test and particularly the kind of knowledge that the child controls about the materials of the test, one can "move" a concrete-operational-thinking child to a formal operational level of thinking.

A second line of evidence comes from an opposite direction. A number of researchers have asserted that up to half of first-year college students are still concrete operational thinkers, this long after Piaget's model would have had them move "up" to formal operational thinking (Dunlop and Fazio, 1976; Tomlinson-Keasey, 1972). And when the American Accounting Association studied a group of upper-class and graduate students, up to half were judged to be either concrete operational thinkers or in transition from concrete to formal operational thinking (Shute, 1979). Is it plausible that large numbers of graduate students think in ways generically similar to ten-year-olds? Possible, perhaps, but put together these two lines of evidence—young children can be taught to think in formal operational terms, and graduate students can seem to think in concrete operational terms—and a more likely hypothesis suggests itself. Perhaps what counts in "higher-level" cognitive processing is not only those abstract and generic operations, but also knowledge, experience, control over specific content (see Glaser, 1984). "Concrete" behavior may in fact indicate thin categories of knowledge, not some intrinsic quality of mind.

This hypothesis is encouraged by a third line of evidence emerging from research into expert vs. novice thinking. Most of the research into this matter involves what is called in cognitive psychology "well-structured" problems,

problems that have a single right answer and a relatively clear-cut algorithm for getting there (Larkin, McDermott, Simon, and Simon, 1980; Chi, Feltovitch, and Glaser, 1981). Experts and novices solve well-structured problems in different ways. Most relevant is that novices (not "lower-level" thinkers, please note) are characterized by relatively concrete thinking, while experts tend to be characterized by more abstract thinking. For example, a novice problem solver in physics might look at a problem containing a picture of a spring and assume that the problem belongs to the category of "spring problems" and begin to think about what she knows about springs. The expert looks at the problem and categorizes the problem not on the basis of its most concrete, physically present feature, but by the abstract character of its intellectual content.

Still more interesting is the line of research into "ill-formed" problems, problems for which there is no obviously "correct" answer, much less obviously correct algorithms for a solution. Voss and others (1985) put the following problem to four groups of subjects: if you were in charge, how would you solve the problems of agriculture in the Soviet Union? The problem solvers were grouped as follows:

1. Novice/low-knowledge: students taking a first course in Soviet affairs
2. Novice/high-knowledge: graduate students in Soviet affairs
3. Expert/low-knowledge: senior chemistry professors
4. Expert/high-knowledge: senior faculty in Soviet affairs

The high-knowledge experts differed from the novices in three ways: (*a*) the high-knowledge experts spent more time decomposing the problem, defining the problem space, explaining why the problem was complex; (*b*) where the novices would propose solutions at a relatively concrete level—more fertilizer, better roads, better farm machinery, etc.—the high-knowledge experts began at a "higher," more abstract level—with the system, infrastructure, or history; (*c*) the novices constructed relatively shorter chains of arguments, moving from point to point without developing any one of them extensively. However, once the high-knowledge experts introduced a topic, they stayed with it, developing a chain of reasoning based on that argument.

The most salient outcome is that of the low-knowledge experts, the chemistry professors. They behaved in ways similar to the low-knowledge novices. This outcome suggests that while there may be some generic quality of expert thinking that characterizes all experts *in their field*, its deployment is crucially linked both to the amount of knowledge one controls about the matter in question, and to the complexity of the structure of that knowledge. Confronting a problem in an unfamiliar area, experts in an alien field seem to behave in ways similar to generic novices.

It seems, then, that extensive, structured knowledge counts for much in good thinking. Some suggest everything. Indeed, it may count for much in development in general. If formal thinking can be induced in a young child by providing substantial experience with the problem materials, if a dualist becomes a relativist once he or she accumulates multiple points of view and sees that all of them are at best intrinsically tentative, if a preconventional moral reasoner becomes a conventional reasoner when that person becomes part of a larger community and understands the shared and therefore abstract values of the community, then the notion of intellectual growth as biological or cognitive epistemology with its own teleology becomes an open question. And so does the model of learning represented by linear movement on a steady or staggered lower-left, upper-right curve.

Progress as Joining the Community. Another—and perhaps more productive—metaphor for growth is the equally familiar one of an "outsider" trying to "get into" a community, a metaphor that models the movement of a learner situated outside a bounded field, who then "enters" the field and so "joins" the community by acting like its members. (This metaphor does *not* place any single community at the upper right of the chart as an ultimate goal.) To join a disciplinary community is, in part, to master a body of knowledge. But that knowledge does not exist "out there," independent of those who control it, just waiting to be acquired. Knowledge belongs to groups of people who have some shared stake in exploring, preserving, and expanding it. The outsider must acquire knowledge from insiders, usually through some form of an apprenticeship. Perhaps we should not, but we draw institutional boundaries around knowledge by locating it in communities defined by experts and by those novices who are trying to learn what experts know. We call those communities by different names—subjects, fields, areas, majors, departments, disciplines. They often overlap, and they consist of subcommunities that also overlap. That these names cut up the pie so differently only reflects the unruliness of communities.

Whatever we call these fields and however we define them, the knowledge they bound is colored by the values, conventions, and styles of the communities that make that knowledge the object of their interest. While the novice is committed to mastering the knowledge that the community thinks is important, the novice is equally committed to acquiring the *ways* of thinking that characterize that community, the tone of voice that identifies one member to another, the required silences whose violation instantly identifies the outsider. However true it is that Shakespeare is a famous writer who wrote many plays, it is usually inappropriate for those trying to join the ranks of literary experts to express that sentiment, either in writing or in speech.

We want to use this metaphor to redescribe the concrete operational thinker or the dualist or the preconventional moral reasoner as a novice standing outside a knowledge community. Of course, our metaphor has its own consequences, particularly in regard to the central interest of this volume—

projects that seek to extend writing "across the curriculum." But we believe that the consequences of our description do more justice to—and do more to help—the novice learner.

The Novice Writer

Those new to a knowledge community often exhibit some characteristic patterns of learning behavior, patterns that teachers can learn to anticipate. First, we should expect from novices behavior that is relatively "concrete" (*not* "lower-level"). A moment of reflection suggests why. Abstraction is at least partially based on the number and variety of instances of a category. By definition, a novice's knowledge is simultaneously very thin and relatively unstructured, with categories defined by as few as a single instance. The student of architecture who knows only classical forms has a very thin category of "architectural style." From the point of view of someone who also knows romanesque, gothic, baroque, modern, etc., that less knowledgeable student's problem-solving behavior would seem concrete operational indeed.

In regard to writing, we can predict a number of "concrete," "immature" forms of behavior: mapping the particular (concrete) language of the assignment into the opening paragraph of the paper; mapping any hint of organization in the assignment onto the paper itself; closely following the sequence of events or topics in an assigned text; and in particular, summarizing rather than analyzing. Novices will tend to say those things that are ordinarily left unsaid by insiders, things that can be left unsaid just because they are shared. Novices will also seize on those features of the "voice" that seem most markedly to characterize the discourse of the field. In a field as stylistically marked as the law, for example, new students typically seize on the *heretofore*'s and *whereas*'s because they are among the most concretely obvious signals of legal language, the language of the tribe.

Second, this "concrete" behavior may be compounded by a predictable deterioration of performance in skills mastered earlier. Someone trying to enter a new community of discourse must bring under control a new body of knowledge, new ways of thinking, new ways of writing and speaking. So it is entirely predictable that some skills already mastered will deteriorate, often by default reliance on the most concrete forms of behavior.

Concrete, novice behavior appears in those aspects of writing that depend on the ability to analyze and synthesize. Here the consequences can be especially damaging because this failing is so often perceived as a sign that the learner cannot think. Because it is so important to our pedagogy, we will examine this behavior at more length and at three different levels: (1) professional school writing, (2) advanced upper-class undergraduate writing, and (3) first-year undergraduate writing. (We might have included professional writing by new attorneys.)

We begin with the mixed professional/academic setting of law school because we want to emphasize that "novice" behavior is not limited to the young and untalented—the effort to join a discourse community invites it even at very high levels of professional writing. Nor are inappropriate judgments of novice behavior limited to teachers of the young: even at "higher" levels, learners write in ways that can by the old, linear metaphor be described as "low-level," "immature," "unskilled," etc., but that we prefer to describe as the predictable response of the novice, independent of any level of development.

Writing by First-year Law Students. Most schools of law require a first-year legal-writing course, but most of those courses do not teach legal writing. They teach research, citation forms, some aspects of legal thinking. This is especially so at the most selective law schools. They understandably assume that students who had A− and B+ averages in college are not merely competent, but proficient writers. And yet in their first weeks and months of law school, many of those writers display the very forms of behavior that characterize writers in their first year of college.

Let us describe a paper given to us by a legal-writing instructor as an example of the work of a student who had not learned how to write well, a paper written by a law student in his fourth week. (Substantial excerpts are reproduced in Appendix A at the end of this chapter.) This student attends one of the country's most selective law schools, has graduated from a prestigious college near the top of his class, and has produced laudatory letters of recommendation, high LSAT scores, and an articulate application essay. The assignment was to analyze how a jurist used precedent while deciding whether a person can be convicted of second-degree murder if that person was coerced into participating in a crime in which another participant commits murder in the first degree.

The faculty person teaching in the legal-writing program was led by a linear conception of development to decide that this writer had never learned to write well. But the essay paradigmatically illustrates the behavior of a novice trying to deal with a new field. First, it precisely tracks the sequence of the jurist's text rather than abstracting from the text the principles of law that the jurist followed. Second, each of the student's middle, supposedly analytical paragraphs (see excerpts) corresponds to one section of the decision and precisely tracks the sequence of its section. It is not surprising, therefore, that the instructor considered this "mere summary." Third, although the conclusion begins to address the abstractions that the jurist considered, it merely lists them in the order in which they appeared in the original text and in the essay.

Finally and most importantly, the middle, analytical paragraphs do not (with a few exceptions) specifically state the key analytical terms of the conclusion, terms first announced only at the end of the paper, where the writer seemed to discover them.

Like so many novice performances, this paper replicates the act of discovery. The writer structured the paper on the narrative of his thinking, discovering the abstract terms of analysis only at the end, where he summarizes them in a list. On the one hand, this might be treated merely as an example of "writer-based prose" (Flower, 1979). But "writer-based prose" is not necessarily a sign of generic "novice writer," as Flower seemed at that time to suggest. It may reflect the concrete behavior of a very experienced writer who is a novice in the field.

The signs of concrete, novice behavior are also evident in the style of that essay. This peculiarly awkward sentence presents the jurist's thinking in the writer's own words:

> The final step in Lord Morris's **preparation** to introduce the precedents is his **consideration** of the idea of **conviction** despite the **presence** of duress and then immediate **pardon** for that crime as an unnecessary step which is in. fact injurious for it creates the stigma of the criminal on a potentially blameless (or at least not criminal) individual.

Pervasive nominalization characterizes bad legal writing in particular and bad academic writing in general. But as we noted above, it also characterizes a kind of stylistic breakdown typical of mature writers trying to wrestle with difficult concepts. The student might have written

> Before he **introduces** the precedents, Lord Morris **considers** a final issue: if a court first **convicts** a defendant who acted under duress and then immediately **pardons** that defendant, has the court taken an unnecessary step, a step that may even injure the defendant by stigmatizing him as criminal when he may be blameless?

This is a complex "if-then" question, involving two conditionals ("if a court convicts . . . and then pardons"), one of which contains an embedded conditional ("a defendant who acted under duress"), followed by a conclusion ("taken an unnecessary step") that itself becomes a cause ("may even injure the defendant") of a complex consequence ("by stigmatizing him as criminal when he may be blameless"). It is not surprising that a novice in legal reasoning should suffer a stylistic breakdown in the face of complex conditions and consequences. But note that his confused tangle of nominalizations is akin to an equally ponderous but professionally deliberate legal style:

> Because the individualized assessment of the appropriateness of the death penalty is a moral inquiry into the culpability of the defendant, and not an emotional response to the mitigating evidence, I agree with the Court that an instruction informing the jury that they "must not be swayed by mere

sentiment, conjecture, sympathy, passion, prejudice, public opinion or public feeling" does not by itself violate the Eighth and Fourteenth Amendments to the United States Constitution. (Sandra Day O'Connor, concurring, *California v. Albert Greenwood Brown, Jr.*)

As turgid as this is, it is not the turgidity of a novice unfamiliar with legal thinking. One of the great ironies of modern prose is that the turgid professional, most deeply socialized into the language of a profession, and the awkward novice can seem to have so much in common.

A related, though less turgid novice response is to concretize in the text too much of the writer's thinking process. In the following example, a new law student as academically distinguished as the previous one tries to adopt the voice of a judge. But in doing so he uses metadiscourse to raise to a level of textual concreteness the machinery of thinking and reasoning—"the main point supporting my point of view," etc.—that experts usually suppress. At the same time, this student raises to the same level of textual concreteness certain substantive matters that any expert would leave unsaid, such as the obvious assertion that a plaintiff must produce evidence against a defendant. (In this passage, we have boldfaced the metadiscourse and italicized the statements that anyone socialized into the world of the law would be unlikely to make.)

> **It is my opinion that** *the ruling of the lower court concerning the case of* Haslem v. Lockwood **should be upheld, thereby denying** *the appeal of the plaintiff.* **The main point supporting my point of view** *on this case* **concerns** *the tenet of our court system which holds that in order to win his case, the plaintiff must prove that he was somehow wronged by the defendant. The burden of proof rests on the plaintiff. He must show enough evidence to convince the court that he is in the right.* **However, in this case, I do not believe that** *the plaintiff has satisfied this requirement. In order to prove that the defendant owes him recompense for the six loads of manure,* he must first show that he was the legal owner of those loads, and then show that the defendant removed the manure for his own use [the paper goes on for several more paragraphs].

A more professional (i.e., socialized, i.e., "expert") version would be, "Plaintiff has failed to show that he was the legal owner of the loads and that the defendant removed the manure for his own use. The court affirms *Haslem v. Lockwood.*"

In both cases, the instructors took these as examples of bad writing and unskilled writers. In our terms, they are examples of novices trying to express themselves in a field that largely baffles them, and displaying the signs of novice behavior—concreteness, saying what can be left unsaid, and occasional breakdowns in stylistic performance in the direction of the most visible and concrete features of the "voice" that characterizes the prose of a field.

These examples illustrate forms of writing familiar to every teacher of freshman composition: summary rather than analysis, thinking out loud, a conclusion discovered at the end, evident stylistic infelicity, etc. In neither case could we assert that the writers were in some general sense immature or unintelligent. And yet they display the generic shortcomings of novice, "concrete" writers.

Writing by upperclass students. As they move into a discipline, undergraduates face many of the conceptual difficulties faced by new professional students. The next example comes from a paper by a third-year student taking a course in Western Civilization, a good student who had written excellent papers in his first-year humanities course, but who had had no preparation in historical thinking. By the concluding paragraph of his paper, he at last reached a point worth making:

> The Popes, Urban II and Gregory VII, used the concept of the Crusades as a means to achieve a form of unity important to them during their pontificate. During Urban's pontificate, he could establish his authority, fight the devil (Muslims), and control fighting amongst the Europeans and direct those energies elsewhere. Gregory VII wishes to achieve unification between the Roman Church and the Greek Orthodox Church. . . . Therefore the Crusade was not just a fight against the Muslims to recapture the Holy Land and to save God's faith, but it was an effort to save the Church and Europe from the dissensions which were tearing it apart.

This paper was given a C+ because it was considered "disorganized," "largely summary," etc. Why? Because all of the first five and most of the next five paragraphs offered only a close summary of the assigned texts, so that the central concept of the conclusion—the Crusades achieving Christian unity—did not begin to emerge until about the tenth paragraph. The introduction was wholly summary and pointless:

> During the eleventh through thirteenth centuries, the Roman Catholic Church initiated several Crusades against the Muslims in the Holy Lands. The Pope would usually instigate and call for armament and support for this endeavor. Pope Urban II started the first Crusade in 1096. His predecessor, Gregory VII, had also petitioned to get support for a crusade in 1074 but did not succeed in launching his Crusade. There are written statements from these Popes concerning the Crusades. Pope Urban II in "Speech at the Council of Clermont" in the year 1095 calls for a Crusade and Pope Gregory VII in a Letter to King Henry IV during the year 1074 also proposes a Crusade.

This is the writing of a student gripped by novice concreteness. Since he does not control the information from the sources well enough to hold it whole in his mind as he thinks through its implications, he predictably summarizes the source, closely following the structure of its text. Once the material is concretized in the form of a linear summary, he is able to draw from it some inferences that qualify as analysis.

Writing by First-year Students. By this point it is almost redundant to offer a typical first-year student paper that might illustrate these same features. Let us briefly look at one from a student with a VSAT well over 600. He was in his third week of college and writing about two speeches in Thucydides' history of the Peloponnesian war, a subject wholly strange to him. This was the assignment:

> In the second chapter of his history, Thucydides presents two speakers asking Athens for help against the other. As we know Thucydides wrote these speeches to represent what "probably would have been said." Compare and contrast the way Thucydides had the Corcyrans and Corinthians rhetorically appeal to the Athenians in different ways.

And here are some indicative excerpts from the paper:

> A Comparison of the Corcyran and Corinthian Speeches
>
> The Corcyran and Corinthian speeches in Thucydides's *The Peloponnesian War* differ in several ways. The most important way that the two speeches differ is in the particular appeals each side gives to support its arguments. I will first discuss the Corcyran speech and then the Corinthian speech in order to show what we can learn from these differences.
> The Corcyrans first apologize. . . . Then they give three reasons why the Athenians should help them and join in an alliance. They say that . . . Then they predict that . . . They say that . . . Finally, they emphasize that . . .
> The Corinthians start out by attacking the Corcyrans. . . .
> The Athenians decide to join with the Corcyrans against the Corinthians because they are sure that there is going to be a war between them soon and that they would have a good ally with the Corcyrans. The speeches are different in that the Corcyrans had the better argument because they understood the Athenians better than the Corinthians since the Athenians were very practical and self-interested at this time. Therefore, the Corcyran speech was a more clever appeal.

We need not dwell on the obvious here: Like the novice problem solver who thinks that a concrete picture of a spring in the problem statement means the problem is a spring-type problem, the student here takes the concrete language of the problem statement—the assignment—and maps it directly into the opening paragraph. The writer takes the sequence of the speeches from the assignment and from the text. In each section, he marches through each speech in summary fashion, at the end discovering his conclusion. While the style of the paper is competent, the organization and thought reflect the student's "concrete" thinking, which is to say, his inexperience in thinking about matters of this kind.

In three cases (new law student, upper-class student new to a field, new college student) we see the same generic pattern—the tyranny of the concrete and the breakdown of control over skills mastered earlier. If our narrative is plausible, the upward curve of growth is at best misleading. While there must certainly be development of some kind, it is not the kind of development that can be graphed like height and weight. A metaphor more insightful and useful than the upward curve is that of the outsider trying to get in, that of the novice trying to join a community of experts, an experience that happens to our best students many times over.

THE CURRICULAR IMPLICATIONS

Once we decided that internalized, controlled experience plays so crucial a role in competent behavior, we tried to find ways to anticipate and accommodate the *entirely predictable* forms of behavior that novices display, not once as "novice writers" but as writers who now and then happen to be novices. A very substantial part of such instruction involves making clear the local conventions of the discourse community. It involves modeling the kind of behavior that we expect of students writing in an exotic field. It involves providing a body of experience in discourse wider than what a single student writes. It involves creating groups in which students can see how other students have solved the same problem in different ways, or can try to solve them together.

More importantly, however, it requires that at every point in the curriculum instructors must be aware of what to expect in the way of "incompetent writing"—summary rather than analysis, inappropriate imitation of obvious and concrete features of a professional style, slavishly following cues in the assignment, stylistic and other breakdowns. It requires instructors to devise assignments that allow or even force students to summarize the complex material they may be unable to hold in their minds. It requires us to anticipate the way novice students will respond "too literally" to complex assignments.

Most important of all, it requires us to prepare students for those experiences they will have as they move through a curriculum, repeatedly enduring the same frustrations of being unable—at first—to move beyond "mere summary," or of discovering only at the end of a paper the conclusions one can draw from the act of summary. We must make the students self-conscious about their own academic and professional progress. It is in this sense that we have tried to redefine articulation. Articulation does not mean simply attaching the output end of one pipe into the input end of the next, higher one so that the students can flow easily through the curriculum. It means teaching the student to articulate himself to a community of knowledge and to anticipate those predictable anxieties—the temporary deterioration of performance and the specific forms it will take.

THE FUTURE

Where the University of Chicago's Writing Programs go from here depends on how much money the university can bring itself to invest in the future and on whether certain political/ideological questions can be settled. At the upper levels, money is in some ways the least important issue because we are able to extract from the graduate and professional schools about as much as we need to support the senior lectors. There is little doubt in our minds—at the moment—that the substantial expansion in the program will come at the upper end, among the graduate and professional students.

The real money crunch will be, first, in expanding the size of the School-house in order to expand the pool of experienced graduate student lectors and, second, in hiring new faculty to help oversee the program, train the graduate students, and monitor their performance in class. The writing programs are labor intensive at the beginning. A graduate seminar that begins the training process must be offered each fall. We necessarily do a good deal of small-group rehearsal with our lectors-to-be, and that takes time. It also takes time to supervise the lectors on the job—reading a selection of the papers they are marking up, visiting their small groups, talking over problems with them. As lectors move on to new jobs, there is a new (though less demanding) round of training, orientation, and supervision. Unless we can expand the number of faculty either by persuading others to participate (unlikely) or hiring new faculty, we will necessarily grow smaller because the faculty now involved in the program are overextended. When they take a break from the program, it means contracting the available resources for training and supervision.

The political problems are more complex, and will be deeply implicated in new hiring. The Schoolhouse has a distinct theoretical bias toward reader-response, text-based analysis. That approach rises to a level of ideology through the entire program. Unfortunately, some of the more belletristically minded faculty suspect that the Schoolhouse has been corrupted by the social sciences, infected by cognitive psychology, linguistics, and other alien practices. In one particularly blunt exchange involving the possibility of bringing in a new director of Writing Programs, Joseph Williams suggested that the Writing Programs should be administratively located outside the Department of English in order to avoid the disciplinary preferences of literary critics and to spare students in other disciplines the preciosity of literary analysis and its emphasis on local textual epiphanies. That did not encourage those already suspicious of the program.

It may also be that some part of the suspicion arises from a perception that too few English department graduate students are selected as lectors and interns. As described above, the selection is anonymous and less than a third of the graduate students selected are from English. Since this is the *only* substantial opportunity for graduate students to teach (the college avoids using graduate students in teaching positions), the positions are perceived as very desirable. It has been difficult to persuade some in the English department that more opportunities for graduate students to teach will arise only if the Writing Programs continue to grow, and that they will continue to grow only if they are not perceived as an English department fiefdom, rewarding its own students or teaching and reading "fine" writing. Only by insinuating the program into a variety of locations in the university, particularly through taking on graduate students from the social sciences, will we get the support we need to expand and thereby draw in increasing numbers of our English department graduate students. And in any case, to subordinate this Writing Program to the prejudices of any single discipline would be to betray its first principles and its greatest success.

Appendix A

A PAPER BY A NEW LAW STUDENT

The case in question, . . . *Lynch*, revolves around the issue of whether the defense of duress is available to the defendant Lynch. The facts of the case are set forth at the beginning of the opinion by Lord Morris writing for the majority and are as follows. Lynch was taken from his home to a meeting with Sean Meehan, a known IRA member and ruthless gunman. Meehan instructed Lynch to steal a car . . . [Meehan kills policeman, Lynch is seized as an accomplice and indicted for second degree murder].

The central issue which Lord Morris and the House of Lords decided upon was whether the defense of duress is available to someone charged with murder in the second degree. . . . In his opinion, Lord Morris attempts to provide a somewhat clear opinion on the central issue of the availability of the duress defense and the implications of this opinion on the related questions.

Lord Morris attempts to clarify and delineate the distinctions used to arrive at the decision to overturn the two lower courts. The opinion first examines the crucial element absent from criminal behavior when acting under duress, *mens rea*. From here it proceeds to ask whether the lack of *mens rea* . . . In order to address the issue and resolve the question of treatment, he considers the idea of reasonable behavior given a set of circumstances in which . . . He is clear to stress that "duress must never . . ."

The final step in his preparation to introduce the precedents is his consideration of the idea of conviction despite the presence of duress and then immediate pardon for that crime as an unnecessary step which is in fact injurious for it creates the stigma of the criminal on a potentially blameless (or at least not criminal) individual.

The first case cited by Morris for its specifics is *Rex v. Crutchly* in which Crutchly broke a threshing machine [recital of facts] . . . The case is significant for Morris's development for two of its essential facts: the legitimate distinction between a criminal act and criminal behavior on the part of an individual in a situation of duress and the idea of resistance to a mob to which the individual did not voluntarily belong. Morris considered both elements to be present in *Lynch*.

The second case cited is *Reg v. Tyler*, which Morris does not intend to use as a valuable precedent. The defendants in Tyler followed a quasi religious leader [recital of facts] . . . Lord Denman [writer of *Reg v. Tyler*], in his opinion, clearly stated that to allow a defense of duress in this case [would countenance murder]. . . . It is this absolute disallowance of the defense of duress which Lord Morris finds unacceptable because he feels that the individual may face no meaningful alternative than to aid and abet. Morris finds that Lynch lacked the alternatives available to the defendants in *Tyler*.

In the next case, *Attorney General v. Whelan*, the defendant acted in consort with others to steal a large sum of silver coin from a railroad. Whelan admitted that he participated in the crime . . . [Jury answers yes to duress/judge finds guilty and suspends sentence because of duress]. Lord Morris uses this case and Lord Murnaghan's opinion to substantiate and cite precedent for his unwillingness to accept duress as a mitigating circumstance instead of a defense. . . .

Lord Morris uses these precedents in order to arrive at his intended point that the defense of duress should be available. Each of the cases cited provides one piece of the scheme by which Lord Morris attempts to show that murder is an offense for which the defense of duress should be available. Dissociation from the criminals as soon as possible (*Crutchly*), non-voluntary association with the criminal (*Tyler*), duress as a defense and not as a mitigating circumstance (*Whelan*) . . . are all components of Lord Morris's reasoning.

Using these cases in this manner, Lord Morris seems to believe that although none of the cases are directly on point, his use of them is a progressive, yet justified interpretation of the relevant precedents of duress as a defense, and that this defense should be available to someone accused of murder in the second degree.

Appendix B

UNIVERSITY WRITING PROGRAMS

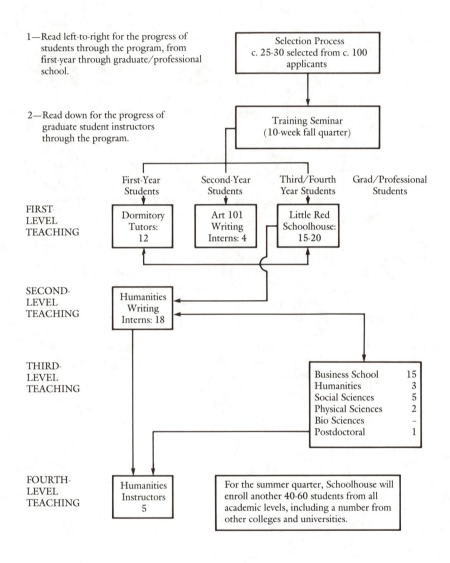

1—Read left-to-right for the progress of students through the program, from first-year through graduate/professional school.

Selection Process
c. 25-30 selected from c. 100 applicants

2—Read down for the progress of graduate student instructors through the program.

Training Seminar
(10-week fall quarter)

First-Year Students

Second-Year Students

Third/Fourth Year Students

Grad/Professional Students

FIRST-LEVEL TEACHING

Dormitory Tutors: 12

Art 101 Writing Interns: 4

Little Red Schoolhouse: 15-20

SECOND-LEVEL TEACHING

Humanities Writing Interns: 18

THIRD-LEVEL TEACHING

Business School	15
Humanities	3
Social Sciences	5
Physical Sciences	2
Bio Sciences	–
Postdoctoral	1

FOURTH-LEVEL TEACHING

Humanities Instructors 5

For the summer quarter, Schoolhouse will enroll another 40-60 students from all academic levels, including a number from other colleges and universities.

REFERENCES

Bryant, Peter. "Piaget's Struggle and the Struggle about Piaget." In *Jean Piaget: An Interdisciplinary Critique*, edited by Sohan Modgil, Celia Modgil, and Geoffrey Brown. London: Routledge & Kegan Paul, 1983.

Chi, M. P. Feltovitch, and R. Glaser. "Categorization and Representation of Physics Problems by Experts and Novices." *Cognitive Science* 5 (1981): 121–52.

Colomb, Gregory G., and Joseph M. Williams, "Perceiving Structure in Professional Prose." In *Writing in Non-Academic Settings* edited by Lee Odell and Dixie Goswami. New York: Guilford, 1986.

Colomb, Gregory G., and Mark Turner. "Computers, Literary Theory, and Theory of Meaning." In *Critical Projections: The Future of Literary Theory*, edited by Ralph Cohen. London: Methuen, 1988.

Dunlop, D., and F. Fazio. "Piagetian Theory and Abstract Preferences of College Science Students." *Journal of College Science Teaching* (May 1976): 297–300.

Flower, Linda. "Writer Based Prose: A Cognitive Basis for Problems in Writing. *College English* 41 (September 1979), 19–37.

Glaser, Robert, "Education and Thinking: The Role of Knowledge." *American Psychologist* 39 (1984): 93–104.

Inhelder, B., and Jean Piaget. *The Growth of Logical Thinking from Childhood to Adolescence.* New York: Basic Books, 1958.

Johnson, Mark. *The Body in the Mind: The Bodily Basis of Meaning, Reasoning and Imagination.* Chicago: University of Chicago Press, 1987.

Kohlberg, Lawrence. *The Psychology of Moral Development.* Vol. 2. New York: Harper & Row, 1984.

Larkin, J., J. McDermott, D. Simon, and H. Simon. "Expert and Novice Performance in Solving Physics Problems." *Science* 208 (1980): 1,335–42.

Perry, William G., Jr. *Forms of Intellectual and Ethical Development in the College Years.* New York: Holt, Rinehart & Winston, 1968.

Shute, George E. *Accounting Students and Abstract Reasoning: An Exploratory Study.* Sarasota, FL: American Accounting Association, 1979.

Tomlinson-Keasey, C. "Formal Operations in Females Aged 11 to 54 Years of Age." *Developmental Psychologist* 6 (1972): 364.

Toulmin, Stephen., R. Rieke, and A. Janik. *An Introduction to Reasoning.* New York: Macmillan, 1979.

Voss, James, T. Green, T. Post, and B. Penner, "Problem-solving Skill in the Social Sciences." *The Psychology of Learning and Motivation* 17 (1985): 165–213.

Williams, Joseph M. *Style: Ten Lessons in Clarity and Grace.* 3d ed. Glenview, IL: Scott Foresman, 1988.

/ / / / / / / / / *Chapter* 6

California State University, Chico

Stephen BeMiller, Lois Bueler, Tom Fox, Victor Lams, Joel Leonard, Anne Nordhus, Elizabeth Renfro, Brooks Thorlaksson

> *Full participation in writing across the disciplines comes when faculty take on the task of teaching their colleagues as well as their students.*

Institution:	California State University, Chico
Institutional Size—Students (FTES):	14,900
Institutional Size—Faculty (FTEF):	800
Student/Faculty Ratio	19:1
Highest Degree Granted— Institution:	M.A.
Highest Degree Granted—English Department	M.A.
Public or Private Institution:	Public

Institutional Mission: small-town, largely undergraduate, residential campus drawing student body primarily from Los Angeles basin and San Francisco Bay area. Admission requires four years of college preparatory courses.

For more information on the program described in this chapter, contact: Lois Bueler, Department of English, California State University, Chico, CA 95929.

Can eight people write a book chapter—and still like each other when they finish? Of course. For they—*we*—have always worked like that. The writing-across-the-disciplines program at California State University, Chico, which has been going for seven or more years (depending on what and how you count), is the product of a long-lived and wide-ranging collaboration among colleagues. This chapter describes that program and the process that has created it. So it speaks for all eight of us, with our individual though overlapping perspectives, and for hundreds of other people as well. I, Lois Bueler, serve as introducer and narrator; having joined this team in midcourse, I can still view Chico State with something of an outsider's memory.

Chico State is a thriving middle-sized state university nestled compactly in the center of a charming small city. Its enrollment is now slightly beyond what the physical plant will accommodate, and the majority of our full-time faculty members are tenured professors hired in the 1960s and early 1970s. These faculty, once encouraged to regard their primary job as teaching and assigned heavy teaching loads accordingly, are now urged to engage in research and publication as well. The student body includes not only local kids looking to be local teachers, but also students from distant urban centers seeking degrees in business and the professions while enjoying the unaccustomed pleasures of small-town life.

This, then, is where we live. The following chapter describes our work and is divided into four sections: (1) what has been built here ("The University-wide Writing Program"); (2) how it has come about ("Imagination and Collaboration"); (3) what the program does best ("Some Distinctive Projects"); and (4) what we hope to do next ("Problems and Prospects").

THE UNIVERSITY-WIDE WRITING PROGRAM

In 1988, Chico State has a well-defined purpose about student literacy: we stress the importance of writing in all fields and help faculty help their students use writing as a means of learning and communicating disciplinary knowledge. And we have a well-defined university-wide program, beyond the mandatory freshman composition course, that consists of three closely connected components: a required junior-level writing test, required writing-intensive courses in each major, and a variety of faculty development projects. Later, various of us will say a little about how this program came about. First, however, let me describe each component.

WEST (our *Writing Effectiveness Screening Test*) is, as its name suggests, a *screen*: a holistically scored ninety-minute essay exam administered twice a semester, WEST must be passed by all students before they enroll in the required upper-division Writing Proficiency course in their major. As a screening rather than a competency test, its pass rate is high, about 80 percent. Students who don't pass WEST take individual tutoring, workshops, or courses before attempting the test again. Faculty members from across campus develop the questions and score the test and are paid for their work from funds generated by the test fee.

Writing Proficiency (WP) courses are required, discipline-specific, upper-division courses in each major. Taught by faculty in the disciplines, they use writing as an integral means of learning and communicating disciplinary knowledge. Students must pass WEST to enroll in WP courses; passing the WP course in the major in turn fulfills the California State University System's mandated graduation writing requirement.

WAD, our *Writing-Across-the-Disciplines* faculty development program, helps all faculty use writing in their courses. University funded and centrally administered, WAD sponsors both extended and part-day workshops for interdisciplinary faculty, helps faculty develop publications of student writing in their disciplines, and provides them with individual consultation, a monthly newsletter, and a library of writing-related books and articles.

Such a program clearly requires careful ongoing administration, by both faculty and staff. Appendix A (at the end of this chapter) gives a schematic overview of how it is funded and who does the work.

These two overviews do indeed describe Chico State's university-wide writing program, which has developed piece by experimental piece over the last half-dozen years. But they give nothing of the real flavor of our work, for they misleadingly suggest a top-down master plan rather than what we really have: a neatening up and institutionalizing of the overlapping initiatives of zealous individuals cooperating with colleagues who believed (or could be persuaded to believe) in a common course of action. So I need to show you something of the acts of imagination and collaboration by which the program came about.

IMAGINATION AND COLLABORATION

When I arrived in the fall of 1982, Chico State already had a years-long history of concern about student writing. That history was at work in a study by the president's cabinet in 1961 which concluded, rightly, that writing ability *can* be tested and is *better* tested by asking students to write an essay rather than have them take an objective grammar/punctuation test. The report recommended that a passing mark on an essay test be required for graduation. Yet, after this serious and extended investigation supported at the highest levels, the university decided *not* to institute a proficiency test. The episode shows us, says Vic Lams (acting WAD historian), that (*a*) in 1961 student writing was conceived and addressed on this campus as essentially a problem in writing pathology (i.e., that what needed doing was for the worst writers to be identified and repaired); and that (*b*) there were serious enough misgivings about a Junior Proficiency English Test to have caused the idea to be scrapped.

But avoiding the error of the pathology-identification model was not enough; by 1975, Chico State was once more studying and recommending and seeing what could be done about student writing. One thing to be done was to reiterate the folly of a one-shot "pass-out" exam and to raise the vision of writing as a schoolwide concern. Yet vision is not policy. As a literacy policy began to be hammered out in faculty committee, biology professor Mike Abruzzo, impatient with his colleagues' discussion of writing as something students take and are tested in rather than something they *do* in the course of learning a discipline, drafted the statement on which our writing-across-the-disciplines program rests: *"All departments shall require their majors before graduation to demonstrate writing ability in their own fields."*

"In their own fields"—in 1976 this "Abruzzo Principle" became university policy, and for some years, responding to a system directive that all campuses certify their graduates' literacy, Chico State hoped that adopting this right-minded notion was sufficient to ensure its effective implementation. The pretense collapsed in 1981 when (in the words of Anne Nordhus, WEST/ WP coordinator) "the Chancellor's Office surveyed its nineteen campuses to learn the effect of their system-mandated Graduation Writing Assessment Requirements. Chico was unique: it was the only campus that had neither delayed nor denied the graduation of any student because of poor writing. Furthermore, it was unable to provide proof that all graduates could—and did—write adequately."

In search of a way to keep the responsibility for good writing with the major departments and yet provide accountability for the program, English department composition coordinator Lams made another visionary leap: Chico State *would* develop a writing test and *would* require it of all students at their junior year. But this test would not attempt to certify competence. Rather, it would screen. An early diagnostic test with a low fail threshold, it would identify students who wrote so badly that they didn't belong in writing proficiency courses in their majors. Students who passed would not thereby be certified as literate—no test can do that—but they would be eligible to enroll in courses in their majors in which writing competently and to disciplinary purpose would be an integral part of their learning.

That concept—the Writing Effectiveness Screening Test—turned the corner for us; it took us toward implementation of the university-wide writing program we have now. Says Nordhus: "The WEST has done more than any other single program to advance the cause of student writing at Chico. It has raised student awareness of the importance of clear writing, has brought together faculty across the disciplines to score student essays, has required students with poor writing skills to improve their writing, has increased accountability of writing-proficiency courses, and has led to the university's active writing-across-the-disciplines program."

The beginning of the implementation of WEST was where I came in, and what I saw, over the next five years, was heroic work: the job of selling WEST to a reluctant university community; the creation of the University Writing Committee, with a faculty representative from each of the eight colleges to help set writing-connected policy and standards for Writing Proficiency courses; the development of a skilled cadre of holistic scorers from faculty across campus and the marshalling of Testing Office resources to make WEST operative; the training of Writing Center tutors to work with student test-takers; fund-raising for faculty workshops and conferences; the development of faculty members as workshop facilitators; publications of student writing; the long-needed and much-heralded WAD newsletter; and more, much more. Who has directed all this work? At various times all eight members of what we think of as the WAD core: one-time English department composition coordinator Vic Lams; one-time Writing Center coordinator and faculty development administrator Brooks Thorlaksson; Lois Bueler, current English department composition coordinator; Anne Nordhus, provost's office WEST/WP coordinator; Steve BeMiller, mathematics professor and Professional Development administrator; Tom Fox, current English department Writing Center coordinator; Elizabeth Renfro, English department, WAD coordinator since 1985; Joel Leonard, geography department and Library Reference staff, WAD co-coordinator from 1985 to 1987. These people, whatever their current titles, keep doing work: Lams, for instance, chairs the WEST question-development committee and Thorlaksson just completed a study of faculty and student attitudes towards WEST and WP. But it's almost .impossible to say who "runs" things; the bright ideas come from whoever feels strongest at the moment and the important decisions are sometimes made by various members of the WAD core, sometimes by individuals.

Such a nonsystem has its flaws, as WAD coordinator Renfro points out:

> Where do my responsibilities end and someone else's begin? Who *should*
> *(will)* handle some of the less appetizing or more onerous tasks? I especially
> have chaffed under this because of my awkward status: part-time, un-
> tenured, yet on paper coordinator of the program. And the difficulties
> inherent in our approach aren't small stuff. They have resulted in occasional
> tensions and, more important, occasional missed opportunities because we

each thought or hoped someone else was handling something. And people outside WAD have sometimes been confused about whom to contact regarding WAD activities.

But let me talk about the great payoffs of this systemless system of ours. First of all, the obvious: it's a given that lots of people's ideas and energies are better than just one person's ideas and energy. What's not a given is how a program can assure a steady stream of those ideas and energies. We've found that when those "lots of people" are all *involved in the running* of a program—indeed, *when all know that the program depends upon their individual initiatives*—they are more likely to come up with, share, and carry through their ideas. If. If they are all sufficiently committed to this dangerous freedom. And so far the commitment has been extraordinary.

Renfro has pinpointed our distinctive feature. Writing across the disciplines at Chico State has had no campuswide writing czar or guru, no single central focus or font of wisdom on whom we could all depend and by virtue of whose existence we could all slack off. So inventing and administering the program has itself been a form of faculty development. Often we aren't sure, at least for a long time, what we have accomplished. But we do know that it is working *together* that has kept us going. Renfro said it most recently. Haunted for months by the relative lack of pizzazz at the January 1987 WAD workshop on collaboration techniques, which she had been tempted to consider a failure, she found herself thinking again about collaboration—and the pervasive influence of the workshop—as she took part in the revising process for this chapter. One thing is certain, she said. We at Chico are collaborators of the first order.

SOME DISTINCTIVE PROJECTS

That decentralized, collaborative, self-initiated and self-educating impulse has been the origin of our most successful projects. Those we will highlight in this section—the faculty development component of WEST, the use of faculty as presenters in WAD workshops, publications of student writing in the disciplines, the WAD newsletter, and the design of specific WP courses—all result from individual faculty initiatives that have attracted attention, and become more or less institutionalized, because they work.

WEST as Faculty Development

Our Writing Effectiveness Screening Test was designed to put teeth in our commitment to Writing Proficiency courses by serving notice to our students that we were serious about writing and by giving WP teachers students they could teach. A side benefit, and one of the test's chief virtues, is that participation in the holistic scoring of the exam is an excellent faculty development tool. Scoring sessions focus strictly on academic issues and give readers the satisfying sense that they are helping the university accomplish something it *should* accomplish. And WEST provides the blessings of smooth administration, thanks to the splendid cooperation and efficiency of WEST/WP coordinator Nordhus and test officer Judy Zachai. It takes place regularly—twice a semester since the fall of 1982—so faculty can count on participating periodically without being trapped by an inexorable schedule. It pays twenty-five dollars per hour for the scoring day. It provides professional training—new readers are introduced to holistic scoring in a two-hour training session before taking part in a live reading. It fosters interdisciplinary collegiality—our fall 1987 reader list includes seventy-five readers from twenty-two departments. It demands energy and competence—we maintain careful reader statistics and table-leader reports which we share with readers who want to know how they are doing. It acknowledges energy and competence (with, we admit, more work)—fine readers are invited (and paid) to serve as table leaders, run test-preview sessions for students, and help develop test questions. When as part of a just-completed evaluation of the WEST/WP program Brooks Thorlaksson asked readers why they read, they cited the money (of course), but significant numbers also mentioned their sense of responsibility to the university, their desire to see more student writing and improve their ability to evaluate it, and their desire to be informed about the test. Four said they did it to have a good time.

Even more important though, two-thirds of Thorlaksson's respondents said that reading the WEST has had a positive effect on their teaching. Some simply feel more confident as evaluators of their students' writing; others use specific WEST-introduced techniques like scoring classroom assignments holistically and showing their students sample papers. Since Reader Training sessions are not restricted to people who actually plan to score WEST, we have encouraged faculty members to attend the sessions specifically to pick up teaching ideas. Inspired by one session's training and follow-up brainstorming with Renfro, for instance, the international relations faculty member newly assigned this fall to teach his department's WP course on international politics conducted (with Renfro) a classroom session on holistic scoring and evaluation criteria, used small groups to critique paper drafts, required students to select and revise papers for final portfolios, and scored those portfolios holistically. As a result, he expects to get more and better writing from his students than he once thought possible.

Faculty as WAD Leaders

Once upon a time, claims Renfro, I uttered a maxim to the effect that full participation in writing across the disciplines comes when faculty take on the task of teaching their colleagues as well as their students. I can't quite remember saying that, but we think it is true. WAD work at Chico State is primarily faculty development work, for if we can reach faculty we will reach students, and faculty members learn most about writing, teaching, and learning when they work with each other. Faculty members who insist in turn upon going about spreading the word not only inform their friends and neighbors; they keep *themselves* professionally alive and flourishing. Early, therefore, we committed ourselves to using Chico State faculty members from all disciplines as leaders and workshop presenters.

On the other hand, prophets have been known to be without honor in their own countries. And we stagnate without new models and new ideas. So we have combined a commitment to local leadership with the use of nationally known writing consultants, and each year have fiddled with timing, formats, and focus as campus exigencies seemed to require. Gradually we have arrived at the formula of "one intensive workshop with star" each year, plus several part-day workshops per semester run by our own faculty. Both formats work: in both, faculty become enthusiastic about considering the uses of writing in their disciplines and devising classroom techniques to widen the range of their writing assignments, lessen their paper load, and help make students more responsible for their own learning. Both formats, in short, provide help with student literacy problems and with classroom teaching. But the faculty members who have become WAD leaders—who administer, make presentations, or work with student publications—have most commonly been "set off" or "sparked" by the intensive workshops. What has struck those sparks has been as idiosyncratic as their results have been various.

Steve BeMiller, mathematics and Professional Development, was hooked before we began, in a sense. "I'm a workshop junkie," he admitted during our first intensive workshop, an invigorating four days with Toby Fulwiler in January 1984. And of course BeMiller's administrative work with the university's Professional Development program practically obliged him to be interested in whatever other faculty members found themselves interested in. It was not obligation, however, but a deep sense of excitement about what writing could do for his teaching of mathematics that overtook him during the workshop and the semester of experimentation which followed:

> I had been frustrated because I had no way of *seeing* students thinking. I hoped they were, but I couldn't get at the process. What I came to realize was that writing is thinking made visible. It was the tool I had been looking for.

Already a master workshop facilitator, BeMiller became a regular presenter at WAD short workshops, contributed a chapter about journals in mathematics to Fulwiler's *The Journal Book*, and made New Directions in Teaching and Learning the most urgent task of the University's faculty development program.

Joel Leonard, geography and Library Reference, was also a participant in that first Fulwiler workshop and also began experimenting with WAD techniques in his teaching. Since he taught a research paper course for the geography department and had devised assignments that would be useful to other faculty members, he made a presentation to our second "intensive," Carol Holder's assignments-focused workshop in August 1985. What Leonard told us in that presentation was useful, without question, but still he had "told" it to us, he hadn't let us try it ourselves, and we wanted something else. At the third intensive workshop, in January 1986, he set out to make his presentation really participatory and got more than he bargained for:

> It was during an "in-class write" that the people in WAD III held. As I was standing in front of the group and the twenty-five of them were doing their writing, all of a sudden the bolt from the blue came down and said "Toby wasn't teaching you about writing. He was teaching you about teaching!" And here I was and they were in control and they were writing what they wanted to write, and they could come back and pound on me or anything, and it was silent for twenty-five minutes or so. I realized that all those years I had controlled students from the minute I walked into the class until the minute it was over. It was really wasting a good amount of *their* time, based on *my* need to be in charge.

Leonard went on to serve as WAD co-coordinator from 1985 to 1987 and now directs our library's student-education program.

Joyce Norman, psychology, also "sparked" in an intensive workshop, and she can identify the precise moment it happened. During August 1984 when consultant Carol Holder asked us to respond to one of several effective assignments that workshop members had submitted, Norman, who had been recognized as Chico State's Outstanding Teacher the previous spring, chose the assignment of a history department colleague:

> In college I had a terrible time with U.S. history. But the question that Dale Steiner read from one of his exams all of a sudden provided one of those "Aha!" experiences. The reason that it shook me was that I was there in a mode of resistance. I was thinking, "I'm here, but I'm not going to take any of this back with me. I mean, this isn't academic, this is—touchy-feely." So coming with that kind of resistance, and then all of a sudden saying "Boy, I would love to have answered *that* question." It created an image. I was in a covered wagon surrounded by Indians and at that moment I stepped back into history and became that person, and I thought "That's a powerful tool, to be able to use imagery and to be able to create that kind of identity." That was the point at which I stopped resisting and started listening and paying attention to what was being said. It had a dramatic effect on my teaching, because it was at that point that I started looking at my tests, and changing all the questions, and introducing in-class writing, and doing a lot of things that didn't turn out to be too successful. But I think that started the whole change from lecturer to process person.

Since that workshop Norman has made frequent presentations showing her colleagues how assignments can be designed to engage students. Norman has special credibility as a WAD presenter: not only can she cite her own conversion experience and its results in her classroom, but as a biopsychologist whose professional specialty is the physiological basis of emotion and thought, she can show us *why* students learn a subject better when writing assignments demand their personal involvement.

Jean Graybeal, on the other hand, arrived at WAD's doorstep as a kind of gift. As we were recruiting for the second Fulwiler workshop of January 1986—a two-day intensive restricted to folk already acquainted with writing across the disciplines and designed to help participants prepare presentations for colleagues, we got wind of a professor in Religious Studies, new that year, who assigned something she called "team journals." We followed up the clue, discovered that Graybeal just naturally belonged in our "second-stage" workshop, and asked her to come. Fulwiler in turn asked her to present her team journal technique as part of the workshop, and ever since she has been showing WAD workshops what she does. (She too has a chapter in *The Journal Book.*) For Graybeal, then, an intensive workshop provided not the spark but the validation. Already profoundly committed to student-centered teaching and learning (and author of a writing-focused technique that colleagues here were eager to adopt and adapt), she found in writing across the disciplines a program that encouraged and publicized her work. And *we* found another gifted and persuasive faculty presenter.

We have seen how the spark effect has led faculty members not only to new teaching techniques but to administrative work and the development of presentations for WAD workshops. Yoshio Kusaba, an art historian who attended the August 1985 workshop and the second Fulwiler workshop in January 1986, also experimented radically with his courses and made presentations about the results. But his most distinctive contribution has been leadership of the project that became *Contrapposto*, the art department's publication of student writing. Like the other participants in WAD, Kusaba's first professional commitment is to his discipline, and his long-standing desire has always been to foster not just student literacy in general but good writing about art in particular. As Kusaba worked with his students, both those in his advanced Writing Proficiency course and the novices in his General Studies introduction to art history, he became increasingly excited by the quality and engagement that resulted from his new-style journal assignments and his radically revised team research and debate projects. Other members of his department began to experiment with their assignments and to collect interesting examples of student writing and, with the technical and administrative help of WAD coordinator Renfro, put together a beautifully designed publication of student writing that rolled off the press in August 1986. The second volume appeared in August 1987 and the third is under way, as are similar publications in other disciplines. For Kusaba, WAD's contribution to this initiative was not just specific teaching techniques (though these were helpful), nor money and technical assistance (though these were essential), but a strongly supportive group of colleagues:

> WAD is the only experience I have at this university that—how shall I put it?—that is so free and so unrestricting in terms of giving and sharing ideas. Not just about writing, but about who we are, how we teach, and what kind of changes we can make. I've never been in any other group that provided me this kind of experience. This is the only one where ideas are really freely flowing, and positive things coming out. This is the only one.

WAD gave Kusaba a new sense of community; Kusaba in turn gave the entire campus a bellwether project of inestimable value.

Publications of Student Writing in the Disciplines

So how did, and does, *Contrapposto* come together? And what specifically has it wrought? *Contrapposto* came together because a few gifted and immensely hardworking people said it would. Kusaba, of course. And his departmental colleague Jim McManus, a WAD participant, and other art department faculty. But also WAD coordinator Renfro, who to our great good fortune is also a professional editor and publisher. She comments here on the process:

> *Contrapposto: A Collection of Student Essays in Art History* is a seventy-page book containing essays, research papers, journal entries, play scripts, and poetry produced by students in the classes of four art instructors. The selections are culled from submissions made by both students and instructors and put into book form with an introduction by the instructors. In *Contrapposto*'s first year, WAD and the art department shared production costs (two-thirds and one-third respectively), with Renfro acting as production editor, and the book was used as a teaching tool and required text in all the basic art history courses. In its second year, *Contrapposto* was funded almost entirely by the art department with money generated by the sale of the first edition, and art students and the art department have entirely taken over the production process. The cover design the second year was the winner of a competition in one of the department's graphic design classes.
>
> Student, faculty, and administrative response to *Contrapposto* has been enthusiastic. In a moment of unbridled zeal, Kusaba at one point even thought about publishing a new issue each semester to accommodate the flood of fine manuscripts students were submitting, before time considerations brought him back to earth. Letters of commendation have come to the art department and WAD itself from Chico State's provost, its president, and even the CSU System chancellor.

Best, perhaps, the publication idea is spreading across campus, with other departments hoping to organize their own publications of student writing. As always, proselytization has taken a variety of routes. Several members of the nursing faculty are WEST readers and others have come repeatedly to short workshops. The leader of the engineering publication attended the first Fulwiler workshop and teaches one of the WP courses described below. The home economics project is being led by its department chair, a longtime WEST reader who also took part in an intensive workshop. The Honors publication is the work of the Honors Program director, who is also English department chair and a WEST reader, and the Honors Program coordinator, from psychology, a WEST table leader and WAD workshop participant. The most recent (and in some ways the most exciting) initiative was taken in the fall of 1987 by three English department graduate students who conceived the idea of an interdisciplinary publication of critical commentary in the arts and humanities. With guidance from WAD, these students enlisted an advisory board of faculty members from English, religious studies, and modern languages, put together a funding package, elicited examples of student writing from throughout the College of Humanities and Fine Arts, and received commitments from faculty interested in making *Critically Speaking* required reading in their courses. Again, WAD administration makes these initiatives work. Renfro helps find seed money, uses the editorial policy guidelines developed by the art department as a model, and serves where need be as production editor, for which you may read "master of all trades." Like *Contrapposto*, these other publications are being planned as teaching tools and showcases for students' writing and publications work, but they are also to be used variously as recruiting devices for departmental majors and faculty, as vehicles for honors projects, and as attractive means of community outreach.

Literacy & Learning

Elizabeth Renfro also started a monthly WAD newsletter, *Literacy & Learning*. It has become within a semester the much-talked-about focus of the WAD program on campus: It is brief (four notebook-sized pages in a single-fold format) and appears once a month, so that faculty remember it from mailing to mailing. Its features are short, focused, commonsensical, and liberally personalized, so that readers find themselves being introduced to the college community and hear their colleagues speaking directly off the page to them. In each issue *Literacy & Learning* has at least one extended profile of a faculty member whose teaching practices are particularly interesting to colleagues. The most recent involved the ways a sociologist uses writing to help both students in his large classes and clients in his stress management workshops at the local hospital synthesize the material he teaches. Always the newsletter has brief teaching hints—how to think about the difference between revising and editing, how to remind students of the meaning of common academic instructions like "analyze," how to make a writing assignment more motivating. And for keeping in touch with faculty on a large campus, each issue provides very brief summaries of three interesting articles about writing and learning accompanied by a tear-off form with which faculty can request copies. Request they do—often asking for several for their friends. Usually they receive back from Renfro not just the articles, but a personal note asking supportive questions about their teaching or suggesting colleagues they might like to talk to.

Four Courses Using Writing in the Disciplines

In addition to the newsletter and to publications of student writing, Chico State has produced several "occasional" publications about writing and campus writing programs. (See Appendix B for a complete publications list.) The most recent is *Writing: Practice and Proficiency*, in which Brooks Thorlaksson talks with faculty about the writing program. The twenty-eight-page booklet includes conversations with instructors of courses in engineering, biology, psychology, and art history, and is designed to spark the interest of faculty members not yet involved in writing across the disciplines or resistant to the notion that writing has a place in their courses:

Bill Gelonek: Civil Engineering 119, Contracts, Specifications, and Technical Reports

"I put my WP students in the same kind of environment they will experience as engineers," Bill Gelonek says. "I give them assignments like the work they will do. They keep journals and write memos, informal reports, formal reports—all the kinds of writing that engineers do. I must admit that at the beginning of the semester they don't believe me. By the end, however, they see how much of their work will depend on writing. And it helps on Alumni Day to have our graduates come back and tell students how much writing they have to do."

Gelonek assigns his students case studies to teach them the different ways engineers write on the job, which means teaching them how to adapt language and formats to a variety of audiences. In one construction project scenario, the students write Progress and Inspection reports, engineer to engineer. When they run into problems on the project, they write Investigative Reports which demand observations, interpretations, conclusions, and sometimes graphs or illustrations. Then they write Evaluation Reports on possible options. All of these assignments lead to their Formal Reports to the client which explain the problems, explore the options, and make recommendations.

While students are working on this assignment sequence, they are also writing short, ungraded, in-class responses to questions Gelonek asks during discussion. And they are keeping journals. Like the in-class writing, journals are not read for errors. Instead, Gelonek responds to the ideas. Journals serve as a way to organize thoughts, encourage introspection, and provide practice. "Civil engineers keep journals as a part of their work," Gelonek says. "They record conversations and the thoughts they have at the time they are making decisions. A classroom journal gets them started on this kind of writing."

Toward the end of the course, students are asked to design and make model structures out of toothpicks. They plan a work schedule in their journals and keep track of their progress. Occasionally they make oral progress reports to the "Boss" and record the reports in their journals. Once the structures are completed, they test them, then write formal reports using the journal notes they kept. After the construction phase is completed, students select a publication for an article about their work. First they write an informal analysis of the publication's readers. Then, following the protocol of engineering firms, they request clearance to submit the article. Finally they prepare an abstract of the article and a cover letter addressed to the editor of the publication.

Roger Lederer: Biology 291, Senior Seminar in Biology

In the capstone course in biology, Roger Lederer teaches students to write about science: "I'm not teaching scientific writing, which requires research and a store of data that students working on a B.S. don't have, but science writing—writing about science to nonscientists." Lederer begins by asking students to read and analyze essays written by professional science writers such as Stephen Jay Gould. "Gould is a good model because he is a practicing scientist who writes incredibly well," Lederer says. "He reaches out in such a way that even complex principles are understandable and readers see how their lives are affected."

After students read and analyze the professional essays, they practice writing short paragraphs modeled on the style of each writer. These are not graded but are read aloud in class. Then Lederer asks his students to try their hand at a science essay designed to inform the reader about a recent scientific issue, such as a new organism produced by genetic engineering or a new drug isolated from a wild plant. The next assignment is more difficult: students write about the sociological, cultural, legal, or historical aspects of their first topic, placing what they know in a larger context. For example, should a scientist be able to patent a new organism? Should Third World countries be allowed to clearcut their forests, given that over 50 percent of our pharmaceutical drugs have come from wild plants?

"It is essential for students to select their own topics," says Lederer. "If they have a topic they know or care about, their papers will be more substantial." And he offers to serve as editor. "I don't require drafts and I don't grade them, but I offer this service because I think it encourages students to be better writers." Only a small percentage take advantage of his offer, and Lederer finds that these are usually the better writers. "It doesn't take much time because these students need the least help. My comments help them polish their skills." Once the papers are collected and graded, Lederer makes copies of the better essays for class discussion and enjoyment. "They have seen the work of professional writers and I want them to know that some of them can do nearly as good a job."

Joyce Norman: Psychology 105, Perception and Cognition

Imagine that you are a student in a biopsychology class and have been given this all-too-typical assignment: *Use the interaction principle to explain intelligence.* There's a problem here. You have just been asked, as a nonexpert, to tell an expert what she already knows and probably has just told you. The assignment requires regurgitation rather than understanding.

Now imagine that you are given this assignment: *You have recently taken an intelligence test sent to you at your request by the Mensa Society. The results show, not unexpectedly, that you have an IQ score of 145 which easily qualifies you for membership in this self-proclaimed society of intellects. In a conversation on the telephone, your father suggests that you have inherited "it" from Aunt Julie; your mother quickly takes the phone and claims that it was clearly a result of the library card she got for you at age five. You have been studying nurture-nature interactionism in your biopsychology class and so after hanging up the phone you carefully construct a letter to your parents explaining to them the current thinking about intelligence. In your letter explain clearly and with illustration the roles of genes and environment in determining adult intelligence.*

This assignment, by contrast, makes you an expert with a problem to solve. It is the kind of informal writing assignment that Joyce Norman became interested in during that WAD workshop and that she uses to help students learn in her Psychology WP class. Norman sees such assignments as practice for the more traditional lab reports, book reviews, and research reports which she also requires. She is convinced that the quality of thought in students' formal papers improves when they get a chance to wrestle with ideas in writing in this informal way. The writing-to-learn assignment must engage the students, however. Explains Norman: "I relate the assignment to their experiences, aim for a specific audience they are familiar with, and include as many details as possible. The assignment will engage them if it strikes them as true."

But the assignment alone isn't enough. "I have to be engaged as well," Norman says. "Students have to know I am paying attention." They get feedback when she reads the answers and responds to how well they have expressed their ideas. "I only put a check, a minus, or a plus. But that is enough." One semester she experimented with not providing any evaluation, but found that students did not do as well. "It doesn't take much time," Norman says. "I spend less than an hour every two weeks reading these review assignments for a class of fifty or so students. For that investment I find out what they are understanding, and they find out right away if they aren't doing well."

Norman uses writing-to-learn assignments because they help create context, which in turn improves thinking. Not all students need it equally, she says; the top 10 to 15 percent seem able to direct their own learning. "But the others don't structure material well, so I give them guidelines. They still learn, and on their own; I only provide a little incentive." And improved thinking goes together with better writing. When discussing their informal papers, "Students often tell me, 'Well, I meant to say' and then I show them that what was in their head didn't show up on the paper. I am helping them express what they are thinking, not teaching writing, but that lesson certainly improves their writing."

Yoshio Kusaba: Art 244, Chinese and Japanese Art

In the humanities, the term paper is supposed to help students develop the intellectual assertiveness necessary to create both meaning and value from what they have learned. But Yoshio Kusaba found that his traditional research paper assignment didn't elicit that kind of thinking from his art history students. "Their papers were simply a collection of quotations. I had a hard time getting them to see that the research paper should be an active synthesis of ideas. I wanted them to see that they should tangle with the ideas, not just recite them."

Yet Kusaba felt there was too much potential value in the research paper to abandon it as a writing assignment. So he decided to work on the thinking process that leads to writing, rather than just focus on the final written product. He began by setting up class debates. The class was divided into two teams and presented with the first topic: Japanese Art, An Original Art Form? The groups were responsible for planning their research, writing critical commentaries on their sources, plotting their strategies, and planning for the debate. While preparing, the students shared ideas and sources, argued, and modified their views. They learned that their opinions had to be supported, that their thinking had to be logical, and that they had to anticipate opposing arguments. Once they had debated the topic, Kusaba set them to work writing the paper. The results were the best he'd seen. "The students enjoyed writing their papers, I enjoyed reading them, and I learned from the papers. The students were able to develop a point of view by synthesizing what others said and thought."

At first Kusaba was worried that this approach would take too much time. "It did take some time to organize the groups and then to hold the debates, but that was when they were practicing what art historians do: discussing ideas, working out problems, agreeing on some points, disagreeing on others. Not only were they responsible for their learning, they were developing an educated point of view. And it was this work—this time of thinking—that led to the improvement in their papers. It was time well spent."

One of the unexpected benefits was increased interest in the subject. "When I came to class, students were already talking about art, continuing discussions, asking me questions they had thought about before class. I felt a real commitment to our work, as well as a commitment to each other." Another unexpected benefit was the publication of several of the papers in Chico's Asian Studies journal, an experience which led Kusaba and his colleagues to develop *Contrapposto*.

PROBLEMS AND PROSPECTS

Do our successes mean that all is well with writing across the disciplines at Chico State? Do we know where we are going next, and how to get there? Only in part. We are uneasy in this spring of 1988, though hope-filled as well. And we imagine that our problems are symptomatic of programs beyond the start-up stage, programs that have already tapped the initial good will of predisposed faculty, have already ridden the crest of the first exciting workshops, have already received the administrative kudos granted newly enthusiastic folk eager to work cheap on great, and greatly fashionable, ideas.

We can state some of those problems as a series of paradoxes:

1. The very success of the WAD program has created a variety of clienteles. Our most experienced and committed WAD faculty, whose energies we have already exploited heavily, need and deserve opportunities for continued personal and professional growth. They need advanced workshops like Fulwiler's second one or the English department's recent Literacy Conference; they need encouragement and support to continue their pedagogical experimentation and to publicize what they are doing. Then there are small groups of faculty within certain departments (as in art or nursing) who are primarily concerned with designing and forwarding projects and curricular change in their own disciplines. WAD energies need to be concentrated on them, too. Above all, there are the vast majority of Chico State faculty still untouched by WAD activities. They need a steady supply of introductory workshops with suggestions about handling the paper load, improving essay assignments, using ungraded

in-class writing, using good student papers as models—all the usual, and useful, staples of our trade. Whom do we serve? When? How much?

2. Because our recruitment model has been successful—because we have skimmed the cream, so to speak—we must change that model. We have relied on a combination of personal contracts and mailed flyers, plus administrative urging, to get the word out, and for the most part our only carrot has been the offer of good company and good ideas. That approach has taken us about as far as it can, says Joel Leonard:

> Faculty interested in using writing to teach and naturally curious and innovative in this area have made themselves known by now, and are involved to various degrees. The past contact techniques are not going to be very effective for the rest of them, at least not alone. New faculty could be targeted and the university's emphasis on writing could be included in hiring information. But currently, it's difficult to *identify* new faculty, much less get them to give time to an amorphous cause.

We need new networks, which will be infinitely harder to establish than the old. We need new sources of funding in order to stipend unreached faculty to attend intensive workshops and give WAD a hearing. *Literacy & Learning* is a strong new publicity and recruitment tool; we need more.

3. We must continue to institutionalize our university writing program, relying upon administrative centralization and funding because the work is simply too complex and important to be carried on without it. We have been blessed with administrative support. But mandated testing, required courses, and programs to help faculty improve their teaching carry their own curses. As coordinator of the English department's Writing Center, Tom Fox deals with WEST fallout and so knows something about both the curses and the possibilities of tests:

> Especially at the beginning of the semester, we tutor *Writing* and not *Passing the WEST*. But WEST's effectiveness as a WAD tool is constantly threatened by limited, counterproductive, and all too seductive ideas about tests. I want to say to Barry-what's-his-name or Marie-failed-three-times, "Come on! Forget what you know, forget what you care about, just string together six paragraphs on topic—you'll pass!" Barry and Marie *are* capable of stringing together the paragraphs, though they both have a great deal to learn about writing before they enter a WP course. It's as easy to teach to the test with a holistically scored essay as it is with a multiple-choice farce. But in doing so, *we* fail. Yet to keep WEST as a positive influence requires more vigilance than most tutors have. When tutoring WEST failees, "humanity" pulls to the short run; pass the WEST and end the suffering.

As for faculty, ours at Chico State, like faculty everywhere, object to anything they construe as meddling in their classrooms, and the notion of including writing as part of course requirements continues to meet with as much indifference or hostility as support. WAD can help overcome the hostility and underlying insecurity only if it continues to be, *and is perceived as being*, a program by faculty for faculty. Yet we *must* have administration sanction, reinforcement, and funding, or we die. How do we manage the balancing act?

4. Much of the impetus and expertise to improve students' reading and writing has come from faculty in the English department, whose professional field it is. But identification of the specific needs of students and teachers, and the language to discuss those needs, must come from faculty in the disciplines. WAD has gained credibility and effectiveness by using workshop facilitators from a variety of disciplines: art, mathematics, religious studies, psychology, geography, management. Good workshop facilitators are a rare breed, however; effectiveness at improving one's own classroom teaching does not necessarily translate into effectiveness as a workshop leader. (No more, of course, than does academic expertise in discourse theory or rhetoric.) We have worked our best facilitators very hard, often (we hope) to their benefit but always with the knowledge that overt professional rewards for such work are far more ephemeral for faculty in other disciplines than for those in English. We need ways to develop and use facilitators from the disciplines without exhausting them or wearing out WAD's welcome.

5. Although we use student tutors with unusual effectiveness and professionalism in the English department's basic reading and writing program, thereby both improving our weakest students' work and teaching our best students about writing and teaching, we haven't even begun to exploit the student tutor potential of writing across the disciplines. Yet doing so would help accomplish every one of WAD's goals: it would help us *talk with each other* about discourse communities in the disciplines, further validate the importance of good student writing, and help our weakest students. We have a model in the English department's tutor training course and Tom Fox, who teaches that course, knows how it would translate:

> Our topics would be questions of genre and disciplinary style, and students would discover, explore, and question the conventions of various disciplines. I feel certain we could get the tutors and the tutees. I imagine we could get the money for the tutors. So how come I'm not doing it? First, I feel busy enough running the Basic Reading and Writing program. I'd want someone else to do it, and that's more money than what tutors cost. And second, there's the problem of space, perhaps the final frontier at Chico State. Our tutoring rooms are in use full-time. We already turn people away.

Yet amid these uncertainties and paradoxes, there are also things we think we know about writing across the disciplines at Chico State. And these things shape our plans. We know, for instance, that we will continue to focus our energies on the willing, the people who want to work with WAD. Many of them don't yet realize that we have something to offer, and reaching them with that information is complicated and slow. But we will continue to operate by what Renfro has called the "contagious colleague" model. Faculty members who have found their teaching lives, and thus their professional lives, changed by what we are learning and doing are the only spokespeople worth having, because they are the only ones who can effect real change in their peers.

We know that the best writing/learning/teaching workshops are interdisciplinary ones. From time to time we have entertained the fiction that we could become more "efficient" if only we would work with a single department or discipline at a time, with some putatively recalcitrant enclave especially in need of "fixing" or some particularly forward-looking group that would make us feel successful. But our history tells us that we all learn most, and are happiest doing it, when we enjoy the stimulation provided by a range of disciplinary views. On the other hand (and this is paradoxical but not contradictory), we know that once an individual department or discipline has achieved a critical mass—a group of faculty who become accustomed to thinking together about writing and learning and who devote themselves to discipline-specific projects—WAD work begins to have the real payoff with students that we too often can only dream it will. We have seen that effect in art history with *Contrapposto*.

We know that publications of student writing will give us opportunities to study the generic requirements that disciplines place on writing. "Student writing is perfect for this kind of exploration," says Tom Fox:

> When student essays "speak" to us as exceptional, we respond because they speak our language. So collections of student writing, aside from their very valuable use in modeling, can also help make conscious the particular demands that a discipline makes on writers. I can imagine an exciting turn in faculty development when more than one discipline has published collections of student writing. Since most knowledge develops dialectically, for art historians to really define how their disciplines shape the form of their writing (and their opinions about writing), they need at least one point of comparison—another discipline's collection of essays. Most disciplinary constraints on writing occur in subtle and habitual ways; we conform by habit without realizing that we are following "rules." A comparison with another discipline can help make us aware of the rules we take for granted.

The possibilities of such comparisons—for our teaching, for research—are enormous.

Finally, we know that the time has come, both despite and because of our history, to find a chief. We need the focus, the campuswide recognition, the infusion of ideas, the surge of team energy that such a person will bring. Hired and housed in English but funded in part by the university administration, this WAD director will be expected to use, build on, and change for the better what is already here. Does this suggest, people have asked, that current writing-across-the-disciplines faculty plan to stop working? Quite the contrary. We are simply improving upon our single most successful mode of operation: finding good colleagues to share the work.

Appendix A

CSU, CHICO'S UNIVERSITY-WIDE WRITING PROGRAM OVERVIEW OF POSITIONS, ACTIVITIES, AND FUNDING SOURCES

	Who	*What*
WEST	WEST/WP Coordinator (Provost's Office) University Writing Committee	Development and interpretation of policy; question-development and advisory committees
	Testing Office Test Officer Office Staff Student Proctors	Test scheduling, administration, record-keeping, statistical analysis
	WEST Readers (75 in fall 1987) 45% from English 55% from other disciplines	Chief readers, table leaders, readers
	WEST "Teaching" Staff English Dept. Writing Center coordinator Faculty and peer tutors	Essay-writing courses, workshops, individual tutoring sessions
	Funds for WEST activities generated by test-taking fees	
WP	WEST/WP Coordinator University Dean University Writing Committee College Deans Department Chairs WP instructors	Designation of WP course(s) in each major; development of WP course guidelines; enforcement of WEST screen; course staffing from within department; GWAR certification (C– or above for WP course)
	Costs of WP courses supported by regular administrative and teaching budgets	

WAD	WAD Coordinator(s)	Annual intersession two-day workshop
	Office of Professional	with outside consultant and Chico faculty
	Development	presenters; two 3-hour theme-focused
	Faculty presenters	workshops with Chico presenters during
	Department student-writing	semester; publications of student writing;
	publication teams	small-group networking; one-on-one
	Outside consultants	faculty consultation; campus newsletter

WAD administratively housed in Institute for Liberal and Interdisciplinary Studies (ILIS); funded annually through university budget process

Appendix B

CSU, CHICO PUBLICATIONS ABOUT WRITING

How To Increase Literacy Without Becoming an English Teacher: Suggestions to the Teacher of Courses other than English Composition about Working with Writing. Five essays by members of the Department of English. 1981.

How to Use Writing to Boost Learning Across the Disciplines: Further Suggestions to Teachers of Courses other than English Composition for Improving Student Thinking Through Writing. Victor Lams. 1982.

What You Need to Know About WEST: Answers to Questions Students Ask About West. Office of the Provost. 2d ed., 1985.

Contrapposto: A Collection of Student Essays in Art History. Vol. 1. Department of Art. 1986.

Contrapposto: A Collection of Student Essays in Art History. Vol. 2. Department of Art. 1987.

Contrapposto: A Collection of Student Essays in Art History. Vol. 3. Department of Art. 1988.

Writing: Practice and Proficiency—A Closer Look at CSU Chico's Writing Program. Brooks Thorlaksson. Office of the Provost. 1987.

Literacy & Learning (newsletter for Writing Across the Disciplines Program). Elizabeth Renfro, ed. 1987–.

Critically Speaking. Vol. 1. College of Humanities and Fine Arts. 1988.

Beaver College

Elaine P. Maimon, Barbara F. Nodine, Gail W. Hearn, and
Janice Haney-Peritz

> *The institution of the [faculty writing] workshop is one of the*
> *major contributions of the writing-across-the-curriculum*
> *movement.*

Institution:	*Beaver College, PA*
Institutional Size—Students (FTES):	2,100
Institutional Size—Faculty (FTEF):	160
Student/Faculty Ratio:	13:1
Highest Degree Granted—	
Institution:	M.A.
Highest Degree Granted—English	
Department:	M.A.
Public or Private Institution:	Private

Institutional Mission: provides a small-college atmosphere with a diverse student population from fifteen states and ten foreign countries. Curriculum offers a strong liberal arts and science background; classes range from fifteen to twenty students.

For more information on the program described in this chapter, contact: Chair, Barbara F. Nodine, Psychology Dept., Beaver College, Glenside, PA 19038.

/ / / / / / / / **Getting the Conversation Started**
Elaine P. Maimon

In the mid-1970s, when writing and learning across the curriculum existed only as the title of a book by Nancy Martin and her colleagues in the British Schools Council Project, Beaver College, a small, independent liberal arts college in suburban Philadelphia, became one of the first sites for a comprehensive writing program. The Beaver College story, like that of many others of its kind, begins in personal narrative composed of many voices. And, as so often happens with personal narratives, the Beaver College story has found several public expressions. This essay is the most recent public statement that derives from a living conversation that has been conducted during the last fifteen years.

Because this conversation is organic, it encompasses change. Yet the principles informing the conversation have retained their integrity. The Beaver College writing program is committed to the concept of writing as an ongoing conversation conducted contrapuntally across the disciplines. Such conversation depends on a recursive process of rethinking, reimagining, reenvisioning—in short, on revision in its broadest and most creative sense. As a consequence, this essay cannot follow a linear format. We intend our narrative to be contrapuntal, as we tell the story of how the writing-across-the-curriculum program emerged and continues.

We tell this story without proposing that we have created a Beaver College model. In fact, one of the major principles that we have learned is that each college, university, or school has its own identity and history that must be taken into account when planning for change of any sort. We can suggest only general principles, not formulas, prescriptions, or tricks. We cannot say, for example, that the ideal faculty workshop should be on campus or off campus, for one day or three days. We can, however, suggest that curriculum planners should function as ethnographers, studying the traditions and mores of their own distinct communities. In that sense, we hope that those teaching at institutions dissimilar from Beaver College will find something of value in this essay, while those teaching at analogous institutions will resist the temptation to import procedures without examining their consequences in another setting.

The opportunity to write this essay provided an occasion for four individuals who have contributed substantially to the Beaver College program to reflect on the last fifteen years. Three of the coauthors—Gail Hearn, Barbara Nodine, and Elaine Maimon—were involved in initiating and developing the program from its earliest stages. In 1986, in order to assume new challenges in other settings, Elaine Maimon left the Beaver College writing program in the capable hands of her colleagues and so has the advantage (and disadvantage) of distance. Janice Haney-Peritz was attracted to accept a position at Beaver College in 1981 because of the reputation of the writing program. As a member of the Beaver faculty, she became a major force in guiding the program into its more mature phases. She has the advantage (and disadvantage) of entering the program *in medias res*. Our narrative will be Ishmaelian, rather than Ahabian. We do not intend to issue directives for finding the white whale. Our quest has more to do with the community in the New Bedford church and the camaraderie on the *Pequod*.

As we discussed procedures for composing this essay, we found that our different points of entering and leaving the program created an appropriately complex pattern for the story we wished to weave. We also determined to keep our eye on you the reader and on your understandable impatience with yet another self-congratulatory personal narrative of how intrepid faculty members and administrators fought curricular inertia, beat the odds, and brought about authentic institutional change. In other words, we have tried to find in the personal history of developing a program those elements that concern public issues in writing across the curriculum. In that sense, the process of writing this essay embodies the essence of what the Beaver College writing program teaches: ways to use writing to discover responses to a broad range of academic material and ways to transform those personal discoveries, if and when one chooses, into public statements appropriate to various and changing contexts.

One of our chief recommendations is to allow time and space within curricular planning for intellectual exploration and discovery. As we have said many times, curricular change, if it is to last, depends on intellectual exchange among faculty members. That intellectual exchange will take different forms at different places—colloquia, workshops, team-teaching with graduate students, assistance from undergraduate writing fellows—but such conversation about principles of writing is essential. Then, just as personal narratives and exploratory notes can be transformed into public statements, such intellectual exploration can be gradually and selectively transformed into public policies and documents: curricular plans, statements in catalogues and in accreditation reports, and, of course, budget lines.

We have divided our discussion into various subtopics, and one especially— the discussion of particular writing assignments—will, we hope, do more than provide useful suggestions for classroom practice; it should also illustrate the intellectual, curricular, and pedagogical developments in the Beaver College program over the last fifteen years. We also allow the styles of the four authors to remain distinct, representative of the contrapuntal harmonies and the fugal dissonances of writing across the curriculum.

First Moments: 1973–1977

In the flux of experience, first moments gain that ordinal distinction only as we ourselves remember them. As the four coauthors discussed their personal versions of first moments, we discovered a number of firsts, ranging in time over a period of several years:

> A biologist and an English teacher, both new to the faculty, talk during lunch in the faculty dining room about students' reluctance to employ the connective powers of English syntax when identifying phyla and classes on biology exams. This conversation—about the response, "wings and feathers," to a request to identify "aves"—leads to some initial cross-disciplinary teaching. The English professor asks her composition students to write a sentence defining *aves*, while the biology professor explains to her students that they will better understand biology if they write about it, sometimes even in sentences. Now, as we think about it, we can see that we were planting a seed in 1973 for what was to become much more ambitious pedagogical collaboration.
>
> The English teacher, who had been on part-time appointment during the "wings-and-feathers" episode, is simultaneously given full-time status and the responsibility as director of composition. (A friend comments that when something like that happens, there ought to be a Rape Crisis Center number to call.) The new director of composition is soon summoned to the office of a new (and brief-tenured) dean, who, in a characteristically dramatic gesture, pitches to her a copy of *Newsweek*, the one with the cover story entitled, "Why Johnny Can't Write," and asks what she is going to do about it. The dean sends the director of composition to see the vice-president in charge of government grants to explore funding possibilities in writing. This incident catapulted an assistant professor, whose preparation for a Ph.D. in English Literature at the University of Pennsylvania had, until that moment, kept her far from the Wharton School, into a world of administration, management, budgets, grants, and fund-raising. It also led her a little later to a 1976 meeting of the Modern Language Association (MLA) to establish a National Council of Writing Program Administrators (WPA), the Depression acronym well expressing the feelings of most of the participants in that crowded room, each in his or her own setting having recently experienced a similarly abrupt and bumpy passage from the gentility of literary scholarship to new uncharted regions.

A faculty committee, led by an outspoken psychologist, demands proof that the second semester of freshman composition actually provides measurable growth in students' writing ability (an early [1975] version of the value-added phenomenon). After checking and rejecting all standardized measures of writing ability, the director of composition appeals for help to the psychologist. "If you want me to come up with reasonable measures of growth in writing ability, you will have to help," pleaded the director of composition, "because to me a measure still means iambic pentameter." But it didn't for long. So began a research collaboration that created an intellectual foundation and justification for what was to become the writing-across-the-curriculum program.

The director of composition cooperates with an anthropologist during one semester and with the outspoken psychologist during another semester to teach their courses as clusters (i.e., to assign a small portion of common reading and to allow students to submit drafts for one instructor's comments and then to submit revised papers to the other instructor, who would assign a grade applicable to both courses).

The biologist and the director of composition talk about adding a writing component to a project that the biologist already has under way, a Student Guidebook for Observational Research in Animal Behavior. This conversation leads to discussions, now involving the psychologist and two other colleagues, an historian and a philosopher, about coauthoring material that would allow teachers of freshman composition to provide students with an introduction to reading and writing in the liberal arts. From these roots grew *Writing in the Arts and Sciences* (Little, Brown, 1981) and *Readings in the Arts and Sciences* (Little, Brown, 1984).

The director of composition attends the 1975 MLA Convention in San Francisco. In a ballroom, in the company of several hundred others, many of whom would also find it a turning point in their careers, she heard Mina Shaughnessy's validating, inspiring talk, "Diving In." After that speech, on a cable car, she meets Harriet Sheridan, dean of Carleton College (Northfield, Minnesota), and learns about faculty workshops and under-graduate writing fellows. Returning to Beaver, the director of composition is armed with what she now calls "the Carleton Plan."

What can we learn now from these selected first moments? Our clear memory was that in each instance we were not trying to save the world—or even the day. We were simply trying to do what seemed sensible, given the demands and constraints of our situation. Although money was a highly desirable commodity from the start, certainly in the mind of the dean, we set the foundation for the writing-across-the-curriculum program without a penny and without really knowing that we were setting the foundation for a program.

Faculty Workshops

After four years of informal efforts, some consciously contrived, others unconsciously accumulated, we moved into the next stage of activity. A small grant from a local Philadelphia foundation, Dolfinger-McMahon, made it possible to conduct the first faculty workshop in January 1977. In the 1970s, January was the Winterim period at the college. Some faculty members taught special month-long courses; others did research. Everyone was expected, officially, to do one or the other, although rule-bending was a common practice. Nonetheless, it was plausible to announce as a Winterim option a two-week morning workshop on the teaching of writing in the disciplines. Since January was part of faculty members' standard nine-month obligation, stipends were not paid.

The idea for organizing a faculty workshop came from Harriet Sheridan's faculty rhetoric seminars that were conducted at Carleton College in 1974 and 1975. Now that such faculty gatherings have become as familiar as committee meetings, we forget that the faculty workshop was something new in the seventies. The workshop at its best is an instance of communal scholarship applied to pedagogic problems, engaging faculty members from across the disciplines in an intellectual exchange that draws on the expertise of all participants. In that way it is different from other faculty activities (the committee meeting, the expert lecture) in that the workshop is (1) scholarly and pragmatic and (2) politically and intellectually nonhierarchical.

The guidance of an outside expert for a portion of the workshop time provides common intellectual material. In addition, the mere presence of an outsider subtly invokes tribal laws of hospitality and civility, allowing the workshop to proceed more politely than it might otherwise. Harriet Sheridan, leading the first workshop at Beaver, raised the enterprise forever from any taint of triviality by her qualifications and demeanor and by her choice of Aristotle's *Rhetoric* as the first reading assignment.

Dean Sheridan's initial workshop attracted 25 percent of the faculty, including the chairpeople of many key departments, including English. The involvement, and perceived leadership, of the English department was crucial—and perilous. Most English department members had valuable experience in teaching writing but little formal expertise, since at that time composition was not readily available as a field of graduate study. English professors also brought to the first workshops a distaste for what they considered the jargon of other disciplines—and the term *jargon* had a broad definition. One of the major breakthroughs in the second stage of the program was the articulated difference between jargon (unnecessary, overelaborated nomenclature) and the efficient use of appropriate technical vocabulary in instances when experts were communicating with each other. The idea of contextual variability would finally begin to take root.

Before that breakthrough, workshops had a subtext of English department arrogance confronting the deep-seated insecurities of other faculty members, who brought vivid memories of humiliation at the hands of their own freshman composition teachers. Scientists, whose own experiences in English classes had made them believe that science writers were microbes from which the English language had to be preserved, found themselves defending the use of subheadings in scientific reports from the charge that such fragmentation was a cop-out to avoid the creation of smooth transitions.

Although such fears were never entirely laid to rest, over the years faculty members developed enough trust in one another to sublimate defensive feelings and to engage in discussions of differing (although not mutually exclusive) definitions for proof, evidence, validity, and significance. Even basic terms like reading and writing could legitimately signify different activities in different contexts. Most scientists, for example, make no apology for reading some sections of research reports and skipping others (thus another secret use for the notorious subheadings that English teachers always distrusted). These discussions were both enlightening and pedagogically useful.

Over the years many different experts presented their theories and ideas to faculty workshops at Beaver College. Because by design we invited multiple experts to present multiple points of view, the faculty group had no choice but to discuss, argue, adopt, reject, synthesize, transfigure, and reimagine a program that became our own indeed. In the 1970s, when writing across the curriculum was new, we had the advantage (and disadvantage) of various outside experts who had little experience in presenting ideas to a diverse group of faculty members from across the disciplines. We could not invite experts in writing across the curriculum per se because no one had yet gained such expertise. As a consequence, with the support of the National Endowment for the Humanities (NEH), we conducted longer, more extensive workshops than might be needed today when veterans of earlier programs can provide syntheses of their experiences. On the other hand, developing faculty ownership of writing across the curriculum has become a more significant problem for programs as we've moved into the 1990s.

Student Involvement

From the start we decided to borrow Harriet Sheridan's idea of involving undergraduates in the collaborative enterprise of teaching writing. (In 1978, Dean Sheridan moved from Carleton College to Brown University, where she established the Rose Writing Fellows Program, the most extensive writing-across-the-curriculum program based on the employment of undergraduate writing fellows.) At Beaver College, we included a selected number of upperclassmen in the Winterim and summer writing workshops. Also, in 1978, inspired by the program developed at Brooklyn College under Professor Kenneth Bruffee, we established one of the first undergraduate writing centers based on principles of collaborative learning. Undergraduates were trained as readers of classmates' work in progress, rather than as junior-grade orthographers and grammarians. Students requesting help with proofreading or with points of usage would find Writing Center consultants who would listen as the writer read the paper aloud or who would demonstrate how to check something in the assigned grammar handbook, but for the most part, the Writing Center gradually gained an identity as a place where writers could find what writers need most—readers.

Early on in the developing program, Writing Center consultants volunteered to provide living models for peer review in the freshman composition classrooms. The yearlong required composition course (English 101–102) had been reconceptualized as a result of faculty writing workshops to encompass the following five major goals:

1. To teach students to respond to classmates' work in progress
2. To introduce contextual variability as exemplified in various academic contexts in the arts and science
3. To introduce the concept of writing as a way of learning
4. To teach processes of transforming private thinking into public statements, through the generative practices of drafting and revising
5. To provide instruction and practice in the conventional features expected in public writing, including the conventions of Standard Written English

Since every freshman began college study at Beaver with English 101, every freshman had the opportunity to understand writing as a complex process related to thinking and learning across the curriculum. Through its emphasis on collaborative procedures, the freshman course also established the idea of writing as a social activity, sometimes conducted in private for personal purposes but always functioning as a connective force. Further, the freshman composition course also served as a road-map for the terrain of higher education. Instructors made conscious efforts (more systematic and efficient after the publication of *Writing in the Arts and Sciences* and *Readings in the Arts and Sciences*) to help students decipher the subtle codes of the various academic communities within the college curriculum. A study of these commonalities and distinctions within academia was at the same time highly sophisticated and elemental, and as a consequence instructors handled the challenge with varying degrees of success.

Remarkably, nonetheless, the most extraordinary changes were taking place in the metaphors that both faculty members and students associated with writing. In a comparatively short time, only an occasional Rip Van Winkle revealed a persisting perversity in defining writing strictly in terms of its surface features. In dormitories and halls, students could be overheard asking each other, "What draft are you on?" "Has your English class gone to the psych lab yet to observe the baby rats?" Instructors in all disciplines—math, studio art, business—were assigning writing as a way to learn, not merely to test, course material. More and more professors were including on their syllabi assigned dates for drafts and peer review sessions.

Often the initiative for writing across the curriculum would come directly from the students. Freshmen who had been taught to submit a page of acknowledgments thanking Writing Center consultants, instructors, peers, and family members for reading work in progress were soon asking professors of physical therapy and economics for permission to attach an acknowledgments page to papers for those courses. Students would also ask professors to review drafts in courses for which drafts had not been assigned. Sophomores, finding themselves eligible for a new writing prize based on a portfolio of drafts and finished work, would ask history professors whether a paper just submitted might be worthy of nomination to the prize competition.

Even more remarkably, biology professors began to report that the emphasis on collaborative learning in writing was carrying a positive effect on teamwork in the laboratory. Instructors felt free to make more realistic laboratory assignments that could at the same time motivate cooperation and reward individual effort. Often students would be asked to pool data and to write a common Results Section, to share references, and then to write individual Introductions and Discussions.

As the 1980s began, writing across the curriculum and collaborative learning pervaded the student and faculty culture at Beaver College. (In 1981, in a report to the National Endowment for the Humanities, the major funder of the program from 1977 to 1981, we wrote an extensive evaluative report—available upon request to Professor Barbara Nodine, Beaver College, Glenside, PA 19038.)

Institutes

During the 1980s, in addition to consolidating and institutionalizing the program at home, Beaver College faculty members have been involved extensively in providing assistance to universities, colleges, and school districts interested in establishing programs according to similar principles. From 1980 to 1983, Beaver conducted a national institute, sponsored by the National Endowment for the Humanities, entitled "Writing in the Humanities." During the summers of 1981 and 1982, teams of college and secondary school instructors from various geographical regions—from El Paso, Texas, to

San Juan, Puerto Rico—assembled on the Beaver campus to study principles of writing, to discuss political strategies to use back home, and to form alliances with each other and with the Beaver staff. In June 1983 in Philadelphia, the institute teams from the two preceding summers joined interested participants from forty states for the first national conference devoted to writing across the curriculum.

From 1983 to 1987, again with funding from NEH, Beaver conducted institutes and extensive partnership programs with twelve local school districts (K–12) in the suburban, industrial, and rural areas surrounding Philadelphia. Although writing across the curriculum was not the only subject of discussion, a shared interest in writing as a mode of learning has helped create nonhierarchical academic alliances across institutional boundaries.

/ / / / / / / /   *Assignments in Psychology:*
Writing to Learn

Barbara F. Nodine

As a psychologist who for many years did not presume to think of herself as a writer, I found my approaches to writing, to teaching, and to everything else I do changed by the workshops and institutes at Beaver. I don't think the changed perspective came in a dazzling flash of light, but looking back, I see my earlier view as that of another person. As a scientifically oriented individual who did not think of herself as having the "talent" to be a writer, I found the concept of writing as a tool for learning to be enormously liberating. If writing could be approached strategically and worked on productively, even without brilliant imagery or scintillating style, then I could help both my students and myself to be better writers. As a cognitive psychologist, I should not have found the connection between writing and learning to be such a novel insight, but perhaps the mystique of the writer aloft in the garret clouded my view of the cognitive capabilities integral to writing. And as a scientist, I was persuaded that writing could be a way of learning because this hypothesis had empirical support—inconclusive and lacking in rigor in absolute terms, but sufficient to involve me in the ongoing process of research.

Not only did I discover that writing to learn would provide me with a constructive means to relabel halting approaches to my own writing, but I could also incorporate these types of activities into my courses. Though this process-conception of writing pervades all the writing assignments described in this chapter, I would like to focus on brief, ungraded writing activities. The particular examples of writing assignments described here are especially useful for the beginning-level courses, though many can be adapted to other courses. These writing activities are not collected by the instructor or graded because their sole purpose is to encourage thinking, not to evaluate the product of that thinking. In the terms that I learned from composition theory, the *audience* for the writing is the self and the *purpose* is for greater understanding of the content being presented in the course.

A frequent complaint of faculty in psychology, and perhaps in other social sciences, is that the textbooks for the beginning course have become too much like encyclopedias, with entries for numerous topics and very little continuity or structure linking the various topics. Thus, some of these activities are directed toward giving students a way of connecting disparate material.

One of the simplest and most widely applicable types of writing-to-learn activities is to ask students to write a one-paragraph summary of a lecture. This writing encourages students to think about the material as a coherent and interrelated unit. To offer a check on the content, I ask for volunteers to read their summaries, and I comment on any omissions or misunderstandings, or I might ask students to share with the person on either side of them. Following a summary writing activity, I have noticed an increase in students' questions about the relations of ideas presented in lecture. Students comment at the end of the semester on how useful these summaries are to them.

Another important type of writing activity requires that students write the legends for visual representations of data or other figural versions of information. The social sciences make frequent use of graphic or tabular presentations, which beginning students often skip over. Students seem to believe that they are relieved of responsibility for those parts of the page not covered with neatly aligned print. I ask students to write legends or titles for figures drawn on the board. Sometimes I present the legend and ask students to create the visual representation. Again, the class can comment on a few volunteered responses, or students can spend a minute sharing with one another.

Another use of writing-to-learn activities quite explicitly includes collaborative groups of four or five students, to whom I present a problem. The students must read the problem, make individual notes on an answer, and then discuss the individual versions and select the best solution to report to the whole class. For example, while studying the experimental method, students might be asked to analyze a brief description of a specific research project, identifying independent and dependent variables, stating the hypothesis, posing ethical considerations, and identifying the variables that can be properly controlled and the possible flaws that might be discovered (beginning students tend to generate many nonexistent flaws). I've also asked students to apply definitions of natural language to chimpanzees' use of symbolic language systems, as a way of defending one side or the other of the controversial issue of whether apes truly have language. Or, students might read a short description of a patient's case history and respond to questions about symptoms, diagnosis, and prognosis.

As an introduction to a new chapter, students might write personal experiences or recollections related to the material; to describe, for example, the celebrations of their sixteenth birthday, their earliest fears, parental methods of punishment, their explanation for the link between their present personality characteristics and earlier ones, or a social interaction at their last meal. Students can be asked to write privately about these matters, without the intent to share, because the point of these writing activities is to connect students' personal experiences with the concepts and data in the lecture material. Such writing exercises highlight the notion that the dry, sometimes numerically or graphically presented results of a psychological study are based on data collected from individuals, interesting people like themselves.

Variations and extensions of the writing-to-learn activities described above have been developed to fit the discipline, level, course size, and, of course, instructor's goals by faculty at Beaver College and elsewhere. As my involvement in writing across the curriculum has progressed from faculty participant at Beaver College to leader of faculty development workshops at other institutions, I find that instructors in various disciplines are most receptive to the connections between writing and learning. Sometimes, as I catch a glimpse of my new self—a psychology professor who has become a purveyor of composition theory—I realize how far the writing-across-the-curriculum movement has come in this decade and a half. When I conduct a workshop on writing-to-learn activities, I do so from my own experience and from the accumulated experiences of hundreds of other professors in business, nursing, sociology, math, political science, and fine arts. We have all come a long way.

/ / / / / / / **Writing in Ecology and the Ecology of Writing**

Gail W. Hearn

I wish that my professors had told me when I was in college more about how scientists actually get their research done. I would have had a much easier time of it after graduation. Although I had a good command of biological facts, and although I had an excellent liberal arts education, I discovered that I wasn't prepared to participate in scientific research at the graduate level. I wasn't familiar with or comfortable with the customs and traditions of real scientific research. Namely:

Collaboration: I envisioned the dedicated scientist working alone in the lab late into the night. While I was right about the late-into-the-night part, the scientist rarely works alone. Whole groups of scientists work late into the night. I discovered that research scientists consult with colleagues at every stage: from designing the experiment, to actually doing the work, to writing up the report for publication.

Repetition: Everything, it seems, gets repeated over and over and over in the course of doing research: the experiment is redesigned and redone until the results are convincing. The report is written and rewritten until it is appropriate and accurate.

Presentation: Making the great discovery public was, I originally imagined, a brief and superficial task for the scientist. A quickly written report with insignificant surface errors that would be corrected by editors somewhere would be more than sufficient because the importance of the discovery would be obvious to everyone. Unfortunately, this is not the way it works. Instead, the final product of research, a written report for publication in a scholarly journal, must be very carefully prepared. The writing must be intelligent, informed, and—most importantly—persuasive, since the importance of research is rarely obvious. There can be absolutely no error in spelling, grammar, or English usage. (Those "editors somewhere" don't exist.) Worst still, tradition dictates that the figures (illustrations) must be carefully and artistically rendered, then reproduced as glossy photographs to give a completely professional appearance to the manuscript.

Why all this concern with how the report looks and reads? Probably because the audience never sees the scientists' laboratory (clean and tidy or messy and filthy) or experimental technique (careful and accurate or sloppy). Therefore, skillfully written, well-illustrated, and error-free manuscripts come to represent to the stranger reading the report the quality of scientific research.

Now as I look around at my contemporaries I realize that these qualities/skills/practices—perhaps in slightly altered form—are important in almost all careers that college students aspire to. But none of these practices seemed very significant during my college years. I worked alone, except for a few laboratory exercises, and certainly never shared ideas or written work with fellow students. Experiments were performed once, and papers were written once; there was never any attempt to repeat and improve on the work. And careful presentation of written work seemed almost goody-goody; I assumed that my professors could see through a few typos to my real abilities.

Fortunately, just as I was struggling with strategies for teaching my students these real-life attitudes and practices, Beaver College began a series of faculty workshops. The workshops focused on teaching writing, not strategies for the real world. But amazingly, the writing strategies that were emerging reflected these very same real-life practices that I was trying to show to my science students.

The workshops also gave me important insights into the traditions of writing in the sciences. By explaining and defending scientific writing traditions to my colleagues in the humanities, I began to understand why we scientists wrote as we did: Why do scientists use subheadings in their writing? Why do scientists use so many unfamiliar words? Are these words just jargon, or is there a real necessity for their use? Why are scientists so fond of the passive voice? Why do scientists need to use pictures (figures and tables) instead of just words alone? And from the other side, why do scientists bother to use any words at all? Why not just pictures?

Upper-level courses in the science curriculum seemed an especially appropriate place to share these real-life skills with my undergraduates. At that stage, the students are close to the point when they will leave college; they know enough biology to appreciate the insights; and they are dangerously far from their English composition experiences.

The course I have chosen to describe here—Biology 329: Ecology—is a typical upper-level biology course, meeting for four hours of lecture and three hours of lab each week. Its prerequisites, including a year of general biology as well as comparative anatomy and physiology, have the effect of restricting the enrollment to between fifteen and thirty students, virtually all junior and senior biology majors. Because the students in the course are relatively homogeneous in their preparation, I am able to build on and to reinforce their previous academic experiences. From their freshman course in English composition, I know they have had practice with appropriate writing techniques, such as paraphrasing and integrating information from different sources. They will also have some experience with collaborative learning and with the peer-review process.

From their previous biology courses they will have learned something about the appropriate style and format for laboratory reports. They might be familiar with library resources including indexes like the Science Citation Index and BioAbstracts. Some students will be aware of the different audiences that exist for written work in biology. As part of an upper-level biology course, it is important to reinforce these experiences, so students don't come to believe that writing is only important in a few isolated, academic situations.

Two general types of writing go on in the course: informal, ungraded writing intended as an aid to memory and learning; and formal, graded writing, intended as apprentice experience in the traditions of scientific writing. Since Barbara Nodine focuses on writing to learn and I use many of the techniques that she mentions, I will focus on the more formal writing that I assign.

I ask students to keep laboratory notebooks—a semipublic but comprehensive record of research. Students are allowed to use these notebooks on the lab practicals—exams intended to evaluate the understanding of concepts and procedures learned in the laboratory. Students quickly learn that sloppy notebooks are little help under the time pressures of a testing situation, and their notebooks soon become more comprehensive and better organized.

I also assign short papers based on questions suggested by their textbooks and longer papers based on laboratory exercises. Short papers provide an opportunity to practice several real-life writing skills. First, because these are questions-to-be-answered, not topics-to-be-written-about, students learn to focus their efforts. Second, students become more familiar with original research reports in a context in which they can already understand why that particular research is important to an understanding of ecology. Third, as part of the process of producing these papers, students gain experience with rewriting (multiple drafts) and peer review.

Three of these short papers are written by each student in the course of the semester, but in-class peer review is used only for the first paper. I generate a list of questions based on the textbook material we are currently covering in the lectures. For example:

The author of your text notes (p. 259) that the extreme breeding strategy of the California condor makes it very unlikely that this bird will be saved from extinction. Locate some of the many articles that have appeared recently in the popular press. Exactly what is the current status of this species?

The author of your text uses the marmot as an example of polygyny (p. 274). What additional information can you learn about marmot social behavior from the paper your author cites (Downhower and Armitage, 1971)? What additional research has been published since then on marmot social behavior? Does this more recent research change the original social system proposed in the 1971 paper?

The short paper is completed in three stages: a rough draft with self-evaluation (required, but not graded); three peer-reviews (graded); and a final draft with an evaluation of the peer-review process (graded). Each student chooses a question to answer (one student per question). At the same time, the students are given extensive details on the assignment, including due dates, maximum length, format, and audience (other students in the course). The students also get a preview of the peer-review process, including directions for peer review, self-evaluation form, and peer-review form.

When the students bring their rough-draft answer to class, they also bring a completed self-evaluation on the status of their project. The evaluation is a one-page set of questions that gives students an opportunity to reflect on their progress. The questions address specific issues:

How close to completion is this draft?

What additional steps do you plan to take in completing a final draft of this project?

How did you locate the sources that you used in preparing your answer? What indexes (Readers Guide, BioAbstracts, Science Citation Index) did you use? What special library services (interlibrary loan; reference section) did you use?

The initial peer review is done in class, with each student commenting on the rough draft of three other students. The peer comments are elicited by asking students to respond to a set of questions for each draft they read. Again, the questions are specific:

In the space below, outline the major points that are presented in this draft.

Is this draft intended for an audience of biology majors? Give an example where the author has assumed some background knowledge of biology on the part of the reader.

Before beginning the peer-review process, the students are reminded that the purpose of the review is to help others write better final drafts. They are also reminded that the peer reviews are graded on the basis of helpfulness and thoroughness.

When the final draft of the project is handed in, it is accompanied by the earlier draft, the three peer reviews, reading notes and photocopies, and an evaluation of the peer-review process. Again, the students respond to questions:

What advice given by your peer reviewers did you incorporate into your final draft? Name the reviewer and describe the advice given.

What advice given by your peer reviewers did you decide to disregard? Name the reviewer and explain why you chose to ignore their advice.

I grade both the papers and the peer reviews. Commenting on the papers is made much easier by the presence of the peer reviews, because in most cases the peer reviewers have already identified the problems in the paper.

The laboratory work centers around two six-week studies of local ecosystems: a deciduous forest and a freshwater pond. In the course of completing these two field studies, the students not only learn some basic methods for measuring and describing such ecosystems, but also experience a steadily increasing need for effective collaboration. Students will, I hope, see the benefit of collaborating, and will be able to produce more detailed and meaningful lab reports describing their work.

Both field studies follow the same overall schedule: three or four weeks of field work, gathering data; one week summarizing class data; one week for each student to write a rough draft of the lab report and to have it reviewed by three other students; and an open lab-book practical and final draft in the final lab period.

Admittedly, ecology has an advantage over many scientific disciplines in that the results of the lab exercises are not entirely predictable. Students are asked to write their lab reports in response to the question: Is this forest/pond typical for this geographic area? Realizing that there is no single right answer to that controlling question, the students, in writing the rough draft, begin to see how the same data can be used to support different conclusions, and they get experience in arranging and structuring the data to support the conclusion that they believe is correct.

The peer review (each rough draft lab report is reviewed by the three other members of the lab group) is conducted during a laboratory period to minimize the problems of plagiarism that can easily arise when all the students are writing on the same topic. On the other hand, borrowing good ideas, with the permission of the original source and with proper acknowledgment of that source, is permitted. Such borrowing frequently occurs when one student, during the peer review, realizes that another student has presented data in a particularly effective form in the results section, or has made especially effective points in the discussion section. At first, stronger students may worry that weaker students will steal all their good ideas, but stronger students, because they are more perceptive, soon see that they don't have a monopoly on good ideas, and that they too can benefit from the peer-review process. The stronger students also receive the instructor's recognition through the frequent public acknowledgment of their peers.

The peer-review process follows the same pattern as that done on the miniprojects: a self-evaluation; peer-review directions; a detailed peer-review form; and a peer-review evaluation. The self-evaluation alerts students to all the places where they can have difficulty in writing a rough draft of a lab report, and the reader's form focuses the reviewer on the usual problems that arise in student-written lab reports. The second field study, done on a small freshwater pond, increases the emphasis on collaboration. New randomly assigned lab groups are formed, and each lab group gathers data together and prepares a common summary.

To what extent did these writing assignments prepare my students for those real-life practices: collaboration, repetition, and presentation? Certainly, the students learned a great deal about collaboration. They had to cooperate with each other at almost every stage of the lab exercises. In some situations, e.g., the gathering of adequate data to describe the ecosystem, the need for collaboration was self-evident. No single student could hope to gather all the necessary information in so short a time period. But in writing the lab reports, the advantages of the peer-review process became clear only after the collaboration had taken place. The advantages, however, were dramatic and convincing. This year the use of peer review worked so well in the first ecosystem study that the students asked to formalize the collaboration on the second study so that each lab group worked together to produce a common Results section.

The concept that repetition leads to an improved product is also something that science students know from other laboratory experiences and, indeed, is reinforced in their ecosystem studies. Overlapping ecosystem measurements provide the repetition that ensures some reliability in collecting data and helps the class identify real discrepancies in the results. But the idea that rewriting like remeasuring might lead to a better result and that checking the result with other equivalent results through peer review leads to greater accuracy represents a transfer of the repetition strategy that is not always evident in advance. Fortunately, the advantages of the drafting process became apparent in the final drafts of both the lab reports and the short papers. Because in writing, students also had a chance to rethink, their papers not only sounded and looked better, they also expressed more substantive thinking.

Likewise, when students are both performing experiments and writing in the ways I have described, they can see the analogy between carefully following the conventions of laboratory procedure and carefully adhering to the conventions of Standard Written English. They will consequently understand the importance of presentation of their work—and of themselves.

In all cases these writing assignments were part of a larger course strategy designed to show students the importance and usefulness of these practices. The writing assignments were, in this way, more than mere expression. They no doubt reinforced understanding of scientific concepts and information—and thereby functioned as a way of learning course material—but their utility went even beyond the learning of course content. Writing provided an opportunity to extend scientific strategies into another situation. Consequently, the writing exercises helped the students to improve in writing up their work and in the overall performance expected of scientists. Moreover, I believe that these activities will also improve the students' general functioning as adults—in collaboration, repetition, and presentation—and that this improvement will not be confined either to writing or to the laboratory.

/ / / / / / / *In Medias Res: Reflections and Assignments in Composition and Literature*

Janice Haney-Peritz

If Ishmael survives the wreck of Ahab's quest, it isn't because he remains aloof. Quite the contrary. From the beginning, Ishmael admits a fondness for the great and mysterious Idea. And later, when Ahab induces the crew to voice their allegiance to his quest for mastery, Ishmael confesses that his fondness made his vow all the "stronger." In fact, Ishmael must work to become Ishmaelian. In the day-to-day venture of keeping the *Pequod* afloat, he makes friends, learns something of Moby Dick's "history," develops a sense of communal responsibility, and realizes both the necessity and value of rethinking, reimagining, and reworking Ahab's putatively providential plot. However, in the revising, Ishmael doesn't lose his fondness for the Idea; instead, he finds a way "to be social with it."

Although there was no Ahab in sight when I joined the Beaver College faculty in 1981, writing across the curriculum soon became my *bête blanche*. Not only would I be teaching the required two-semester freshman composition course, but I would also be serving as advisor to the student-run Writing Center. Since both the composition course and the center were considered fundamental to the success of Beaver's venture in writing across the curriculum, I set out to learn the exact meaning of this venturesome idea. Fortunately, I never found it. In conversations with my colleagues, I learned that there had been faculty workshops on writing, a series of institutes, and some collaborative research projects. Over the years, various writing assignments had been developed, tried out, revised, and in some instances, abandoned. But even though each faculty member had some story to tell about his or her engagement with writing across the curriculum, no one purported to know it all—to be in possession of the true meaning, the Ultimate Idea.

At first, this proliferation of stories and meanings was disconcerting. However, as time went on, I learned not only to be social with the idea of writing across the curriculum but also to value this kind of knowing as a way of bridging the gap between outside and inside. When I came to Beaver, I was more or less an outsider, a newcomer in pursuit of an idea. But as I conversed with those on the inside about how writing figured in our different disciplines as well as in our courses, my position changed. In learning to be social with the idea of writing, I became a coworker, a member of a faculty that was engaged in the difficult process of initiating students into an academic culture.

Believing that what worked for me might also work for my students, I base my pedagogical practice on the principle that writing is a social act which varies according to the context and aims of its production. So, for example, students in my freshman composition course collaborate with each other in all phases of the writing process—from generating ideas to analyzing drafts to editing the work they have decided to make public. They compose discourses for a variety of contexts, aims, and audiences. And, they read and respond to a wide range of academic and nonacademic texts.

To get the conversation about writing across the curriculum started, I often ask students to make a list of the writing they will be doing for their other courses, to share their lists in small groups, to note the sections of *Writing in the Arts and Sciences* that might be of use to them as they work on specific writing projects, and to present their small-group findings to the rest of the class. Since students usually forget to list such tasks as notetaking, journal writing, and test-taking, I use this opportunity to question the commonplace notion that the only writing that counts is writing typed up for a grade. Such questioning not only turns the conversation toward more process-oriented issues but in so doing introduces the possibility of a revised relation to writing.

Occasionally, I have "clustered" my composition course with the yearlong introductory psychology course. On these occasions, my colleagues in psychology provide me with copies of their syllabi, textbooks, and assignments. In consequence, I know when my students will be dealing with such issues as memory, language acquisition, and personality theory—a knowledge that makes it possible for me to design assignments that encourage students to use psychological concepts to achieve various aims in different contexts. Although I give students some class time to collaborate on their psychology projects, my main concern is to help them understand the discursive context of these assignments. So, for example, while the students are working on the "Mama Rat" assignment—an assignment that emphasizes observation and description—they are also reading and rhetorically analyzing a wide range of academic and nonacademic descriptive writing; using their journals to produce descriptions for different audiences and aims; and doing some in-class exercises that raise philosophical questions about the relation of words and things, questions that broach the possibility of revision by complicating the students' understanding of the role convention plays in the production of descriptive writing. Since I do not grade the "Mama Rat" papers, students are required to choose one of their journal pieces, to develop it into a set piece of description, and to submit it to me for evaluation along with a "metacommentary." In this, students compare the writing (both process and product) of the "Mama Rat" paper with the set piece of descriptive writing they are handing in.

If clustering works at Beaver, it may be because the composition course is founded on an attempt to put the principles of social learning, contextual variability, and conceptual revision into practice. Hence, even though students are required to purchase *Writing in the Arts and Sciences*, teachers are not expected to cover the text chapter by chapter. Indeed, I teach students to use this book the way I do: as a resource for anticipating, identifying, and dealing with the problems academic writing assignments pose. Moreover, since there is no departmentally mandated syllabus, I can work out my course as the class moves along, keeping in mind that the point is not only to keep the conversation about writing going but to do so in a way that will assist students to become active participants in an academic culture.

For me, bridging the gap between outside and inside was not an especially difficult task. Since I had been teaching at the college level for some years before coming to Beaver, I was already familiar with the ritual and symbolic practices of academia. Not so the typical college freshman. Although freshmen have already had twelve years of schooling, most have only a rudimentary understanding of the workings of an academic culture. What makes matters even more difficult is that many of my students are habituated to mass culture, a culture that tends to alienate people from their native capacity for conceptual thinking and critical reasoning. Hence, even though my students enjoy recounting their personal experiences, they seldom relate them to a significant conceptual or critical framework. Similarly, even though my students are fond of expressing their opinions, they rarely substantiate those opinions with anything other than appeals to common sense, declarations of "that's just the way it is."

Since conceptual thinking and critical reasoning are central to the workings of an academic culture, we professors are often tempted to discount both the experiences and opinions of our students. However, if we give in to this temptation, then we will find ourselves in the ivory tower that so many presume we already inhabit. In that tower, experts teach a body of abstract knowledge in ways which belie not only the conceptual and critical practices that would differentiate academic culture from mass culture but also higher education's claim to make an existential difference in the lives of its participants.

As I see it, the experiences and opinions of students are not the problem; rather, it is the students' relation of—and therefore their relation to—those experiences and opinions that (re)presents a problem. But if this is, in fact, the case, then the problem can also be conceived as an opportunity for revision. With a little help from their teachers and friends, students can revise their relation of and to their experiences and opinions. In so doing, not only may students learn to appreciate how writing works, but they may also come to understand why it is so important to academic culture. Indeed, until it is coupled with some such revisionary aim, the principle that writing is a social and contextually variable act is unlikely to have the existential and cultural significance it should.

With this aim in mind, I begin my freshman composition class with a set of assignments that focuses on the revision of personal experience. On the first day of class, students are given fifteen minutes to write an account of some experience that disturbed, confused, or angered them. Although I read and respond to these written accounts, my response is composed solely of questions. Drawing on Richard Young's particle-wave-field heuristic, I ask questions like the following: If you had been older, would you still have reacted in the same way? If your friend had been male rather than female, would you still have refused to go? Is there a relationship between the way you responded to Mary and the way you respond to characters in films, novels, and TV programs? When students read these responses, they are taken aback, in part because they had expected an evaluative commentary. What, they ask, are they to do with my response? When I ask them what they would like to do, most of them say that they feel the need to answer some of my questions. I encourage them to do so in their journals.

At this point, I put the students into storytelling groups and give them instructions on what to do in their groups. Basically, what happens is that each person reads his or her story aloud, answers questions of clarification posed by others in the group, works with the others to identify the story's center of gravity, listens as each peer recounts some experience associated with the initial story, discusses with others the likenesses and differences among all the stories, and either generates a categorical name for this collection of stories or defines in writing what these stories exemplify. Whereas my questioning response encourages students to explore further the specificity of their experience, these small-group exercises encourage the students to produce a conceptual frame for their personal experience.

During the ensuing two weeks, students use their journals to recount personal experiences, to pose and then answer questions about specific aspects of the experience, and to posit various conceptual frameworks within which their experience might be seen as a case in point. At the same time, students are reading and responding to a number of texts that draw on personal experience to explain a concept, pose a generalization, or raise a problematic issue. Since some of these texts are by academics, not only do students have to deal with such disciplinary concepts as ritual, class, and the oedipal complex but they also see how the relation of and to personal experience can be mediated by something other than the commonplaces of our mass culture.

All this writing, reading, and storytelling culminates in that conventional staple of the freshman composition class: a familiar essay. However, since students are asked to develop such an essay from the journal writing they have been doing, even their rough drafts show signs of something less familiar: the attempt to use concepts to mediate their relation of and to experience. As peer review makes the issues of audience and aim more real to the students, further conceptual and rhetorical revisions occur until that limit called a deadline is reached. But even though a deadline institutes a limit, my hope is that students will continue to revise not only their relation to experience, but also their relation to the various bodies of knowledge they encounter in academia.

As a graduate student in English, I learned a body of knowledge about literature, in large part by writing numerous scholarly papers. Hence, when I began teaching my specialty, I not only assigned my students numerous papers to write; I also assumed that writing-across-the-curriculum programs were meant for others—for all those nonliterature professors who didn't require numerous formal papers. However, as my understanding of writing across the curriculum changed, so too did the way writing figured in my literature-based courses. Nowadays, I usually require only one of the kinds of papers that have traditionally been central to literary study: a reading of a text, a review of contemporary approaches to a text, or a research paper on some aspect of the context in which a literary text was produced. But even though I now require only one formal paper, students in my courses do much more writing. Indeed, they write something for every class—usually a response sheet to the text for the day.

Twice a semester students are required to review their response sheets and to analyze them not only in terms of what is said but also in terms of the literary and cultural ideologies that underwrite their relation to and opinions about the literature they are reading. Drawing on this analysis, the students identify issues and define problems for further exploration. To assist them in doing these tasks, I provide them with a textbook (McCormick, Waller, and Flower, *Reading Texts*, D. C. Heath, 1987), as well as with two diagrammatic representations of the conceptual framework within which most literary critics work. That literary criticism has a conceptual structure surprises most of my students in a way that encourages them to revise their relation of and to their reading of literature. Building on this revisionary relation, students proceed to write a formal paper that goes through multiple drafts and peer review before it comes to me for a grade.

By encouraging response, revision, and collaboration, I am trying to make my pedagogical practice principled, rather than providential and predictable. And even though old habits die hard—especially those I developed while learning a specialized body of knowledge about literature—I have had the good fortune to learn about something else: writing across the curriculum. Yet, finally, it is the way I have learned—and continue to learn—about this venturesome practice that encourages me to believe that if I keep working at it, I may eventually become Ishmaelian.

Some Concluding Remarks

From its beginnings, Beaver's writing-across-the-curriculum program has depended on conversation. Keeping that conversation lively has proven to be a difficult task. Like students, faculty members come and go. To address this problem, we periodically hold faculty workshops on some aspect of writing across the curriculum. But even though most newcomers attend these workshops, many veteran instructors don't. Furthermore, the structure of these workshops is not quite what it used to be. In the 1970s when writing across the curriculum was new to all of us, nonhierarchical intellectual exchange was the order of the day. In these later times, this kind of intellectual exchange is much more difficult to achieve, in part because the workshops are led by one or two faculty members who are presumed to be the ones who know. This presumption—reinforced as it is by the relative scarcity of veteran faculty members—tends to make the conversation about writing less exploratory and revisionary than it used to be (or should be).

Moreover, there is a problem with resonance. In the past, faculty were involved in weeklong and sometimes even monthlong workshops and institutes. Nowadays, however, we steal a morning here and a day there. Consequently, faculty who are new to writing across the curriculum often experience difficulty in becoming social with the idea. They feel the need for more stories, more support, and more intellectual play before going public with their understanding. Fortunately, the recent institution of an M.A. in English program has made it possible for us to respond to this need in a new way, that is, by assigning graduate students to work with new faculty members who are interested in integrating writing into their courses.

Veteran faculty members—especially those who don't participate in the workshop process of initiating new faculty to the idea of writing—present a more difficult problem. In this case, the tendency is to fall back on former habits, a tendency noticeable both inside and outside the English department. Writing-to-learn assignments are squeezed out of the syllabus to make room for more reading, more discussion, more dissemination of information, or more testing. Paper assignments are given with little or no indication of the audience, aim, context, or conventional characteristics of the kind of writing at issue. Suggestions about process and opportunities for peer collaboration are less frequently offered. And complaints about plagiarism, grammatical errors, and spelling mistakes increase.

Those of us committed to writing across the curriculum have sought to address this problem in various ways. We hold workshops on specific issues of concern to the faculty such as plagiarism and its next of kin—the research paper that takes the form of a string of quotations and paraphrases; we involve ourselves in the local public and parochial schools, often offering programs on writing across the curriculum for elementary and high school in-service days; and we attempt to make connections between writing and other issues of interest such as higher order reasoning.

Indeed, the writing-across-the-curriculum program took on new life in the early 1980s when the faculty became interested in critical thinking and problem solving. In workshops made possible by the Fund for the Improvement of Post Secondary Education (FIPSE), we explored and debated numerous theoretical models of thinking, reasoning, and problem solving, generated various practical proposals for curricular and pedagogical change, and recognized anew the centrality of writing to the intellectual development of students.

From the start, we worked toward weaving the writing program into the fabric of the institution through paragraphs in the college catalogue, mission statements, and descriptions in accreditation reports. But now, in the program's second decade, we are attempting another kind of institutionalization through curricular requirements. Recently, the Beaver faculty approved a modified core curriculum which requires that core courses emphasize the processes of learning—including, of course, writing—rather than the mere coverage of information. Since core courses are offered in seven areas (science, cross-cultural studies, Western history, the arts, texts of Western culture, quantitative reasoning/computer science, and individuals and society) and since students are required to take coursework in all seven areas, the writing-across-the-curriculum program will now go beyond voluntarism to develop institutionalized courses over and above the yearlong required course in freshman composition.

Although institutionalization policy will now play a stronger role in maintaining our commitment to writing across the curriculum, we have by no means given up our belief that conversation is fundamental to the success of our efforts. Indeed, the institution of the modified core is already providing new occasions for intellectual exchange. Workshops for faculty involved in designing and teaching core courses are being held, and there is a major proposal in the works that would provide core teachers with the time, support, and recognition they deserve for developing courses that engage students in writing to learn and learning to write.

Keeping the conversation lively is no easy task. Nevertheless, Beaver's writing-across-the-curriculum program is likely to enjoy a long life, not only because it stresses contextual adaptability but also because it values conceptual revision. As the concerns of the Beaver community change, so too will the workings of the writing program. Our hope, however, is that these sea-changes will enable us to discover yet more ways to be social with the idea of writing across the curriculum.

Michigan Technological University

Elizabeth A. Flynn, Robert W. Jones with Diane Shoos and Bruce Barna

> *[Technical faculty] value calculating and computing over writing, and they are resistant to the idea of "expressive writing" because they don't see their role as encouraging students to explore attitudes or values. They want their students to become efficient problem solvers, not introspective evaluators.*

Institution:	*Michigan Technological University*
Institutional Size—Students (FTES):	6,300
Institutional Size—Faculty (FTEF):	420
Student/Faculty Ratio:	15:1
Highest Degree Granted— Institution:	Ph.D.
Highest Degree Granted—English Department:	M.S.
Public or Private Institution:	Public

Institutional Mission: a selective, rural university that emphasizes undergraduate education in science and engineering; in recent years MTU has also developed as a research-oriented institution with a number of fully developed graduate programs.

For more information on the program described in this chapter, contact: Elizabeth Flynn, Department of Humanities, Michigan Technological University, Houghton, MI 49931.

The writing-across-the-curriculum movement in the United States has had its most significant impact on liberal arts curricula. Most of the institutions represented in this book, for instance, have a liberal arts orientation. Only one, Michigan Technological University, has a specifically technological orientation. And Michigan Tech's writing-across-the-curriculum program, one of the first and most influential in the country, has, perhaps ironically, had its greatest impact—on its own campus and on other campuses—on liberal arts faculty rather than technologically oriented faculty. The movement has not yet developed a model that addresses the specific needs of students and faculty in nonliberal arts curricula. At Michigan Tech, we are attempting, in the second phase of our program, to develop such a model.

Although rooted in research and theory that arise out of the work of James Britton, Janet Emig, and James Moffett,[1] the American writing-across-the-curriculum movement has been developed, for the most part, by individuals trained in the liberal arts. Typically, composition specialists actively engaged in developing such programs received their training in traditional graduate programs in English, specializing in literature, and they became familiar with education research and theory only after obtaining positions and redefining themselves as composition specialists.

The values and attitudes that inform the movement are deeply humanistic. Writing, which is seen as an art, is placed at the center of all curricula, including technical curricula, and writing that is exploratory ("expressive") is valued more highly than writing that is practical ("transactional"). At many faculty development workshops, all faculty, regardless of discipline, are asked to write expressively, to keep journals, perhaps to generate a narrative essay and to submit the essay to peer review. They are also asked to encourage their students to keep expressive journals that involve introspection and value assessment.

The approach works well with faculty who share the prevailing perspective. The following course description, for instance, is testimony to the power of writing-across-the-curriculum workshops on faculty who are predisposed to accept their fundamental assumptions and the practical strategies that arise out of them. Diane Shoos, an assistant professor of French in the Department of Humanities at Michigan Tech, restructured her first-year language courses after attending a two-day workshop. She describes the innovations she introduced as a result of the workshop, as follows:

In my French classes I routinely ask students to keep loose-leaf notebooks. Although the specific contents vary according to the student's level, the notebooks are in all cases both an opportunity for creative communication and, perhaps more importantly, a place where students can "step back" to reflect on their own learning process.

At the introductory level the notebook serves as a personalized workbook in the foreign language. In the first quarter French classes, for example, I often ask students to create in the notebook lists of descriptive words (adjectives, gerunds) and later brief descriptive sentences about culturally authentic visuals such as advertisements. As their skills develop, students invent short narratives to go along with pictures or photographs chosen by them, or write short compositions about themselves or someone else, incorporating new structures and vocabulary. From time to time I ask students to exchange their notebooks in class so that they have the opportunity to see, comment on, and help revise each other's work. Although these same assignments could be completed and handed in individually, compiling a notebook helps students connect material and gives them a sense of language acquisition as a cumulative process. In addition each person's notebook becomes a concrete, personalized record of their progress.

At the first-year level students also use their notebooks as journals to react (at first in English, then later as much as possible in French) to aspects of the culture they encounter in the media or in their own lives, as well as to comment on their own experience as second-language learners. In this way the notebooks serve as a diagnostic and, even more importantly, self-diagnostic tool: given the opportunity to identify their own particular learning problems, students appear much more likely to seek solutions to them. This is crucial at a school like Michigan Tech where students are often reluctant to speak with instructors. In addition, because students have the chance to give regular feedback about the class, including their reactions to specific activities and assignments, the journals serve as an informal, week-by-week teaching evaluation. On more than one occasion the journals have given me important clues to the collective "mood" of the students.

A professor of French language and literature is no doubt quite willing to accept the idea that writing is integral to learning and that students should be encouraged in engage in "creative communication." Shoos has found expressive writing to be a valuable supplement to conversation because it is a considerably less constrained form of communication. Students are less anxious when experimenting with language in the quiet of their dorm rooms than when confronting each other and a knowledgeable teacher in the classroom. Journals also provide Shoos with insight into how the course is going and what the students are experiencing as they proceed through the course, information that she clearly values.

Those of us who have conducted numerous workshops on and off campus recognize that not all liberal arts faculty are receptive to writing-across-the-curriculum theory or practice. In fact, some humanities faculty, such as literature specialists and philosophers, are among the most resistant. Some literature teachers are convinced that the best way to teach writing is to expose students to the best literature that has been written, as if the connection between reading and writing were direct and uncomplicated and as if epic poetry and the student essay were not two entirely different genres. Some philosophers are so committed to their discipline that their primary allegiance is to their field rather than to their students. Still, on the whole, liberal arts faculty are ready for our message because their disciplinary training predisposes them to it. Usually, they already assign writing in their courses and are highly motivated to explore ways to construct more meaningful assignments and to improve the language abilities of their students. A brief workshop is often sufficient to alter the pedagogical approaches of these faculty.

Our program at Michigan Tech has had considerably more impact on faculty in the College of Sciences and Arts than in the College of Engineering. The most dramatic transformations have occurred within the Department of Humanities and among particularly enthusiastic faculty in the Department of Social Sciences and the Department of Biological Sciences.[2] Within the Department of Humanities, for instance, almost all teachers of first-year English ask students to keep journals and provide opportunities for peer critiquing and submission of multiple drafts. The department also supports the Reading/Writing Center, a facility that provides students an opportunity for one-on-one tutoring in both writing and reading and the Center for Computer-Assisted Language Instruction, a facility that provides opportunities for interaction among students and between teacher and students through netted computers.[3] Most of the department's general education courses are writing-intensive and are limited to thirty-five students per section so that faculty have opportunities to assign considerable formal and informal writing and to conference with students.

Nonliberal arts faculty, however, have not usually developed a predisposition to accept the concepts advocated at writing-across-the-curriculum workshops. Their disciplines, by definition, are practical, functional, and "transactional." They have been trained to solve technical problems efficiently, and they see their job as helping their students attain similar skills. Often they value calculating and computing over writing, and they are resistant to the idea of "expressive" writing because they don't see their role as encouraging students to explore attitudes or values. They want their students to become efficient problem solvers, not introspective evaluators.

Failure to convince engineering and technology faculty of the merits of writing-across-the-curriculum pedagogies has often resulted from an inability of composition specialists to convince such faculty that the ways of learning in engineering and the ways of learning that writing make possible possess common ground enough to warrant including writing at the expense of subtracting some valuable current component of a course.

WRITING ACROSS THE CURRICULUM
AND THE ENGINEERING CURRICULUM

At Michigan Tech, where approximately 40 percent of the faculty are in the College of Engineering, we have had ample opportunity to experience the difficulties of convincing engineering faculty that writing, especially exploratory writing, should be an important component of their course structures. Although over three hundred MTU faculty have participated in faculty development workshops, participation by faculty from the College of Engineering has not been proportional to their representation on the faculty as a whole. And often those engineering faculty who do attend are among the most resistant to the ideas presented there. They complain that they teach large classes and cannot possibly add grading student papers to an already heavy work load. Or they say they would feel foolish interrupting a lecture to ask students to summarize in a journal entry what they have heard so far. Or they insist that much of their teaching involves imparting basic information best learned through lecture and examination.

Not surprisingly, the program evaluation that we conducted several years ago revealed that we had had the least impact on the engineering curriculum and on engineering faculty. In a curricular practices survey of former workshop participants conducted in 1982, for instance, we found that only 22 percent of the engineering faculty had tried one or more writing-across-the-curriculum activities, such as assigning journals or ungraded writing, compared to 41 percent of humanities and social sciences faculty and 84 percent of the composition faculty (Kalmbach and Gorman, 1986: 78). In another study, an examination of portfolios of the writing of five engineering students over the course of their career at Michigan Tech, we found that the writing the students did in their first-year composition and humanities courses demonstrated the influence of the writing-across-the-curriculum program in that they kept journals and wrote multiple drafts of papers, but the writing they did in their engineering courses (primarily lab reports) demonstrated very little influence (Kalmbach, 1986: 182; Kalmbach and Gorman, 1986: 81–82). We concluded that attendance at a writing-across-the-curriculum workshop and the presence of a nationally visible program on campus were no guarantee that classroom practices in the College of Engineering would actually change. Occasional successes did occur, of course. Cynthia Selfe of the Department of Humanities and Freydoon Arbabi of the Department of Civil Engineering, for instance, described a successful collaborative project involving the use of journals in Arbabi's civil engineering class in an article that won the William Elgin Wickenden Award for the best article of the year in the journal *Engineering Education*. But these exceptions usually demonstrated the value of one-on-one collaboration between composition specialists and engineers rather than the effectiveness of workshops in introductory writing. We decided, therefore, that the workshop model that had brought so much national visibility to the Department of Humanities and to the university had to be supplemented by a collaborative model if we were to have an impact on the College of Engineering.

Collaboration is, by definition, reciprocal, dialogic.[4] Two or more individuals representing different, though compatible approaches, value systems, or epistemologies come together to create a new solution to a problem, or a new way of doing things. The collaborating agents need not necessarily be equal partners; one may take the upper hand in the relationship. What is essential, though, is that both agents contribute and that one approach, system, or epistemology not be effaced by the other. The resulting product represents a new synthesis of different ways of thinking or behaving.

The collaborative model works well with engineering faculty because it encourages mutuality and respect. Faculty resistant to the idea of expressive writing or pedagogical approaches that seem foreign to them need not give up their own traditions, their own pedagogical purposes and goals. Rather, they come together with composition specialists to see how writing might most appropriately be used in their particular context. They needn't become writing-across-the-curriculum converts, true believers. They needn't learn to speak an entirely new language or create entirely new structures. They need only be willing to exchange ideas, to converse with individuals who have a new perspective on what writing is and how it can be used in classroom settings.

The challenge, initially, is to identify common ground. No communication can take place if the individuals involved cannot establish what Kenneth Burke in *A Rhetoric of Motives* calls "consubstantiality" (1969: 21). Dialogue must begin by emphasizing similarities, shared assumptions, and goals. It is useful for composition specialists to remind themselves, for instance, that they are dealing with other faculty members, not practicing engineers. Most engineering faculty have had very little industrial experience and approach their teaching from an academic rather than an industrial perspective. Like humanities faculty, they have elected to teach and conduct research at a university. They can be approached, therefore, as colleagues rather than as strangers who speak a foreign language and have access to difficult and obscure knowledge.

It is necessary, too, to look for common language and concepts. This is not always as difficult as it may seem. Here, for example, is a definition of design proposed by the Engineers Council on Professional Development:

> Engineering design is the process of devising a system, component, or process to meet desired needs. It is a decision-making process (often iterative), in which the basic sciences, mathematics, and engineering sciences are applied to convert resources optimally to meet a stated objective. Among the fundamental elements of the design process are the establishment of objec-

tives and criteria, synthesis, analysis, construction, testing, and evaluation. Central to the process are the essential and complementary roles of synthesis and analysis [Lynn, 1977: 150].

Such terms as "process," "synthesis," and "analysis" are certainly familiar to writing-across-the-curriculum proponents as they are often used to describe the activity of writing. Engineering design and the composing of an essay are problem-solving processes that have much in common.

If these commonalities are not always recognized, it is perhaps because problem-solving models congenial to engineers don't always appear to resemble those that are congenial to composition specialists. Numerous researchers in engineering, though, have emphasized the recursiveness rather than the linearity of the problem-solving process, an approach that bears a strong resemblance to currently accepted models of the composing process. Billy V. Koen, professor of mechanical engineering at the University of Texas at Austin, for instance, describes the problem-solving process as follows:

> The more candid authors admit that engineers cannot simply work their way down a list of steps, but that they must circulate freely within the proposed plan—iterating, backtracking and skipping stages almost at random. Soon structure degenerates into a set of heuristics badly in need of other heuristics to tell what to do when [1984: 155].

Throughout his article, Koen promotes heuristics as a means of defining engineering methods and understanding engineering design.

INITIATIVES IN THE COLLEGE OF ENGINEERING

Two initiatives now under way are designed specifically to engage engineering faculty in conversation and thereby have an impact on the engineering curriculum. Robert Jones of the Department of Humanities has a three-year grant for $45,000 from the General Electric Foundation to examine writing done in industry and to work with faculty from a variety of engineering disciplines teaching a variety of different kinds of courses to alter the writing component in their courses so that it reflects current thinking about the nature of the composing process and is informed by research into writing done on the job. Elizabeth Flynn has a three-year grant for $75,000 from the Whirlpool Foundation to focus specifically on writing done in the upper-level capstone design courses in the various engineering disciplines. Like Jones, Flynn will work collaboratively with engineering faculty to determine the most effective way to structure writing assignments and to provide feedback on them. She will also train tutors in both the Reading/Writing Center and the Center for Computer-Assisted Language Instruction to deal with the specific problems of students in design courses.

Following are descriptions of the two initiatives. Jones's project is in its second year and aims to improve student writing in a variety of courses in the engineering curriculum. Flynn's is in its first year, but was piloted for two years in the Department of Chemistry and Chemical Engineering.

Initiative One

Jones is collaborating with engineering professors either to include writing in a course for the first time or to revise the writing component of the course. These courses range from first year through master's level and from laboratory courses to design courses. His goal is two-fold—to expose engineering students to various types of writing experiences, and to promote the use of process in the courses. Jones assumed that the students taking the courses had been introduced to the writing-as-learning approach and had kept a journal in their humanities courses, but that they had not been introduced to a process approach to writing in their engineering course work and that they viewed technical writing solely as a matter of communicating rather than learning.

As of June 1988, work has been completed in five mechanical engineering courses. The types of writing assigned in these courses varied greatly, as did the degree of involvement by the professor. However, throughout all the courses, there was one constant: that writing should be a carefully considered activity that can lead to both increased learning and accurately communicated ideas. The following summaries provide details of the project:

Course 1. In a junior-level design course, students were required to work in groups to produce a full-scale report. They were introduced to the project requirements in a class discussion, then submitted a preliminary proposal of the report, followed by a draft of the report itself, on which they received feedback from peers. Individual members of the group generated the various parts of the report including introduction, discussion, and conclusion; the group as a whole worked on visuals. Jones and the instructor of the course designed detailed instruction sheets, self-checklists, and peer critique forms.

The instructor reported that the students responded much more positively to this assignment format than had the students in any quarter over the past two years. He reported, as well, that the average grade rose from 75 percent in 1985–87 to 84 percent in the summer of 1987. While this is a significant increase, the more important result is that the reports themselves improved dramatically, especially in the areas of clarity, organization, and technical accuracy of the writing.

Course 2. The writing took quite a different form in this junior-level problems course. Here, the professor wanted the students to use writing to clarify and explain how they reached answers on homework problems. He had become convinced over the years that students often couldn't explain why and how they had arrived at answers to problems, and he suspected that they sometimes simply memorized approaches and applied them randomly until one worked. In an attempt to remedy the situation, he required students to write out the assumptions on which each homework problem was based and, three times a quarter, to write out explanations of specific definitions or concepts.

On a preinstruction questionnaire, 48 percent of the students indicated that they "sometimes" to "always" wrote out answers to technical problems, while 52 percent indicated that they "almost never" or "never" did. On the postinstruction questionnaire, 72 percent said they believed that writing out explanations was "helpful" to "extremely helpful" while only 16 percent said the practice was of "little help." Interestingly, 80 percent of the students felt that their writing skills remained the same during the course, indicating that students recognize that writing can assist in learning material even though no improvement in so-called "skills" occurs.

Course 3. This first-year course, Engineering Graphic Communication, provided the most challenges of any course revision undertaken. First, the enrollment was large—sixty students. Second, the students, virtually all first-year, did not anticipate that writing would contribute significantly toward their grade or their learning in this course, especially since the course emphasized graphics.

While writing had been included in this course in previous terms, it was always of the "one-shot" kind: students were assigned topics, wrote the papers, and turned them in for a grade. For the first time, this professor agreed to use a sequenced approach, including student-selected topics, topic proposals, preliminary drafts, peer critiques, and short conferences with the professor. Both the students and the professor were enthusiastic about the method. On the course evaluations, the students commented that they had a very precise idea about requirements for the paper and that the sequenced approach contributed toward improving their writing and their understanding of the topics. The professor reported that overall there were "no negative comments" from the students about the new system. In fact, he said that the new system was "what we ought to be doing. It's what the students are looking for." He also reported that the grades on the reports averaged one-half a grade higher for the class using the sequenced approach.

Course 4. In this master's-level course, the concentration was on revising lab-report formats and reducing the number of reports to emphasize quality of writing. While students reacted well to the changes in the writing component, two additional benefits resulted: (1) students made several suggestions which should complement those changes initiated by Jones and the professor of the course; (2) both the professor and the students felt that the written work prepared students very well for required oral presentations, thus integrating speaking and writing skills.

Course 5. Oftentimes, engineering students object to writing lab reports because too many are assigned, and report formats are repetitious. Some courses will require seven to nine long reports (six to eight pages in length) in a ten-week term. Often students must do as much as fifty-five pages of writing for one or two hours credit. Students often felt, too, that in preparing the reports, they used the same phrases again and again. Both problems were in evidence in the sophomore-level lab course. Additionally, this course has the reputation of being a "weeder" course, one which poses extreme difficulties for students.

The writing component in this course was revised more dramatically than any of the others. Since so many changes in this course were needed, a two-stage approach was used. The first stage included the following:

1. Revising completely the laboratory instructions manual
2. Reformatting the measurements, calculation, and procedures sections
3. Increasing the emphasis on the discussion section of the report
4. Reducing the number of reports from seven to three

Four experienced graduate teaching assistants taught the labs and graded the reports for the course. They reported the following results:

1. The new format was much easier for the students to follow than the previous one, which often led to vague and incomplete reports.
2. The reduced number of reports allowed the GTA's to increase the emphasis on the writing quality, and the students responded very favorably to this increase.
3. The increased emphasis on discussion and results led to more creative problem solving.
4. Because the students were producing more acceptable reports, the grading time was reduced.

In the future, the GTA's will concentrate on increasing the quality of the writing by building in revision work (including peer review and self-critiques) and encouraging students to generate questions for their conclusions.

The changes made in this course are especially important because of students' negative attitudes prior to revising the writing component. As in all the other courses, students responded very positively to the new approaches, increasing the possibilities for understanding the subject matter and for achieving higher grades.

Follow-up Work. While all professors wish to continue the work they began this past year, some have suggested changing certain procedures, and two have indicated that changes are needed to reduce the time required to read and grade reports, especially in courses where enrollments reach forty or more students. Jones and several professors are presently working on coded grading systems and comment formats to reduce the time required, as well as establishing evaluation instruments to determine whether concentrating on writing affects the acquisition of technical information and knowledge. Finally, two professors wish to further emphasize efforts to increase the quality of student writing, now that such broader issues as student response to writing requirements, integration of writing into course grading systems, and formatting procedures have been addressed.

Projects for 1988–89. At this writing, eight courses from several engineering disciplines will be the focus of the year's efforts. Many of the changes made in 1987–88—sequenced assignments, peer critiquing, learning notebooks—will be integrated into other courses for the school year. However, some efforts will be new:

1. There will be more emphasis on higher-level cognitive skills. Courses in geological engineering and civil engineering will include assignments specifically designed to develop synthesis and evaluation skills; most of this work will be done in academic/learning notebooks, and in one case, introduction to word-processing skills will be combined with the notebook work.

2. In an electrical engineering orientation course, writing will be included for the first time. In part because of the large enrollment (250 students), electrical engineering seniors who have had coop work experience will be trained as readers for the three required papers.

3. Lab-report requirements in a chemical engineering course will be changed significantly to promote conceptual skills and to acknowledge the importance of the learning component, as well as the communication component.

Viewing both the process and the results of the Writing in Engineering project clarifies and strengthens the goals of writing-across-the-curriculum efforts and the place of writing in the education of engineering students. Further, conversing with engineering faculty demonstrates that technologists and humanists share a common language, one which can articulate exciting changes in the educational process.

Initiative Two

Flynn will be working with instructors of capstone design courses, mandated by the Accreditation Board for Engineering and Technology (ABET). These courses, by engaging students in open-ended problem solving and in writing reports, aim to prepare them for the work they will be doing on the job. She piloted the project by working with two faculty who team-teach "Chemical Engineering Plant Design," a three-course sequence required of seniors in the chemical engineering curriculum. Both instructors had attended writing-across-the-curriculum workshops.[5]

Bruce Barna, one of the instructors, describes the course as follows:

> The chemical engineering plant design course is a senior-level capstone course in which students are asked to apply the material learned in other courses to realistic design problems. The projects are similar in scope to those chemical engineers might encounter after several years as process, project, or design engineers.
>
> The design sequence consists of three courses of three credits each, which are offered in the fall, winter, and spring quarters. In the first two quarters the students work in groups of four to five and proceed in stages through a major design project. The students are free to form the groups with the constraint that high achievers (GPA > 3.0) should try to stay together. They meet in lab sessions where they are assigned a project, have an opportunity to work together as a group to complete the project, and report on their results to members of the other groups.
>
> The reports themselves necessitate role-playing. The class is told that it is part of a hypothetical chemical company, the Design Division of the Fictitious Chemical Company. They are also told that the instructor is the division manager. Groups are then given an open-ended assignment such as, "Should we manufacture chemical X?" *or* "Do the lead phasedown regulations provide an opportunity for us to enter the market with octane enhancers such as oxygenates?" The project is divided into four segments to provide opportunities for grading and feedback: (1) the technical feasibility and market survey, (2) the description of the equipment design, (3) the economic evaluation, and (4) the economic optimization of the project. Each group submits a formal report and makes an oral presentation at the end of each segment.

Flynn's approach was to observe the first course and part of the second course in the three-course sequence and to discuss her observations with the instructors as the course proceeded. She observed them twice, once in the fall and winter of 1985 and again in the fall and winter of 1986. The observations and discussions produced modifications in the way the writing assignments were handled. In the fall and winter of 1986 she also interviewed members of one of the writing groups, wrote up a description of her findings, and gave it to the instructors of the course. The report also resulted in modifications of the writing assignments.

When Flynn first started observing the course, students were required to change topics each time they completed a segment of the larger report, so that with each report they were building on the work of other groups. The idea was that by shifting to a new topic, students would become familiar with the work of their classmates and would gain the experience of working out problems in a variety of different areas. Flynn suggested, though, that the approach perhaps intensified the difficulty of an already difficult assignment. Students had to generate four reports of approximately twenty-five pages each in a short period of time (thirteen weeks). In addition, they had to do research on

four different topics. At her suggestion, the instructors modified the assignment so that the following year, students did not change topics from report to
report. The following year, too, students were encouraged to revise their work
as they went along. After each segment of the report had been graded,
students had to revise it and resubmit it when they submitted the next
segment of the report. This innovation was the idea of the chemical engineering instructors.

Flynn's assessment of the new course structure, based on observations and
interviews with students in one of the groups, was that it was definitely better
than the original approach. Students were less pressured and had more time to
spend on each assignment. They were also encouraged to conceive of each
report as a draft that could still be improved upon rather than as a finished
product. Interviews with the students suggested, though, that there were still
problems with the new course structure. For one thing, the students reported
that they were seriously overworked, often staying up very late to complete
course assignments and spending far more time on the plant design course
than on their other courses. They also said that they were unprepared to do
the library research or the report writing required in the course because
previous chemical engineering courses entailed reading material in a textbook
and being tested on it or writing up laboratory reports. They talked of wasting
hours in the library because they were employing unproductive research
strategies, and the approach they described was usually entirely unsystematic.

They also talked of avoiding writing if they possibly could—the two female
members of the group did most of the writing while the two males preferred
to do the calculating. They mentioned feeling that the hard work they were
doing was not useful since they couldn't see that it bore any resemblance to
the work they would have to do on the job. It also became clear that the
students were not taking full advantage of the opportunity to revise their
previous work since they based their revisions entirely on the instructor's
comments rather than on a re-viewing of the work itself. Two members of the
group admitted, in fact, that they had not read the segments of the report as
they were generated. They didn't have to since they were not responsible for
doing any of the revising.

Flynn's summary of her interviews with the students motivated the instructors to rethink the course once again. They concluded that the students were
still overworked and so they lengthened the amount of time the students had
to produce the reports. Students wrote two reports per quarter for the first
two quarters rather than three reports the first quarter and one report the first
three weeks of the following quarter. They also changed the assigned topics so
that students would have to do less original research. They used design
problems previously used in a national design contest and provided students
with information that they could use in their reports. In other words, they
reduced the amount of research required to produce the reports. They also

rethought the report content—combining the market survey and technical feasibility study into a single report, for instance—and integrated those assignments with lecture material more effectively. They say they are not yet convinced that topics from the national contests worked effectively. They were very happy, though, with the revised report assignments and felt that they made for a much more tightly organized course.

Another component of Flynn's project is to train tutors in the two facilities sponsored by the Department of Humanities—the Reading/Writing Center and the Center for Computer-Assisted Language Instruction—to work with students taking engineering design courses. The Reading/Writing Center is staffed by professional consultants who provide students opportunities for one-on-one tutorial sessions, usually to discuss ways the student might improve a draft of a paper. Although the center is available to students from all departments, its primary constituency has been students enrolled in the first-year English program. The Whirlpool grant, however, will make it possible to train consultants to work specifically with engineering students and to encourage senior-level students to make use of the facility.

The Center for Computer-Assisted Language Instruction is a facility available to all MTU students and faculty, although it primarily serves humanities faculty teaching courses in the department's undergraduate Scientific and Technical Communication Program. The center has a system of networked computers that allows for electronic interaction between teacher and student and among students. Students enrolled in computer-intensive or computer-assisted courses can store their journal entries and drafts of formal assignments on disks, receive on-line feedback from classmates and from the instructor, and reconsider journal entries or revise formal essays on the basis of the feedback they receive. The Whirpool grant will allow us to develop ways of using the facility in support of the engineering design courses.

CONCLUSIONS

The writing-across-the-curriculum program at Michigan Tech has evolved in unexpected ways since its beginnings in the mid-1970s. The program was initially centered in faculty development workshops intended to introduce faculty from a variety of disciplines to the idea that writing enhances learning. A grant of $250,000 from the General Motors Foundation allowed humanities faculty to conduct two four-day workshops per summer over a period of five years and to involve over three hundred MTU faculty in the program. The in-house workshops became the model for the workshops that Tech faculty and former Tech faculty (most notably, Toby Fulwiler, who initially developed the workshop model, and Art Young, both of whom have moved on to other institutions) conducted and still conduct at numerous colleges and universities nationwide. Almost from the beginning, however, workshops were complemented by collaborative projects designed for publication. Initially, those projects were generally among humanities faculty and resulted in the collaboratively produced book edited by Fulwiler and Young, *Language Connections: Writing and Reading Across the Curriculum* (NCTE, 1982). Eventually, some projects began to develop between humanities faculty and faculty in other disciplines. The second collaboratively produced book, *Writing Across the Disciplines: Research into Practice*, edited by Young and Fulwiler (Boynton/Cook, 1986), includes four of these. The new collaborative initiative in the College of Engineering described above, then, is a natural outgrowth of this increased interest in developing collaborative projects with faculty beyond the Department of Humanities.

Unquestionably, the first phase of the program was dominated by the workshop model (what might be called a dissemination model) and was centered in the Department of Humanities. The General Motors Grant funded released time for composition faculty and increased travel funds for humanities faculty. It also made possible the hiring of fifteen communication specialists in support of the program over the five-year period that the grant was in place. Not all fifteen have remained at Michigan Tech, but more than half have, most of whom have distinguished themselves nationally as composition experts. Not surprisingly, then, the faculty who benefitted most from the first phase of the program were members of the Department of Humanities. Almost all full and part-time faculty in the department have participated in a writing-across-the-curriculum workshop, and almost all have tried to incorporate writing-across-the-curriculum techniques in their classes. Given that the department is an interdisciplinary one—encompassing English, speech, communication, technical communication, philosophy, foreign languages, psychology, music, theater, and art—this is a considerable accomplishment. As Shoos's course description demonstrates, humanities faculty operate in a climate where writing, especially exploratory writing, is valued very highly and where ideas about how to incorporate writing into courses are freely exchanged.

The present program has no curricular component in the sense of mandating that writing-intensive courses across the curriculum be developed or in requiring students to take a writing course designed to prepare them for the academic writing they will do in college. The spirit of the program has always been collegial, and efforts have always been made to work with faculty who are genuinely enthusiastic about incorporating writing into their courses. However, the program does have a curricular center that first-year students are required to take at least two first-year English courses, and these courses are taught by faculty (full- and part-time) and graduate students who are committed to the idea that writing enhances learning and who routinely have students keep journals, critique papers in groups, and provide them opportunities to revise their work one or more times. In this way, students from all university curricula are introduced to a process-approach to the composing of assigned writing. This becomes a distinct advantage when faculty from other disciplines attempt to incorporate journals or group critique sessions into their courses. The approaches may be new to them, but they are not new to their students.

The first-year program is currently supported by the Reading/Writing Center described above. Most of the professional consultants have attended a writing-across-the-curriculum workshop, and all attend weekly development sessions in which composition theory is introduced and discussed. The center is designed to engage students more fully in the process of composing. They are provided more opportunities than they would normally have to discuss their drafts with a writing specialist and to revise them again and again on the basis of the feedback they receive.

The department's major programs also reflect the strong influence of the writing-across-the-curriculum program. The undergraduate program in Scientific and Technical Communication (STC), one of the largest in the country, offers courses in communication theory and in composition and rhetorical theory, courses that are often taught by the same faculty who conduct writing-across-the-curriculum workshops. The Center for Computer-Assisted Language Instruction, which has been described above, was designed originally to support the STC program. Its system of netted computers has created new possibilities for enabling students to use writing to facilitate learning. Computers provide increased opportunities for feedback and for revision. They also invite students to explore and experiment as they compose.

The developing master's program in Rhetoric and Technical Communication, now in its third year, is even more firmly rooted in communication theory and composition and rhetorical theory than is the undergraduate program. Students are required to take courses in these areas. Sometimes their reading and writing assignments involve them directly in writing-across-the-curriculum projects. In one composition theory course, for instance, students interviewed faculty from disciplines other than English in an attempt to determine the nature of academic writing in that field. Also, many of the graduate students teach in the first-year English program and receive weekly instruction in the teaching of writing. They work from a common syllabus and regularly require students to keep a journal and to submit multiple drafts of essays.

Michigan Tech is an institution fully committed to the idea that faculty from all disciplines have a responsibility to participate in the effort to improve student writing and to the idea that writing is a heuristic that facilitates learning. That commitment is as strong on the upper-administrative level as it is on the departmental level. The president of the university, Dale Stein, clearly takes great pleasure in recounting the department's achievements in developing an awareness of the importance of writing, both locally and nationally. The Office of Corporate Relations is committed to assisting humanities faculty obtain corporate funding in support of the program. The dean of the College of Sciences and Arts, William Powers, has allocated funds in support of writing-across-the-curriculum conferences and has been encouraging in countless other ways.

Michigan Tech's writing-across-the-curriculum program was initiated and developed by Toby Fulwiler and nurtured by Art Young, who headed the Department of Humanities for eleven years until his resignation in 1987. In addition, many Michigan Tech faculty have distinguished themselves as composition or communication specialists and supporters of the writing-across-the-curriculum movement, including Carol Berkenkotter, Marilyn Cooper, Elizabeth Flynn, Randall Freisinger, Diana George, Jack Jobst, Robert Jones, the late Bruce Petersen, Cynthia Selfe, and Billie Wahlstrom. It is hard to imagine a climate more conducive to successful program development.

NOTES

1. Texts that have become central to writing-across-the-curriculum research and theory are James Britton's *The Development of Writing Abilities*, Janet Emig's *The Composing Processes of Twelfth Graders*, and James Moffett's *Teaching the Universe of Discourse*. (See References).

2. Several faculty from the Department of Social Sciences and the Department of Biological Sciences have applied writing-across-the-curriculum techniques in interesting ways. See, for instance, Bradley H. Baltensperger's "Journals in Economic Geography" and Flynn, Mc Culley, and Gratz's "Writing in Biology: Effects of Peer Critiquing and Analysis of Models on the Quality of Biology Laboratory Reports."

3. For a description of Michigan Tech's Center for Computer-Assisted Language Instruction, see Thomas DeLoughry's articles in *The Chronicle of Higher Education*.

4. The term "dialogic" is used by Mikhail Bakhtin in *The Dialogic Imagination* to suggest a mode of interaction among the multiplicity of voices that comprise a novel. It derives from "dialogism," which Michael Holquist, editor of *The Dialogic Imagination*, glosses as "the characteristic epistemological mode of a world dominated by heteroglossia. Everything means, is understood, as a part of a greater whole—there is a constant interaction between meanings, all of which have the potential of conditioning others. Which will affect the other, how it will do so and in what degree is what is actually settled at the moment of utterance. This dialogic imperative, mandated by the pre-existence of the language world relative to any of its current inhabitants, insures that there can be no actual monologue. One may, like a primitive tribe that knows only its own limits, be deluded into thinking there is one language, or one may, as grammarians, certain political figures and normative framers of 'literary languages' do, seek in a sophisticated way to achieve a unitary language. In both cases the unitariness is relative to the overpowering force of heteroglossia, and thus dialogism" (p. 426).
   Joseph Comprone has applied Bakhtin's concept of dialogism in an interesting

way in his essay, "Concepts of Textual Pluralism and Dialogic Literacy: Ways Into Collaborative Learning in Writing Across the Disciplines Courses." He also makes use of the concept in "Reading Oliver Sacks in a Writing Across the Curriculum Course."

5. The course closely resembles the design course described in Anne Herrington's "Writing in Two Academic Settings: A Study of the Contexts for Writing in Two College Chemical Engineering Courses."

REFERENCES

Bakhtin, M. M. *The Dialogic Imagination: Four Essays*, edited by Michael Holquist. Austin: University of Texas Press, 1981.

Baltensperger, Bradley H. "Journals in Economic Geography." In *The Journal Book*, edited by Toby Fulwiler. Portsmouth, NH: Boynton/Cook, 1987.

Britton, James, et al. *The Development of Writing Abilities (11–18)*. London: Macmillan, 1975.

Burke, Kenneth. *A Rhetoric of Motives*. Berkeley: University of California Press, 1969.

Comprone, Joseph J. "Concepts of Textual Pluralism and Dialogic Literacy: Ways Into Collaborative Learning in Writing Across the Disciplines Courses." (Unpublished Manuscript).

———. "Reading Oliver Sacks in a Writing Across the Curriculum Course." *Journal of Advanced Composition* (forthcoming).

DeLoughry, Thomas. "For Many Writing Instructors, Computers Have Become a Key Tool." *The Chronicle of Higher Education* 34, no. 35 (11 May 1988): A9, A16.

———. "Writers, Not Machines, Are Focus of Michigan Tech Computer Center." *The Chronicle of Higher Education* 34, no. 35 (11 May 1988): A16.

Emig, Janet. *The Composing Processes of Twelfth Graders*. Urbana, IL: NCTE, 1971.

Flynn, Elizabeth A., George A. Mc Culley, and Ronald K. Gratz. "Writing in Biology: Effects of Peer Critiquing and Analysis of Models on the Quality of Biology Laboratory Reports." In *Writing Across the Disciplines: Research into Practice*, edited by Art Young and Toby Fulwiler. Portsmouth, NH: Boynton/Cook, 1986.

Fulwiler, Toby, and Art Young. *Language Connections: Writing and Reading Across the Curriculum*. Urbana, IL: NCTE, 1982.

Herrington, Anne. "Writing in Two Academic Settings: A Study of the Contexts for Writing in Two College Chemical Engineering Courses." *Research in the Teaching of English* 19 (1985): 331–61.

Kalmbach, James R. "The Laboratory Reports of Engineering Students: A Case Study." In *Writing Across the Disciplines*, edited by Art Young and Toby Fulwiler.

Kalmbach, James R., and Michael E. Gorman. "Surveying Classroom Practices: How Teachers Teach Writing." In *Writing Across the Disciplines*, edited by Art Young and Toby Fulwiler.

Koen, Billy Vaughn. "Toward a Definition of the Engineering Method." *Engineering Education* 75 (1984): 150–55.

Lynn, Walter R. "Engineering and Society Programs in Engineering Education." *Science* 19 (1977): 150–55.

Moffett, James. *Teaching the Universe of Discourse*. Portsmouth, NH: Boynton/Cook, 1983.

Selfe, Cynthia L., and Freydoon Arbabi. "Writing to Learn: Engineering Student Journals." *Engineering Education* 74 (1983): 86–90.

Young, Art and Toby Fulwiler, eds. *Writing Across the Disciplines: Research into Practice*. Portsmouth, NH: Boynton/Cook, 1986.

Robert Morris College

Jo-Ann M. Sipple and Chris D. Stenberg

> *[Workshop] participants saw writing assignments as an aid to learning . . . [and] planned their writing assignments as an integral part of their course design. . . . Nonparticipants saw the writing assignments as finished products . . . with all the correct features of spelling, punctuation, and grammar.*

Institution:	*Robert Morris College*
Institutional Size—Students (FTES):	5,400
Institutional Size—Faculty (FTEF):	180
Student/Faculty Ratio:	30.1
Highest Degree Granted— Institution:	M.S.
Highest Degree Granted—English Department:	B.S.
Public or Private Institution:	Private

Institutional Mission: a private, urban college specializing in undergraduate education in business disciplines.

For more information on the program described in this chapter, contact: Jo-Ann M. Sipple, Department of Communications, Robert Morris College, Corapolis, PA 15108

In the growing body of literature about writing across the disciplines, special-purpose institutions of higher learning are rarely predicted as the most likely places to foster write-to-learn programs. Yet, Robert Morris College, specializing in undergraduate and graduate programs in business administration, has firmly rooted itself in write-to-learn theories and practices throughout its five years of program planning, development, and evaluation. We believe Robert Morris College is the first business college to establish a lasting program with distinctive, transportable features. This essay focuses on four aspects of the Robert Morris "Writing Across the Business Disciplines" (WABD) program: (1) our structural approach to integrating writing-to-learn activities into courses throughout the academic programs; (2) a description of an exemplary course in cost accounting with integrated write-to-learn tasks; (3) some notes on administrative aspects of our program; and (4) our multiple-measure evaluation, featuring teacher protocol analysis.

A STRUCTURAL APPROACH TO WRITING TO LEARN

At the outset of our endeavor in 1981, we tied ourselves to the then prevailing theories that allowed us to exploit the many functions of writing beyond what James Britton has labeled "transactional" writing (1975: 28–31). We looked to the work of Fulwiler and Young in *Language Connections*, Richard E. Young in "Paradigms and Problems" and *Rhetoric: Discovery and Change*, and Janet Emig in "Writing as a Mode of Learning." These were our major sources for justifying various uses of writing to aid students in learning concepts, developing an inquiry process peculiar to a discipline, and applying general knowledge to a particular field. Since that time we have found further theories that have enabled us to fully integrate writing-to-learn tasks in courses across the curriculum—for example, Kenneth Bruffee's concepts of collaborative learning (1985: 231–39), Maimon's notions of integrative writing in particular discourses of various disciplines (1986: 9–15), and others. Out of this complex network of theories about the nature and multiple functions of writing, we have tried to advance one dominant principle: to use writing as a learning tool rather than as an exclusively evaluative one in the specific disciplines. Simply stated our expected outcomes are these:

1. Faculty reenvision their courses, planning the full integration of writing as means to helping students better achieve course objectives.

2. Students use writing-to-learn tasks more frequently and variously in targeted courses across the disciplines to achieve more sophisticated thinking and learning in a discipline.

3. Both faculty and student attitudes toward writing change significantly when faculty and students engage in courses containing fully integrated writing-to-learn principles. Students and faculty see writing as more than a means for testing student knowledge at the end of the learning experience and are inclined to use it more and variously during the learning experience and on the way to more finished products. Writing is the means to the end rather than the end itself.

4. Through a multiple-measure approach toward program evaluation, we can identify expert teacher-planning processes and corresponding student-learning processes, discipline by discipline.

In the process of planning and implementing our version of a writing-across-the-disciplines program, we believe we have created a model program to be shared with institutions of higher learning around the country. Our approach has been described by a team of external evaluators from Writing Program Administrators in 1985 as "structural": rather than asking faculty across the various business, arts, and science disciplines taught at Robert Morris to add various writing tasks to their courses, we have instead called upon selected faculty to combine their respective disciplinary or field expertise with their newly acquired knowledge of writing-education research. To ease this merger, we have worked closely with Richard E. Young at Carnegie-Mellon and with other researchers at the newly established Center for the Study of Writing at Carnegie-Mellon and the University of California at Berkeley. Based on the premise that we can make cross-disciplinary research and practices happen, we have asked faculty to target one of their courses in which they integrate writing-to-learn tasks as a means of helping students gain entry into the discourse community (defined by Clifford Geertz) of the discipline they are studying.

To provide ample context for such an ambitious task, we have established the following kind of environment: Representative faculty from each of the academic departments are chosen each year to participate in forty-five hours of intensive seminar work for the purpose of considering the uses of "writing to learn" in a particular targeted course culminating in an exemplary course design. Not until the subsequent semester do these faculty implement their course designs, which integrate writing to learn for their students. Both during and after the implementation semester, these faculty, as well as the program director and outside evaluators, measure the results of the faculty's planning processes and the students' corresponding learning processes, discipline by discipline.

The following description of Chris Stenberg's upper-division cost accounting course for accounting majors illustrates our structural approach to course design and implementation. This course typifies design and implementation features that transcend the discipline-specific characteristics of cost accounting or a targeted course in any specific discipline.

THE DESIGN AND IMPLEMENTATION OF AN EXEMPLARY COURSE IN COST ACCOUNTING

Cost accounting is generally the first accounting course in which our accounting majors are required to justify their applications from the two perspectives of accounting theory and utility. My course deals with two distinct areas of accounting practice called cost accounting and management accounting. The first area involves a detailed investigation of how the "cost" of a product is developed in a variety of manufacturing environments. The second area requires investigation into the development of meaningful financial information to support management's decision-making process. Both areas contain complex theories and applications.

My first step in designing this course was to step back and question what the course ought to achieve. To answer this question competently, I had to identify the knowledge and skills possessed by successful ("expert") cost and management accountants. In order to corroborate the literature available in accounting journals, I consulted a sufficient number of practitioners to insure that both scholars and practitioners were pointing in the same direction. The published work in the accounting journals does in fact corroborate the word of successful practicing accountants. Both conclude that application skills are mandatory and that higher reasoning skills are equally important.

The journals provide evidence that there is need for fundamental restructuring of accounting education especially in light of the present academic environments. In *Accounting Students and Abstract Reasoning: An Exploratory Study*, George Shute points out that in many accounting courses professors stress content over the thinking process, their examinations do not test higher level reasoning skills, and their instructional strategies are most frequently focused on application skills at the expense of developing abstract reasoning (1979: 37–39). In February 1987, Stephen Collins in the *Journal of Accountancy* cites a study that characterizes the accountant "as having interests flowing mainly to the world of ideas and concepts, gathering information in a practical manner, undertaking decision making by objective, impersonal logic, and dealing with the outer world in a planned, orderly manner" (p. 54). And in this same article, Collins quotes Sheridan Biggs, the national director of human resources of Price Waterhouse, who says that "entry level [accountants] must be first-rate business people with broad understanding of the business world and the measures needed to advance financial reporting to more informative and useful levels" (p. 58).

"Accounting Bores You? Wake Up" by Ford Worthy in *Fortune* magazine highlights some of the deficiencies in cost-accounting practices and the resulting inappropriate management decisions by manufacturers. Many companies are using procedures that are simply no longer appropriate in their new manufacturing environment (p. 43). One must ask if this result would exist if the educational process that produced these practicing cost accountants stressed the higher learning levels. Would the accountants have challenged the validity of the procedures being used and made changes in their methodology? Would the accountants have questioned or probed for the real information needs of management and made appropriate modification in what was furnished?

Among successful practitioners, application is a given. And successful practice requires even more. Business needs accountants who can give meaning to the data, who know the cause-effect relationships among variables, who can assess the merits or detriments of an application, and who can transfer what is known in order to deal with new situations. Successful practitioners view themselves as more than "number-crunching technicians." Their self-image is that of a professional. They view application as a vehicle to help them develop relevant accounting information in order to solve some larger, more significant business problem. Thus, both scholars and practitioners alike call for a change in accounting education if it is to appropriately reflect the needs of the marketplace.

Once I was able to rely on the expected outcomes validated by the field experts, it was easier to define objectives for the exemplary cost-accounting course. From the faculty seminars, I remembered to attend to cognitive and affective levels that account for both the higher and lower levels of the inquiry processes. Benjamin Bloom's cognitive and affective taxonomies as well as Robert Mager's instructional objectives provided me with a useful framework for identifying those levels of knowledge and skills.

In short, there was a difference between this exemplary course plan and the official college syllabus. While the official course objectives emphasize "an awareness" of techniques and applications "in a typical manufacturing concern," my reenvisioned course design includes objectives that take students to precisely identified higher levels of analysis, synthesis, and evaluation. Unlike the objectives in the official course, which keep students at the application level and do not serve the real-world needs of accounting majors, the reenvisioned course forces students to move up and down the entire cognitive and affective ladders.

The course objectives, after reenvisioning the course from these new perspectives, are the following:

Course Objectives: Cognitive Domain

1. To identify and define technical concepts associated with cost and managerial accounting including terminology, conventions, and problem-solving procedures
2. To apply technical concepts to a variety of fact situations in a problem-solving format
3. To explain an application by interpreting the cause-effect relationships of problem elements
4. To criticize an analysis regarding its theoretical merits and limitations
5. To relate an analysis to disciplines other than accounting

Course Objectives: Affective Domain

1. To distinguish the professional accountant from a back-room technician
2. To link academic study to current financial events
3. To develop a professional style in application of technical concepts
4. To accept and use writing as an effective problem-solving tool for accountants

I believe these course objectives are relevant and responsive to both the academic and professional needs of the students and the profession. The topics of instruction remain essentially the same in both the official and exemplary courses. However, the way they are treated in each course is radically different. In the exemplary course, I relate the broad course objectives to each topic.

For example, in the area of job-order cost-accounting systems, these are the enabling objectives:

Enabling Objectives

A. Define and justify the design of job-order cost systems
B. Explain how costs flow through a job-cost system in terms of accounting theory
C. Compute and use the predetermined overhead rate
D. Justify the use of estimates for overhead application
E. Justify the use of departmental overhead rates
F. Explain how and justify why the overhead account is used as a control device
G. Prepare journal entries and financial statements for a manufacturer using job-order cost accounting.

At the intersection of course objectives and topics of instruction in each area, faculty who are designing exemplary courses develop enabling objectives

Figure 9–1
Intersection of Objectives and Topics

Topics of Instruction	
Course Objectives	*Job-Order Cost-Accounting System*
1. Identify terminology, conventions, and procedures	A. Define system design
2. Apply technical concepts	C. Compute and use predetermined overhead rate
	G. Prepare journal entries and financial statements using job-order costing
3. Explain an application	A. Justify system design
	B. Explain cost flows
	F. Explain use of overhead account in control
4. Criticize an analysis	D. Justify use of estimates in rate calculation
	E. Justify use of departmental rates
5. Relate an analysis to other disciplines	No enabling objective

that very often include writing as a learning tool. Figure 9–1 is a sample of that intersection for job-order cost accounting. To illustrate this intersection of course objectives and topics of instruction, I have used a cross-sectional format like that described in Algo Henderson's "The Design of Superior Courses." This chart graphically depicts the depth of coverage for each topic of instruction at particular cognitive and affective levels of development. The chart also shows that at the intersections of objectives and topics, the enabling objectives (more often including integrated writing tasks to help students achieve those objectives) allow comprehensive planning to take place.

To understand how these writing-to-learn tasks fit in, it is important to see writing as the means to the end—the end being the achievement of particular course objectives. The following three writing tasks illustrate the point:

Writing Task 1

I'm having trouble understanding the design of job-order cost-accounting systems. Maybe my problem is that I don't understand the job-cost environment. Can you help me by listing some operating characteristics of a job coster and then explaining why this accounting system makes sense under these circumstances?

Writing Task 2

Let's pretend that you manage a print shop. I stop at your shop and ask if you can print 100 copies of an audit report. The report is fifteen pages long and should be printed on a high-quality white bond paper measuring 8.5 x 11 inches using black ink. You agree to print this job. I then ask you how much you will charge me. You set your selling price by multiplying your production cost by a factor of 2. If the cost of a job was $100 then you would set the selling price at $200. Before responding formally to my price inquiry, you must estimate the total production cost of this job. Write some notes describing how you will make this estimate. Be precise in describing your methodology.

Writing Task 3

As an accountant, I like working with facts. I feel uncomfortable with the computation of the predetermined overhead rate because it is based on estimated overhead cost and estimated production activity. Estimates can be wrong. I propose that it would be better to use the actual overhead cost and actual activity from the last accounting period since these would be real values as opposed to estimates. Can you justify the use of estimates in this accounting system and explain why my proposal is not acceptable? Do this by outlining the major arguments you will use to justify the use of estimates.

After designing this course in the spring of 1985, I first implemented it during the subsequent fall 1985 term and have since conducted it every term. The writing-to-learn tasks shown above force my students to address typical problematic situations. I use the tasks to help the student focus on and explore a theoretical issue. Private writing or writing to learn is, for my courses, the bridge between application and higher levels of reasoning and inquiry. Ultimately, many problem-solving assignments require students to define the problems and prepare lists of procedures that will be used to solve the problems. This activity forces the student to engage in the thinking process used by successful practitioners before an application is started. For example, the student must precisely identify what the customer's need is, what steps are appropriate to reach this outcome, and what information will be needed to perform the procedure. After executing the procedures, students are asked to prepare narratives explaining what the numbers mean, now that they have been "crunched." After the students apply the procedures, they critically examine and evaluate the results; in other words, the student is forced to evaluate why the application has utility and meaning as well as why the application is relevant. This redesign does not eliminate application. Rather, it requires students to engage in higher-level reasoning and uses certain writing tasks to insure that this level of learning is taking place.

The implementation of this exemplary course is not without problems. The early terms of implementation especially weren't perfect for either my students or me as we encountered three major problems: First, I presented my students with significant problematic situations in class and asked them to take several minutes to do some personal, exploratory writing. In those early days most students did not perform well. The problems were not broken down into small enough segments. Students were overwhelmed by the massive, complex, theoretical issues. They needed more time to think through and explore the complex issues before offering something good.

Second, students were accustomed to immediate rewards for their efforts. I didn't collect the homework or private writing. Diligent students still did all requested work, but not all students are diligent. In addition, many students could not break the rote habit. It was easier for them to listen to a lecture and memorize the content for a test than to do the explorations through writing. The new course requires students to learn actively, and this isn't as easy. Letting the students know that I am looking at the writing is important. The risk is that students will concentrate more on the communicative aspects of their writing versus exploration and discovery. But the risk in *not* doing so is that students come unprepared for the meaningful discussion in class that must take place if they are to enter the mainstream debates of the accounting profession.

Third, the course design requires considerable planning and commitment. Not all faculty are willing to devote the necessary time to this process. Therefore, not all courses in a department can be exemplary. Yet for those faculty who do commit the time, there must be support from the remaining members of the department. Otherwise, the departmental curriculum will become, as Ernest Boyer warns, fragmented rather than coherent and confuse the students (1987: 92).

To offset these and other problems like them, there are a number of successes worth mentioning. First, it is surprising to discover how many students expand the use of private writing beyond that assigned them to help solve the problems in class. Some students create their own writing tasks and ask for review and suggestions for improving their quality of thinking. The improved self-image resulting from this kind of activity is astounding. Knowing why a procedure is performed helps them view themselves as members of the profession and not as mere clerks.

Second, students engage in more sophisticated thinking when they are presented with a series of smaller, more manageable problems prior to class meetings. Then they devote as much time as is personally necessary to deal with the issues. Class discussions are more lively and more students are actively engaged when they have thought through the issues prior to class. Consequently, there is not as much need to lecture. The ineffectiveness of the lecture method relative to retention of material is well documented. Students are able to deal with the problems they are encountering, and this makes class meetings more interesting and worthwhile for both faculty and students.

Third, the implementation of the exemplary course makes me feel more like a professor than like a presenter. Faculty-student relationships are much more direct, and student successes and failures become more personal to the faculty member. In the case of this course, the textbook became more of a student aid and not the driving force of the course. The class is custom-designed for the needs and backgrounds of the students I teach. In many areas, I am able to fully integrate concepts that have yet to be published in texts rather than having to tack these new developments onto the text coverage.

Without a doubt there are many differences between the official and exemplary course implementations. In the official course students are usually very passive. They listen to lectures, observe demonstrations, solve problems for homework, and view transparencies or the professor's transcriptions of the problem's solution. On tests, students are typically asked to reperform problems or transcribe lecture notes. Rote memorization is a successful strategy to use in order to pass the course with a high grade. The reasons for the solution are not important; only the solution matters.

In contrast, the exemplary course has much more to offer the aspiring accountant. Students are now responsible for much more than discrete applications. Problems that students must solve are more realistic, multifaceted, and complex. Students are expected to participate actively in discussions just as they would be expected to in their professional lives. Students must acquire the successful inquiry procedures of the expert accountant and can no longer rely on rote memorization to pass the course with a high grade. Further, students must be able to explain both orally and in writing the reasons why they have offered a particular solution. So it goes in the real world of practicing accountants.

NOTES ON THE ADMINISTRATION OF WRITING-TO-LEARN PROGRAMS

The administration of the Robert Morris writing-across-the-business-disciplines (WABD) program may help others learn from its successess and failures. Our program is paradoxically fraught with the typical promises and threats that such programs bring to college campuses. While writing to learn as a concept has become one of our chief instruments for improving learning "about whatever we're studying" (Zinsser, 1985), it is in practice one of the most volatile political issues in our colleges and universities (Knoblauch and Brannon, 1983: 465–74). Our case is no exception.

At the risk of oversimplifying the administration of writing-across-the-curriculum programs, we can reduce much of what we have learned to three overriding principles: First, plan comprehensively (before trying to implement) for funding, implementing, evaluating, and giving position to the program in the institution. Second, the success of implementation rides on the people directly involved. Only committed faculty and students can make the program really work. Recognizing and compensating faculty for their efforts should be an administrative priority. And third, administration's ability to cope with both anticipated and unanticipated problems that inevitably arise will cause the program to last or drive it into extinction.

Through some serious planning for three years before trying to implement our program, we regularly consulted Richard E. Young at Carnegie-Mellon University. Jean Silvernail, our director of academic funding, and Jo-Ann Sipple wrote the initial grant proposal to the Buhl Foundation. The director of the Buhl Foundation saw merit in funding us for the first year of implementation and also invited us to return for much-needed supplemental funds. This resulted in yet another grant for conducting evaluation and continuing the close collaboration with our research institution, Carnegie-Mellon University. It was through planning with the advice of our consulting partners at Carnegie-Mellon that we were able to lay out the details of our structural approach to the faculty seminars, establish the method we would use to help faculty integrate writing-to-learn tasks in their particular courses, design our multiple-measure evaluation, and create some practical experiments for further research. As we predicted throughout our planning for funding, implementing, and evaluating, it would be the participating faculty across all disciplines who would establish the program. This program administrator regards faculty as the dominant resource for initiating and maintaining the essential work that must go on if the program is to succeed.

The Buhl Foundation's grant initially supported each faculty with a $2,100 stipend for redesigning a targeted course with fully integrated writing-to-learn tasks and then implementing and evaluating that course during the subsequent semester. Since the external grant expired, the college has continued to fund the program—offering a more modest stipend of $1,200 to each faculty member in successive cycles for the extraordinary effort in redesigning each course. Executive administration at the college had to be convinced to concur with the foundation's view: there is extraordinary faculty effort required, and it is worthy of compensation. Since the first year, we have engaged in established processes for designing, implementing, and evaluating all program activities and personnel: faculty, students, administrators.

It would be misleading to leave anyone with the impression that we have a paradise for writing across the curriculum at Robert Morris College. Problems abound even here. The usual battles over funding, program design, and evaluation are regularly fought. The program director spends many restless nights before having to face financial constraints, unconvinced administrators and faculty, or reluctant students. Yet, the history of this program reveals that it will not be discarded, at least not lightly. A recently formed advisory council made up of faculty, administrators, students, trustees, and business executives regularly advises program and executive administration of new ways to integrate our approach through individual departments. In fact, the current issue is to use the approach to reenvision whole department curricula using WABD technology.

It should be noted that certain program administrators can bring with them charismatic qualities to help programs succeed. Those leaders who have left their institutions have more often taken with them something of the program they helped build and maintain. But programs that are well planned and comprehensively evaluated can succeed even after the departure of a strong administrator. There is no doubt that the political complexities of continuing to fund these programs, giving them stature beyond the scope of English departments and writing centers, and keeping open communication between the program administrator and other constituencies inside and outside the institution depend heavily on the people who make the program work. Every success and failure we have encountered can, in some way, be traced to these political realities.

Institutions serious about writing to learn as a significant educational reform movement view these programs from perspectives other than the political as well. The faculty and student activities and, just as important, the comprehensiveness of evaluation—these are what successful programs are made of. Ideally, colleges should try to build programs that can transcend an individual's qualities, for only then can they really claim success. Perhaps at this point it is best to return to the issue of comprehensive evaluation.

A MULTIPLE-MEASURE EVALUATION APPROACH FEATURING TEACHER PROTOCOL ANALYSIS

If the faculty are the first population called upon to plan and implement writing to learn, it seems reasonable that faculty ought to be the first population called upon in the institution's evaluation effort. At Robert Morris we have found teacher protocol analysis particularly useful in the context of our multiple-measure evaluation effort (see the Evaluation Chart—Figure 9–2). The protocol methodology has given us insights into teacher planning processes and corroborated the qualitative research we have conducted through several other evaluation instruments such as analysis of faculty, administrative, and student surveys; outside evaluation-team reports; course designs and evaluations by individual faculty; and others. As an evaluation tool, verbal protocols enable us to collect quantitative, raw data "in as hard a form as could be wished" (Ericsson and Simon, 1984: 4). Talk-aloud protocols, defined by Ericsson and Simon, have been used to discover models of problem-solving processes. For example, in 1979 and later, Flower and Hayes used this same research method to discover cognitive models of the composing process. However, protocol research has not yet been explored as a means to discover the planning processes that *teachers* use as they design and integrate writing tasks in particular courses across the disciplines. This tool, then, allows us to make truly original contributions to the evaluation of writing-to-learn programs. What follows next is an illustration of teacher protocols accompanied by an analysis of these protocols taken from WABD participating and nonparticipating faculty at Robert Morris College.

For example, we have asked faculty to perform the following task for a talk-aloud protocol (faculty talk aloud into a tape recorder, and these tapes are later transcribed for analysis):

> Devise one writing assignment for your course (name course). While you are devising the assignment, describe as fully as you can your main teaching/learning concerns. Talk aloud about what is going on in your mind while you are doing the task. Write the words for the assignment, which you would have typed to hand to your students.

While providing examples of full transcripts with complete analyses is the subject of another essay, let us describe some results of these analyses taken from nine pairs of participating and nonparticipating faculty. One of the faculty in each pair, respectively, reenvisioned a targeted course for our writing-to-learn program. Perhaps the most striking contrasts between participants and non-participants appear in two transcriptions taken from faculty who teach an upper-level course in management information systems. On the one hand, the participants saw writing assignments as an aid to learning—to achieving a specific course goal, e.g., "distinguish between information and data." Participants thereby planned their writing assignments as an integral part of their course design to help students achieve the course objective. On the other hand, nonparticipants saw the writing assignment as the finished product of their students' thinking—as a "persuasive communication to a superior" with all the correct features of spelling, punctuation, and grammar. There are other distinguishing features worth noting between participants and nonparticipants. (See Table 9–1.)

At first glance, one may be surprised to find that 75 percent of the nonparticipants were trying to improve student writing while *none* of the participants was trying to teach writing or improve writing skills. On closer analysis one can find that the participants were trying to use writing in many ways to aid students during the learning process. The well-intended nonpar-

Figure 9–2
Evaluation Design

What Is to Be Evaluated	Kinds of Evaluation			
	Formative	.... Internal .... Summative	External	Metaevaluation
Effectiveness of Planning Seminars	writing responses by faculty participants faculty-participant surveys	faculty participant survey	XXXXXXXXXXXXXX	XXXXXXXXXXXXXXX
Effectiveness of Targeted Courses	contribution to taxonomy of writing evaluation by ind. faculty participant writing activities throughout pre- & post-course design	pre- & post-course designs evaluations by individual faculty course plans	on-site WPA evaluation visit	evaluation designs by individual faculty participants evaluation design of whole program
Integration of Writing-to-Learn Activities in Targeted Courses	taxonomy of small genres faculty-participant surveys student-participant surveys	final copy of taxonomy faculty-participant surveys student-participant surveys	on-site WPA evaluation-team visit protocol interviews protocol analysis	protocol analysis— experimental design

Effectiveness of Winter Research Seminars	participants' written responses to weekly agendas and writing materials	faculty-participant surveys course plans	on-site WPA evaluation-team visit (analysis of data by external team)	analysis & conclusions drawn from pre- & post-faculty surveys designs by faculty
Impact of Writing-to-Learn Activities in Targeted Courses	preimplementation information faculty surveys administrative surveys student surveys	post-course design info: faculty surveys student surveys administrative surveys	design of sets of writing activities performed by students pre- & post-implementation of targeted courses	coding schemes & analysis of pre- & post-implementation protocols
Implementation of Targeted Courses	class visits protocols interviews	analysis of class visits, protocols & interviews Writing Program progress report	on-site WPA team protocol analysis	design of protocol analysis protocol analysis of faculty/students
Probability of Long-term Establishment of *WABD*	XXXXXXXXXXXXXX	analysis of: administrative surveys faculty surveys student surveys	on-site WPA team recommendations	longitudinal case studies research design

Table 9–1
Teacher Attitudes Toward Planning Writing Assignments

Teacher Attitude Toward Planned Writing Task	Participants in WABD	Nonparticipants
	(percent agreeing with stated attitude)	
The teacher realizes that creating an assignment is a rhetorical task.	30	13
The teacher is concerned that students see the purpose of the writing.	30	0
The teacher has thought about the task in concrete, operational terms—has considered the subtasks involved.	100	88
The teacher is sensitive to students' abilities and acts on that information by modifying the writing task, providing extra guidance, etc.	90	25
The teacher hopes that the writing assignment will help improve the students' writing skills.	0	75

ticipants thought that their formal writing assignments, used to test student knowledge, would teach students how to write as well.

We have been able to draw some conclusions about our program based on these data and others like them. First, in a formative way, the data we have been accumulating through protocols continue to help us monitor the faculty seminars, classroom practices, and other writing-across-the-curriculum activities. Through analyses of these data we have not only been able to discover what's right and wrong with our program, but we have also been able to make necessary adjustments along the way.

Second, there are a number of summative evaluation statements that teacher protocol analysis permits us to make:

1. We can judge the success of our forty-five-hour intensive faculty seminars. Our protocol analyst, Nancy Penrose, offered these summative statements about these data:

> Overall, seminar participants differed from nonparticipants on measures of attitude and teaching behavior. Participants typically view writing as a means for learning rather than as a testing device or an opportunity for practicing writing skills. Their use of writing in the classroom reflects these attitudes. Participants are more likely than nonparticipants to develop assignments that further the learning objectives of their courses and that are integrated into the

course structure. . . . The results of the present analyses indicate that the faculty seminars provide an effective means for communicating the fundamental principles of the writing-across-the-curriculum program and for changing the way writing is used in courses at Robert Morris [1986: 54–55].

2. The protocol analysis corroborates the findings from our analyses of teacher-attitude surveys: participants have changed their conception of writing assignments and their place in course designs and, more importantly, have acted on that information in their own courses and in trying to influence their departmental colleagues about the various uses of writing.

3. The protocol analysis reveals that participating faculty know how to plan for and design writing tasks that aid learning and that, further, they know how to plan courses that integrate writing-to-learn tasks.

4. The protocol analysis reveals that faculty participants view writing much differently from nonparticipants. (This was especially true in the first two years of the program.)

5. The faculty's experience with protocols has shown them the significance of their contributions in the institution's evaluation effort and has also provided them with a data base to pursue collaborative and individual research.

Thus, the research methodology helps us get an idea of what the participants take away from the seminars and of how this training affects their work and attitudes. It is important to note that some of this information is not readily available through our other evaluation measures such as surveys or classroom visits.

In *Writing Across the Disciplines*, Young and Fulwiler explain why they kept pursuing their multiple-measure approach to evaluation: "Collect all the data possible because it simply gives us more information on which to base our overall assessment" (1986: 52). We heartily concur with their approach, and in addition we recommend using teacher protocol analysis in the context of multiple-measure evaluation. Teacher protocols specifically lend insight into ways that teachers can more effectively integrate writing tasks within their course designs. Furthermore, the protocols can guide teachers in planning writing assignments into their respective courses so that students will more efficiently achieve their course objectives. This has been our experience at Robert Morris in course design and implementation, in administration and evaluation.

REFERENCES

Bloom, Benjamin S., ed. *Taxonomy of Educational Objectives. The Classification of Educational Goals. Handbook I Cognitive Domain.* New York: Longman, 1954.

Boyer, Ernest. *College: The Undergraduate Experience. The Carnegie Foundation for the Advancement of Teaching*. New York: Harper and Row, 1987.

Britton, James. "Language and Learning Across the Curriculum." In *Forum: Essays on Theory and Practice in the Teaching of Writing*, edited by Patricia Stock. Portsmouth, NH: Boynton/Cook, 1980.

Britton, James, and others. *The Development of Writing Abilities (11–18)*. London: Macmillan, 1975.

Bruffee, Kenneth. "Liberal Education, Scholarly Community, and the Authority of Knowledge." *Liberal Education* 71 (1985): 231–39.

Collins, Stephen H. "Recruiting and Retaining the Best and the Brightest in Today's Economic Market." *Journal of Accountancy* (Feb. 1987): 52–58.

Davis, Ken, Marian Arkin, Harry Crosby, and Richard Gebhardt. "Robert Morris College's Writing Across the Business Disciplines Program: A Progress Report for the Council of Writing Program Administrators" (1985).

Emig, Janet. "Writing as a Mode of Learning." *College Composition and Communication* 28 (1977): 122–28.

Ericsson, K. Anders, and Herbert A. Simon. *Protocol Analysis: Verbal Reports and Data*. Cambridge, MA: The M.I.T. Press, 1984.

Fulwiler, Toby, and Art Young, eds. *Language Connections: Reading and Writing Across the Curriculum*. Urbana, IL: NCTE, 1982.

Geertz, Clifford. "The Growth of Culture and the Evolution of the Mind." *The Interpretation of Cultures*. New York: Basic Books, 1973.

_____. *Local Knowledge*. New York: Basic Books, 1983.

Henderson, Algo. "The Design of Superior Courses." *Improving College and University Teaching* 13 (1965): 106–109.

Knoblauch, C. H., and Lil Brannon. "Writing as Learning through the Curriculum." *College English* 45 (1983): 465–74.

Mager, Robert F. *Preparing Instructional Objectives*. Belmont, CA: Pitman, 1984.

Maimon, Elaine. "Collaborative Learning and Writing Across the Curriculum." *Writing Program Administrator* 9 (1986): 9–15.

Penrose, Nancy. "Analysis of Faculty Protocols and Post-Protocol Interviews." *Close-Out Report to the Buhl Foundation*, edited by Jo-Ann M. Sipple. Pittsburg: Robert Morris College, 1986.

Shute, George E. *Accounting Students and Abstract Reasoning: An Exploratory Study. A Research Report*. Sarasota, FL: American Accounting Association, 1979.

Worthy, Ford S. "Accounting Bores You? Wake Up." *Fortune* 12 Oct. 1987: 43–46.

Young, Art, and Toby Fulwiler, eds. *Writing Across the Disciplines: Research into Practice*. Upper Montclair, NJ: Boynton/Cook, 1986.

Young, Richard E. "Paradigms and Problems." In *Research on Composing*, edited by Charles E. Cooper and Lee Odell. Urbana, IL: NCTE, 1978.

Young, Richard, Alton Becker, and Kenneth Pike. *Rhetoric: Discovery and Change*. New York: Harcourt, 1970.

Zinsser, William. "A Bolder Way to Teach Writing." *The New York Times*, 13 April 1985, Education section.

University of Massachusetts

*Sylvia Helen Forman, Julia A. Harding, Anne J.
Herrington, Charles Moran, and William J. Mullin*

> *An essay that uses metaphors bears an analogy to the struc-
> ture of physics itself.*

Institution:	*University of Massachusetts at Amherst*
Institutional Size—Students (FTES):	27,800
Institutional Size—Faculty (FTEF):	1,400
Student/Faculty Ratio:	20:1
Highest Degree Granted—	
Institution:	Ph.D
Highest Degree Granted—English	
Department:	Ph.D.
Public or Private Institution:	Public

Institutional Mission: a public, land-grant, research university
with a compound mission—the production and dissemination of new knowledge; teaching at both undergraduate and
graduate levels; and service to the Commonwealth of Massachusetts.

For more information on the program described in this
chapter, contact: Anne Herrington, Department of English,
University of Massachusetts, Amherst, MA 01003.

At the University of Massachusetts at Amherst, "writing across the curriculum" means that each of the university's academic units—from Afro-American Studies to Zoology—offers a junior-year writing program for its majors. This junior-year program is an aspect of the University Writing Requirement, which has two components—first-year students must complete a three-credit writing course, English 112; and juniors must complete a writing program designed, staffed, and offered by their major department.

The University Writing Requirement is founded on these assumptions— that writing is an activity central to the work of the academic community, both as an instrument of thought and of communication; and that for college graduates, knowing how to write includes not only mastery of the shared conventions of "good writing" but of the conventions particular to the student's major discipline. It follows from these assumptions that faculty from all disciplines share with the English department responsibility for the teaching of writing.

PROGRAM ADMINISTRATION, FUNDING

The first-year component is administered by the director of the Writing Program, a member of the English department. The junior-year component is administered by the associate director of the Writing Program, currently a member of the physics department. Both director and associate director report to the University Writing Committee, a cross-disciplinary group appointed by the Faculty Senate and charged with the maintenance and review of the Writing Program.

Funding for the Writing Program, both freshman and junior-year components, is established in the Writing Program budget, which is a separate, identifiable item within the larger budget of the Faculty of Humanities and Fine Arts. The Writing Program sends a small budget supplement to each department offering a junior-year writing program. The size of this supplement is a function of the number of junior majors in a given department.

PROGRAM HISTORY AND DEVELOPMENT

The university's Junior-Year Writing Program came into being in fall 1982 as part of the new University Writing Requirement. This new requirement replaced an existing Rhetoric Requirement, a two-course, entry-level sequence required of all undergraduates. The Rhetoric Program, which had since 1970 given courses to fulfill the Rhetoric Requirement, had by 1980 fallen upon hard times. Forced to beg for funds each year, it had been unable to provide enough sections for students required to take the courses. The resultant backlog, accompanied by rumors of the requirement's impending demise, caused students to postpone their rhetoric courses in the hopes that the requirement would be canceled before they graduated. By spring of 1982 the backlog was estimated to be three or four thousand students—an administrative nightmare.

In addition to its administrative problems, the Rhetoric Program had lost clear curricular focus. In an attempt to respond to the university's many constituencies, it had diversified its offerings to include such courses as "The Rhetoric of Film," "Technical Communication for Engineers," "Public Speaking," and "Writing about the Social Sciences." As the course offerings diversified, it became more difficult to argue for the requirement's special status as the only specific course requirement in the undergraduate curriculum.

The Rhetoric Program's greatest liability, however, was that it belonged to no one. Because it was a "special program" and not a department, it had no faculty who had an interest in its survival. It depended for its teaching upon faculty borrowed from departments, chiefly communications studies and English, and upon a legion of teaching assistants and part-time lecturers. And since it was administratively difficult to credit departments for the on-loan teaching they did in the Rhetoric Program, the program was increasingly seen as a drain on departmental resources.

As these forces gathered, the English department was accumulating expertise in the teaching of writing. A seminar on the teaching of writing given to English M.A.T. candidates in 1976 produced a link with the Springfield (Massachusetts) public schools. This connection led to a Walker Gibson–inspired application to NEH for extended teacher institutes in the teaching of writing. During the period from 1978 to 1982 five members of the English department—Walker Gibson, James Leheny, Charles Moran, Joseph Skerrett, and C. K. Smith—led yearlong teacher training programs for writing teachers in the Massachusetts public schools. In the course of this work they gained both knowledge in, and enthusiasm for, the emerging field of composition theory.

So it was, in hindsight, inevitable that in the fall of 1981 the provost would convene a Rhetoric Study Group charged with recommending changes in the existing Rhetoric Program. It was also inevitable that this group would draw upon the newly accumulated and visible expertise now available in the English department. The Rhetoric Study Group issued its report in January 1982. The report recommended that the six-credit rhetoric requirement be replaced with a six-credit writing requirement. First-year students would be required to complete a three-credit course given by the English department. This course would be tightly focused on students' writing. It would have no literature or reading component. Students would write, offer critiques, receive feedback, revise, proofread, and publish. The teacher would function as editor and coach. (For a full description of the first-year writing program, see *New Methods in College Writing Programs*, published by the Modern Language Association in 1986.)

The second half of the requirement was to be taken in the junior year as part of the student's major, and would be designed and taught by the student's major faculty. The Study Group moved the second course into the junior year because it wasn't convinced of the value of a six-credit entry-level sequence that "prepared students for" the curriculum to come. It was difficult, they reasoned, to predict the kinds of writing students would be asked to perform in the variety of majors available to them at the university. So it seemed to make better sense to move the second course from the freshman year into the junior year, when the undergraduates had committed themselves to a major field.

The Study Group located the course in the department of the student's major rather than in the English department for three reasons: First, the English department could not know the conventions of the many worlds of discourse represented by the university's undergraduate majors. (Good advice for an English major might not be good advice for a student majoring in hotel and restaurant management.) Second, the English department did not have, nor was it likely to obtain, the resources necessary to staff a two-course university requirement. Third and most important, the committee believed that the work of the first-year writing course had to be reinforced by the rest of the curriculum. If the English teacher was the only university person who actively taught students' about writing, students would think that only English teachers—a small fraction of the "real world"—cared about it. The most powerful support for the first-year course was to come from the most significant professionals in a student's program: the faculty of the major the student had chosen to follow.

The Study Group's report was presented to the Faculty Senate's Academic Matters Council, which took the group's recommendations to the full senate. In April 1982 the senate overwhelmingly endorsed the recommendations and created the Ad Hoc Committee for the University Writing Program to oversee the development of the program. Included in the report of the Academic Matters Council was the recommendation that the Writing Program should be located in the English department but should report to a pan-University Writing Committee, which would itself then report to the Faculty Senate.

In the fall of 1982 the Ad Hoc Committee began to prepare the ground for the junior-year program, which was to be in place by fall 1984 to serve the first juniors who would come through under the new dispensation. The committee established a task force led by Professor Brian O'Connor, from the Department of Zoology. The task force developed guidelines for junior-level writing courses and published these in a November report to the Faculty Senate. Among the guidelines were these:

The upper-level writing course should be one in which extensive writing is used to teach the subject, not vice versa.

Ideally a department should not create new courses to satisfy this requirement; regular courses, preferably those already required for the major, might be revised to include enough writing to satisfy the upper-level writing requirement.

The quantity of writing is less important than how the writing is incorporated into the course. For example, frequent short writing assignments (two or three pages) on which the student receives comments and which the student has an opportunity to revise are more effective than long research assignments submitted at the end of the course and returned with the final examination.

Correct usage, spelling, and syntax should be expected, not taught, in student writing at this level. Instructors should attend rather to organization, logic, and clarity.

The task force also included this statement in its November report:

We have learned through discussions with department representatives that there is no all-purpose syllabus which can be readily adjusted to suit the various disciplines. On the contrary, specific disciplines offer unique opportunities and challenges for planning writing courses. To assist departments in making plans for their students, staff from the Writing Program are prepared to consult with department representatives or undergraduate curriculum committees.

The task force further recommended that a portion of the old Rhetoric Program budget be allocated to departments by the Writing Program, on a per-junior-major basis, to defray part of the cost of adding writing to departmental curriculum.

Development of the academic programs took place in an eighteen-month period, beginning in January 1983 and ending in May 1984. During the January intersession break, the task force met with representatives from each of the university's sixty-five major-granting academic units. At these meetings task force members and departmental representatives discussed the planned junior-year writing courses. In February the Ad Hoc Committee issued a call for draft proposals, due in April. Attached to the memorandum were copies of proposals under development in the anthropology, history, and zoology departments. The draft proposals arrived in April, were studied by the task force, and were returned to the departments, with the committee's comments, by 15 May. The departments returned their revised proposals to the committee by 1 August. In September 1983 the committee began the approval process. By May 1984 every major-granting academic unit had in place an approved junior-year writing program.

As we write this chapter in the spring of 1987, the program is in its fourth year. Professor William Mullin and the University Writing Committee now oversee a writing-across-the-curriculum program that includes sixty separate junior-level writing programs given in and by academic departments for their majors. Although the initial guidelines suggested that the writing requirement be built directly into existing major courses, most departments (72 percent) have found it administratively and pedagogically preferable to create freestanding, three-credit courses. Physics, anthropology, and business management, the three programs described in detail in the following sections, are of this sort. Some departments, the economics department among them, have connected one- or two-credit satellite writing seminars to existing upper-level courses already required of their majors. In other departments such as theater, sports studies, and communications disorders, the writing is fully integrated into existing major courses. A small number of departments, including engineering, hispanic languages, and mathematics, contract with the English department and send their majors to English courses in technical and expository writing.

FACULTY DEVELOPMENT

The University Writing Committee sponsors regular workshops for faculty and teaching assistants in the Junior-Year Writing Program. The committee also meets regularly with all departments to review their specific programs. In addition, the Writing Program maintains a library of materials on writing and the teaching of writing that are available to any and all teachers at the university. The materials include program descriptions and sample syllabi from all junior-year writing programs on the campus, and multiple copies of books and articles on the teaching of writing.

Three Junior-Year Writing Courses: Anthropology, Business, and Physics

The character of the Junior-Year Writing Program is best understood by looking at specific courses. The three we describe here illustrate the range of aims, course structures, and staffing to be found in the program. The courses described have been developed and taught by three faculty members who have been central figures in developing the university's Junior-Year Writing Program.

/ / / / / / / / *Writing in Anthropology*

Sylvia Helen Forman

Sometimes the logistic complexities of Anthropology 333 ("Writing in Anthropology") seem overwhelming to students and instructors alike. There are reading assignments, paper due dates, peer critiques, research activities, classroom discussions, and, one semester, even a Chinese banquet to attend. The powers of concentration of both students and instructors are tested as both parties attempt to manage a complex set of tasks in various stages of completion. At one point in the course the students may be trying to avoid severe confusion as they begin library research for their third assignment while continuing to mull over potential revisions on their second assignment, the second drafts of which have just been turned in to the instructors for comment. For their part, the instructors (a TA and myself) have to cope with twenty-five individual research topics which span cultural, biological, and archaeological themes. One is constrained to ask—as the students and the TA occasionally do—if this complexity is necessary and what purposes it serves. I can address these questions best by explaining a bit about the nature of anthropology as a discipline and by delineating the array of goals set for this course.

Anthropology is a wide-ranging field: the social behavior of monkeys, the development of early civilizations in Peru, the structure of the Arapaho language, and gender relations and agricultural practices among the Hausa people of West Africa are a few of the research interests of departmental faculty. Our majors mirror this breadth and usually have focused interests in distinct areas of the discipline. They object to being denied the chance to develop their own interests in a required course. Thus, the writing course works best if it has flexibility of subject matter and points at which students can choose their own topics for elaboration.

The major goals of Anthropology 333 emphasize on the one hand acquisition of anthropological knowledge and research skills, and on the other, development of an understanding of writing as a personal and intellectual process and as a tool for communication. As described in the syllabus, this is "a writing-intensive anthropology course." It must, and does, have substantive content from the body of anthropological data and theory. Each instructor (so far, three faculty have taught the course) selects a topical focus for her own version of the course. (One selected "North American Indians"; I have used both "The Anthropology of Conflict and Law" and "Foods and

Culture.") These sorts of topics are typical of upper-level courses in the field, and they allow sufficient breadth for student choice of research issues and for design of assignments that develop appropriate skills in research and writing. Subject matter is provided in the forms of assigned readings, lectures, films, and discussions, as well as through the students' individual inquiries. Intellectual and data analysis skills are honed in the contexts of paper assignments and short writing exercises, including peer critiques of paper drafts.

The first assignment is a formal review of a key book within the subject matter of the course. This assignment provides all the students with a common starting point on the subject. Sample book reviews, from a major journal but of varying quality, serve as models of the form and examples of appropriate types of criticism. The emphases in this assignment are on getting to know the domain of the subject, considering the critical dimension of reading anthropological literature, and writing about the content and organization of a book in a clear, informative manner.

Our second assignment requires definition of a small-scale research topic on which the individual student conducts a field study and writes a descriptive report. Such topics as "How do foreign students at the university react to American foods?" and "Why do local people shop at a 'health foods' grocery store?" turn out to be interesting and manageable for this project. Emphases in this assignment are on generating a research theme, developing skills in interviewing and in analysis of "raw data," and articulating one's research process and results in a logically organized report. Fieldwork is at the center of anthropological methodology. In this assignment, the students have their first real, albeit miniature, experience in dealing with the research progression that goes from idea to data collection methods to data analysis to writing description and results in a professional format.

In many respects, the third assignment—a research paper in the form of a scientific journal article—is the most difficult of the lot. As the students do not have extensive knowledge of anthropology, delineation of a meaningful research question is often perplexing for them. Moreover, they have only a few weeks in which to carry out relatively extensive library research on their topics and prepare a draft of the paper to journal specifications. This project is also difficult because it seems to students to be similar to the essay or term paper form that they are all too familiar with and around which they have firmly established bad habits in most cases. Term papers appear, to me, to be documents that students write in an effort (starting with the top of page one) to cram in all available facts, please a teacher, and earn a grade. In contrast, a research article requires defining a meaningful question, analyzing appropriate material, selecting and arraying relevant facts, and demonstrating the relation of those facts to the research question in a logical manner. Consequently, in writing their journal articles our students are forced to confront, and unlearn, past habits of paper preparation, in addition to mastering new material. We underline the professional and scientific nature of this paper by having the second drafts read and assessed, in a simulation of the "blind review" process, by graduate student volunteers from the department. The comments of these external reviewers are provided to the students on the same review form used by the major anthropological journal and seem to bring home to the students the concept that someone other than "teacher" could read and evaluate their work. The emphases in this largest assignment are on anthropological approaches to research reasoning, library research techniques, critical assessment of information sources, and rigorous, formal exposition of an argument derived from data and aimed at a knowledgeable audience.

The final assignment invites the students to manipulate and transform the material they have collected and analyzed in the third project by asking them to present it in the form of a popularized scientific article. Our model here is the sort of article published in *Natural History* or *National Geographic*. It requires a reformulation of the research question from the third paper and the development of a "hook" that will draw a lay reader into the article. Canons of professional accuracy must still be met, but a lively and less technical style of writing is necessary. Emphases this time are on understanding how information can be used differently for different purposes and audiences and on lucid writing that places a minimal burden on the reader.

Beyond the four formal assignments, peer critiques constitute a major form of writing in the course. Students are provided with detailed guidelines about why and how they are required to react to the draft papers of their classmates. The first draft of each paper is subject to a peer critique before the instructors see it. Suggestions and criticisms to an author are in written form, and these are eventually read and commented on by the TA and me. The stress in peer critiques is on being helpful and specific, rather than negatively critical.

In an effort to avoid the punitive connotations of grading, and to place the focus on the process of writing, papers in this course are not graded until ultimate versions (i.e., at least third and often fourth or fifth drafts) are submitted as a portfolio at the end of the semester. At that point, each paper receives a letter grade based on a holistic reading for factual content, organization, format, clarity, tone, style, and technical correctness of the writing. The grades are then weighted, with the latter two papers counting more than the first two, and averaged. This letter grade comprises 60 percent of the student's course grade. The other 40 percent is based on a point score that includes attendance and participation, completing all course activities, and submitting work on time.

This year, the TA position associated with Anthropology 333 increased from half-time (ten hours per week) to two-thirds time. The TA each year is a semivolunteer: one of the regular anthropology TAs who expresses an interest in working with the writing course. These TAs are graduate students in anthropology and in at least their second year of graduate study. They are not specially screened for writing skills, but they work closely with the faculty instructor on methods of assessing students' work in the course and attend training workshops offered by the University Writing Program each year. A TA's primary responsibility is to read and comment on draft papers in the course. He or she also consults with individual students about both subject matter and writing, participates in the class meetings and, generally, provides at least one substantive lecture during the semester. I, as the faculty instructor, do the grading of the students' portfolios, although I consult with my TAs about students' final course grades.

Student response to Anthropology 333 has been largely positive. For the most part, the students assert that they gain from the peer-critique experience, not only through the feedback they receive from peers, but more importantly from enhancement of their ability to criticize their own writing as a result of learning to assess the work of others. As one student commented, ''At first I was embarrassed to give my paper to one of my peers, but then I learned how helpful it was. When I wrote them myself, I turned around and looked at my paper and found the same problems in my paper that I had pointed out in my peer's.'' Another commented, ''It made you look upon your own writing in a new way.'' Students say that they especially appreciate working with different writing formats, and, in the case of the popular science article, of learning to express the same material in distinct forms. As one wrote, ''The variety allowed us to speak to different audiences.'' Another student saw the value of the various assignments in terms of their helping her ''become aware of the different purposes writers serve when expressing an opinion.''

Students are less positive about the work load in the course. They are not accustomed to producing so much writing and find this writing, in conjunction with having to assimilate the subject matter, quite demanding. Yet their complaints on this front are tempered by their sense that they do benefit from the experience and that they accomplish a great deal during the course. In a comment typical of others one student said, ''The course is very effective but if it were four credits instead of three, I think I would have expected the rigorous requirements I have experienced.'' Students do not object to the postponement of grading until the end of the course. From the students' perspective, the greatest frustration in the course seems to be carrying out so rapidly the library research for the third assignment.

I believe, although I can't prove it, that one reason students accept the rigors and complexities of ''Writing in Anthropology'' as gracefully as they do is that I make the rationale for each step and requirement explicit to them. The syllabus explains the goals of the course, and of particular components of it, in great detail. Each paper assignment discusses the nature and purposes of the specific type of writing requested. Classroom dialogue includes consideration of the types of writing students may encounter in future study or in jobs. Therefore, as in the School of Management course described below, students can see how the structure and demands of Anthropology 333 address their needs and interests and why their cooperation and participation is worthwhile.

/ / / / / / / /   *Writing in Business*
Julia A. Harding

Newcomers often think that business writing is a matter of learning new formats: client reports, marketing plans, or correspondence within an organization. Business writing, in fact, begins with understanding the values of the business world. The junior-year writing course in the School of Management (SOM 491) attempts to simulate the business environment while recognizing that students are novice writers. The course creates two kinds of pressure familiar to all business writers—the unrelenting pressure of time and the requirement for unmistakable meaning, usually after a single reading.

Business writers feel the pressure that comes from knowing someone down the hall or across the country is waiting for their finished product. Students, on the other hand, have trouble understanding why the management writing program requires them to submit every paper by a specific deadline. To a student, these deadlines may seem arbitrary, but they are based on the fact that delay on the business writer's part makes it unnecessarily difficult, and sometimes impossible, for others to complete their jobs.

Effective business writing also requires something else students object to— the writing must be perfect. Rightly or wrongly, résumés and cover letters with typographical errors are ignored. So, the management writing course emphasizes the surface features of writing, simply because business writers jeopardize their credibility if they commit errors in spelling, word choice, format, and sentence structure. Instructors in the writing course also assess students' work using an employer's standards of performance. The quality of work matters, not the time spent or the method used.

The aim of the writing course in the School of Management, then, is to help students understand the requirements of the different kinds of writing they will produce in their professional lives. Underlying this simple aim is the assumption that business writers need to be versatile, adapting their writing to specific situations as effective managers adjust their leadership skills to the needs of differing groups.

Students complete five assignments in the writing course, each of which is more cognitively demanding than the previous one. Early on, students prepare an executive summary on a timely business topic such as the hurdles to a new bilateral trade agreement between the U.S. and Canada. Over time we have observed that students find this summary difficult, and we conclude that student writing problems often have their origins in reading. As a result, the course has a secondary focus on expanding vocabulary, following the development of an argument, and drawing warranted inferences.

Assignments are also drawn from the real lives of business professionals, such as preparing a cover letter (to accompany the student's résumé) that responds to an actual job vacancy notice, and writing succinct memos. Because our students will possibly act one day as spokespersons for their companies or industries, they also prepare a persuasive piece, usually a letter to the editor, on a controversial business topic such as drug testing in the workplace.

The fifth assignment is a research essay in which a student formulates an independent position on an issue for which there is no widely accepted answer. One assignment, in which students were asked whether Cadillac will ever recapture its leadership in the luxury car market, illustrates the difficulty in constructing this assignment. Students need to have some interest in the topic, access to ample research material, and a question narrow enough to answer in six to eight pages.

As assignments become more difficult, they carry greater weight: the executive summary counts for 15 percent of a student's grade, but the research essay counts for 30 percent. Taken together, the five writing assignments make up 85 percent of the student's grade, while the remaining 15 percent is accounted for by quizzes, the final exam, and tests of grammar, reading, and editing skills similar to the Graduate Management Admissions Tests. Most students report that the course is valuable but demanding. One student in a typical comment noted that learning a range of styles would be valuable in the future. The same student went on to say, "The grading is tough, but if it remains consistent, then I think the students will understand." Another student concluded her evaluation with this comment: "Thank you! I finally had an opportunity to work on business writing. I'm tired of writing about compare and contrast the moon and the sun."

The management writing course serves the general needs of students in business, but it doesn't address the needs of particular subspecialties as different as accounting, general business and finance, management, and marketing. The program also faces the pressure of a large enrollment: seven hundred students annually. To accommodate such a large number of students, this course is offered as an intensive, two-credit, half-semester, seven-week course given four times during the academic year. After three years of this arrangement, debate continues about the structure of the course. Student opinion has been evenly divided: half the students report they like a course that approximates the demands of what they call the real world, while the other half describe the course as too much like boot camp. Many students included a comment like this one on their teacher/course evaluations: "This should be a three-credit course that runs the full semester. This is much too important a subject to have a condensed course."

The program is designed and managed by a full-time faculty lecturer. The five or six teaching assistants who are hired each year are usually Ph.D. candidates in English or Masters of Fine Arts students in fiction or poetry. Occasionally, an MBA student comes to work in the program, but in general the clock-hour requirements of the MBA program preclude them from accepting this assistantship. Teaching assistants generally attend lectures in the writing course on Monday and Wednesday and meet a discussion section of thirty students on Thursday or Friday. In discussion sections, students have an opportunity to discuss the nuts and bolts of the upcoming assignment. One discussion meeting is usually reserved for peer editing, and in place of the last discussion class, each student meets individually with the TA to review the student's preparation for the research essay. The primary responsibility of the TAs is to respond to student questions and concerns as they prepare each assignment and to respond to each assignment before the next is due.

It is probably already obvious that this course requires close coordination among the staff. As a rule, the faculty person and the TAs meet every other week to exchange information and to address instructional issues such as grading assignments, using the discussion meetings to the best advantage, and selecting upcoming assignments. These meetings also provide a chance for a group of writing instructors, each of whom may have an individual perspective on teaching business writing, to learn to work together and develop a sense of common purpose. When the idea of functioning as a team does become a reality, faculty and teaching assistants alike share one of the more satisfying experiences that teaching offers.

/ / / / / / / *Writing in Physics*
William J. Mullin

A student in my course wrote an essay comparing an obsolete particle-detection method with more modern techniques. She wrote, "The Wilson cloud chamber produces photos, like silent movies, that are black and white. Each photo, like one frame of a silent movie, records an instant in time." She later stated that a newer instrument, the time-projection chamber, is more like "MTV with quadraphonic sound." I liked her similes and suggested that she extend the analogy in the essay. Unfortunately, the revision came out less pleasing than the draft. However, I don't feel our effort was a failure. The student had found what works and what doesn't; and she had explained the basic physics accurately and clearly.

What in the world is a physics professor doing working with students on similes? There are a number of answers: My students are satisfying a writing course assignment that must be taught in the physics department. As long as I must read their papers I prefer reading colorful ones. Analogy and metaphor are powerful ways of explaining hard concepts. Moreover, analogies are an intimate part of the structure of physics. Nevertheless, the arrangement is a bit unusual.

In thinking about how we might establish the junior writing program in our department we realized that previously existing courses required almost no writing other than lab reports and a rare term paper. Problem sets are, quite properly, the rule. We could not have easily adapted any of our courses to serve as a junior-year writing requirement. Our curriculum contained another deficit that we repaired by designing a new course. Our undergraduate students typically concentrate on pre-twentieth-century physics in their required courses. They rarely come into contact with modern research before the senior year. So we incorporated faculty lectures on current topics into a new course, Writing in Physics. The faculty member giving the lecture suggests outside readings at an appropriate level (for example, from *Scientific American* and *Physics Today*) on his or her topic. As instructor in charge of the course during its first three offerings, I designed writing assignments to complement these faculty lectures.

The assignments involve qualitative thinking and writing. They require little use of the mathematics or rigorous argumentation characteristic of most of physics. Most textbooks and course lectures are mathematical, even if they have been simplified to the appropriate level. But the initial and comprehensive insights professional physicists have about physical systems are quite different from the presentations in journal articles and textbooks. The rigorous discussions in written work are usually highly refined versions of the subject. Calculations analogous to those on the backs of envelopes or on napkins are more commonplace than is generally believed. However, students have trouble learning these approaches; they are not often required to produce them themselves. Because they are unfamiliar with these modes of thinking, students tend to grope for a formula to plug into. They have not been shown how to understand what the formulas really mean. Before we instituted this new course, there was no place where physics majors could receive formal practice in using heuristic argumentation.

A few of the writing assignments from the course are discussed here—first the assignment itself, and then a brief gloss. I require six essays during the semester. The standard length is four to five pages.

> *Assignment 1.* Write an essay explaining to a freshman Physics 141 student why an airplane flies. [Physics 141 is an introductory mechanics course without calculus.] Assume that the student already has seen the Bernoulli

equation in his course and now wants to know why it works. Emphasize physical (qualitative) arguments—on the molecular scale—when possible. After all, the forces on the wing arise because air molecules hit it; does the faster horizontal motion of this air over the top of the wing somehow imply that the molecules hit the wing with less vertical speed, or less often, or what? And why does the air move faster over the top of the wing?

The Bernoulli equation is a powerful tool that can be used to consider airflow and lift on an airplane wing. Derivations of the equation arise from abstract principles. But what the equation is saying in terms of molecular activity is not so clear. Textbooks don't usually get into such a discussion. Writing this essay to the audience mentioned forces the student to view the processes in a new, deeper way.

> *Assignment 2.* Write a newspaper article for the Science section of the *New York Times* on the subject matter of Eugene Golowich's talk ("Strings or related matters in elementary-particle theory"). Assume the audience is made up of college-educated nonscientists. The title of the essay should be a headline.

Science writing is characterized by, among other things, concise explanations of complicated issues and by explanations using analogy, for physics is substantially based on analogy. As an example, the ideas and mathematics of fluids are very similar to those in the theory of electromagnetic fields. In quantum mechanics we learn that electrons travel as waves, in some regards similar to light. Current cosmology holds that the early universe underwent a phase transition analogous to that occurring when iron becomes magnetic. If you understand an idea about one aspect of nature, you may have a head start on figuring out an entirely different one. An essay that uses metaphors bears an analogy to the structure of physics itself.

> *Assignment 3.* This assignment is based on Robert Hallock's talk, "Superfluids and Superconductors." The physics department is attempting to upgrade the Advanced Laboratory course for senior physics majors. The Undergraduate Studies Committee is considering various possible experiments. Write a proposal addressed to this committee, suggesting a particular low-temperature experiment (or set of closely related experiments).
>
> The proposal should include a thorough discussion of why low-temperature physics should be an area studied, what the experiment is, the motivation for choosing the particular experiment, the equipment required, and the value and cost (insofar as you are able) relative to possible experiments in other areas of physics.
>
> The committee is composed of faculty who do research in several areas of physics and who can be presumed to have only a vague knowledge of the field of low-temperature physics. To make your case you must provide background information and convincing arguments.

This writing task is different from the usual laboratory report of an experiment carried out by following a cookbook-like recipe. In this assignment the student must design the experiment herself and even estimate the cost of setting it up.

> *Assignment 4*. Professor Ann Ferguson of the philosophy department, in her talk to us, will examine the possibility that physics and other sciences may involve sexism, just like other human activities. Since most physicists do not closely examine the foundations of the scientific method, they often have a myth-like belief in its perfection and find this claim surprising.
>
> Your assignment is to write about the scientific method, as it is applied to physics, with specific emphasis on its human aspects. The precise specification of the subject is up to you. You may, for example, want to respond to the question of sexism or to look at fundamental ethical issues involved in practicing physics. Identify your audience.
>
> Please back up your discussion with adequate reference to the literature on your subject. Several items on reserve may help you, particularly these books: Sandra Harding's *The Science Question in Feminism*, Evelyn Fox Keller's *Reflections on Gender and Science*, and Thomas Kuhn's *The Structure of Scientific Revolutions*.

The field of physics includes a number of important subsidiary issues that the faculty never seem to cover in regular courses. The study of the history, or the structure, or the ethics, of the field has never been a regular part of the curriculum. Writing projects like that required in Assignment 4 get the students thinking about these issues.

The structure of Writing in Physics is centered on the writing, not the class meetings. I present the assignment at the time of the faculty lecture and establish a due date for the midprocess draft (a second or third draft of the essay). On that day the students have a peer-review session in which three students interchange and criticize each other's work. Usually each student receives one written peer review (I hand out a form) and one oral one. Student reviews vary from excellent to ignorable and no revisions are based solely on them. A teaching assistant and I read and comment on the papers. The final work is due a week or so after we return the drafts. The teaching assistant, Elizabeth Lambert, who has been helping me in the course since its inception, is an advanced graduate student from the English department who has had considerable experience in science writing. While she is not able to detect all errors in physics made in student papers, her perspective as a writing specialist is valuable.

The existence of writing courses taught by physics and other non-English faculty is somewhat unusual. A few of my colleagues' question the arrangement, feeling that writing instruction belongs in the English department. Having been influenced by the same prejudices, an occasional student in Writing in Physics will ask, "This is an 'English' course, isn't it? How come there's so much physics in it?" Perhaps the student's question answers my colleagues' objections.

PROGRAM ASSESSMENT

In addition to each department's regular course-evaluation procedures, the University Writing Committee conducts a biennial program evaluation to determine the health of all departmental junior-year writing programs. More specifically, the aim of the evaluation process is to identify programs in difficulty so that problems can be dealt with, and stellar programs so that these can be promoted.

To conduct this sort of programmatic evaluation, the committee decided that it would be important to gather information about the following topics: each department's commitment to their writing course (using such indices as degree of faculty involvement, faculty attitude, and course size), students' and instructors' evaluations of the course, the department's perceptions of strengths and problems with the course, and aspects of the course itself (e.g., staffing, structure, aims and content, number of writing assignments, writing and teaching techniques used).

While some of this information can be reported on paper, it is important to talk with the faculty directly involved in teaching the junior-year course and, in some cases, with the department head. To this end, members of the committee, with assistance from other interested faculty, conduct interviews with representatives of each department. Completing all of these interviews with fifty-eight programs is time-consuming but worthwhile: in combination with the written reports from each department, the interviews provide the Writing Committee the fullest sense of each program; equally important, they create an occasion for teachers to reflect on their junior-year course and discuss its strengths and weaknesses with others.

Committee members prepare written reports on each program they have evaluated. These are then reviewed by the committee, most importantly to discuss what kinds of advice and assistance to offer departments having problems. Each department receives a copy of its program's evaluation. For those departments having problems, a member of the committee is assigned to advise them. For those departments doing well, the evaluation report serves as a way to provide positive feedback so that those faculty who teach the writing course may be recognized.

MAJOR SUCCESSES AND PROBLEMS

The most recent Junior-Year Writing Program evaluation provides a picture of the successes and problems of such programs. On the basis of the evaluation of fifty-eight programs, the University Writing Committee designated fifteen as exemplary, thirty-one as satisfactory, and twelve as needing additional monitoring or modification. Interestingly, the fifteen exemplary programs represent a diverse range of departments across the university. These include not only such logical candidates as history and anthropology, where extended writing would already seem to be a central concern in disciplinary activities and learning, but also such less likely departments as physics and entomology.

The success of the Junior-Year Writing Program in such diverse subject areas suggests to us that the important factor in determining that outcome is not whether a discipline has traditionally relied on writing as a means of inquiry or problem solving. Instead, its success derives from the degree to which there is (a) direct involvement of faculty from that discipline and (b) integration of writing into students' studies in their major field. We will discuss each of these, being candid about problems as well as successes.

The direct involvement of faculty from the particular discipline or department is important for conveying to students the sense that the writing course is valued. Of the fifteen exemplary programs, eleven were taught by faculty from the department, either alone or with a graduate teaching assistant. (Sixty-five percent of the fifty-eight evaluated programs were taught by faculty.) Of the other four programs, three were taught by lecturers and one was taught by a graduate teaching assistant. In all exemplary programs, however, the department clearly expressed its commitment to the program and fully integrated the program with the undergraduate major.

In contrast, programs that were having difficulties had little faculty support. This was evident both in the staffing of the courses and in faculty attitudes. For example, in one department no faculty had direct involvement with the writing course; TAs were assigned to teach it. Further, the TAs were reportedly reluctant to teach because the average class size was over twenty-five, and they perceived the teaching demands for the courses as detracting from their own studies. Their negative attitudes were shared by the faculty, who expressed chagrin over the burden the course had placed on their department. For the faculty from this department and a few others, their negative attitude reflects in part a belief that the teaching of writing is an onerous, unrewarding chore, one that should be left to the English department. It reflects also the burden of having many majors and too few faculty to teach these majors. In departments with exemplary programs the enrollment pressures are felt also, but faculty in these departments seem to see the value of teaching writing within their undergraduate major program.

The second important factor that distinguishes exemplary and satisfactory programs is that writing be skillfully integrated with students' studies in their major field. In these programs it is clear to students that the writing they are doing is related to their learning or future professional activities. The descriptions of the anthropology, management, and physics programs illustrate the diverse ways such integration can be achieved. This integration is also evident in nontraditional departments such as the University Without Walls Degree Program developed by Gail Hall. As part of this program, students prepare an extensive Prior Learning Portfolio of their prior nonacademic learning experiences in order to receive university credit for these experiences. Since this portfolio requires extensive writing, the UWW Program designed its junior-year writing course, "Writing About Experience," to help students prepare the portfolio while teaching them more generally applicable ways of prewriting, organizing, and working with peer review groups.

In exemplary and satisfactory programs, such integration is achieved through various course structures, the most common one being a specially designed "freestanding" course that connects writing instruction with learning about the subject matter and the discipline's methods of inquiry or with genres of writing associated with discipline-related professions. Seventy-two percent of the junior-year programs evaluated in 1987 were freestanding, including eleven of the fifteen exemplary courses and the three in this chapter.

Four of the exemplary junior-year programs used other structures. One integrated writing into two existing courses required of majors. Three used tutorials. While the structures of the tutorials varied, in all cases they were either taught by departmental faculty or at least closely linked with a departmental course. Either way, the writing instruction was connected with substantive intellectual work that students were doing for their major.

In programs having problems the course structure made integration more difficult. The most obvious problems arose in the few instances where the "writing instruction" was offered through tutorials that didn't have a strong link to existing departmental courses. In one extreme instance, the "writing program" consisted of a number of one-credit tutorials attached to regular upper-division courses. Graduate students from the department ran the tutorials with little or no coordination with the faculty member teaching the parent course. In some tutorial sections the TAs had sole responsibility for selecting writing assignments. Students were required to meet with the TA only three times during the semester. Not surprisingly, the program evaluation indicated that TAs had difficulty getting students to come to the tutorials and that students resented what they perceived to be the "extra" work involved. Further, both TAs and faculty expressed frustration with the arrangement. In instances where TA-run tutorial linkages have succeeded, there was close coordination between the professor and the TA in planning assignments and responding to students' writing, some presence for the TA in the regular course, and some inclusion of the writing in the regular course.

We have cited two extreme problem cases to illustrate some of the challenges a writing-across-the-curriculum program is likely to face, especially if the responsibility for program development and execution is given to the academic departments. These cases also point to the need for a group of colleagues, like the Writing Committee, to monitor the program periodically and work with departments having difficulties. Fortunately, at this point, the problem cases have been the exceptions.

A LOOK TO THE FUTURE

Knowing the vicissitudes of academic institutions, we are not much inclined to make long-term predictions about the future of our Junior-Year Writing Program. Still, given the present health of the program, we are optimistic: Over 80 percent of the programs evaluated in 1987 were found to be satisfactory or exemplary. Further, there are some signs that the program is having indirect effects on other courses. Importantly, the university's revised General Education requirements include the recommendation that courses that satisfy these new requirements include a substantial amount of writing.

Another reason for optimism is that the Junior-Year Writing Program is a faculty-initiated and faculty-run program. The specific components have not been imposed by administrators nor imported from elsewhere: the program arose as a particular academic community's attempt to address a perceived curricular problem. Its continued success depends on the support and active participation of that community.

Helping keep that support alive is an underlying aim of much of the work of the University Writing Committee. On the basis of the recent evaluation, the committee has identified weaknesses in the program that we as a faculty must address. For one, we need at least to maintain—and ideally to increase— the level of direct faculty involvement in junior-year courses. That means reducing the percentage of courses now taught solely by TAs (currently 21 percent of the junior-year courses). It also means working to increase the involvement of faculty from the handful of units like the School of Engineering that send their majors to English for their junior-year writing courses. More generally, it means involving new faculty in junior-year writing programs so that participation and support is not limited to just one or two faculty in each department.

Obviously, we need also deal with those courses that have been identified as having problems. The way the program is designed, resolution of difficulties depends on the success of collegial consultations between members of the Writing Committee and the department offering the course. While the committee has the ultimate authority to withhold approval of a course that it feels does not fulfill the junior-year guidelines, it has not had to invoke that authority.

The success of these collegial consultations reflects the general faculty support for the program and its starting assumptions: that writing is an activity central to the academic community, both as an instrument of thought and of communication; and that for college graduates, knowing how to write includes not only mastery of the shared conventions of "good writing" but of the conventions particular to the student's major discipline. It follows from these assumptions that faculty from all disciplines share with the English department responsibility for the teaching of writing. As one student asked rhetorically in a Junior-Year Writing Program Evaluation, "Who better than someone in our own discipline to teach us how we may someday have to write?"

Note: In addition to those people mentioned specifically in the chapter, we want to acknowledge the contributions of members of the University Writing Committee, and particularly those of the 1986–87 committee—Jeremiah Allen, Maria Brazill, Christopher Hurn, William Patterson, and Judith Solsken—who conducted the program evaluation. We gratefully acknowledge as well the work of two graduate research assistants, Bonnie Auslander and Deborah Cadman, who compiled the evaluation materials and prepared an invaluable *Research Guide to the Junior-Year Writing Program*.

George Mason University

Christopher Thaiss, Kathleen Campbell, Robert Clark,
Stanley Zoltek, and Donald C. Holsinger

> *The biggest achievement of this decade-long endeavor is the
> high "language consciousness" of both faculty and admin-
> istrators. There's a lot of writing going on; where it isn't,
> faculty wish it were.*

Institution:	*George Mason University*
Institutional Size—Students (FTES):	19,000
Institutional Size—Faculty (FTEF):	760
Student/Faculty Ratio:	25:1
Highest Degree Granted—	
Institution:	Ph.D.
Highest Degree Granted—English	
Department:	M.A. and M.F.A.
Public or Private Institution:	Public

Institutional Mission: a regional state university serving an
urban/suburban area. Average age of students is twenty-six,
95 percent are commuters, and average SAT of entering
students is 1050.

For more information on the program described in this
chapter, contact: Christopher Thaiss, Department of English, George Mason University, Fairfax, VA 22030.

/ / / / / / /   *Introduction*

Christopher Thaiss

George Mason grows. We have 19,000 students now, 30,000 are projected for 1995. New full-time faculty are being hired steadily, many of them for vanguard graduate programs in information technology, engineering, and computer science. Meanwhile, class size, especially in the lower division, keeps increasing. Some freshmen have no class with fewer than one hundred students. The proportion of part-time to full-time faculty keeps rising. Even at twenty-five students per section, freshman composition can't deliver enough sections to preclude a large backlog of students; Advanced Composition (English 302), the four-year-old junior-level required writing course (created to reinforce writing across the curriculum), has developed its own dangerous overflow. A move we have resisted—allowing students to exempt junior-level composition through a proficiency exam—has become inescapable.

Nevertheless, GMU remains genuinely committed to undergraduate teaching, despite the hazards of large class size and underexperienced, undersupervised faculty—plus tightening "publish or perish" pressure on tenure-track teachers. As one indication of this, a recent survey of students in the forty sections of junior-level composition revealed that almost every course in almost every major at the upper-division level requires writing, usually one or more papers, plus essay exams, with a number of courses requiring journals in various forms, plus other types of writing. At the freshman-sophomore level, two general education programs, PAGE (the Plan for Alternative General Education) and BA/SIC (Bachelor of Arts and Sciences Integrated Curriculum), offer about 25 percent of the freshmen and sophomores an interdisciplinary, language-intensive curriculum. The 150 faculty in these programs take summer workshops in teaching and work in teams throughout the year to refine their courses.

With the success of these ventures has come the desire to redesign the general education program for 100 percent of the students. Currently, a cross-colleges task force, headed by philosophy professor Debra Bergoffen, is meeting with faculty from all departments as part of its two-year agenda. The task force has reviewed many core models and is seeking from the departments a consensus on both the shape of the program and the kinds of courses to include. Using data gathered thus far, Bergoffen has designed a core model with courses spread over four years. Most pertinent to this essay is the language intensity of the proposed core. At a recent meeting of the cross-disciplinary task force, members expressed strong support for centering writing and speaking in the content courses, with faculty development funds devoted to regular workshops on the writing process and writing-and-speaking-to-learn activities. Rather than designating a few courses as "writing-intensive," every course would teach uses and forms of writing and speech appropriate to the curriculum. For example, a proposed first-semester course on the Western tradition might take students through a multidraft process from discovery to peer feedback to editing on several papers, while the core science course, taught the same semester, might include a reading-response log and in-class thinkwriting. These uses and forms would be just as central to the particular course as would the selected readings and lecture topics.

The task force feels that faculty and administration will support this re-design because our prior work has created a climate in which most faculty accept some responsibility for helping the students achieve linguistic sophistication and versatility. Moreover, we have a large nucleus of faculty across departments who regularly build language-rich classes. As one task-force member, a music professor, put it: "Writing has become so important in my music classes that I know we can do this successfully throughout the general ed program."

What have we been doing since 1978 to help create this climate?

WEEKEND WORKSHOPS AND FOLLOW-UP MEETINGS, 1978–81

In 1978, spurred on by the success of our first institute of the Northern Virginia Writing Project, director Don Gallehr and I asked for a small grant (about $2,500) from the discretionary funds of the deans of Arts and Sciences, Business, and Professional Studies to fund a weekend workshop for George Mason faculty at an off-campus conference center. Though we had no money for stipends, we still drew sixteen professors from nine disciplines. Their commitment was not only for the weekend workshop; each one also promised to attend monthly three-hour meetings and to prepare a presentation on his or her own use of writing in teaching. These presentations were given either at the monthly meetings or at meetings of the participant's own faculty.

This first workshop produced many happy surprises, among them the physical education professor who became a publishing phenomenon and whose aerobics and weightlifting classes intensified students' experiences with freewriting; the English teacher who discovered his talent for autobiography and the value of small groups in his classes; the historian whose students now wrote plays and stories for him as well as essay exams.

The first program ended with a presentation of certificates by the deans and their promise of renewed funding for the second year. In spring 1981 the third GMU faculty-writing conference was held: the main difference between the 1978 workshop and the 1981 version was that by then the workshop leaders— not only the participants—came from such departments as psychology, education, and business law.

STATE-SUPPORTED SUMMER INSTITUTES, 1980–81

The second major boost to WAC at George Mason came in 1980, when the State Council of Higher Education chose us as one of four Virginia universities to receive a two-year grant of $110,000 to develop our program. The four schools (GMU, Virginia Commonwealth, Virginia State, and Virginia Tech) promised to form a consortium to exchange ideas and practices and to spread the word to other Virginia schools.

The grant allowed us to support faculty from the weekend workshops for five intense weeks, eight hours per day. Our summer institutes were seminars based on the National Writing Project model. Each person was responsible for one three-hour presentation on such topics as learning journals in statistics classes, the design of a writing-intensive psychology curriculum, multiple revisions of philosophy papers, and writing-to-learn techniques in history.

During this biennium, we had also received state funding for a Writing Research Center. Under this grant, six of our teacher/consultants—the title we gave to graduates of the institute—carried forward controlled research studies and played a major role in conducting the first Virginia Conference on Writing Across the Disciplines. This conference, held at GMU, featured presentations by teacher/consultants from all four funded faculty-writing programs and from three other member schools in the consortium.

As a capstone project for the grant period, fifteen of the teacher/consultants drafted and revised essays that became the first version of the collection we later published as *Writing to Learn: Essays and Reflections on Writing Across the Curriculum* (Kendall/Hunt, 1983).

THE ENGLISH COMPOSITION REQUIREMENT

In the wake of the state grant program, the University Senate approved a controversial redesign of the English composition requirement. Designed to support an emphasis on writing in the majors, this plan designated one half of the six-hour requirement to be fulfilled at the junior level, in sections built according to the interests of three curriculum areas: humanities, natural sciences, and social sciences. Each section would focus reading and writing tasks on one of the three areas; students would have the option of doing one research project for both English 302 credit and for credit in a major course. Currently, all of these sections are taught by English faculty, full- and part-time, though the approved plan allows for teaching to be done by faculty from other departments.

This course has been a great success. The faculty enjoy the interdisciplinary experience and the students find the course valuable preprofessionally and as a definite aid for the formal work assigned in major courses.

LANGUAGE ACROSS THE CURRICULUM AND PAGE, 1982–

Just as the two-year Faculty Writing Program grant ended, the university received $381,000 from the state to begin an experimental program in general education, this program offering its first classes to more than 250 students (currently 400) in fall 1983. This interdisciplinary program (the Plan for Alternative General Education—PAGE) features student writing in many forms (e.g., journals, library papers, critiques, lab reports) as a mode of learning. Writing instruction in appropriate form occurs throughout the four-semester program; there is no separate composition course. PAGE courses are built by interdepartmental teams and focus on interdisciplinary themes (e.g., cross-cultural perspectives, technology and society, conceptions of the self). Writing helps to reinforce the interdisciplinary emphasis; for example, in the first two semesters, students keep a single "PAGE journal," in which they make connections among the diverse courses they are taking.

More than 140 GMU faculty have taken part in one- to five-week workshops since 1982, all of which include attention to writing as a mode of learning and to such topics as assigning and evaluating written work. PAGE has given one-course release time since 1983 to a specialist in writing—and speaking—across the curriculum (PAGE also fulfills the university's three-hour speech requirement), who works with individuals and course teams toward the constant improvement and variation of assignments and methods. This person also conducts meetings on topics of common interest (e.g., small-group process), and publicizes teaching innovations by PAGE faculty.

SOME ACHIEVEMENTS

The biggest achievement of this decade-long endeavor is the high "language consciousness" of both faculty and administrators. There's a lot of writing going on; where it isn't, faculty wish it were. Those of us who have been involved in the WAC effort since the beginning decided at that time to create a grass-roots program through workshops that would involve interested faculty. We felt that a "seed" program would eventually provide a strong base for more ambitious plans. Rather than beginning the program from the top, as has occurred recently at many institutions where "writing-intensive" courses have been mandated before faculty training has begun, we felt that massive curriculum change would occur naturally through pressure from experienced faculty. This has occurred, though when one builds from the ground up—and depends much on informal sharing from teacher to teacher—it's often hard to see the patterns of growth clearly, even when one can see the growth.

This favorable climate produces some abundant flora. For example, the current general education requirement for all students includes the two semesters (freshman and junior) of composition and one or two required writing-intensive courses in literature (in English or another language). It also produces a remarkable energy in faculty to take part in such time-consuming endeavors as PAGE. Another manifestation of the environment is that a newly developed doctoral program for community college faculty has made writing to learn part of its program core.

Of course, no one is satisfied that we are doing enough. Hence, the desire of the task force to enrich the writing and speaking content in all required courses. Hence, a recent spontaneous motion by the university's Board of Visitors (our version of the Board of Regents) "that the Office of Academic Affairs do all in its power to sustain and expand the writing-across-the-curriculum program." Hence, also, the ambition of the top administration to seek grant funds, up to $ 2.5 million, to create at George Mason a (tentatively titled) Interdisciplinary Center for Writing, to include such elements as faculty development, new faculty positions, and student scholarships.

I should also mention among achievements the impact of the writing and publishing that our faculty have done as part of the writing-across-the-curriculum program. Part of the philosophy of the National Writing Project has been that the teaching of writing improves as teachers learn more about themselves as writers. Our workshops and seminars for faculty have always included opportunities for faculty to work in small peer-response groups on projects of their own choice. We find that many faculty are just as hesitant to share their writing as our freshman are, and that those who have given and received feedback have broadened their views on writing and their own confidence. These groups have been cross-disciplinary; faculty learn to see the value of sharing their professional writing with people who are not accustomed to their disciplinary assumptions and jargon. The sharing alerts them to ideas they had taken for granted and forces them to explain their writing for a less specialized audience. Indeed, one purpose of the cross-campus newsletter in 1980–82, the 1982 research volume, and the 1983 book *Writing to Learn*, was to extend this phase of our program.

In a university that becomes ever more publication-conscious, such personal development in writing can be essential for all faculty, especially the new and the dormant. In fact, several individuals were boosted toward publication

—and tenure or promotion—by this work. As we have put most of our language-and-learning emphasis on classroom techniques and curriculum design, we haven't been able to bring to most faculty this opportunity for personal growth. However, this element will be part of whatever plan for the new Interdisciplinary Center for Writing is eventually approved.

NEEDS

What are the most pressing needs of our language-across-the-curriculum program at George Mason? First, we don't have consistent channels of communication between the faculty at large and those who have learned the most about language-to-learn. Since the end of the first state grant in 1982, we have not had, except in PAGE, a regular publication of the methods and discoveries of faculty using language as a mode of learning in their classes. Funds to revive our campuswide newsletter would be welcome. Also important would be a detailed survey of all writing in all colleges. While we know that much writing is being assigned and read, we do not know how deeply and broadly writing-to-learn techniques are being applied, nor the questions and concerns that individual faculty have. The survey and the newsletter would awaken our many new faculty, especially in the burgeoning technical programs, to the benefits of the program.

Perhaps even more basic is a central, interdepartmental writing committee, with some released time for members, to channel the energies of faculty and administrators and coordinate the many current and proposed activities. The proposed Interdisciplinary Center for Writing might serve this function. Certainly, the committee to oversee the new general education program, if it is approved, will have to fulfill this need for faculty teaching the core. Currently, several professors are partially released to administer phases of our effort: the director of English composition, the director of creative writing, the director of the Northern Virginia Writing Project, the writing/speaking specialist in PAGE, the chair of the general education task force, the director of the writing lab, and the coordinator of word processing. But as our program continues to expand and diversify, we'll need more released time for faculty who can keep the multipart enterprise together. No doubt the program will thrive on the intrinsic rewards teachers and students receive from the language-rich environment, but as the administration has been learning, faculty development and curriculum improvement require people with the time to devote to them.

REPORTS FROM REAL PEOPLE

The four reports that follow come from faculty who have been part of the language-across-the-curriculum effort for at least four years. Kathleen Campbell of Fine and Performing Arts brought innovative techniques with her from Texas and has developed her own unique strategies in PAGE and in her theater courses. Gifted teachers Robert Clark of public affairs and Stanley Zoltek of mathematical sciences were introduced several years ago to language-and-learning techniques in the general education program. Donald Holsinger of history joined the WAC seminar in 1981 and wrote one of the chapters, "Writing to Learn in History," in the volume that came from those institutes. He too has successfully used language-and-learning strategies in both PAGE and his courses in the history department.

/ / / / / / /   *Nature-Object Exercise*
Kathleen Campbell

One of my favorite exercises is a variation of one developed by Professor Paul Baker during his years as head of the drama departments at Baylor and later Trinity University and as artistic director of the Dallas Theater Center. (His description of the original exercise, along with others he developed, is recorded in his book *Integration of Abilities: Exercises in Creative Growth*.) I use the exercise often in my theater and general education courses at George Mason because it can be easily varied to suit a specific course or the needs of a particular group of students, and because the results, especially in terms of stretching the students' ideas about their own abilities, are so exciting. It increases students' powers of observation, provides material for writing assignments, introduces them to the creative process, and increases their appreciation of artistic work.

I begin the process by asking students to choose an object from nature that will be the focus of a six- to eight-week creative exercise. At this point I never tell the class what they are going to be doing with the object, although I caution them to select with some care, suggesting they choose something they believe will hold their interest over a long period of time. Despite this, many grab the first object that strikes their eye on the way to class the day they are to bring their objects in for approval. In the long run, it doesn't really make much difference, but there are some kinds of objects that don't work well and should be avoided. Most students work best with something they like or are intrigued by, although students who select a souvenir often find it hard to disassociate the object from its history. Living animals, especially pets, don't work well, but growing plants often do. (Flowers, leaves, or other parts of plants that are picked are likely to die during the course of the exercise; some students are able to use this, others find it disconcerting.) It is helpful if the objects can be easily carried so that students will have no difficulty taking them home for weekends to keep up with daily assignments.

Once the objects are chosen, I ask the students to write daily detailed descriptions of them for at least one week, sometimes two. If I am using a journal for the course, which I often do, the observations go there; otherwise, I ask students to use a folder to keep all the assignments together so that each time I take up the work I can review all entries made from the beginning of the exercise. I encourage the students to involve as many senses as possible in their observations, not just sight. (I suggest they can imagine how something might taste or sound if their object is one they cannot directly observe.) The emphasis at this stage is on detail; the problem is to observe carefully and describe rigorously. At first they will look for changes in the object and complain when none occur: "I looked at my rock for five minutes today, and it hasn't changed." By being forced to continue to study the object, they gradually notice things that they missed in their early observations, and often the object begins to be invested with meaning as they work with it. A week later the student with the uncooperative rock described intricate details of color and texture and expressed curiosity about the rock's origins.

During this period, students will tend to become frustrated and often angry, especially if the observations last into a second week. I ask them to write down all of those feelings too. They can also be encouraged to study their resistances to the exercise and write about those. The biggest complaint is usually that the exercise isn't any fun, or simply that they don't like doing it. I help them work past this by acknowledging their reactions, even agreeing with them, but insisting that they return to the basic assignment. (I always do the exercise along with the students, and I know that it isn't particularly entertaining; sharing my own frustrations often helps them get past theirs.) Often they find that they react similarly to other tasks; such discoveries give them more control over their own work processes.

The next step is to ask students to draw the object. This phase can also last a week or two, but unless the class has some art background they will become very frustrated if asked to draw too long. I ask them to begin with more or less realistic drawings of each side of the object, but I stress that no one expects beautiful, polished drawings. Then they are asked to try abstracting lines or shapes from the drawings and working with them as independent design elements. The curve of a shell or the angles of branches and twigs may become elements in an abstract design. They may want to begin to play with color at this time if they are not already using it.

During this period they continue writing, but I encourage them to focus more on the feelings the object evokes than on descriptions: a student working with a shell brought home from a vacation wrote eloquently about the loneliness and sadness evoked by a beautiful object out of its element; another imagined how her stick felt being hauled around in her book bag; a third, whose flower was gradually drying up, recorded her guilt about having caused its early death. They can also continue to write about their frustrations, resistances, reactions to the exercise, which are likely to increase when asked to respond in a form (the drawings) in which they don't feel secure. At this point anxieties appear: "I don't see what drawing this acorn has to do with literature"; "I hope you know why we are doing this, because it sure seems dumb to me"; "my roommate asked me why I am carrying this rock around and I just told him I have a crazy English teacher—sorry." Students who have learned how to do what they think the teacher wants have a lot of trouble with this exercise, and this is the point where it is most likely to surface in their writing.

After they work with the drawings, I ask students to look over all the work they have done with the nature object and to select several things they want to develop further. These "things" may be ideas, feelings, drawings, pieces of writing—anything generated during the course of the exercise that interests them as a possible starting point for a creative project. They should develop these possibilities in any media they want to experiment with to see what happens, sharing the results with others and getting some feedback on what works and what doesn't; they may want to work with the same basic concept of feeling in more than one form. At this point small groups can be used effectively, since many students are shy about showing such "works in progress" before an entire class. To an outsider, the results may have no obvious relationship to the objects the students have been studying, but the connection can usually be seen clearly in the record of observations and reactions.

After about a week of experimentation, the students select from this small group of ideas one to carry through to a "finished" work. (All of these are really still works in progress, so I don't push the idea of "finished" too hard; the idea is to go beyond the exercise phase, though, toward something that has an aesthetic form and the power to communicate like a work of art.) If a class is otherwise focusing on a particular art form, students may be asked to develop their ideas in that form. Generally, though, I encourage works in any media, visual or verbal; the most important thing students gain from this exercise is an awareness of their own work process, which helps them in approaching many kinds of projects—so the more options they have, the more successful they usually are. These works should be shared with the entire group, but with an emphasis on the process as much as the product. I recognize technical success, but since few students will be accomplished artists, I try to keep the focus on the creative experience.

The exercise can end at this point, but I often use the small work of art as a warm-up for a larger project—the creation of a character. This requires students to return once more to the fund of ideas, feelings, and images they have created through the study of the nature object and to draw on them to develop a much more complex creation. Their development of this character should be as complete as possible. I ask them to think not only about the obvious facts such as age, race, sex, family background, occupation, physical description, but also about hobbies, favorite foods, colors, or music, clothes, pets, and dozens of other possible details that help to individualize a person. This assignment seems like a big jump to them at first, but when they begin working on the project, they usually find it surprisingly easy. The successful completion of the work up to that point has introduced them to their own creative potential, so students are less afraid to tackle an assignment that seems difficult or risky. Also, they have a great deal of flexibility in how they present their character. They may create a short story, a biography or autobiography, or a detailed character description, any of which may be accompanied by drawings or other visual materials. For example, an older student who began with a shell wrote this short poem about growth and independence:

LIFE BEGINNING

You lay placid, warm and
connected on the rocky, dusty
surface of the land—
within the part that made
up your whole—

Through the powers of good
and evil—you were split,
separated, touched by the seed
of life—thrown into the
abyss of dark strangeness—

There to lie until your needs
push you to seek the light,
your curiosity to seek the
answers—your fragmentation
to seek its wholeness—

From the same cluster of ideas, she wrote a character description of a housewife attempting to manage a catering service and a household at the same time.

Another student created this extended metaphor from his object:

THE LOOM AND THE THREADBEARER

Dream away Dreamer.
Weave your way into life.
The loom or the threadbearer
Who is the real god?
Do they deal in fate
Or do they deal just in life?
The loom lashes down,

And the threadbearer pulls her thread
Silently through life.
Lash down!
Silently through life.
Lash down.
Dream away Dreamer
Can you control your life?
Little and small
Can you control your life?
A pebble in the sand
Can you control your life?
Lash down!
Silently through through life.
Dream on dreamer.
Stop
And live.

In theater classes, I offer students a further opportunity to work with the characters they have created by developing a more specifically theatrical project. Some write and perform monologues or short scenes; students interested in visual design may develop set or costume designs for a projected play involving their character. The student mentioned above performed a delightful monologue for the class in which her businesswoman/housewife tried to dissuade a client from celebrating the couple's original meeting place by including a golden-arches motif in their wedding while she juggled with her own increasingly petty domestic problems. Two other students, who had each created older characters, wrote a one-act play in which the two senior citizens joined forces and escaped from a nursing home. Usually, large numbers of students—most of whom are not theatre majors—elect this optional assignment even though they had been strongly resistant to the exercise in earlier phases, a testimony to the personal strength they have discovered through the exercise.

Early in the project students usually raise the question of grades. Because this exercise emphasizes personal development and creativity, it is difficult if not impossible to grade by an objective grading system. Further, working to get a good grade often prevents students from giving in to the experience of the exercise; they may spend the whole time trying to figure out how to do it correctly instead of just doing it. At the same time, the exercise takes a lot of student time and they properly expect some kind of recognition in their course grade for their work on it. My solution is to give them a single grade at the completion of the project, although I give them substantial comments to guide them during the course of the exercise. This final grade is based principally on my sense of their commitment to tackling the exercise rather than on the results, although in fact those who give the exercise a real try usually produce the most exciting work. In gauging the students' participation I look for a number of things: volume of written entries and drawings, timeliness of entries (since one part of the exercise builds on the previous part, it is essential that students keep up with the work as assigned), honesty of observations of object and personal reactions, depth and originality of final projects.

Most students find doing the exercise a frustrating experience; they look for a right way to complete the project, or expect a specific answer to appear at some point. Because the assignments are given one at a time, they must do the work "blind," not knowing where the exercise will lead them. Living with this frustration and confusion is part of how the exercise works. For many students who have learned very well how to play the game of discovering and delivering what a teacher wants, this open-ended assignment (which truly has no "right" answer) is a frightening experience to which they will develop intense resistance. If they can work past their anger and confusion, however, the experience can be a liberating one, for it shows them that the ability to create lies within them, and that that power can be used in a myriad of effective ways. Leading students through this exercise can be frustrating and frightening for teachers also, for to do so one must abandon the security of a system of right and wrong answers and enter with the students into a world of imagination in which results can be unpredictable and intensely personal. Even though I have done it many times, I still find it hard to throw away my own opinion of "right and wrong" or "good and bad" work and to have the courage, generosity, and open-mindedness to recognize and encourage a student whose original work may challenge these long-held conceptions. Honestly doing the exercise along with the students is difficult, but it is the most effective way I have found to enter the creative realm with my students and thus be better equipped to successfully guide them through it.

/ / / / / / / *Communicating Across the Curriculum in Two General Education Courses*

Robert Clark

GMU's experimental general education program, PAGE, calls for substantial communication—both oral and written—in all its courses. I have been directly involved in planning and teaching two PAGE courses with quite different communication requirements. Cross-Cultural Perspectives involves students in detailed study of cultures quite distant in either time or space from their own (e.g., the Hausa-Fulani of Nigeria, Mid-Pacific Islanders, Medieval France). Technology and Society deals with the interplay between these forces by focusing on a specific technology as a case study (e.g., computers, television, the space program). Though the communication dimension of these courses is different, communication still plays a vital role in successfully teaching each course.

CROSS-CULTURAL PERSPECTIVES: THE FOUR-PART JOURNAL

Students in Cross-Cultural Perspectives keep a journal as their principal written record. The journal makes explicit their reactions to the culture they are studying. It includes four kinds of entries:

1. One-page reactions after each class
2. In- and out-of-class reactions to something the instructor assigns (music, video programs, etc.)
3. Reactions to assigned readings
4. Collected materials, such as press clippings, pertinent to the course

We emphasize keeping the journals complete and up-to-date; we encourage authentic reactions. We don't particularly emphasize writing style, but that has not created a problem. Students submit the journals monthly throughout the semester, and we record our reactions to the entries in the journal itself. Most instructors don't assign a grade to the journal until the semester is over. The journal is, however, a substantial part of the final grade, in some classes as much as 40 percent.

Journals are important in the course because we want students to engage psychologically with a culture quite different from their own. The journal encourages them to do that without feeling threatened. By means of journal entries, students can begin, we hope, to see parallels with their own lives. For example, in my section, which deals with traditional Basque mountain culture, I try to show students how apparently "irrational" life choices of Basque shepherds are more correctly understood as "nonrational," meaning that the ends-means relationship cannot be shown empirically, but instead exists in another realm of life, where reality is defined by tradition, faith, or some other immeasurable characteristic. I ask students to write a journal entry describing some recent event from their lives in which their choices were influenced by similar nonrational cultural forces. Many of them write about intimate personal events involving family, other loved ones, religion, and long-term hopes. These feelings, which I could never have elicited orally in class, helped greatly toward the students' empathizing with a remote, strange people and understanding that these Basque shepherds' reactions to life were not "irrational" or "crazy," and in fact were not unlike some of their own life choices. I find the entries remarkably well written, too.

There are few costs connected with the journal other than the outlay of time required for the instructor to read and evaluate each one several times during the semester. The benefits far outweigh this cost, especially if the class is kept small. For me, the principal benefit of the journal is that it fosters dialogue between the students and me in a much more direct and trusting way than is possible through class discussion. No matter how hard we try, it's difficult to stimulate all students to speak out in class, but the journal overcomes that hurdle. I have been both surprised and pleased with the openness and confidence with which my students address important issues of the course in this medium. I feel that it significantly helps to make the course a success.

TECHNOLOGY AND SOCIETY: COLLABORATIVE PROJECTS

The communication that takes place in Technology and Society contrasts sharply with that of Cross-Cultural Perspectives, for it stresses public, oral communication rather than private interactions through the journal. In Technology and Society, a fourth-semester course, students are assigned to small teams of four or five. Each team is given problem-solving tasks that involve discovering features of the interplay between society and the team's selected technology. Since my sections have focused on information technology, I have my teams choose an aspect of that, such as the telephone or the typewriter, and trace it back to the origins of its component parts (which almost invariably come from abroad). Periodically, perhaps four times a semester, each team comes before the class to report on its findings. Thus, communication for these students has two important dimensions—the interactions of the group members as they plan and carry out their projects; and the oral reports themselves.

Writing becomes important as the team discovers that it must develop written plans, notes, and drafts to guide them through the research and reporting. Nevertheless, these projects do not result in a permanent written record. Students are graded on the quality of their oral presentations, and they also share in a group grade—although we reserve the right to award differential grades to students whose contribution (or lack of) to the project has been noteworthy. Professors give feedback to the students after each report on a special form developed for this purpose; we usually spend much class time discussing the reports.

Team projects aren't easy to use in a teaching setting. They require much time and attention by the teacher, and they usually cause anxiety among the students. When used correctly, however, the team projects generate the right amount of creative tension and the students learn more from each other than they could from us. In any event, the professional world that awaits them moves on the basis of committees and other small groups, so it is essential that these students master the art of collaboration.

/ / / / / / / /   *The Electronic Journal in Required Mathematics*

Stanley M. Zoltek

As a mathematician, I have not until recently had much interest in writing as an aid in teaching mathematics. However, my experience teaching a course in the PAGE program with student electronic-journal writing during the past three years has significantly changed this feeling. The PAGE program encourages each instructor to incorporate writing into the curriculum whenever possible. Analysis and Solution of Quantitative Problems I & II are mathematics courses that require students to use a CDC Cyber 830 mainframe computer. Given the program's commitment to writing and my students' background in computing, I decided to have them keep an electronic journal on their mainframe accounts. This allowed me easy access to their journals and created an environment that elicited student responses seldom encountered (as colleagues pointed out) in a paper-and-pencil journal format.

My early attempts at having students write journals did not meet with great success. I found that it worked better in my classes if I gave some direction. At first I asked students to keep a weekly journal about whatever they wanted. Some students kept a careful account of their experiences in the classroom and kept in touch with me as to what was working for them and what was not. Other students, however, turned their journals into a sort of private psychoanalytic session in which they would spill their life stories out to me. I would hear about why they couldn't get along with their parents, how much it hurt them that they couldn't find a girlfriend or boyfriend and so forth. Some students simply stopped writing since they felt the points weren't worth it.

During this first year of experimentation, I learned how I could focus these journals into tools that could help both me and the students to function better in the classroom. These observations came from noting what students were writing in their journals and what changes were occurring in the classroom.

Most teachers of mathematics are aware that many of their students are very much afraid of the subject and have a mental block against learning mathematical concepts and principles. Now, one of my first journal entries asks students to tell me something about themselves. I ask them for a phone number at which they can be reached, which math courses they have taken prior to this course, and some of their favorite and least favorite things. (Often math is listed in the latter category.) I find that this first journal entry gives students a chance to get used to writing to a "math professor" and to express any doubts or fears about the course. At the next class meeting I always make a point of letting students know that I have read their journals and that we are going to have a very safe atmosphere in which students won't have to fear being ridiculed by me or by their classmates.

Below are two examples of students' first journal entries. The first example is in the form of a list of responses to my questions, while the second is in an almost conversational style. However, both students exhibit a comfortable feeling about expressing themselves in this electronic journal format.

Example 1

—I have taken geometry, algebra 1 and 2, and PAGE 125.

—I live in Arlington this year—I decided to try off-campus, plus I have a job there.

—I will give you my number when I get a phone installed.

—My favorite things are art and music. My least favorite are computers, unfortunately.

—This class is the type that I'm really going to have to concentrate hard on. In a way, it seems interesting though.

Example 2

Now to begin my journal. I was in Advanced Placement math in high school, and got as far as very basic Calculus. All I actually remember now is integration and derivatives. I've only taken PAGE MATH so far in college, but I'm sure I'll have to take some more difficult classes before I'm through.

I live off campus, but it isn't very far away. I walk to school when I'm not feeling too lazy.

You can reach me at 273–0853. If I'm not home you can always leave a message with one of my roommates, or on the machine if it answers. Don't leave any messages with the dog—she never gives us our messages!

My favorite things include: #1 Science Fiction, #2 Unique clothing and makeup, #3 Unusual and old music, #4 School (really!), #5 People (with open minds)

My least favorite things include: #1 Boring writers, #2 Mundane clothing and music, #3 People (with closed minds)

Many mathematics students are poorly prepared for class because of their elementary and high school training. The result is that many concepts that should be easy to get across can take several tries and require unique approaches to convey. For me, this extra effort draws much of its energy from the feedback students give me in their journals. I make myself aware of my students' preparation by asking them to write a mathematical autobiography.

The next example shows that this student has done remarkably well in classes in which the instructor was willing to prepare careful notes and handouts. Such feedback is encouraging in the face of thinking that most extra efforts are just a waste of the instructor's time. The student has also pointed out the importance for her, and most likely for many of her peers, of collecting homework on a regular basis. More importantly, she is making a plea for a structured learning environment.

Example 3

Dear Dr. Zoltek,

   In elementary school, I used to love math. I excelled very quickly, and I was doing algebra on the seventh grade level in sixth grade. Only two other people were on my level, and a student teacher taught us instead of the teacher. I really enjoyed it because I did well. Unfortunately, the book was too easy, and they didn't provide us with harder books. The school didn't carry any. There was one girl though, who went to junior high for part of the day to take math class there, but she was really smart. So we mediocre people missed out on learning anything new.

   When I got to junior high, I came to the sad realization that the book I used in elementary school was so easy because it didn't teach me what I really needed to know to understand the fundamentals of Algebra I. I had a real hard time understanding the concept of x and y replacing numbers and I ended up getting out of honors math and into a regular course. Finally, in ninth grade I understood algebra really well and got straight A's, and I was loving math again. I had a really good teacher so that helped.

   In high school, I took geometry which I hated. The teacher was really old and he couldn't see. He used to yell a lot, too. I didn't understand geometry so I didn't like that class either. In eleventh grade, though, I was back in algebra again and I did very well. I had a very organized teacher who gave us very good notes in class. In twelfth grade, I took advanced algebra and did well in that too after I switched to the right teacher. The first teacher was confusing and didn't give any notes. The second was great. His class was good because he gave good notes and was always available for help. The only thing I didn't like was that he only collected homework once or twice a semester. I tend to fall behind under that kind of system because I know that I can do my homework at a later date. This is what is happening to me in Strand.

   Bye!

   Further, journals let students give me feedback about exams and the pace of the class. Although I have a relatively fixed amount of material to cover, student comments do play an important part in the pacing of the class.

   The following example shows how a specific student has prepared for an exam and how she views the pace of the class. The student was upset about what she had not studied but essentially felt the exam was quite fair. She added that her good work was directly related to our going at a pace with which she felt comfortable.

Example 4

> I think that the first quiz was very reasonable. I did a lot better than I thought I would while I was taking the test. I was very nervous and it took me a while to get the hang of things. I didn't think I was doing the problems right. The only thing I messed up on was the permit and the catlist commands. The night before the test I was even going to study all the commands and the problem solving guide, but I decided that you would only test us on the problems. Boy was I mad when I saw that we had to know the commands. I have a problem remembering them, so whenever I do my journal I always bring my class notes and "Using the Cyber."
>
> I think I am doing so well because we are always going over everything again and again. Sometimes I get bored and restless when I already understand what has been taught and you go over it again for others who don't understand, but sometimes you go over it three or four times. I think that I will never forget $An = P (1 + i/m)^{\wedge}mn$ as long as I live. Don't get me wrong, though. I'd rather be in a math class that moved a little slower than be in one that was faster because I probably fall in between the two and wouldn't do well in a faster class. I enjoy math more and attend class more when I understand.

My experiences with an electronic journal have encouraged me to try writing as a means of dealing with specific topics that students are having trouble learning. For example, this semester students in the first course have had a great deal of difficulty in the section entitled "Charting the Earth." Invariably, when a student comes to my office hours for help, the following scenario occurs: I start to explain the setup of the problem to the student and soon find that he or she doesn't know what the terms in each mathematical expression represent. Specifically, when we try to find the distance between two cities on the earth that lie on the same circle of latitude, we need to understand concepts such as radius of a circle, longitude lines, circles of latitude, hypotenuse, adjacent side, and opposite side. Even though in class I carefully define the needed terms, I find that the students quickly forget or do not understand the definitions.

The next time I cover these topics, I plan to give homework problems in which I have drawn a sphere and labeled specific lines, angles, and directions and then ask the students to tell me what the specific items are and to detail in writing why they think their answers are correct. That is, I will have them in their own words define the terms we have been using. When I have done this in a one-on-one setting in my office, I have found that the student remembers what he or she has learned and can still use this knowledge the following day.

(This cannot always be said for what a student acquires from a "standard" mathematics lecture.)

I find the benefits of keeping electronic journals for instructors and students to be threefold. First, journals provide a private place to express opinions and concerns about the class, specific topics, materials, and personal matters that affect class performance. Second, for the instructor with a home- or office-computer terminal link to a university mainframe, accessing "electronic" journals is much more convenient than carrying around an armful (or boxful!) of traditional notebook journals. Also, the instructor can make an instant reply by electronic mail after reading a student's journal entries. And finally, electronic journals encourage more individualized, personal dialogue between student and teacher, resulting in a greater effort to produce positive results.

/ / / / / / / /   ***A Historian's View***

Donald C. Holsinger

Since my first contact with the writing-across-the-curriculum movement during a 1981 summer seminar, I have accumulated an ever-expanding tool kit of classroom methods in the teaching of courses in non-Western and global history. Once I had overcome the initial barrier of inherited assumptions about the "proper" place of writing in learning, I found that the classroom could become a history "laboratory" that engaged students in many dimensions of learning. My teaching techniques have been based on the following propositions: (1) writing necessarily involves deep thought, (2) writing, a mysterious interaction between conscious and subconscious thought, is a process of discovery—about ourselves and about our knowledge of the world around us, and (3) writing for another reader is an act of self-transcendence that cultivates a detachment basic to an educated person.

My attempts to apply these principles in university teaching over the past half dozen years have had mixed results, as any innovative approach is bound to have. Among the greatest benefits have been a confidence and a spontaneity in my teaching that have helped draw students into a joint quest to understand the world of past and present. History courses are natural arenas for experimenting with writing-to-learn techniques. Short writing assignments are a good way to engage students in subject matter foreign to them. For example, in a course on global history since 1500, students start out not with a list of facts about Columbus; rather, they themselves assume the roles of historians in the year 2025 assigned to write a chapter on the 1980s. By "doing" a history of several pages on the era of their experience, they are forced to reflect on the nature of history as a process of selection, analysis, and narration, at the same time as they come to see the global connections in the present-day world. If this exercise is successful, "history" will become for them a living, evolving process that connects the past with the present in an ever-unfolding dialogue between the illumination of the particular and the illustration of the general.

Similarly, in a course on African history, I ask students on the first day to write down the first words that pop into their minds when they hear the word "Africa." They then compose a paragraph incorporating the words and divide into small groups to compare their work. Students usually benefit in several ways. Some students, assuming they have little sense of Africa, discover that they possess vivid images of it, often misguided, stereotypical. They are enlightened and relieved to discover that others share their preconceptions. This exercise leads naturally into a discussion of common myths and stereotypes about Africa and of the origins of popular misconceptions. It also helps to set the hoped for tone for the course, one of free but serious exchange of ideas. Even more importantly, it engages the students by drawing connections between their own experience and the subject of the course.

One of my goals in teaching is to enable students to comprehend the shifting frontiers of cultural, economic, and political interaction that have shaped the world over the past five centuries. It is crucial that students overcome the natural tendency to view global change solely from a Western-centric vantage point. When cultures encounter each other for the first time, there are always at least two different human experiences. One of my favorite writing exercises to illustrate both the meaning of Western-African interaction in Africa during the nineteenth century and the nature of historical analysis is a role-playing task involving an encounter between American journalist Henry Stanley and African leader Mojimba in central Africa in 1877. Students are given two one-page documents describing the same incident, a violent clash between Stanley's expedition and Mojimba's group of local inhabitants. Stanley's description of events pictures a group of brave pioneers savagely assaulted by cannibals. Mojimba's account describes an African welcoming party treacherously attacked by foreign invaders.

Students are required to assume seriously a new role, that of a journalist with an international reputation for objectivity and detachment writing in 1877 for a newspaper with a similar reputation. Using only the two accounts, they must compose a one-paragraph account of the incident that they will be satisfied to have appear on the front page. The word count is strictly limited to prevent them from trying to describe the incident from both points of view. They are forced to sift the probable from the improbable, to decide what is most likely to be true. They then meet in small groups and compare their accounts, this time assuming the role of editors who now recommend changes. Here are two student samples, the first from a first-year graduate student and the second from an upper-level undergraduate. I would consider both among the better student responses to this in-class assignment that I have seen.

Graduate:

A violent encounter between the exploration party of Henry Stanley and members of the Basoka tribe took place recently on the Lualaba River. As the Stanley party travelled north by canoe, they met a large group of Basokas in fifty canoes, in ceremonial dress, coming toward them. Stanley's party fired on the Basoka advance canoe, and when the Africans retreated, Stanley's men followed them to their village, inflicting heavy casualties. According to a Basoka representative, Mojimba, they were outfitted to welcome the white men, but Stanley maintains his party was threatened by the Africans with spears.

Undergraduate:

A violent confrontation occured in the Congo basin between the party of european explorers led by Henry Stanley and a local tribe led by Chief Mojimba. The fighting erupted when the 2 parties met on the waters of the Congo river although the reasons have not yet been clarified. The europeans armed with guns inflicted serious casualties on the natives who possessed only spears, causing them to flee towards their village closely chased by Stanley's party. The fight then proceeded in the native village resulting in considerable destruction on the side of the African tribe.

Such an exercise can be mined at great length and in many different ways. Rarely do I have enough time to exploit it as fully as I would like. After the exercise, the class discusses how they went about doing the exercise, thereby raising questions involving historical method and how the task of the journalist compares with that of the historian. Students are then asked to become historians in the 1980s assigned to find out what really happened back in 1877. They normally come up with a variety of ways to proceed, ranging from doing anthropological research in Zaire to detailed analysis of Stanley's other writings. Once we have explored the methodological implications of this exercise, I make a number of substantive comments on what the incident itself illustrates—mutual ignorance, negative cultural preconceptions, technological disparity in military encounters, the legacy of bitterness among the defeated, how typical such encounters were in nineteenth-century Africa, Stanley's influence in shaping Western images about Africa, and finally, the key role that Stanley played in setting off the European "scramble" for Africa.

Thus, one simple writing exercise becomes a gateway to learning about the African past as well as about methods of historical analysis. Sometimes it isn't until they look back on the exercise that students become aware that they wrote an authentic piece of history. They discover, some for the first time, that historical analysis can be fun. They are also reminded that it is demanding and, above all, illuminating.

The Minnesota Writing Project

Keith A. Tandy and Rosemary L. Smith

> *The notion that our effectiveness as teachers may be as impor-*
> *tant as our knowledge of our field is pretty radical and*
> *threatening stuff.*

Institution:	*Moorhead State University for* *Minnesota Writing Project*
Institutional Size—Students (FTES):	7,100
Institutional Size—Faculty (FTEF):	330
Student/Faculty Ratio:	22:1
Highest Degree Granted— Institution:	M.A.
Highest Degree Granted—English Department:	M.A.
Public or Private Institution:	Public

Institutional Mission: one of seven regional multipurpose state universities. Primarily a teaching institution where research is conducted to enable faculty to remain current in their disciplines.

For more information on the program described in this chapter, contact: Keith A. Tandy, Department of English, Moorhead State University, Moorhead, MN 56560.

The Minnesota Writing Project is a writing-across-the-curriculum program sponsored by the Minnesota State University System (MSUS). Supported by the Bush Foundation of St. Paul. MSUS is composed of seven state-supported universities, varying widely in size, age, and mission. The seven campuses enroll approximately 52,000 students, and employ about 2,100 faculty and a similar number of support staff, with an annual budget approaching two hundred million dollars. A governing board appointed by the governor sets broad policy for MSUS and selects a chancellor for the system. Each campus, under its own president, enjoys considerable autonomy.

The five original campuses, beginning with Winona in 1860, and including St. Cloud, Mankato, Moorhead, and Bemidji, were founded as normal schools, becoming four-year teachers' colleges in the 1920s. They became state colleges in 1957 and were authorized to develop master's programs six years later. In 1971, Southwest State opened at Marshall as a technical and liberal arts college, and Metropolitan State in Minneapolis–St. Paul as an upper-division school serving nontraditional students in the Twin Cities. In 1975 all seven campuses became universities, while retaining their primary mission as teaching institutions.

In the mid-1970s, recognizing that almost two-thirds of the MSUS faculty were tenured and that enrollment had stabilized (slowing future hiring), Chancellor Garry Hayes began putting special emphasis on faculty development. Legislative funding supported nineteen innovative programs within MSUS in 1978 and 1979, and seven of these were continued in 1980 and 1981. The aim was to find ways to keep teaching vital even as the average age of faculty increased and the influx of new ideas and energy with young faculty diminished.

As the economy in the state and the nation worsened in the early 1980s, legislative support decreased, and MSUS successfully approached the Bush Foundation in St. Paul with a nine-part faculty-development grant proposal. Covering a three-year period beginning July 1981, and renewed for an additional three-year period, this grant provided just under two million dollars, matched by MSUS, for faculty development. Included in the grant was support for the Minnesota Writing Project.

PROGRAM AND PHILOSOPHY

With the Bay Area Writing Project as our model, we designed and tested a series of five-day faculty writing workshops, generally held at the beginning or end of the summer, starting at Moorhead State in 1978. The workshops included substantial advance reading and writing assignments, nearly forty hours in daytime sessions, and additional writing and revising assignments at night. These workshops became the basic design, with interesting variations, for the other six campuses in MSUS.

Our program philosophy was heavily indebted to the assumptions of the National Writing Project, though we recognized that our workshop participants were nonselective, and—unlike K–12 teachers—not accustomed to group work. Like many in the field, we began with a concern for literacy and evolved quickly into interest in the uses of writing for purposes of teaching and learning. Equally important, we found that our five-day workshops served to gather faculty in noncompetitive groups, to break down the isolation of most academic lives, and to focus our attention on our successes and problems as teachers. In short, our workshops served to build a sense of community among participants that was simply unavailable in traditional university structures. Given the opportunity to escape from the usual territoriality and self-serving politics of departmental curriculum committees, for example, we found ourselves mutually renewed by the visible and exemplary energy of our colleagues, as discussions of writing and learning expanded to incorporate broader matters of good teaching.

Very early we found our colleagues intolerant of lectures (of course!) and of writing theory per se, but eager to participate in a wide range of model writing activities, including peer critique groups. Thus, most staff presentations came to include a period of trying out a type of student writing activity (summarizing, journal writing, case histories, various systems for discovering content, and so on), and then discussing possible uses in their own courses with the staff member most experienced with and knowledgeable about that kind of assignment. Other presentations on teacher activities, such as responding to and evaluating student writing, also included hands-on activities followed by discussion. The final workshop sessions were always given over to assignment designing; participants chose from the smorgasbord of alternatives to the term paper and adapted what they found most consonant with their own subject matter and teaching styles.

During the school year we scheduled follow-up sessions for past participants (these were often poorly attended but lively sessions), reviewing their work and sometimes testing new presentations for the summer. At various times we targeted special groups of faculty, either with divisional workshops or special staff consulting or both. As a result, on one campus a number of business departments now require all their majors to add a course in practical or technical writing to their yearlong freshman English sequence, and all candidates in two master's degree programs take required writing courses taught by Project staff members. Several special workshops have enabled business faculty to negotiate the nature and content of the technical and practical writing courses with the English faculty who teach them; consulting funds allowed us to introduce individual faculty to word processing, which is now used in over 40 percent of the freshman English classes on one campus.

ASSUMPTIONS

The ten-year history and substantial support for this program (approaching $1.4 million and over 1,200 faculty participants in the MWP program alone) invites reflection, but also the warning that what now may seem very simple and obvious was not so at the beginning, and if there is clarity now, it was often won through costly, painful, and foolish mistakes. We believe that MWP grew and flourished because (1) we had ongoing contact with and guidance from James Gray and the exemplary staff development design he created in the Bay Area Writing Project; (2) we enjoyed extraordinary administrative support, especially from President Roland Dille and Vice-President William Jones at Moorhead State; and (3) we came to understand and operate on the following assumptions (many of them extensions of BAWP assumptions into the university setting):

Faculty Needs. University faculty share a long tradition of respect for good writing; but in the rapid expansion of American universities in the late 1950s and 1960s much of the writing previously expected of students across the curriculum was abandoned in favor of objective examinations. Thus many faculty feel a strong obligation to contribute to the literacy of their students, without being at all clear on how to go about doing so. Most faculty outside of English are dismayed at the poor quality of student writing, but feel they lack the training or "authority" to judge, mark, or evaluate it. MWP leaders approached this problem in a variety of ingenious ways, with short presentations on common errors by "Ye Olde Grammarian" (Bob Gremore at Metro State) or on language philosophy (Harry Solo at Mankato State), for example. Many participants found encouragement in Samuel Johnson's remark ("Sir, I do not have to be a carpenter to see that the table is wobbly") and in David Robinson's (Winona) characterization of the traditional English teacher, treating student writing to saturation error-marking, as "Conan the Grammarian."

Faculty Isolation. We assume that university faculty are often terribly isolated, partly as the result of recent growth, the fact of rigid departmentalization, and the emergence of faculty unions that often diminish traditional collegiality. But isolation is built into university traditions in other, more ancient ways as well: in the structure of the individual researcher perfecting his or her expertise at the close of a career as a graduate student; in the tradition of the closed classroom; in the competitive realm of research and publication; in the fact that few university faculty have any training to speak of in *how* to teach and are consequently reluctant to talk about teaching; by the traditional forms of staff development (research leaves, sabbaticals) which are usually isolated and individual; even, at worst, by the unprofessional dependence on the traditions of academic freedom and tenure as protection against being held accountable for poor teaching. As a result, most of our workshops incorporated some element of planned group-interaction or trust-building as part of the rather new *collaborative* staff development in writing-across-the-curriculum workshops.

Faculty Teaching Skills. Because the university focus has traditionally been on mastery of disciplinary content, many faculty have ignored or even held in contempt the methods, skills, processes, and arts of teaching and learning. M.A. and Ph.D. programs demand enormous investments of time, energy, and emotion to mastering the field, but rarely is anything approaching that investment given to learning how to teach—nor are career rewards in the university very clearly attached to good teaching. Even in so-called "teaching universities," new administrators are likely to try to make their mark and ensure their own advancement by raising the standards for production of research, not for teaching. Young faculty know that publication is likely to count more than teaching in tenure decisions. Beyond the issues of job security and advancement, our traditional focus on our expertise leads many faculty to exclusive dependence on the traditional information-transfer model of teaching: I'll lecture, you listen. Yet so much research on learning generally and language learning specifically suggests that learning is most effective when it is interactive, that a strong thread of content evolved in MWP workshops concerning the learner-centered classroom generally. Sr. André Marthaler and Patrick Riley at Bemidji State used role-playing to present typical and ideal office conferences; Southwest and Winona incorporated presentations on learner types; several campuses used "Three Strategies for Using Writing to Learn," a videotape by Mary K. Healy (available from Boynton/Cook) that advocates and demonstrates quick, in-class modes of writing as functional and nonevaluative. Our participants wrote, read their writing to peer critique groups, and discussed that experience as a model of collaborative learning adaptable to many classrooms. Often we found ourselves sharing our best *teaching* practices, whether or not they were more than marginally related to issues of literacy. Thus while faculty may enroll in a WAC workshop out of concern for literacy, they welcome opportunities to experience and discuss a wide range of good teaching practices, even if the connection to student writing is very slender.

Faculty Writing Assignments. Many faculty have experienced only a very narrow and traditional kind of academic writing—the end-of-term paper, the library research project, the review of relevant secondary sources. While these models help faculty evaluate students' progress toward professional skills, they may thwart many students who do not plan to follow us into academic careers, and they neglect many effective, imaginative, and efficient ways of using writing to enhance learning. Thus MWP workshops presented a broad spectrum of kinds of writing, from learning logs and journals to microthemes to freewriting to summaries, abstracts, and précis, to case studies, to concept-mapping, to writing-to-get-ready-to-learn, and so on. Our aim was to broaden the options available, and to include writing assignments that could actually *reduce* the paper load many faculty fear when they think about assigning more writing.

Faculty Individuality. We assume that teachers differ—in personality, in style, in their need for varied degrees of distance from their students, as well as in the pedagogical approaches traditional in and (not necessarily the same thing) appropriate to their differing subject matter. As a result of such differences, they need to see the eclectic presentation of varied types of writing assignments discussed above, so that they can choose or modify those that best match their individual approaches to teaching and their disciplinary content.

Faculty Experiencing Writing Types. We assume that faculty need to *experience* writing assignments before they can know whether a given type (the journal, the summary, the case study, the sequence of drafts, etc.) will fit their style and classroom context, and which of their teaching problems a given type of assignment might best address. So just as MWP workshops presented a smorgasbord of assignments, so we insisted that each presentation include an opportunity to try out the kind of writing being presented.

Faculty in Community. Beyond the initial issue of literacy and the supplemental matter of productive teaching practices, or perhaps because of them, most WAC leaders recognize that their programs offer the beginning stages in building a community of scholars, a community denied us, traditionally, by the isolating conditions of graduate work and of our workplace. Generally we are more confident of our expertise in our field than in our effectiveness as teachers, and if our teaching seems shaky, we're likely to blame the students and avoid conversations about teaching and learning, even to assume they are trivial topics. When such postures result in a kind of elitism, little progress can take place. But part of the genius of the Bay Area Writing Project's design was in providing opportunities for teachers to talk about what *works* in the classroom, about their successes rather than what they *believe*—and to discover, from thoughtful reflection, how to separate what they believe from what does, in fact, work. So our workshops intended from the start to open conversations on things that work, and in those open exchanges of good teaching practices from all areas of our campuses, our participants discovered others around them who also are committed to good teaching.

Faculty Ownership. Our workshops succeeded when faculty ownership and invention of the programs were acknowledged and respected by administrators (and at times suffered badly from interference and ill-advised policy decisions imposed on the faculty leading the programs). State-level administrators insisted on controlling our complex budget (but never mastered it) and decentralized control without discussing it with us, informing us of the change, or providing for uniform procedures for handling money. At one point the seven campus project directors were told that our meeting to plan for the renewal of the first grant was "inappropriate"; four months later we were ordered to produce a revised design, rationale, and budget for the renewal grant within a week. But ownership is no simple matter of avoiding top-down interference. Within campus leadership teams, personnel actions were extremely difficult: not all emerging presentations were equally effective, and we had great difficulty remedying those situations. Frequently, presentations crystallized, ceased to evolve, or became private turf. Within a team, the time and energy expended was always uneven, and often that was painfully visible. Among the campuses, an initial honeymoon period of sharing and inventing was followed by some unseemly and destructive competitiveness and territoriality. As campus teams became confident of their capacity to deliver solid, effective workshops, they often became resistant to any form of outside comment other than praise, and some campus leaders became greedy over all discretionary funds in our unstable budget. Still, at any one time during a six-year period, teams of six cross-disciplinary faculty at each of the seven campuses were exchanging ideas with their local colleagues and with other teams across the state. Ownership and collaboration are linked subjects, and the best we can suggest is to engage in long reflective conversations about these issues with the wisest colleagues and administrators available.

RESULTS

The Minnesota Writing Project has had a long history, as staff development programs go, and impressive numbers, whether measured in financial support, faculty enrolled, or impact on neighboring institutions. But as in all programs with intent to produce change and growth in teachers, change is difficult to quantify. We know that faculty by the hundreds have reestablished writing as a functional part of their classroom teaching, and that they have done so in thoughtful, informed ways. We hear the howls of protest from students who are facing higher standards and more writing assignments in courses that they had assumed were safely divorced from that art. We find our colleagues are more closely bound in a community of teaching and learning, and more thoughtful and better informed about their role in that community.

MWP Leaders' Growth

We also feel that the deepest impact of the program has occurred with those most closely and extensively involved in it—those leaders of MWP programs who have persisted in their commitment to the program. So, we have seen one campus director who became acting vice-president for Academic Affairs as an interim appointee at his university; any number of MWP staff members elected as chairs of departments and of university-wide task forces and committees; a remarkable increase in publication and other scholarly and research activities, including a staff member on one campus who was invited to appear on an international panel at a conference on Canadian literature. MWP leaders have been sought out for, and have accepted, important leadership responsibilities within their institutions, and have exhibited remarkable levels of professional growth and activity.

MWP Participant Growth

MWP workshop participants have also shown substantial growth as a result of their taking part in the program. One colleague—Lou DeMaio, in speech pathology—reports insistently that his two workshop experiences "taught me to write *twice*: once in acquainting me with process and heuristics, and then in introducing me to word processing." His publication record is enviable. One support staff member at Moorhead State had over fifty short articles and reviews accepted for publication in professional journals within three years of his participation in a workshop.

The Invisible Dimension

Beyond these examples, there is an invisible level of impact, represented in our minds by a colleague—Del Corrick—who directs an open-admission division of our campus. In 1978 he drafted two short stories as part of his preworkshop writing assignment, and in 1987, while on sabbatical leave, he finally was able to return to those stories, one of which has been accepted for publication; the other is being considered by another journal, and he has a substantial part of a novel underway. He had moved from a master's in creative writing through a doctorate in American studies to an administrative post; his sabbatical leave allowed him to complete a creative moment growing out of his early training, renewed by our workshop assignment, and finally brought to fruition. One of the Prairie Writing Project's staff members, Mary Gardner, is now teaching in Texas. She ascribes to her experience with the PWP staff the fact that she found courage to begin (and eventually publish) her first novel (*Keeping*

Warm, Atheneum), which was favorably reviewed in the *New York Times*. Her second work, a series of letters titled *Milkweed*, is in final editing, and her third, another novel, is in its third revision.

Besides these individual achievements, we believe that MWP has raised the level of professionalism and improved the degree of consciously humane teaching that exists in MSUS. Sometimes this shows up best in the metaphors participants create during their struggle to incorporate new ideas and attitudes. We have enjoyed the wit of the teacher who wrote, the first day of a workshop, "Sometimes I think students write on the model of the squid—throwing up clouds of ink and hoping to escape in the confusion"—but recognize also, at least possibly, some negative and self-protective comment on students there. From the middle of that workshop, we recall an earnest question about starting to write: "How do you get the first olive out of the jar?" And another participant, reflecting on his workshop experience a year later, said, "I learned that writing is not a *shadow* of thinking, or just a way to *report* on learning; it is itself a way to think and to learn." Growth at a very deep level is evident in that thought.

PROBLEMS

Follow-up. One major problem was our inability to design a program for following through, either after annual workshops or at the end of the major grant period. Bemidji succeeded in gathering many of their series participants at some follow-up sessions and, along with St. Cloud and Winona, published new assignments designed by participants on a regular basis. Mainly, it was difficult to find dates and participants for weekend review and renewal sessions during the academic year.

Internal Revenue Service. Our problems have also involved a crippling debate between administrators and MWP staff on the interpretation of Internal Revenue Service regulations governing honoraria and stipends for participants and staff. (Essentially, those in our kind of program who provide a service should be salaried, with attendant deductions; those who do *not* provide a service—participants, for example—can receive support that does not go through salary and deduction mechanisms; but while that seems the clear intent of IRS language, WAC administrators should be aware that in some regions of the country the IRS has found exotic alternative readings.)

Burn-out. Our problems have also included burn-out of leaders: the preparation for and delivery of a presentation on the uses of writing in the classroom is a demanding task, particularly for faculty from outside of English departments who may not have much sense of authority on their subject, and turnover of staff within MWP has been fairly heavy. Coordinating and integrating six such presentations plus other parts of the program (with careful timing of writing groups, evaluation, discussion sessions) places extraordinary demands on those who direct the workshops.

Divisiveness. Both during and as a result of workshops, we have experienced (and, in fact, unintentionally contributed to) a kind of polarization of teachers. The notion that our effectiveness as teachers may be as important as our knowledge of our field is pretty radical and threatening stuff for many. Some participants become very uncomfortable with ideas such as the decentered and interactive classroom. Some will whisper and giggle and refuse to engage in assigned tasks—in fact, behave in ways they would not tolerate for a second from their students. Departments can and have become bitter battlegrounds, as authoritarian teachers resist change, defend lofty academic standards and the sanctity of "the major" and their own academic freedom. Students can be caught up in such battles, as can junior colleagues. While we know of no MWP staff member directly hurt by engaging in the program, the full casualty count from all departments isn't in.

Administrative Interference. If any one thing hampered the effectiveness of the Minnesota Writing Project, though, it was—paradoxically—administrative interference ("paradoxically" because, at the beginning, the Prairie Writing Project enjoyed splendid support from Moorhead State administrators and the MSUS chancellor's office as well). And as the Project grew and progressed, we could count on local support and assistance almost always, almost everywhere. But at the system level we were more often than not met with implicit distrust of faculty, whether in our capacity to conceive or administer or to deliver a responsible program. We found system administrators demanding control of both budget and policy matters, but incapable of administering the first or addressing the second intelligibly. Repeatedly, through the two grant periods, we were told that we needed to create new ways to spend money, but we were not told the amounts we had to work with. Withholding information seemed to be a systematic management philosophy for a number of years, as was the sense that MWP was an attractive thing for an administrator to claim to be administering.

The major defenses against bad policy decisions and management were campus administrators who were fully committed to protecting the program, an established and effective program design, a strong track record with that design, and a clear philosophical base for the program.

Obviously, such mismanagement consumed a great deal of the MWP leadership's time and energy. Without such problems, we might well have a stronger continuation of the consortium program. As of now, on three of the seven campuses, MWP activities continue. One will offer two workshops in an ongoing series, under on-campus funding, and with its third full staff; two others will continue single workshops. Other campuses have incorporated parts of the MWP design into ongoing faculty development programs, at modest levels of support.

Appendix

A BRIEF HISTORY OF THE MINNESOTA WRITING PROJECT

The Minnesota Writing Project began as a replication site of the Bay Area Writing Project—the Prairie Writing Project—at Moorhead State University. To the well-known structures of the National Writing Project (a five-week Summer Institute for select teachers, K–13, training a cadre of leaders for school-year in-service programs) we were urged to add a program in writing across the curriculum for college and university faculty. Administrators at the three campuses of Tri-College University (a consortium including Moorhead State, Concordia College, and North Dakota State University) provided about $16,000 in release time for eight faculty selected from the three campuses to prepare for and lead both summer programs.

Initially, we received $30,000 from MSUS, supplemented by the Stern Foundation, for two workshops in 1978 and two in 1979. The Prairie Writing Project (PWP) staff spent winter and spring quarters of 1978 studying writing theory and available information about writing-across-the-curriculum programs, including those at Beaver College and Michigan Tech. We designed a five-day, forty-hour workshop, initially for faculty in English; we were able to pay stipends of four hundred dollars to the participants—prorated on attendance.

Under special legislative funding ($90,000), PWP offered four workshops in 1980 and five in 1981. We were also invited to expand the workshop series to include the other six MSUS campuses in the Minnesota Writing Project, as a large part of an MSUS grant proposal to the Bush Foundation for faculty development, and Moorhead State became the training site for new project leaders from sister campuses. In 1981 three of our workshops enrolled such leaders from St. Cloud State, Mankato State, and Winona State, and one workshop was reserved for working with those leaders on the theory and practice of WAC workshops and programs.

Under Bush Foundation funding for this WAC program (approximately $100,000 a year, matched by MSUS), the Minnesota Writing Project offered workshops on four campuses in 1982, seven campuses in 1983, six in 1984 and 1985, and seven in 1986 and 1987. In addition, we held a theory workshop at Moorhead State in 1982 for new leaders from Bemidji State, Southwest State, and Metro State, and several leadership training workshops over weekends as campus staff changed and as similar programs evolved in our region. Workshops have ranged in size from eighteen to fifty-seven participants.

Prairie Writing Project also provided leadership training workshops for Bush Foundation–supported WAC programs at four state college campuses in North Dakota and three in South Dakota, and for nineteen community college campuses in Minnesota. In all, some sixty campuses have sent faculty who have participated in our workshops and returned to lead writing-across-the-curriculum programs on their own campuses.

The University of Michigan

Liz Hamp-Lyons and Eleanor McKenna

> *The writing-across-the-curriculum program springs directly from the faculty consensus that all students should write throughout their time in the college, and from their further consensus that student writing ability is the responsibility of all faculty.''*

Institution:	*University of Michigan—Ann Arbor*
Institutional Size—Students (FTES):	34,800
Institutional Size—Faculty (FTEF):	2,750
Student/Faculty Ratio:	13:1
Highest Degree Granted—	
Institution:	Ph.D.
Highest Degree Granted—English	
Department:	Ph.D.
Public or Private Institution:	Public

Institutional Mission: A state-supported institution with students from 50 states and 106 foreign countries. A selective university that offers a diverse curriculum.

For more information on the program described in this chapter, contact: Eleanor McKenna, English Composition Board, The University of Michigan, Ann Arbor, MI 48109.

The undergraduate college of Literature, Science and the Arts (LS&A) at the University of Michigan is one of eighteen schools and colleges that interact to form the university. It is a liberal arts college with an enrollment of 13,000 students.

The writing center for the college, the English Composition Board (ECB), funded in its first year (1978–79) by the Andrew W. Mellon Foundation and since then by the university, came into being as a result of faculty response across disciplines to a perceived lack of improvement in the writing abilities of undergraduates at Michigan during their college years.

In 1976 the University of Michigan's Graduation Requirements Commission stated their desire to participate in improving undergraduate literacy. Between that time and January 1978, six university faculty, who formed the ECB, worked to develop a proposal for a new composition requirement for the College of Literature, Science and the Arts, which enrolls the majority of Michigan's undergraduate students. The six members came from five departments: English (two), chemistry, Far Eastern languages and literature, journalism, and psychology.[1] At the best-attended faculty meeting in a decade, the proposal was passed with only three dissenting voices. The cost of the new writing program in its first year was estimated at $250,000 for 1978–79 and more than $1.3 million for the first three years. It is a measure of the college's concern about undergraduate literacy that no one described that cost as excessive.

The writing program was supported by a grant from the Mellon Foundation in 1978–79, its experimental year, of $450,000. The program also received a grant from the Ford Foundation for 1979–80 to conduct research into the new writing requirement, primarily to develop and evaluate the writing assessment. Further grants from the Mellon Foundation for a final total of over $500,000 supported the center's outreach activities to Michigan high schools and two-year colleges that sent students to Michigan. However, throughout the ten years of its existence, the greatest proportion of the cost of the writing program has always been borne by LS&A itself; in 1987–88 that cost was close to $770,000.

THE WRITING ASSESSMENT

The underpinning for the writing program was, and is ten years later, the writing assessment. Every entering student, first-year or transfer, must take this fifty-minute direct writing test. This was intended to place undergraduate students along a continuum of writing instruction so that in any class the instructor would encounter a narrower range of writing needs than in the former composition courses taken by everyone. But it was also intended to have an impact on Michigan high schools.

In discussions with high school teachers across Michigan and beyond, teachers made it clear that their desire to provide frequent writing opportunities for students was frustrated by teaching loads of five classes of thirty to thirty-five students each week. They stressed the value of a rigorous university entrance assessment in communicating a clear message back to the schools about the importance of writing: they hoped that this emphasis would in its turn bring about a reduction in class size.

After ten years of the Michigan program, this hasn't happened. High school teachers still complain about large classes and heavy teaching loads, and the Michigan State Writing Committee still finds that eleventh and twelfth graders do less writing than teachers wish. However, these Michigan teachers have worked with the assessment instrument long enough that they are able to familiarize their students with it and alert them to the significance of the test, which is binding on all takers within LS&A. As the years pass, more and more of the university's other schools are also joining the program, including their entering students in the assessment, and holding them to placements.

Critical to the Michigan program is that individuals may take varying paths through it. There are two levels to the introductory part of the program: transfer tutorial and transfer composition; beyond this all students must fulfill the upper-level writing requirement in their junior or senior year; and all placements may include the specification of a mandatory "writing workshop," which calls for students to attend one-on-one conferences about actual writing in the students' classes until they are certified as competent writers. The role of these mandatory visits to the writing workshop has increased in recent years, and students are no longer held to a lower writing placement because of a lower level of writing skill in just one area of their writing. However, fewer students have been exempted from introductory writing courses: while 25 percent were exempted in the first year, this percentage has fallen steadily each year until in 1987–88, when only some 8 percent of students (almost all transfer students) were exempted. Equally, the number of students placed into tutorial has risen steadily, from 5 percent in the first year to 12 percent in 1987–88. Much of this can be explained by regulation changes for different units and schools; however, there has been a gradual fall in the standard of writing among entering students, as measured by the Michigan writing assessment.

In its first two years, the English Composition Board received funding for research from the Mellon Foundation. Since that time, there has been no funding specifically for research. However, in 1986–87 the position of Associate Director for Assessment was created, making possible larger-scale research investigations. A comprehensive program of research into the assessment was put into place in 1986–87 and 1987–88, and will culminate in 1988–89 with the introduction and validation of a new assessment instrument.

WRITING ACROSS THE CURRICULUM

The final element in the Michigan writing program is the writing-across-the-curriculum program (WAC), a highly ambitious and innovative program for juniors and seniors that involves faculty and administrators from every department in the college. An evaluation of the writing-across-the-curriculum program is planned to begin in 1989–90 and to continue for several years.

Professor James Sledd, speaking at a conference at the University of Michigan in 1981, described the Michigan program as "the most intelligent and resolute undertaking which has been made in the field for forty years." He went on to highlight two particular strengths.

> One, the program dramatizes the university's official commitment to good writing by creating courses in composition in *all* departments, not in English only; and two, by enlisting the cooperation of the schoolteachers of the state, the program acknowledges that the professoriat cannot work in arrogant and selfish isolation but needs the knowledge, help and guidance of its fellow-workers in schools.

Richard Bailey, then director of research at the English Composition Board, was able to say in 1981 that "faculty view the acquisition of writing skills in the same way that they view the acquisition of other kinds of knowledge."[2] The junior-senior writing program required all students, in their junior or senior year (preferably the former) to take a course, usually in their concentration, but in some cases as part of their distribution requirement, in which they study a disciplinary area and simultaneously focus their attention on the expression of knowledge and ideas through the medium of writing.

The program is directed by the ECB but taught by faculty in the various disciplines. Each faculty member designs his or her own course and presents it to the ECB for review and approval. While course descriptions vary greatly, all courses are expected to require extensive writing (a minimum of thirty pages is suggested, but many courses exceed that); opportunities for revision are a major focus, as well as writing experiences that are staged or sequenced throughout the semester, rather than one long term paper due at the end of the term or written midterm and final examinations. However, courses that require long papers written in stages throughout the term are regularly approved and fairly common.

The college acknowledges the additional expenditure of time required for a writing-intensive junior-senior course and spends most of the junior-senior program budget each year on the provision of teaching assistants (TAs) to support the work of the faculty member in the course. These are graduate students in the discipline concerned, and they are chosen to work in WAC courses by their departments. The ECB runs a training seminar each semester for TAs who are new to the junior-senior program. Since 1987 TAs receive graduate credit for the seminar.

Approximately 1,600 students during registration each semester "modify" the seventy or so ECB-approved WAC courses in the natural sciences, the social sciences, or the humanities that can be used to satisfy the college's junior-senior writing requirement. To modify WAC courses—courses that combine teaching of content with teaching of writing—is to signal the intent of using such courses to fulfill the junior-senior writing requirement.

Modifying course registration is a routine process for current Michigan students. Today more faculty in the disciplines are directly involved in English Composition Board policy decisions. The Policy Committee advises the director of the ECB on all matters pertaining to the writing program at Michigan. This committee is composed of seven faculty from the three major branches of LS&A (natural sciences, social sciences, and humanities), the director of the ECB, and two ECB faculty elected by ECB faculty to serve on the committee. In specially scheduled meetings the Policy Committee reviews and discusses for approval all new course proposals for the WAC program and awards a small number of citations for outstanding proposals each year. The Policy Committee with two annual $250 awards now also recognizes outstanding contributions to the junior-senior writing program by graduate student teaching assistants.

Forces from within have shaped the program over the years: in the early phases of the program "regular faculty members read and evaluate(d) students' writing."[3] Today, however, TAs take on the responsibility of evaluating and commenting on students' writing and help faculty to design diverse writing activities. If we find that teaching assistants have *replaced* faculty in evaluating and commenting on student writing (the exact extent of TA-versus-faculty involvement is speculative at present) then we will have witnessed a fundamental shift in the WAC program at Michigan since its conception.

As the program reaches the end of a successful first decade, the faculty across disciplines are becoming less directly involved in talking about the issues in writing than when the program began. It is less obvious in 1988 that faculty place the same emphasis on the acquisition of writing skills as they do on the acquisition of other knowledge. For example, since the early days of the WAC program, each semester the ECB has presented a term-long seminar in the teaching of writing to the Michigan faculty in the disciplines, which was at first well-attended. Over the years, however, the number of faculty attending declined, in part as faculty became experienced in WAC courses. In 1979 all faculty in the WAC program were new in the junior-senior writing courses, while in the 1987–88 academic year only 20 in a program of 170 courses are new. Gradually, the faculty seminar evolved to a faculty-and-TA seminar, with fewer faculty each year. Today, this seminar is perceived for the most part to be primarily for TAs; faculty are welcome at the seminar but even faculty new to the junior-senior writing program seldom attend. In the 1987–88 academic year seventy-two TAs and one faculty member have attended these seminars, now required for TAs funded by the ECB and new to the WAC program. TAs now receive one unit of graduate credit for the thirteen hours of training in tutoring writing in the disciplines. The transition from faculty seminar to graduate student course seems complete.

In response, the ECB has introduced a separate series of seminars designed for faculty new to the WAC program and other seminars for faculty new to the college but not yet involved in writing-intensive courses. It is promoting collaboration between new and experienced faculty. For example, a round-table discussion in the fall of 1988 included faculty newly experienced in teaching writing-intensive courses who presented descriptions of their courses and discussed problems and successes in teaching such courses with faculty newly arrived on campus and those about to teach a writing-intensive course for the first time.

ECB faculty have also researched faculty experiences in the WAC program during the past decade and have used this research to promote writing to learn in the disciplines.[4] Since not all faculty have the time or inclination to explore contemporary theories of writing for themselves, the ECB now provides a manual for faculty, drawing on the success of experienced faculty in the program over the years to describe a variety of ways writing can enhance learning. It is not meant to define and narrow what counts as a junior-senior writing course; rather, the manual includes descriptions of different writing-intensive courses in the disciplines as well as models for using writing that can help guide inexperienced faculty in proposing and implementing writing-intensive courses. These varied descriptions make concrete the philosophy implicit in the manual and basic to the WAC program at Michigan that writing in the college is a way of learning as well as a way of communicating and participating in a variety of academic communities.

WAC courses at Michigan are just as varied in terms of numbers of students. Some in biology, psychology, English, and communications, for example, are large; entire teams of TAs assist in the writing instruction. Many, such as the WAC seminars in history, limit enrollment to twenty. Some are restricted to students majoring in a particular field; others attract students from across the curriculum who use such courses to fulfill distribution requirements and/or fulfill the junior-senior writing requirement.

Linguistics 316 exemplifies a new course (offered for the first time in the WAC program in the winter 1988 term) that can be used to satisfy distribution requirements. The assignments are designed to train student writers to examine differences in a number of academic genres, to think critically about discoursal features of these genres (and ultimately discoursal features of their particular disciplines), and to provide a generalized preprofessional training to students from a variety of disciplines. The sources for the following description of Linguistics 316 are observations of the course and discussion with the instructor and students by Eleanor McKenna. The source for the description of Biology 301 is notes of an extensive interview with the course instructor shaped into a description by Liz Hamp-Lyons. In both cases, we had access to TA's teaching journals (required for credit in the TA seminar).

Linguistics 316

According to the course description, Linguistics 316 hope[s] to demonstrate "the value of linguistics as an interdisciplinary enquiry and to provide perceptions that will assist participants in becoming members of future discourse communities." It was an experimental course with an enrollment of eleven that met twice weekly for hour-and-a-half periods. The writing assignments included several short papers spaced throughout the semester and one term paper due at the end of the term. Both the instructor, John Swales, and the TA, Michele Chan, evaluated and commented on student papers. Both conferred with students. Michele noted in her teaching journal that "all pieces of writing receive detailed comments from both John and myself, and all members of the class conference with one of us (sometimes both of us) often." However, Michele's rather plaintive observation near the end of the course was that, when it came to revising a paper for a better grade, the students paid attention to John's comments on their papers and not hers.

Swales said that his course was not set up for people in particular disciplines, but that it dealt with student writing, didactic (textbook) writing, and research writing across the curriculum. He said students in this course analyzed the language out of their disciplines, "learning to do this as linguists do it." Swales maintains that even the skeptical begin to see that rhetorical strategy is not trivial. They begin to notice "finer distinctions of language and to understand the process of interaction of discourse and the community." Comments from his students support this claim. For example, an economics student said that he was more conscious since taking this class of what a thesis really represented and added, "I never looked at writing from a textual basis before." This student demonstrated in a final paper a high level of awareness of rhetorical features of the discourse of economics he was examining. Another student's comments suggested that he had been surprisingly unself-conscious of variation in a writer's voice in the disciplines. He said he had never seen much point in writing from a formal standpoint before this course. Another student said she "became more aware of technique. It helps me when I'm writing other papers, starting is not so overwhelming. I'm more aware of [rhetorical] strategies especially in introductions."

Swales said he wanted students "to find out what is needed to give a good impression." He wanted them to write up "good" findings, to know how to make claims and to leave out those that should be left out. He commented that in one of the first writing assignments "the data collection was worthwhile and the analysis first-class, but they didn't know how to deal with the analysis, didn't know what to do in writing up the data." Michele seemed to echo similar feelings when in her teaching journal she wrote that in student papers in response to an early course assignment "the biggest problem was no purpose." She continued that she found some of the students lacking in a sense of "what it all means." On the matter of style in student writing, John said surface features at the sentence level might not receive feedback but anything in the paper that was "off-register" would. In her teaching journal Michele articulated a strong stance against over-zealous marking of grammatical/mechanical errors on student papers:

> I also find that marking all grammatical/mechanical mistakes (just because a teacher can't bear not to, or because a certain problem is easy to fix once students know the rules) has to be considered with caution. Many mistakes are not due to ignorance but to carelessness. Marking grammatical mistakes constantly will give students a clear message that grammatical correctness is what you value, perhaps more than content. I'm sure there is a middle ground, but I'd rather err on the side of not over-marking grammatical mistakes.

When I talked about classroom interaction in general with these students in 316, they said they didn't participate as much in their other courses. They felt they participated more in this course partly because Swales involved himself in their writing. John encouraged the students to involve themselves in each other's writing in a variety of ways. Each set of assigned papers was put in a folder and made available for anyone in the class who wanted to examine one or all of the papers. Michele brought the folder to class and students could pick it up from her.

I discussed with Swales this approach to fostering learning in a WAC course; he said that he was narrowing "the gap between profs and students." He wanted to "give the students a forum for saying what other people may not have said before, actually original things to say." He added, "This reinforces a feeling of worth in what they (the students) are saying, helps them to analyze critically."

Biology 301

Like most other departments, when the junior-senior writing requirement was introduced the biology department had a short list of its courses that could be taken to fulfill the requirement. However, none of these was a compulsory course and increasingly it was found that students either didn't like the choices or were constrained by scheduling problems. In 1985 the department introduced "Biology 301: Writing for Biologists" to overcome these problems, and it has been taken by from sixty to a hundred students each semester during these three years. The course has so far been taught as a lecture course alternately by one member of a small group of three dedicated faculty, each assisted by a team of up to five TAs, who individually lead discussion sections.

One of the three faculty is Ed Voss, a research botanist who was, as he says, influenced while still in high school by a great journalism teacher who emphasized the importance of excellence and clarity in writing. Professor Voss feels that the sciences have a reputation for "sloppy writing" which is particularly unfortunate because writing in science requires accuracy most of all, and sloppy writing is inaccurate writing. Wordiness is another problem in a field where "it costs several cents a word to get a paper published." His course outline and his handouts reflect these concerns. In accord with the stated philosophy of Biology 301, he considers that the course is more about learning to write than about writing to learn. As we talked, however, it became clear that there is a focus on the nature of scientific endeavor, on experimental methods, the use of controls, the drawing of conclusions, and so on, although in, for example, critiquing scholarly papers the students have to be required to look for internal textual contradictions rather than external scientific ones, since they don't know the specialist field well enough for the latter.

Professor Voss stresses the relationship between correct grammar and clear meaning—his concern is for accuracy and style, and especially for appropriate evidence and style for varied assignments. He works with abstracts early in the course as a way of focusing on meaning, conciseness and clarity. For one assignment, the students read journal articles without abstracts, construct abstracts for the articles, and then see the original abstracts. Voss has never used student papers or examples from students' papers in his plethora of exemplary overheads and handouts, although TAs sometimes do so in the discussion sections for this course.

An important part of the course is the review paper, in which students are asked to choose their own topic in biology and carry out library research. Voss stresses primary sources (*Index Medicus* for the premed students; *Biological Abstracts; Science Citation Index*—not simply general periodicals) and requires ten to fifteen of them. Each student gives an oral report on his review paper in progress in the discussion sections: Voss believes that the oral presentation is good preparation for a final draft and shares our belief in the benefits of talking about your subject. He also believes that listening to your paper being read helps with stylistic choices and that reading aloud highlights editing needs. Because many students seem to be intimidated by the library, one of the developments in Biology 301 has been the inclusion of formal instruction in the use of the specialist library.

In Biology 301, students meet in two-hour sections weekly with a TA in addition to the lectures with Ed Voss. Conferencing is also done by the TA, but if a student misses a lecture she has to get the handout from Ed— "not to keep track of them but to try to get to know them." The TAs (there are often five, but the number varies with the number of enrolled students) meet weekly with him, and they pass papers around to decide the standards to be set, discuss exercises and answers, and talk about students who are having problems. The TAs have been provided with a thick handbook prepared by the team of three faculty and TAs involved in earlier courses; there is also at least one TA who has taught the course previously to lead the new ones, so Ed feels able to let the TAs get on with a fairly free hand. This supportive structure for TAs in the WAC program works very well. Each TA is given considerable freedom and responsibility, but she is also helped by both ECB/WAC faculty and biology faculty as she learns how to handle these new and critical activities.

Biology TAs, like other TAs who have them, find their discussion sections a very fruitful part of the program, both for talking about writing in the subject, and (at least as important in our experience) for getting close to the undergraduates they are working with. This closeness is increased by the biweekly conferences built into Biology 301 (which is exceptional in the junior-senior writing program). The individual conferences are highly valued by TAs and students.

Voss sees the purposes of Biology 301 as being to help the students improve their own writing and to help them learn how to critique the writing of others, acquiring a "healthy skepticism" that he finds too often lacking. As seems to be so often the case, he finds it hard to pinpoint evidence that the students' writing improves as a result of the course; he finds it necessary to have faith in the TAs to work with the students and monitor their progress. Although few students fail to certify, there is some self-pruning by students who are struggling. He tells the story of a former chair of biology who was reading letters of support from the students of TAs seeking the GSTA excellence award. He found that letters from students supporting TAs in upper-level writing courses were much better than letters from students supporting TAs in other courses.

TAs in Biology 301 find it a worthwhile though exhausting experience.

They share the concern about clarity and appropriate style to suit a particular audience with Voss and the other professors. Reading the journals of the biology TAs in the training seminar, we can see that they learn a good deal about working with students and about the discourse of their discipline. TAs believe that students in this course improve their writing, as this comment from one of them indicates: "By the end of the semester most people were submitting papers with solid organization, significant content, and appropriate examples and explanations written with the reader in mind."

/ / / / / / / / *Problems and Successes*
Liz Hamp-Lyons

My own involvement with the junior-senior program has been wholly in terms of the training of TAs, and therefore the problems and successes I see start from that perspective. The primary problem with the program is the lack of centralized control. While the ECB supervises the program, it would be a misrepresentation to say that it "controls" it. The program is entirely dependent on faculty across the disciplines being willing to propose and mount such courses, which means that in some semesters there is a shortage of courses in specific areas. Neither does the ECB control what happens in a junior-senior writing course, except in the loosest way. A new course is proposed formally and reviewed for approval by the ECB's Policy Committee, but if approved thereafter it is not monitored. Some courses incorporate a good deal of prewriting, revision, conferencing, staging of assignments, etc., while others hold to a model that looks pretty much like one in any other course with one or two long papers added. A recurring bone of contention for new TAs is that although the junior-senior writing course is a requirement for graduation, the ECB does not set standards for certification. Each faculty member in each course must make those decisions, and TAs often feel that this is too heavy a responsibility if they are asked to make such decisions, especially in their first teaching semester. Further, while we run seminars for faculty teaching in the junior-senior writing program, they cannot be required to attend: some don't, and even for those who do the seminar can provide only a very rapid survey of major issues.

At a large, major research university such as Michigan, preparation for teaching is not given a very high priority, especially since it does not figure highly in the criteria for promotion and tenure; therefore faculty members limit the amount of energy they give to these courses: this sometimes means that TAs carry more of the burden for the course than was ever intended. In a few cases, TAs are left to read and respond to student writing and make certification decisions, even to decide course grades, without having worked with the faculty member to establish criteria or standards for writing in the course. The TA sometimes does not have a section meeting with the students, and finds it hard to get to know them and encourage them to talk about their writing. Occasionally, a TA is unable to attend the lectures and is thus out of touch with the content the students are writing about. There have been scattered reports of TAs who have, after more than half a semester, been unable to find the faculty members in order to meet them.

All of these problems relate to the issue of control and spring directly from the decentralized model of the Michigan program. But for every problem there is also a success, and the greatest success is that after ten years the program is still alive and vigorous. Most of the faculty at Michigan seem still committed to excellence in writing for our graduates, and still believe that this goal is best achieved when faculty in all disciplines take responsibility for it. This continuing commitment came through powerfully in a recent survey of faculty. Faculty continue to propose and teach new courses that fulfill the requirement—Linguistics 316 by John Swales is an example—and every student is still required to fulfill the junior-senior writing requirement, ensuring that at least one course in the junior or senior year is writing-intensive.

It is now difficult for a student, whatever his major, to find a route to a degree at Michigan that substantially avoids writing. The faculty know that the program depends completely on them, and this knowledge means that departments resist the temptation to stop offering courses, to "leave it to the ECB." A loose hand on the reins of curriculum is an essential corollary of that, since if we placed too many restrictions on the shape of a junior-senior writing course, faculty and departments would be less inclined to offer such courses. Leaving the setting of certification standards to faculty and their TAs means that for every course in every semester, establishing the basis for certification is a problem that must be solved. Working to solve the problem focuses attention on the course and on questions about the relation between writing and the discipline, between writing and the other goals of the course, in a way that would not occur if those standards were more firmly set by the ECB. In the TA seminar a main focus is on criteria for writing, in the academy generally and in each discipline specifically, and on the articulation of these criteria into standards. Thus a three-way interaction is set up, between the faculty member and the ECB, through the TA.

The use of TAs in the program allows those TAs as well as the students they are working with to learn to talk about the linguistic and discoursal conventions of their discipline, and to begin to understand the reasons for those conventions. For me the greatest success of the program, and its real hope for the future, lies in the TA training seminar, in the developing specification of the essential skills a tutor-instructor of writing in a discipline needs. But even more, it lies in the group of graduate students (some experienced teachers, some very advanced in their graduate work, some dedicated professional writers) who must cope with the pressures of working with students while taking course work or writing dissertations. It is hard work, and many of them leave after a semester to take easier assistantships, but they take the experience with them. One past participant in these seminars is now on the Michigan faculty; some are teaching other upper-level writing courses; most move elsewhere when they graduate. We look on the seminar as consciousness-raising at least as much as training, and we believe that in working with each new group of TAs we are working with some college and university writing instructors of the future.

/ / / / / / / *Problems and Successes*
Eleanor McKenna

As coordinator of the WAC program, I keep the bureaucratic wheels turning as smoothly as I can and act as consultant for faculty and students on a range of issues related to the junior-senior writing courses. I am also responsible in part for training TAs and developing faculty seminars about writing instruction in the disciplines. I am in touch on a daily basis with faculty and students in the disciplines as well as administrators in each department. I serve as liaison between the ECB Policy Committee and faculty proposing new courses during proposal review procedures each semester.

I agree with Liz that one of the greatest successes of the WAC program at Michigan is in the training of TAs to assist faculty in writing-intensive courses, but this training needs to be continually improved. The greatest challenge I see is to explore even more ways to support faculty who introduce extensive writing in their courses.

Liz has also raised some very specific concerns about the WAC program—the same concerns that I hear almost daily from people with various perspectives on the junior-senior writing program. When I respond to such concerns, as I will here, I draw on the various perspectives my position as coordinator allows. First, centralized "control" of faculty in the disciplines is not and never has been at issue in the junior-senior writing program at Michigan. The ECB need make no decisions about keeping "a loose hand on the reins" on curriculum or faculty in the disciplines when it comes to what and how they teach in writing-intensive courses. The question of centralized control was settled when it was collectively decided that only faculty in the disciplines would make certification decisions. They would decide whether or not students in their courses had satisfied the junior-senior writing requirement needed for graduation based on criteria and standards for certification set within their individual courses. ECB faculty are never involved in certifying that a student has or hasn't fulfilled the junior-senior writing requirement, although we do act as consultants and give support in a variety of ways to help students certify when we are asked. Guidelines for the design of upper-level courses have indeed been set by the ECB faculty in the role of writing specialists. These guidelines, however, are fairly basic—amount of writing and types of assignments. If these basic guidelines were not met, a course could hardly qualify as writing-intensive. Individually, ECB faculty can act as consultants to faculty in the disciplines on matters of course design, and they often do when new courses are proposed. However, the ECB Policy Committee, comprised mainly of faculty from other disciplines, now makes decisions on the approval of new courses.

The ECB does control funding for TAs in the disciplines who assist in approved courses, and faculty have to ask for this funding from the ECB. Sometimes this hand on the purse strings can be used as a measure of control. As a condition of funding, the ECB requires TAs new to junior-senior writing courses to take the training seminars discussed above. (Only if a TA is funded by the ECB does this requirement apply.) In general, then, we can better say that the ECB collaborates with faculty in the disciplines in directing the WAC program.

The central issue here, as I see it, is not one of control but of responsibility. I too am aware of faculty in the disciplines who take the writing requirement lightly and who exploit the assistance of TAs: the course instructor (new to the program) who does not respond to repeated invitations to attend faculty seminars on writing in the disciplines, for example, then claims to know little about the ECB (when asked by his TA) except that it is "a bureaucratic agency which requires training and with whom (I) must dicker to get funds"; the course instructor whose assignments on the new course proposal submitted to ECB don't match the papers his TA is working with in the training seminar is another example. But for every irresponsible instructor there are many who are responsible. Some faculty in our junior-senior courses have been working with student writing, tirelessly it seems, since the establishment of the program.

Second, if TAs are taking on more responsibility in dealing with student writing, this is not necessarily negative. The quality of writing instruction from many of these TAs is excellent in terms of the amount and quality of conference time they give students. The problem arises sometimes when TAs' involvement *replaces* that of faculty in writing instruction altogether, especially when a TA is inexperienced. But many courses work well with faculty supervising groups of assistants (as in Biology 301) or one assistant (as in Linguistics 316). Finally, experience in teaching writing doesn't necessarily produce good writing teachers. Some of the most insightful readings of student papers (from descriptions in teaching journals) come from TAs in the training seminar with no formal writing instruction background.

When we contemplate the diversity and decentralization at Michigan and the nature of the student body and faculty, the idea of a single set of criteria and standards for certification in all junior-senior writing courses seems unlikely. If we then contemplate the complexity of written communication in the diverse communities formed at this university, a single set of criteria and standards seems impossible. But there is a great deal of common ground among these diverse communities. Focusing on the differences among disciplines—differences in the nature and structure of theories and applications of theories, support for those theories, as well as differences in conventions—tends to obscure this common ground. For this reason, in the TA/training seminar we start the training with an examination of common factors in academic communication and move slowly toward developing particular criteria and standards that relate not only to a particular course but to individual assignments within that course. Nevertheless, despite this careful movement from general to particular criteria and standards using material first from two disciplines in LS&A then assignments and papers from the TAs' courses, some TAs still look to the ECB to set criteria and standards for their assignments. In a survey of TAs at the end of the training seminars one writes about her relationship with the students in her course:

> I think I have a good working relationship with my students. They are putting quite a bit of effort into making improvements in their first drafts; and they want to learn how to improve their writing. At times, they may feel my standards are too exacting, but I make an effort to justify all my criticism and suggestions. Having ECB handouts to appeal to as the "authoritative word" on matters of style and criteria on which papers are graded has made this a lot easier. Criticism is easier for them when they know I go to training sessions and I try to work with them to get their writing up to "ECB" standards.

This despite our focus in the seminar on the consultancy nature of the ECB's role in setting standards within particular courses. The ECB's expertise in helping establish criteria and standards is central to the process in the WAC program, but the final responsibility (that word again) rests with faculty and TAs in the disciplines.

THE FUTURE

As a starting point in the writing-across-the-curriculum program at Michigan, we acknowledge and accept the way things are at large research universities and at large teaching universities: faculty are under intense pressure to produce research and obtain research grants on the one hand while, on the other, managing teaching loads that leave little extra time for writing courses that are labor-intensive and time-consuming. Therefore, one goal in the writing-across-the-curriculum program is to exploit existing but underused support for writing-intensive courses; another major goal is to find every conceivable way of extending that support.

To this end, our writing workshops faculty have established themselves in places other than the central ECB office facility. They are available for writing conferences in the dorms, in the undergraduate library, and in word-processing labs on campus. Our after hours writing workshop means students no longer have to get help with papers only during regular business hours. We are lobbying hard for as much space as possible in an extensive word processing lab complex now under construction. We propose to establish a new kind of workshop lab in this complex, staffing it with ECB faculty and specially trained TAs from across disciplines. We want to offer workshop labs to course instructors so that they can assign course time for supervised writing. (We will be proposing that their teaching assistants and ECB faculty do the supervising and give conference time where needed.)

In addition to exploiting our existing workshop program, we have begun to do the same with our relatively new peer tutoring program. The peer tutors have established times when they are regularly available on a walk-in basis or by appointment. They have established too a highly visible place of their own in the undergraduate library with the cooperation of the library staff. This program is being advertised as an extension of the workshop support for students in writing-intensive courses. We target in this advertising campaign those TAs who are assisting in writing-intensive courses for the first time so they can take full advantage of the support available here. We are talking in training seminars with teaching assistants about the strengths they bring to discussion in conferences with students about the writing process: their knowledge of subject matters; their intuitions about the nature of text structure and argument in individual discourse communities. But we also relieve them of the worry that they must suddenly become experts in style and grammar to do a good job, and lay out for them instead how they can utilize the ECB faculty's specialized training in rhetoric and grammar and the specialized training of the peer tutors. We are advising faculty who fret about doing (in the words of one faculty member) "the English department's work," that we stand ready through the workshop and peer tutoring programs to help their students learn to edit their work for style and grammar. In faculty seminars we use a variety of materials to trigger discussion on the difference between using writing to learn in their courses and teaching the basics of writing style.

Our efforts at improving writing in the disciplines are not confined to the junior-senior writing program. That was the starting point a decade ago. On request we now conduct seminars in tutoring writing for teaching assistants who work with student writers at any level of undergraduate study. We give seminars in tutoring writing in campuswide conferences for faculty involved in TA training programs. Some ECB faculty are experimenting with "linked" courses: linking their introductory composition courses to introductory courses in the natural and social sciences, usually large introductory lecture courses. In these courses ECB faculty work closely with the subject matter of the writing assignments. They attend the lectures and discussion sections so when they work with their composition students the focus is on disciplinary content.

As we hope you can see from this whirlwind tour of the Michigan writing program, we are committed to the extensive use of writing as a way of learning at every level of study during our students' college years.

We consult also with Schools outside of LSA about writing programs for different levels of college study. The Music School, for example, recently asked us about the feasibility of implementing a writing requirement for their sophomores. We are not even limiting our efforts to improving undergraduate writing. In 1989 we will begin to extend our efforts to graduate student writing. We proposed to the graduate school that we extend our workshop services for undergraduates to graduates across disciplines on an experimental basis. The graduate school accepted our proposal and we are preparing to go ahead on a new front.

We are committed to the extensive use of writing as a way of learning at every level of college study. We will continue to recruit heavily for WAC courses. As a postscript, we are discovering that TAs might represent an unexplored source for recruiting WAC courses in the future. For example, one department this spring term, because of a series of unrelated changes within the department, had not been able to schedule even one of their usual course offerings to fulfill the junior-senior requirement for fall term. Discussions between the chair of that department and the ECB produced no remedy. But a newly trained TA from our seminar in tutoring writing in the disciplines, without being aware of the problem with course offerings, convinced a professor in that department to offer an upper-level course as a junior-senior writing course for fall term. She convinced the professor that she had experience and training in tutoring writing and could assist with the assignments in that course. She secured a position for herself and did the junior-senior program some good at the same time.

NOTES

1. This section was prepared drawing on unpublished papers describing the program and discussion with colleagues who have been associated with the English Com-

position Board in various roles since its inception. An unpublished paper by Professor Dan Fader, the English Composition Board's first director and member of the original Composition Board ("Scribo, Ergo Sum"), has been central in the preparation of this section.

2. Bailey, R. B. "This Teaching Works" (For the English Composition Board, 1981, Mimeographed).

3. Patricia L. Stock. "The University of Michigan." In *Teaching Writing in the Content Areas: College Level*, edited by Stephen N. Tchudi. Washington, D.C.: National Educational Association 1986.

4. Helen Isaacson. "The Junior/Senior Writing Course: A Manual for Faculty." (Prepared for the English Composition Board, the University of Michigan, 1987).

/ / / / / / / / / *Chapter* ***14***

The Baltimore Area Consortium

*Barbara E. Walvoord and H. Fil Dowling, Jr. with John
Breihan, Virginia Johnson Gazzam, Carl E. Henderson,
Gertrude B. Hopkins, Barbara Mallonee, and Sally McNelis*

> *As it matures, the consortium is moving in two major
> directions—toward greater involvement in research and
> toward expertise in broader, interconnected areas such as
> critical thinking and reading abilities.*

Institution: *Towson State University for BACWAC*
Institutional Size—Students (FTES):   15,500
Institutional Size—Faculty (FTEF):   880
Student/Faculty Ratio: 18:1
Highest Degree Granted—
    Institution: M.A.
Highest Degree Granted—English
    Department: M.A.
Public or Private Institution: Public

Institutional Mission: provides comprehensive opportunities
for undergraduate and graduate education and offers a variety of programs in the traditional arts and sciences and in
specialized professional fields.

For more information on the program described in this
chapter, contact: H. Fil Dowling, Jr., Department of English, Towson State University, Baltimore, MD 21204.

This chapter is intended as a guide to consortium building. It reflects the experience of the Baltimore Area Consortium for Writing Across the Curriculum (BACWAC), headquartered at Loyola College in Maryland (1980–82) and at Towson State University (1982–present). The consortium, an arm of the Maryland Writing Project, also based at Towson State, has for eight years been serving its members—more than twenty Baltimore-area colleges, community colleges, and universities, as well as virtually all the public and private school districts of Baltimore and the surrounding counties. This essay will show how a consortium is a valuable asset for writing across the curriculum, either alone or in tandem with a National Writing Project site. Figure 14–1 shows BACWAC members, four of whom are also presented in fuller profile. A fifth consortium member, Prince George's Community College, is described in Chapter 4 of this volume.

The main reason for forming a consortium is to help schools operate cost-effective yet productive writing-across-the-curriculum programs. Consider how such programs usually develop in a region lacking a consortium, as was the case in Baltimore before BACWAC's founding in 1980. Indigenous efforts by a college's or school's own faculty are brave and sometimes effective, but are hampered by isolation and lack of funds. Funding for extensive faculty training usually occurs only when a grant proposal is successful. Expensive outside speakers and consultants are brought in, a program is built from the ground up, it runs until the grant runs out, then most of it is disbanded. If a college five miles down the road then gets a grant, it builds its own program and expertise the same way. Often the two campuses don't even know about each other's programs.

If there is a National Writing Project site in the region, the situation may be more positive. However, a consortium can help a National Writing site extend school-college and cross-disciplinary collaboration. The typical National Writing Project is run from a single college campus, with strong participation and perhaps codirectorship from the surrounding K–12 school districts. The National Writing Project holds annual, intensive, credit-bearing five-week summer institutes to train "teacher-consultants," primarily K–12, who in turn serve as presenters and coordinators for less intensive workshops or credit-bearing courses in surrounding K–12 schools during the academic year. The summer institute tries to award a stipend for teachers, but even if it doesn't, K–12 teachers are earning academic credit, and most are receiving at least partial tuition rebate from their home schools.

Figure 14–1

A Profile of Selected BACWAC Member Schools, 1980–1987

K–12 School Districts and Associations
Association of Independent Maryland Schools (representative schools):
    Calverton School 2, 3, 4, 5, 6, 7, 9, 10, 12, 13
    Park School 2, 3, 4, 5, 6, 8, 9, 10, 12, 13
    Roland Park Country School 2, 3, 4, 5, 6, 8, 9, 11, 12, 13
Baltimore City Public School (representative school):
    Baltimore City College High School
      2, 3, 4, 5, 6, 9, 10, 11, 12, 13
Baltimore County Public Schools (representative school):
    Perry Hall High School 2, 3, 4, 5, 6, 7, 8, 9, 10, 11, 13
Catholic Schools in the Archdiocese of Baltimore
    (representative school):
    Calvert Hall 2, 3, 4, 5, 6, 8, 9, 10, 11, 13
Harford County Public Schools 2, 3, 4 (MWP), 5, 9

Community Colleges
Anne Arundel Community College 2, 3, 5, 6, 9, 12
Catonsville Community College 2, 3, 4, 5, 8, 9, 12, 13
Chesapeake College (new member) 3 (four faculty), 5, 11, 13
Community College of Baltimore 1, 2, 3, 5, 8, 10, 11, 12
Dundalk Community College 2, 3, 5, 9, 10, 13
Essex Community College 1, 2, 12
Harford Community College 2, 3, 4, 6, 12
Howard Community College 2, 8, 9, 11
Montgomery Community College 1, 4
Prince George's Community College 1, 2, 5, 6, 7, 8, 9, 11, 13

State Colleges and Universities
Coppin State College 1, 2, 3, 4, 5, 6, 8, 9, 10, 12
Morgan State University 1, 2, 3, 4, 5, 6, 8, 9, 12, 13
Towson State University 1, 2, 3, 5, 6, 7, 9, 12, 13
University of Baltimore 1, 2, 3, 5, 6, 9, 12, 13

Private Colleges and Universities
College of Notre Dame of Maryland 1, 2, 3, 4, 5, 6, 9, 11
Goucher College 2, 3, 4, 5, 6, 7, 8, 9, 10, 11, 13
Lincoln University (PA) 1, 4, 5
Loyola College in Maryland 1, 2, 3, 4, 5, 6, 7, 9, 12, 13
Mount St. Mary's College 5, 6, 8, 10
Villa Julie College 2, 3, 5, 8, 9, 11, 12, 13
Washington College 2, 4, 5, 6, 8, 9, 11, 13
Western Maryland College 4, 5, 6, 9, 10, 11, 12, 13   *(Continued)*

BACWAC Services:

1. School sent at least one faculty member to the 1982 or 1983 semester-long BACWAC institute (30 contract hours).
2. School hosted at least one WAC workshop using BACWAC presenters on its own campus.
3. At least ten faculty from the school have attended BACWAC meetings or workshops away from campus.
4. School used BACWAC personnel as consultants to help plan its WAC program.

    Note: Since K–12 schools usually make heavier use of MWP training than BACWAC training, numbers 1–4 in K–12 schools reflect use of both BACWAC and MWP services.

WAC Activities

5. School had at least one of its own faculty make a WAC presentation at its own school.
6. School had at least one of its own faculty make a WAC presentation to an audience away from its own school.
7. School had at least one faculty member publish something about WAC in an off-campus publication.
8. School effected a change in its curriculum as a result of WAC activity.
9. School has documented changes in teacher classroom behavior as a result of WAC activity.
10. School has made changes in procedures for institutional assessment of writing as a result of WAC activity.
11. School has established or made changes in a writing center as a result of WAC activity.
12. School has had one of its faculty serve on the BACWAC steering committee.
13. School has distributed written information about WAC to its faculty.

However, college faculty cannot use master's level academic credit, nor do such faculty automatically receive remission of tuition from their employing schools. Because their efforts to improve their pedagogy are less highly rewarded than publication in their disciplines, they are loath to devote a summer to a pedagogical institute, especially if most of its participants are K–12 English teachers.

A second problem is that, though a National Writing Project site often establishes a WAC program on the home campus, it may be difficult to extend that program to nearby colleges and universities and then to bring about coordination between faculty at those campuses and the K–12 teachers in their regions.

The consortium model offers a way to address these problems, whether or not it works in conjunction with a National Writing Project site. In this model, a consortium of coequal schools, elementary through university, pools resources to support writing programs in all of them.

ESTABLISHING THE CONSORTIUM

A basic principle is to work from the bottom. Committed teachers and lower-level administrators are the ones who will make the consortium work. BAC-WAC began in 1980 when three friends, representing two local colleges and the Baltimore public schools, invited twenty colleagues from other institutions, elementary through university, to an informal meeting to share information and discuss ways to collaborate. Committees were formed to write a constitution, gather other interested teachers, and submit a grant proposal for a National Writing Project site. Monthly meetings drew a close-knit, enthusiastic crowd. Each person tapped his or her institution for membership dues (now $175 per year per college or school district). Membership entitled the school to have its faculty vote or hold BACWAC office and to pay reduced fees for workshops sponsored by the consortium.

GOVERNANCE

BACWAC has been led by an unpaid, six- or nine-member steering committee, elected by the membership for a one-year, renewable term, and equally representing K–12, community college, and college levels. For daily administration, the steering committee elects an unpaid coordinator, who serves a three-year term. The coordinator's campus—or in BACWAC's case the Maryland Writing Project—serves as fiscal agent and headquarters.

BACWAC's experience indicates that both the coordinatorship of the consortium and the coordinatorship of its workshops/institutes must be *strong* and *consistent* positions, while the steering committee must be *large, revolving*, and *representative*. The three coordinators of the consortium who have served since 1980 have provided stability, consistency, and leadership. The coordinator must be patient with the frustrations of trying to communicate and negotiate decisions and actions with teachers and administrators from a variety of schools who often don't pay attention to what's in their mailboxes, forget what BACWAC is from one year to the next, don't return things on time, and ask innocently, "What do we get for all that dues money, anyway?"

Filling the second strong position, the coordinator of workshops and institutes must be familiar with the presenters trained in the institutes, must be tactful about selecting only the best presenters to send out to campus workshops, must know the network of writing-across-the-curriculum activists in all the member schools, and must be a good organizer.

Service on the Steering Committee is one of the best ways to engage the informed commitment of a person and that person's school, and to provide workers for BACWAC activities. Coordinators were at first afraid that a large steering committee might prove unwieldy, but experience has proved otherwise.

RELATIONSHIP TO A NATIONAL WRITING PROJECT SITE

BACWAC launched the Maryland Writing Project in 1980, but today BACWAC is an arm of the MWP. The Maryland Writing Project, with its more complex activities and large grant-fed budget, needs a more centralized governance than BACWAC. Led by codirectors who receive salary or released time, and based at Towson State University, the Maryland Writing Project operates a highly successful program following the traditional National Writing Project model discussed earlier, with summer institutes, courses and workshops in local K–12 schools during the year, summer workshops for student writers, an institute for teacher-researchers, monthly meetings for teacher-consultants, a newsletter, and a biennial writing conference that attracts teachers from English and other disciplines, elementary through college. BACWAC members are often involved in Maryland Writing Project activities. BACWAC, with its more democratic governance, operates within the MWP and carries out the four main activities discussed in the next section.

BACWAC PROGRAMS

The Consortium's four major activities help the Maryland Writing Project to serve the unique needs of college faculty, to involve faculty at community colleges and colleges other than Towson, and to encourage contacts between those faculty and K–12 teachers. BACWAC's programs reflect a wide variety of philosophies and approaches to teaching, but there are some dominant themes: writing is viewed as a process, as a mode of learning, as the making of meaning, and as a social act shaped by its context. Classroom teachers are treated as equals and professionals, no matter what their disciplines or levels of teaching. Workshops are participatory and practical. Workshop leaders function as classroom teachers talking to teaching colleagues.

Academic Year Institutes. The Consortium runs institutes that meet during the year rather than during the summer and that draw primarily college, community college, and some high school teachers from disciplines outside English. (Maryland Writing Project runs the summer institutes, located at Towson; they draw primarily K–12 English teachers, though BACWAC activities have helped them draw several college-level non-English teachers.) Typically, an institute will meet for two or three hours once a week for a semester. Faculty participants sometimes obtain released time from their home schools. Institute locations are rotated among member schools to demonstrate the consortium-based nature of the institute.

The BACWAC institutes can succeed because college faculty unwilling to give up a summer will attend an institute during the school year, especially if the college grants them some released time—often easier for the college to find than a large summer stipend. Each BACWAC member college paid only $250 to have a faculty member attend a thirty-hour semester-long institute—including doughnuts at each meeting. Since 1980 the consortium has sponsored two institutes, with a total of twenty-eight participants representing fifteen colleges, community colleges, and high schools. More than half the graduates are non-English teachers. In addition, BACWAC has worked closely with the NEH-funded summer institutes at Loyola College from 1982 to 1985.

Workshops on Campuses. Using non-English faculty presenters trained through BACWAC and Loyola College institutes, BACWAC, at the request of member institutions, has provided twenty writing-across-the-curriculum workshops on fifteen college and community college campuses. The fee to the school can be kept reasonable, since a single administrative structure and a single corps of trained presenters serve all the campuses.

In addition, BACWAC-trained faculty have made presentations at eleven local conferences and at a number of national and regional professional conferences. Five of the non-English faculty and a number of the English faculty have published essays about writing across the curriculum in professional journals. Institute graduates have organized programs on their own campuses.

The Fall Conference. At the consortium's fall conference (held on a Thursday afternoon from four to six), everyone on BACWAC or the Maryland Writing Project's mailing list is invited to a central location to hear BACWAC presenters trained in the institutes. These well-attended conferences lead to invitations for writing-across-the-curriculum workshops on various campuses. The conference includes a BACWAC business meeting and offers a structured opportunity for participants to form writers' groups and special-interest groups that may continue to meet independently throughout the year.

Nationally Known Speakers. BACWAC sponsors an annual February meeting, featuring a nationally known speaker who offers a general hour-long talk to a large crowd and, the next day, a daylong workshop or two half-day workshops for twenty-five to sixty participants. At this meeting college, community college, and K–12 people mingle with one another. The location has rotated among member schools and colleges to demonstrate the consortium base. The Thursday speech is free (BACWAC dues cover the cost); the Friday daylong workshop costs schools from $25 to $35 per person, including lunch. Attention to detail and a sense of elegance in refreshments, meeting rooms, and other details are BACWAC trademarks. As John Trimbur, an early BACWAC steering committee member, always said, "The consortium that eats together stays together."

BACWAC'S PROBLEMS

Here are some difficulties that a consortium may face:

1. We learned the hard way how important it is to properly initiate steering committee members at the beginning of their terms, to keep them all engaged in worthwhile activities, and to insist that they regularly attend committee meetings. At one point, we initiated a rule that any steering committee member who missed three meetings would be automatically replaced. We also have published the monthly meeting time before elections, and elected only those people who were free to come at that time; otherwise, there's little likelihood that nine academic schedules can be made to coincide.

2. Getting dues from all the member colleges has been an ongoing hassle. Our best successes have come when we have presented the request to the chief academic officer as an invoice, not as a letter, and have notified a loyal consortium contact person at each institution who can follow up if dues are not forthcoming. One year, when a financially hard-pressed college had cut from the institutional budget all money for organizational memberships, one activist on that campus squeezed the consortium's dues out of her department's budget for paper. This is the kind of ground-level support that the consortium must nurture at every member school.

3. Demonstrating to member schools what they get back for their dues, to members what BACWAC is all about, and to funding agencies what has been achieved requires more careful record-keeping than a volunteer organization with rotating leadership can easily handle. A "history and records" subcommittee of the steering committee might work, though we've not yet tried it.

4. Elections of steering committee members are something of a charade, since most of those voting at the annual meeting don't know the nominees and many have come just to hear the speaker, and may not have attended any consortium meetings previously. So a strong nomi-

nating committee is important, and ours now nominates just one person for each spot (accepting, however, nominations from the floor). Nonetheless, the election does place the governance procedures before the scrutiny of large numbers of people, reinforcing the concept that this is a democratic consortium, not one school's pocket borough.

5. Our current membership list is outdated and full of names of people who have left the area—or this vale of tears altogether. We don't have the records or the staff or the computer capability to update it easily. Volunteers have recently computerized the mailing list on personal computers, and the new plan is for steering committee members to divide the responsibility of contracting people and updating the list. We should have collected better records of attendees at meetings, used personal computers in the first place rather than a quirky and often inaccessible institutional mainframe, and had committee members who were fanatics for detail take charge of ongoing updates of the list.

6. Quality control of presentations is crucial but difficult. Someone must decide which of the institute graduates is to be used for the presentation at Dundalk Community College next week and at Goucher College the week after. The coordinator of workshops must be strong, knowledgeable about the presenters, and willing to make tough choices. Most presentations are made by the six or seven non-English consortium graduates who have become most experienced at presentations before other faculty. English faculty are less in demand because they have less credibility in front of an audience of non-English teachers—the normal audience of BACWAC workshops. A serious attempt must be made to use the talents of nonpresenters or they will fall away. One can work them into the governance structure or ask them to help plan and organize activities, plan workshops for their own campuses, or write for a newsletter. A Maryland Writing Project-sponsored research institute has also engaged the efforts of some BACWAC institute graduates. In the research institute, about twenty-five teachers, elementary through university, meet to encourage one another's classroom research efforts. BACWAC has also sponsored writer's groups, which meet to read and respond to one another's writing, and special-interest groups, which meet to discuss special topics or readings.

7. To make institutes attractive to faculty is challenging. Two BACWAC institutes were successful—one for non-English faculty under a Danforth grant that awarded a small stipend, and one that enrolled mostly English teachers without a stipend. However, the most recent institute attempt, again for non-English faculty, failed for lack of enrollment. The consortium had no stipends and no way of helping hard-pressed colleges to support released time for the participants. Faculty are reluctant to commit themselves to a thirty-hour institute during a semester in which

they have no reduced load and no stipend. The one point at which the consortium, therefore, is dependent on grant funding is to offer stipends or released time for faculty participants in the institutes.

BACWAC's ACHIEVEMENTS AND FUTURE

When the consortium began, the Baltimore area contained two schools that had writing-across-the-curriculum programs and many that wanted to, but didn't know how to begin. In the intervening eight years, as Figure 14–1 shows, virtually all of the twenty-odd area college and community college campuses have had at least one faculty workshop, most under BACWAC auspices, and most of the campuses have developed strong programs with regular follow-up meetings, additional workshops for faculty, writing-intensive courses, and other features. Most school districts, both public and private, have at least some middle and/or high schools that have had workshops for faculty across the curriculum. Consortium meetings bring together faculty from K–12 with college and community college faculty, historically black with historically white colleges, and college and community college faculty with one another. The consortium continues to attract a steady membership, good attendance at its meetings, and dedicated leaders. The fact that a number of campuses have asked for a second or even third workshop illustrates that BACWAC's work is not done when it has led one workshop on each member campus. The consortium continues to be a strong and well-respected force within the region.

As it matures, the consortium is moving in two major directions—toward greater involvement in research, and toward expertise in broader, interconnected areas, such as critical thinking and reading abilities. Under the leadership of Barbara Walvoord, a group of six faculty from three BACWAC institutions is currently writing a book presenting the results of a four-year study that investigated the writing and thinking processes of college students as they completed college writing assignments in courses in a variety of disciplines. Half a dozen other pairs of researchers, some including non-English faculty, are also at work on research, some of which is resulting in conference presentations and/or in publications. In turn, these research results are becoming the spur for new and more varied presentations to be taken to workshops on member campuses. The greatest challenges now facing BACWAC are to offer another institute to increase the presenter pool, and to serve the changing needs of those member campuses that now have maturing writing-across-the-curriculum programs and have already had BACWAC's basic workshop.

In the next section, four representative institutions reflect on how BACWAC helped them develop writing across the curriculum at their schools.

/ / / / / / / /   ***Towson State University***

H. Fil Dowling, Jr., and
Virginia Johnson Gazzam

The Baltimore Area Consortium came along at just the right time to give a significant boost to Towson State University's writing-across-the-curriculum efforts.

Towson State is a comprehensive university with 15,000 students. It offers a variety of programs in the liberal arts and sciences and in several specialized professional fields. Beginning in 1976, every student was required to take a discipline-specific advanced writing course, but significant training for the faculty across the disciplines who would teach these advanced writing courses was lacking. BACWAC has helped train these faculty. In 1981, Dowling, after attending the first Maryland Writing Project summer institute, was named coordinator of Towson's Advanced Writing Course Program. He then became codirector of the 1982 BACWAC institute, drawing as participants five Towson State faculty from three departments (including Gazzam from biology). One other Towson State faculty attended the 1983 BACWAC institute. These participants helped form a strong core for Towson's writing-across-the-curriculum program: all teach writing or advanced writing courses in their disciplines; four have served on Towson's cross-disciplinary advanced writing course subcommittee; several have led workshops; two have authored conference presentations or publications on writing; one supervises a department's second writing course; two are involved in research on writing; and one, Keith Martin, in 1986 became codirector of the Maryland Writing Project.

After the initial two intensive BACWAC workshops, Towson State has continued to offer daylong and two-day workshops each January, for faculty in all disciplines, using Towson faculty and sometimes BACWAC presenters from other institutions. The workshops have been so well received that, typically, over thirty faculty voluntarily attend on their own time and without remuneration. Dowling, as advanced writing course coordinator, using the consortium model of "teacher-consultant" rather than "supervisor," works with faculty across disciplines by participating in classrooms, watching assignments develop, doing the writing assignments along with the class, and talking to the students and the instructor about writing and learning in that classroom.

/ / / / / / / /   ***Perry Hall High School***

Sally McNelis

A resourceful principal, a $3,000 Carnegie Foundation grant, the words of Ernest Boyer, and the response of BACWAC to the plea of a would-be in-service coordinator shaped the Perry Hall High School writing-across-the-curriculum program, upon which the total Baltimore County School System would base its program.

Perry Hall is a large, suburban high school of approximately 1,800 students with diverse socioeconomic backgrounds. Its writing-across-the-curriculum project, begun in 1984, was sponsored by Principal James Bowerman and coordinated by two members of the English department. Ernest Boyer's focus on the centrality of language provided a vehicle for this high school staff to use language as the medium through which subject-matter learning takes place. The first forty-eight-contact-hour in-service program involved fifteen teachers from disciplines as diverse as social studies, business education, special education, and science. English teachers were invited to participate only to the extent that they would be resource teachers in disciplines not represented in the in-service program. BACWAC provided three speakers who demonstrated practical applications in all content areas.

Barbara Walvoord also coached the leadership on the need to establish ownership of the program among participants; the English department leadership had to end. And so it did. An advisory board was elected and soon teachers from content areas outside English were in charge of the staff development and growth of writing across the curriculum at Perry Hall High School.

The consortium influence continues to be felt at Perry Hall. Two BACWAC teachers have returned to present workshops for the entire faculty. Perry Hall teachers have participated in BACWAC programs twice a year since 1984. Perry Hall's writing-across-the-curriculum program is now directed by a social studies teacher; a recent in-service course was planned and coordinated by a social studies/English teacher team. The direction is clear for these committed teachers and school-level administrators. Curriculum improvement is a priority at Perry Hall High School, and its success is a tribute to the solid foundation of a staff development program nurtured by BACWAC.

/ / / / / / / *Loyola College*

John R. Breihan,
Barbara Mallonee, and
Barbara E. Walvoord

A college that hopes to establish a strong writing-across-the-curriculum program profits by initiating consortium activity, as Loyola's example illustrates.

Loyola is a medium-sized, very selective Catholic college in Baltimore. In 1980, Walvoord, a new Loyola faculty member, initiated Loyola's first faculty WAC seminar. Mallonee and Breihan, both members of that first Loyola seminar, became codirectors with Walvoord of the first BACWAC seminar. Then they won for Loyola a six-year NEH grant.

The grant project used summer seminars plus yearlong pairings between faculty in writing and in other disciplines to bring about growth and change in teaching. Participants could choose between two types of pairings: In Type-A pairs, a single group of twenty freshman students were enrolled in composition and in another core course (for example, history); the instructors blended the two courses into one six-hour semester-long or three-hour yearlong writing-intensive experience. In Type-B pairs, the writing instructor served as consultant to the instructor of an upper-class course in a discipline. The reexamination, growth, and change that occurred as pairs struggled over course plans and responses to student papers ensured that the excitement and ideas generated in the summer seminar were translated into genuine, enduring change. (For a deeper insight into the struggles of one pair, see Barbara Mallonee and John Breihan, "Responding to Students' Drafts: Interdisciplinary Consensus," *CCC* 36 [1985]: 213–31.)

Many of the pairs systematically observed their students to answer questions about student writing and learning. Colleagues from other BACWAC schools then became involved in similar collaborations, all nourished by the Maryland Writing Project's teacher-researcher seminars. Improved teaching as well as several published articles resulted. Walvoord and five other instructors, representing five disciplines and three BACWAC colleges, are now collaboratively authoring a book that reports their four-year study of college students' thinking and writing in classrooms across disciplines and institutions. The project grew out of a Loyola pairing. (For further description of this and other BACWAC and Loyola collaborative research, see Lucille McCarthy and Barbara Walvoord, "Models for Collaborative Research in Writing Across the Curriculum," in *Strengthening Programs in Writing Across the Curriculum*, edited by Susan McLeod [San Francisco: Jossey-Bass, 1988].)

The NEH project also included a survey of faculty attitudes/practices both before and after the project, and a collaboratively written handbook about writing in every discipline at Loyola. Both these aspects extended the research and the collaborative emphasis of the project.

In addition to the research collaborations that grew out of Loyola-BACWAC-MWP cooperation, there were other interchanges. BACWAC semester-long institutes helped train several Loyola faculty, who then went on to become leaders in the Loyola/NEH project. BACWAC provided presenters for Loyola summer institutes, and in turn, faculty who had participated in the Loyola summer institutes enlarged BACWAC's pool of presenters. Money and audiences were combined to bring outside speakers. Loyola's leadership in the consortium enhanced the college's local visibility and the impact of its NEH project. Certainly, from Loyola's standpoint, involving neighboring—even rival—campuses in a consortium effort has brought significant advantages.

/ / / / / / / /   *Harford Community College*
Gertrude B. Hopkins and
Carl E. Henderson

The roots of writing across the curriculum at Harford Community College lie in a sabbatical leave by an enthusiastic English instructor who became involved in the Maryland Writing Project and the Baltimore Area Consortium for Writing Across the Curriculum.

Gertrude B. Hopkins, associate professor of English at Harford, received a sabbatical leave to examine new theories in the teaching of writing. As a Summer Fellow in the MWP, she met BACWAC members who shared her interest in establishing strong writing-across-the-curriculum programs. Ms. Hopkins' enthusiasm for promoting WAC, fueled by her BACWAC colleagues, was contagious on the HCC campus. She encouraged other faculty, including Carl Henderson, who became an MWP Summer Fellow and a member of the BACWAC steering committee. These common experiences helped establish a philosophical basis on which to build a program at Harford.

Ms. Hopkins' efforts, coupled with earlier work done by James Galbraith, an HCC English professor and past president of the Maryland Association of Departments of English, created, in the minds of the HCC administration, a strong interest in developing a WAC program on our campus.

This convergence of activities resulted in the establishment of a collegewide writing lab that includes computer-assisted instruction. In addition, HCC strengthened its ties to BACWAC when Barbara Walvoord conducted a workshop in the spring of 1987 for HCC mathematics faculty who wanted to use writing in the classroom. Then Harford hosted the fall 1987 BACWAC meeting during which Homer H. Morris, associate dean for humanistic studies and Carl Henderson demonstrated the use of the Writer's Workbench software in teaching writing.

Thus, Harford continues to strengthen its functional relationship with the Baltimore Area Consortium for Writing Across the Curriculum which began with a meaningful dialogue between colleagues.

The Enemies of Writing Across the Curriculum

Art Young and Toby Fulwiler

The fourteen writing-across-the-curriculum programs in this volume tell us of a renewed academic spirit on college campuses, of a genuine sense of inter-disciplinary community, of increased opportunity and expectations for student writers, of increased commitment to undergraduate teaching by faculty. They tell us of programs designed not only to improve student writing, but because writing is integral to other academic activities, of programs designed to improve student learning, reading, speaking, listening, critical thinking, and problem solving as well. They tell us of programs designed to enable students to master the content as well as the discourse of various disciplines—that is, to master accounting or zoology even as they learn to read, write, think, and solve problems like an accountant or zoologist.

Then why the need for an "Afterword" with such an ominous title? The need arises from the experiences shared with us by numerous colleagues from varied institutions across the country. Almost everyone that has administered a writing-across-the-curriculum program knows that such programs can create a better academic environment for both students and faculty and achieve ringing campus endorsement. But we also know that writing across the curriculum is still an adjunct program on most campuses, still on tenuous budgetary footing, still without clear administrative positioning within the academy, still, as it were, operating on the fringe of academic respectability. Undoubtedly, some of the success of writing across the curriculum is due to its easy ability to cross disciplinary lines and bureaucratic structures to bring teachers and students from across campus together around teaching and learning practices central to education in all disciplines. However, we need to recognize certain problems germane to writing across the curriculum, problems that threaten its effectiveness and staying power.

UNCERTAIN LEADERSHIP

Specially trained or retrained faculty often act as program administrators for writing across the curriculum and/or as teachers of upper-level writing courses. The experience, expertise, and leadership of these people are a necessary ingredient of a successful program. Writing-across-the-curriculum faculty conduct workshops, collaborate with faculty in numerous disciplines, administer large budgets and numbers of people, and conduct research in appropriate areas. However, such vitally important leaders may or may not have full faculty status or participate equally in the academic community. They often are appointed as non-tenure track faculty, as lecturers, as adjuncts, or academic staff. Some even have part-time appointments. Their area of expertise, so central to the academic enterprise, is not considered an academic discipline, an area of inquiry in itself where serious, valuable research and teaching are performed. Thus, many faculty in such positions are treated as temporary and transient, emblematic of the fact that the academic community considers writing across the curriculum itself that way—a national fad to counter the perceived lack of commitment to undergraduate education, a fad to remediate years of neglect in the precollege years. Thus academic communities (at least those who represent them) are reluctant to grant full and equal status to faculty who administer and teach in such programs. Often when programs are successful after several years, upper administrators find themselves having to turn over the key people who have made their programs successful and who have gained immeasurable experience in doing so. This unstable leadership and lack of community commitment inevitably lead to the decline of once successful programs.

ENGLISH DEPARTMENT ORTHODOXY

Most successful programs receive their impetus and leadership from faculty within English departments supported by colleagues in other departments. Often, English departmental administrators and senior faculty support these efforts, and such programs are clearly embraced as an important aspect of the English department's role on particular campuses. But just as frequently, English department faculty and administrators do not support these efforts, fearing their department's literary mission will be diluted by even more writing programs. They don't see why they should provide leadership to a campuswide program as important to history or chemistry as to literature.

Traditional English faculty may not see rhetoric and composition as an important area of teaching and scholarship in English and often are content to leave the teaching of writing to graduate students, lecturers, and part-time faculty. This in spite of the teaching of writing taking up two-thirds of the instructional load of the typical English department. Senior faculty in such departments don't support the hiring of tenure lines in writing, and they don't look favorably on scholarship and program administration in writing when faculty in these areas are reviewed for promotion or tenure. They are inclined to see any published article on John Donne or Henry James as more substantial and significant than any article on composition theory pedagogy, no matter what the quality of the contribution such articles might make to the discipline. Although some English faculty have the cavalier attitude that just about anyone can teach writing—thus first-year graduate students and adjuncts with varying credentials and experience do much of the instruction— ironically, they are uneasy with the idea that untrained faculty in other disciplines might teach writing in other than English courses.

More than one viable writing program has been dismantled by a change in departmental administration or by the curricular or personnel decisions of unsympathetic senior English faculty.

COMPARTMENTALIZED ACADEMIC ADMINISTRATION

Universities, colleges, and schools are organized by academic disciplines— philosophy, physics, political science, and so on—which generates consequences, often hidden and little understood. While such organization might be credited with driving the development of knowledge within disciplinary constraints, it often neglects important areas of inquiry that are interdisciplinary or that don't fit comfortably within a traditional discipline's boundaries. Some activities, such as reading, writing, and critical thinking, we might call foundation abilities on which all other academic enterprises are based. As such, they are the province of all the disciplines and yet of none of them. They fall through the cracks of academic organization and disciplinary emphasis, just as many students fall through the cracks in education, jobs, and participatory citizenship because they do not build the foundation at the same time they learn disciplinary knowledge.

Thus, many newly formed comprehensive writing programs do not fit comfortably into the academic structure. They are often given special status outside of academic departments, but not equal to them. Such programs are created by the immediate perceived need of faculty, administrators, or legislators, but they remain vulnerable to the budget axe in ways that academic departments do not. Sometimes they are identified with remedial or study-skills programs, with the implied assumption that once students write better, or once faculty and employers perceive that students write better, or once the political pressure for educated graduates eases, such programs will be phased out.

Those programs administratively housed in English departments do not necessarily enjoy better status than those housed in isolated units (sometimes called programs, centers, boards, or institutes). They are add-ons to the real business of the department—the literary education of majors, minors, and graduate students—and as such wield no influence within the department and do not contribute measurably to the department's central role as a constituted academic discipline. Because the writing-across-the-curriculum program plays little role in the life of the department, it can be dropped from the department's activities without affecting any other area of the department. The same could not be said of dropping the departmental major, or graduate program, or even specialized courses in Chaucer, Shakespeare, and Milton. Because we have not found a way to administratively state that the writing program is central to the education of all students, writing programs remain isolated and vulnerable to the unpredictable whims of social and educational factors such as the balance of trade or the appointment of a new departmental chairperson.

TRADITIONAL REWARD SYSTEM

At many colleges and universities, faculty know that funded research, refereed publication, and the specialized training of graduate students is valued more than undergraduate teaching. Of course, "good" undergraduate teaching is expected, and it becomes a baseline for mediocrity that teachers are not encouraged to rise above. Promotion, tenure, merit increases, departmental work load, and local and national recognition all depend on the quantity and quality of published research, not on the quantity and quality of undergraduate teaching. Faculty who invest significant time in attending workshops, changing course structures, conferencing with students, reading student writing, and collaborating with other faculty on pedagogical projects are seen as diminishing their research commitment and concomitantly their salary and status. Traditionally within English departments themselves, reward for being promoted through the ranks has been less undergraduate teaching, with the teaching of writing "escaped" altogether. To remain productive, the reasoning goes, scholars need the opportunity to lecture repeatedly on familiar subjects, not the time-consuming drudgery of teaching maturing thinkers and writers.

Because institutions increasingly derive their status and funding based on a research record of solving state, regional, and national problems, they use undergraduate education as the base from which to launch new initiatives: research institutes, graduate programs, subsidiary corporations, technology transfer centers. Nationally, undergraduate tuition has risen at substantially more than the rate of inflation throughout the 1980s, and yet undergraduate classes appear to have grown larger and to be taught increasingly by graduate students, adjuncts, and part-time faculty. Most universities claim to seek a balance between teaching and research, a goal that would be supported by proponents of writing across the curriculum. In practice, however, as evidenced by the faculty reward system, they encourage the continued development of a faculty member's research expertise and accomplishments, while remaining content with what is perceived to be adequate but static undergraduate teaching. Writing across the curriculum is founded on the premise that integrative writing tasks will improve undergraduate learning and communication abilities, and the faculty reward system explicitly devalues faculty efforts to realize that premise.

TESTING AND QUANTIFICATION

With the rise in the number of students attending institutions of higher education and with the increased specialization of most professional training, quantification of testing and grading has become commonplace. Students often sit in large lecture halls and take tests that have been designed to be machine-scored. Test scores are then machine-averaged to produce a final grade. Final grades are then machine-averaged to produce the grade point average (GPA). And even though studies have shown no correlation between a student's GPA and his or her performance after college, the GPA is a crucial ingredient in all sorts of decisions, from admission to graduate and professional school to opportunities for job placement.

In such an atmosphere, the teaching of writing has little place. Perhaps the most significant problem is that writing is viewed almost exclusively as another evaluation instrument, an opportunity to test students on whether they have read the textbook or paid attention to lectures, an opportunity to enter one more grade in the grade book. The opportunities to take risks in order to create new knowledge and then to communicate information as a writer who has learned something to readers who want to know it too, opportunities which when experienced are crucial to the development of writing abilities, are generally ignored. Another problem is that writing doesn't fit very well in the quantification paradigm. Evaluating writing appears a much more subjective process than machine-scoring "objective" tests, and, therefore, inherently unfair to the enterprise of putting the important GPA number on a student. In addition, the grading of writing is a much more time-consuming task for the teacher or the graduate students assigned to the teacher.

Quantification affects teaching generally, not just the teaching of writing. We can calculate fairly accurately the amount of research dollars and number of publications on a professor's record, but because we don't know how to quantify good teaching, we devalue it in favor of the numbers associated with research during tenure and promotion decisions. Such practice contributes to faculty belief that to succeed in academia one need only teach adequately and then spend as much time as possible on research and publication.

Testing mania is even more severe in the nation's schools. Not only do teachers, administrators, and departments of education subscribe to the same thinking as their college counterparts, but they have greatly increased the presence and importance of standardized testing. Not only are students labeled with a standardized test score, but so are teachers, schools, school districts, and states. Standardized test scores can now even predict if the nation is at risk. They are given with increasing frequency and, not surprisingly, teachers often give up control of the curriculum and their pedagogy and teach to the tests. If teachers don't voluntarily reduce the amount of time spent on writing, they are often required to do so by vigilant administrators. Incidences in which teachers were reprimanded for asking students to write before they had completed workbook exercises—the required preparation for an upcoming test—are not uncommon.

Teaching grammar and usage is not teaching writing, and tests of grammar and usage do not test the ability to write, but such practices absorb most of the school time allotted to instruction in writing. Because schoolteachers have demanding workloads—often three or four preparations and five or six sections of thirty students each, they are acutely aware of the emotional investment and time involved in designing effective writing assignments and then responding to 150 student essays. No wonder many are seduced by workbook exercises that someone else has designed and that can be marked quickly and efficiently, objective grades in the grade book, standardized test preparation complete, principal and superintendent pleased, the nation secure. In such an environment there is little commitment to write to learn rather than write to be tested, little commitment to develop a pedagogy that models what writers do so that children can imagine themselves as writers and begin to act as writers do.

ENTRENCHED ATTITUDES

There are many entrenched attitudes that undermine the goals for writing across the curriculum. They are shared to some extent by faculty, administrators, students, and the general public. Collectively, these attitudes may be the most significant enemy of all.

Some attitudes, perhaps the easiest to confront and change, have to do with self-interest. Many administrators believe or want to believe that writing across the curriculum is a quick fix. They seek the immediate gratification of a visibly successful program, one that quiets legislators and enhances administrative careers. They are unwilling to make the long-term commitment to resources, faculty development, and institutionalization that is necessary to sustain a program.

Many faculty are apathetic, others insecure, even hostile, to any program that offers to assist them with their teaching. They see such efforts as a subtle indictment of their current teaching and feel threatened by any attempt at collaboration centered on teaching. They believe that teaching is a matter between teacher and students, and any organized attempt to change their teaching strategies is an attack on academic freedom. Similarly, many students feel threatened when writing is introduced into a course. It is an unfair obstacle to getting the desired grade and an odious interruption in their career training. They will write whatever is necessary to successfully pass the course, but they don't see the point of developing their writing and thinking abilities. They are conditioned by the rote memorization and regurgitation of test taking, and they say that all they want is for their teachers to tell them what to say and how to say it.

Such attitudes undoubtedly confront those who seek to develop any cross-curricular, university-wide program. However, there are numerous entrenched attitudes about writing and the teaching of writing that when combined with the general inertia of educational systems hinder the development of writing programs. Some of the most obvious are: students should learn to write in high school and no further instruction in writing should be necessary; students should pass a test that certifies that they can write now and for all time; writing instruction equals remediation; learning to write is a series of discrete skills that can be taught in isolation removed from any functional or communicative context; writing is not connected to learning; writing cannot be taught; writing can be taught by anyone with a college diploma; writing research is not real research; and, the new writing pedagogy is ''soft'' with its opportunities for collaboration and revision, not to mention its opportunities for reflection and sustained critical thinking, especially when compared to the rigors of the go-it-alone, one-time-only, machine-scored test.

These familiar attitudes, coupled with the fact that there is little reward for doing otherwise, reinforce many teachers' tendency to teach as they were taught, that is, to assign very little writing in classes across the curriculum, and when it is assigned, to read it for evaluation purposes exclusively. Such teaching also assumes that the teacher's job is to disseminate knowledge and that the student's job is to memorize what the teacher disseminates. It undermines the goals of most writing programs that promote active student involvement in the creation of knowledge and its effective communication. It also paves the way for the pervasive attitude that teachers cannot be trusted to disseminate the correct information and the counterpart attitude— standardized tests can be trusted to measure students' learning of the correct information. Thus the phenomena of teaching to the test and teaching standardized lists of cultural literacy have effectively taken the responsibility for curriculum, pedagogy, and evaluation away from teachers and placed it in the hands of the state and its test makers. One of the main promises of writing across the curriculum is the renewed empowerment of informed teachers in the educational process.

David R. Russell in a recent article ("Writing across the Curriculum and the Communications Movement: Some Lessons from the Past," *College Composition and Communication*, May 1987) states that "the fundamental problem of WAC is not so much pedagogical as political, not how to create a sound program (that has been possible for decades), but rather how to administer it, how to place it firmly in the complex organizational structure of the university" (p. 191). Russell's analysis of well-conceived, initially successful programs at Colgate and Berkeley in the 1950s and 1960s is extremely helpful. He points out that the enemies these programs faced—academic bureaucracy and indigenous attitudes—are the same ones that programs of the 1990s face. Both programs eventually succumbed when advocates' enthusiasm faded.

Certainly, there are enemies within—from misplaced self-interest and aggrandizement to amorphous and ill-conceived programs—but the immediate challenge for writing across the curriculum is to change attitudes, ways of thinking, and academic structures. All of the programs in this book have had some success in doing so. But the process is a continuing one as faculty, students, administrators, and national reports come and go. Institutions must develop a more or less permanent structure whereby writing-across-the-curriculum advocacy is ever renewed and expanded. Otherwise, the best that can be hoped is to keep the enemies at bay.

Bibliography

C. W. Griffin

This bibliography describes materials important to the history and development of writing across the curriculum as well as those that contribute to its evolving body of theory and that describe specific writing-across-the-curriculum programs. Materials that discuss specific classroom techniques and the uses of writing in particular disciplines are not included. The phrase "writing across the curriculum" will be abbreviated WAC.

Adams, Barbara, Olivia Bissell, Angela Bodino, and Myrna Smith. "Writing for Learning: How to Achieve a Total College Commitment." American Association of Community and Junior Colleges Convention, San Diego, April 1985. ERIC ED 258 666

Four papers describing the WAC program at Somerset County Community College, including its theory of writing as learning, the development of faculty workshops, lessons learned from the project, and the possibility of developing collegewide consensus on writing standards.

Anson, Chris M. "The Classroom and the 'Real World' as Contexts: Reexamining the Goals of Writing Instruction." *The Journal of the Midwest Modern Language Association* 20.1 (1987): 1–16.

Argues that two instructional ideologies currently compete with each other in English studies, one of which holds that the purpose of writing instruction is to indoctrinate students into an academic culture, while the other holds that its purpose is to teach certain context-neutral writing skills. Suggests that this clash can be resolved by an approach to composition teaching informed by recent work in WAC, by which students would "become ethnographers of language, gathering, analyzing, responding to, writing about, and practicing different forms of discourse" that they see and hear about them.

———. "Toward a Multidisciplinary Model of Writing in the Academic Disciplines." In *Writing in the Academic Disciplines*, edited by David A. Jolliffe, 1–33. Norwood, MA: Ablex, 1988.

Through an extensive review of existing research, this important contribution to WAC theory points out major gaps or discrepancies in our knowledge of writing in the academic disciplines and suggests that "three perspectives on writing in the academic disciplines—the professional, the curricular, and the developmental"—be further explored.

Anson, Chris M., J. E. Schwiebert, and M. M. Williamson. *Writing Across the Curriculum: An Annotated Bibliography*. Westport, CT: Greenwood Press, in preparation.

This first complete bibliography of WAC materials will include about 600 entries in categories such as theory, research, history, programs, and faculty development, as well as a series of "pedagogical" categories grouped into disciplinary areas: social sciences, humanities, physical sciences, business, etc.

Bailey, Richard W. "Writing Across the Curriculum: The British Approach." In *Fforum: Essays on Theory and Practice in the Teaching of Writing*, edited by Patricia L. Stock, 24–32. Portsmouth, NH: Boynton/Cook, 1983.

Describes the assumptions for, recommendations about, and impact on WAC in Great Britain of *A Language for Life*, the Bullock report published in England in 1975. Notes that the report and the publications related to it assume that the best learning is active, that articulation in all its forms is the basis for understanding, and that writing is the preferred vehicle for expressing the process by which understanding is achieved.

Baker, Sheridan. "Writing as Learning." In *Fforum: Essays on Theory and Practice in the Teaching of Writing*, edited by Patricia L. Stock, 224–27. Portsmouth, NH: Boynton/Cook, 1983.

Borrowing from an earlier article entitled "Writing as Discovery," *ADE Bulletin* 43 (1974): 34–37, this author argues that writing is a way of learning because "it teaches us how to move from the circumscribed self-center of childhood and adolescence into mature thinking, how to generalize from our attitudes, emotions, hunches, and private ideas into mature and valid thought."

Barnes, Linda Laube, and Isaiah Smithson, eds. "Writing Across the Curriculum." *Illinois English Bulletin* 74.1 (1986). Papers from the Annual Composition Conference, Edwardsville, 1986.

The papers in this collection discuss the pedagogical implications of WAC, two extensive WAC programs, the role of the writing center in WAC, and the part played by writing in learning and its transfer. The issue contains a brief bibliography.

Beach, Richard, and Lillian Bridwell. "Learning through Writing: A Rationale for Writing across the Curriculum." In *The Development of Oral and Written Language in Social Contexts*, edited by Anthony D. Pellegrini and Thomas D. Yawkey, 183–98. Norwood, MA: Ablex.

Basing their claims on research in reading and writing, these authors claim that writing can help students learn new information in subject area classes, can help them develop problem-solving strategies for organizing both old and new information, can teach them writing conventions and audience awareness, can help them evaluate critically the information they are learning, and can teach them to perceive and analyze their own experiences.

Bean, John C., Dean Drenk, and F. D. Lee. "Microtheme Strategies for Developing Cognitive Skills." In *Teaching Writing in All Disciplines*, edited by C. Williams Griffin, 27–38. New Directions for Teaching and Learning Series, vol. 12. San Francisco: Jossey-Bass, 1982.

This particularly useful article describes a method for formulating short writing assignments, which are short enough to be used in large classes and graded quickly and yet complex enough to pose different kinds of cognitive problems for students.

Behrens, Laurence. "Memo from the Faculty Senate to the English Department." *Freshman English News* 8.2 (1979): 13–15.

An ironic comment on freshman composition courses, making the point that they seem to serve the interests of English teachers rather than prepare students to write in other disciplines.

_____. "Writing, Reading, and the Rest of the Faculty: A Survey." *English Journal* 67.6 (1978): 54–66.

Reports the results of a survey of faculty attitudes toward student writing conducted at American University. Results indicate that faculty perceive student reading and writing skills to have declined over the past five or ten years, that the most frequently encountered problems are mechanical ones, that faculty downgrade less for mechanics than for organization, that they assign papers fairly frequently, and that students in the humanities are less likely to get detailed instructions in class about the preparation and presentation of their papers than students in science, social science, and professionally oriented courses.

Berger, Jeffrey. "Beyond the Workshop: Building Faculty Development into the WAC Program." Conference on College Composition and Communication, Minneapolis, March 1985. ERIC ED 257 079

Describes the WAC program, which restructures the classroom situation to focus on the revision process in faculty-led peer groups, at the Community College of Philadelphia. Develops a heuristic for revision that addresses the rhetorical concerns of writing teachers and draws content area teachers away from informational models of writing.

Bernhardt, Stephen A. "Writing Across the Curriculum at One University: A Survey of Faculty Members and Students." *ADE Bulletin* 82 (1985): 55–59.

Results of a survey of faculty and students in the College of Liberal Arts of Southern Illinois University at Carbondale indicate that, contrary to expectations of many English faculty, students and faculty do value writing abilities highly, agree that writing instruction is a responsibility shared by all departments, assign writing fairly frequently, and have students write for a variety of purposes and audiences.

Bertch, Julie. "Writing for Learning: Starting a Writing Across the Curriculum Program in the Community College." Conference on High School–College Articulation in Writing, Tempe, April 1985. ERIC ED 256 387

Describes the steps followed in implementing a WAC program, including stating the rationale and goals, enlisting faculty support, and involving faculty through workshops and individual contact. Also describes methods faculty can use to incorporate more student writing into their classes: note taking, class logs, study guides, writing assignments, essay tests, and conference evaluations.

Blair, Catherine Pastore. "Only One of the Voices: Dialogic Writing Across the Curriculum." *College English* 50 (1988): 383–89.

Because "true writing across the curriculum should be based on dialogue among all the departments," this author argues that "the English department should have no special role in writing across the curriculum—no unique leadership role and no exclusive classes to teach—not even freshman composition." (But see Louise Z. Smith's article cited later in this bibliography for an opposing point of view.)

Bogel, Fredric. *Teaching Writing: A Handbook for Instructors in the Freshman Seminar Program*. Ithaca: Cornell University, privately printed, 1984.

Presents the writing program at Cornell as a "yeasty mix of instruction in writing and introductory study in a wide range of disciplines." Contains chapters on organizing the course, classroom methods, correcting and grading essays, as well as a bibliographic guide, etc.

Bridgeman, Brent, and Sybil B. Carolson. "Survey of Academic Tasks." *Written Communication* 1 (April 1984): 247–80.

Reports results of a survey of 190 academic departments in 34 universities to determine the academic writing skills needed by incoming undergraduate and graduate students. Major findings were as follows: (1) writing skills are important to success in graduate training and even more important to success after graduation; (2) even departments whose writing requirements are light do require some writing of first-year students; (3) descriptive skills are considered important in engineering, computer science, and psychology, while in other disciplines skill in taking a position is important; (4) in evaluating student writing, faculty members focus more on discourse-level features such as content or organization rather than on sentence-level skills; (5) different disciplines do not uniformly agree on writing-task demands or on a single preferred mode of discourse to use for evaluating entering undergraduate and graduate students.

Britton, James. "Language and Learning Across the Curriculum." In *Fforum: Essays on Theory and Practice in the Teaching of Writing*, edited by Patricia L. Stock, 221–24. Portsmouth, NH: Boynton/Cook, 1983.

A succinct summary of Britton's theories of writing as learning.

———. *Prospect and Retrospect: Selected Essays of James Britton*. Edited by Gordon Pradl. Portsmouth, NH: Boynton/Cook, 1982.

Reprints various well-known pieces related to WAC, including "Writing to Learn and Learning to Write," "Shaping at the Point of Utterance," and "Reflections on the Writing of the Bullock Report."

Britton, James, Tony Burgess, Nancy Martin, Alex McLeod, and Harold Rosen. *The Development of Writing Abilities (11–18)*. London: Macmillan (for the Schools Council), 1975.

This classic in WAC literature reports on research conducted by the authors between 1966 and 1971 to inquire into "the processes by which the written language of young children becomes differentiated, during the years of eleven to eighteen, into kinds of written discourse appropriate to different purposes." The concepts that Britton's team developed in their study of 2,122 pieces written by students in the first, third, fifth, and seventh years of school have become part of the conceptual fabric of WAC, including the idea of writing as a process involving such stages as conception, incubation, and production, and the classification of writing both by the writer's relationship to the audience and by its function—expressive, transactional, or poetic. The team concluded that as children moved through grade levels, they wrote more and more in the transactional mode for the teacher-as-examiner audience.

Burnham, Christopher C. "Tapping Non-English Faculty Resources in the Literacy Crusade." Conference on College Composition and Communication, Dallas, 1981. ERIC ED 202 022

At Stockton State College basic writing courses are staffed by volunteer faculty from across the college who are trained in writing theory and pedagogy as well as in grading techniques.

Chamberlain, Lori. "Gadamer, Hermeneutics, and Composition." Modern Language Association, Los Angeles, December 1982. ERIC ED 232 140

Holding that neither the empirically based composition position nor the reader-response literary position offers a sufficiently broad theory of reading and knowing, this author argues that Hans-Georg Gadamer's theory of understanding can provide a basis for developing a "writing across the curriculum disciplinary approach in which the reading and writing are tied to a disciplinary methodology, a genuine context, a set of conventions, and a content."

Collins, Terrence. "Necessity, Invention, and Other Mothers—Going Interdepartmental." Minnesota Conference on Composition, 1977. ERIC ED 149 354

This early piece provides a rationale for going "interdepartmental" in thinking about writing instruction and suggests ways of accomplishing this shift in perspective. Includes an annotated bibliography on interdepartmental responsibility for the teaching of writing skills (1966–76).

"Comprehensive Writing Programs." Elaine Maimon and Harvey Wiener, eds. *The Forum for Liberal Education* 3.6 (1981). Publication of the Association of American Colleges. ERIC ED 200 172

Describes comprehensive writing programs at nine colleges and universities, including Beaver College, Grinnell, Gonzaga, Maryland, Michigan Tech, Saint Edward's College, the University of Michigan, Wheaton, and Yale.

Comprone, Joseph J. "Literary Theory and Composition: Creating Communities of Readers and Writers." Conference on College Composition and Communication, Minneapolis, March 1985. ERIC ED 254 855

Argues that "a theory of interpretation developed from the composition scholar's reading and revision of literary theory could effectively serve as a core theory in writing across the curriculum programs." Explores the implications of various theoretical perspectives as they may be used by writing teachers in constructing a theory of interpretation.

———. "The New Rhetoric: A Way of Connecting Community and Discourse Conventions in Writing Across the Disciplines Courses." Conference on College Composition and Communication, Atlanta, March 1987. ERIC ED 279 019

Argues that "two concepts from the new Rhetoric—S. Toulmin's 'warrants' and C. Perelman and L. Olbrechts-Tyteca's 'universal audience'" can "give English teachers the strategies they need to provide the balanced perspectives on texts that will assure both the rigor and breadth required of good writing."

Connolly, Paul, and Teresa Vilardi. *New Methods in College Writing Programs: Theories in Practice*. New York: Modern Language Association, 1986.

Contains twenty-eight descriptions of recently revised college writing programs, including WAC programs at Beaver College, Brown, Cornell, George Mason, Michigan Technological University, the University of Michigan, and the University of Washington.

Connolly, Peter J., and Donald C. Irving. "Composition in the Liberal Arts: A Shared Responsibility." *College English* 37 (1976): 668–70.

Description of an early series of WAC seminars held for faculty at Grinnell College.

Covington, David H., Ann E. Brown, and Gary B. Blank. "An Alternative Approach to Writing Across the Curriculum: The Writing Assistance Program at North Carolina State University's School of Engineering." *Journal of the Council of Writing Program Administrators* 8.3 (1985): 15–23.

Describes the methods, costs, and effectiveness of a program in which faculty from the writing center serve as consultants on writing to teachers and students in technical courses.

Cullen, Robert J. "Writing Across the Curriculum: Adjunct Courses." *ADE Bulletin* 80 (1985): 15–17.

Reviews Kinneavy's three program models and argues for the superiority of a fourth model, as developed at UCLA and the University of Washington, in which "advanced writing seminars taught by writing program instructors are offered as adjuncts to courses in other disciplines."

Davis, David J. "Writing Across the Curriculum: A Research Review." Information Analysis, 1984. ERIC ED 254 848

A review of articles and books on WAC which reveals that the following basic assumptions characterize most WAC programs: (1) writing is a complex and developmental process; (2) writing should be used to promote learning; (3) the teaching of writing is the responsibility of the entire academic community; (4) the teaching of writing should be integrated across departmental lines; (5) writing serves several functions in the educational context; (6) the universe of discourse is broad; (7) the teaching of writing should occur during the entire four undergraduate years. Studies also support the assumption that writing increases student learning.

DeBlois, Peter. "Inventional Theory and Writing in the Content Areas in Freshman English." Conference on College Composition and Communication, Washington, D.C., 1980. ERIC ED 185 570

Argues that "the focus of content writing instruction should be to prescribe the inventional techniques that are common to all forms of writing, and to survey the writing skills and structural constraints that are peculiar to the discourse of specific disciplines."

Dick, John A. R., and Robert M. Esch. "Dialogues among Disciplines: A Plan for Faculty Discussions of Writing Across the Curriculum." *College Composition and Communication* 36 (1985): 178–82.

Describes a series of questions that WAC practitioners can ask about writing in other disciplines in order to familiarize themselves with its nomenclature, purpose, audience, stylistic features, and contexts.

Donlan, Dan. "How to Involve Other Departments in Helping You Teach Writing."
National Council of Teachers of English, Chicago, November 1976. ERIC ED
145 452

An early set of practical suggestions for an English department wishing to involve
other departments in improving student writing skills. Suggests that the department proceed through four phases: (1) development of a rationale for involving
other departments; (2) administration of a writing attitude inventory to colleagues in other departments; (3) compilation of a needs assessment for each
department participating; (4) development of an ongoing in-service education
program for faculty members.

Dowling, H. F., Jr. "Towson State University's Approach to Improving Writing Across
the Curriculum." *College Composition and Communication* 65 (1985): 240–42.

Describes this college's WAC program: "second writing courses" taught by
faculty from various disciplines and a coordinator of the program with one-half
released time, who has helped develop guidelines for all second writing courses,
tutored students from second writing courses, and sponsored workshops and in-
service aid to faculty teaching such courses.

Dowst, Kenneth. "The Epistemic Approach: Writing, Knowing, and Learning." In
Eight Approaches to Teaching Composition, edited by T. R. Donovan and B. W.
McClelland, 65–85. Urbana, IL: National Council of Teachers of English, 1980.

Argues that writing is a way of knowing, a way of "making some sense out of an
extremely complex set of personal perceptions and experiences of an infinitely
complex world" and describes a sequence of assignments designed for a writing
course based on this premise.

Draper, Virginia. "Formative Writing: Writing to Assist Learning in All Subject
Areas." Curriculum Publication no. 3. Berkeley, CA: University of California,
Bay Area Writing Project, 1979. ERIC ED 184 115

This helpful handbook describes techniques that teachers in all subjects can use to
enhance student learning without becoming expert markers of grammar or punctuation errors themselves.

Duke, Charles R. "Survey of Writing in Various Disciplines." Research/Technical
Report, 1982. ERIC ED 232 167

Results from a survey of 400 faculty in the six different colleges at Murray State
University, Kentucky, suggest that faculty members: (1) strongly support both
the basic freshman composition requirement and the emphasis upon writing in
general education courses; (2) accept responsibility for teaching writing skills in
their own disciplines, and endorse the offering of upper-division writing courses;
(3) endorse the idea that writing can be used to teach concepts; (4) see students as
having major problems in controlling their subject matter and proofreading and
editing their work; (5) take interest in their students' writing difficulties and offer
help during the writing process; and (6) express interest in learning more about
using writing in their disciplines.

Eastman, Arthur M. "The Foreign Mission of the University English Department."
Modern Language Association, New York, December 1981. ERIC ED 215 349

Argues that the home mission of an English department is the teaching of reading
and writing. The foreign mission is the "converting" to a higher literacy those
outside university English departments, especially teachers of high school English
and university teachers in disciplines other than English.

Eblen, Charlene. "Writing Across-the-Curriculum: A Survey of a University Faculty's Views and Practices." *Research in the Teaching of English* 17 (1983): 343–348.

A two-page questionnaire sent to 471 full-time instructional faculty at the University of Northern Iowa (and returned by 266) resulted in these findings: (1) as a whole, faculty assigned importance to overall quality of ideas, followed by organization, development, grammatical form, and coherence, in that order; (2) problems cited by faculty fell into two major clusters, one associated with communicative maturation and the other with standards of edited American English; (3) frequency and types of writing varied across academic divisions, but the writing required was almost exclusively transactional.

Emig, Janet. "Writing as a Mode of Learning." *College Composition and Communication* 28 (1977): 122–28. Reprinted in *The Writing Teacher's Sourcebook*, edited by Gary Tate and Edward P. J. Corbett. New York: Oxford University Press, 1981.

The earliest major article describing the ways in which writing "represents a unique mode of learning."

Ferlazzo, P. J. "Writing Across the Curriculum from the Point of View of a Department Chair." College English Association, Houston, April 1982. ERIC ED 215 368

Describes the development of the WAC program at Montana State University, a program funded first internally and by the state and later by a two-year federal grant. Included in the program are workshops for small numbers of non-English faculty in designing and evaluating writing assignments, the development of a writing center to serve remedial students, released time for English faculty to work with faculty in other disciplines, and training of English faculty in collaborative learning and writing assignment design.

Fleming, Margaret, ed. "Writing Across the Curriculum." *Arizona English Bulletin* 27.1 (1984).

The articles in this journal issue focus on various aspects of WAC, including descriptions of particular programs, the place of the writing center in a WAC program, the history of WAC, fringe benefits of WAC, etc.

Fletcher, S. L. "Gracing Our Work: Generating Theory from Writing Across the Curriculum." Modern Language Association, New York, December 1981. ERIC ED 218 644

Argues that theoretical thinking is now needed to help establish WAC as a real field and not just as a passing fad. Suggests that theory should come in three forms: (1) administrative theory, which considers how a cross-curricular writing program should organize itself; (2) pedagogic theory, which asks how best to teach writing within particular classrooms and disciplines; and (3) speculative theory, which inquires into the two common denominators across fields—mental operations and language.

Forman, Janis. "Notes toward Writing Across the Curriculum: Some Collaborative Efforts." *Journal of Basic Writing* 2.4 (1980): 12–21.

Describes an experimental course called the Composing Process offered first in the fall of 1979 at Goucher College. By preparing students to assist others in writing papers required outside of English, this course was to become the center of the new WAC program at Goucher.

Freisinger, Randall. "Cross-Disciplinary Writing Workshops: Theory and Practice." *College English* 42 (1980): 154–66.

A detailed rationale for WAC programs and a description, in particular, of the program at Michigan Technological University.

Freisinger, Randall, and Bruce Petersen. "Writing Across the Curriculum: A Theoretical Background." *Fforum, A Newsletter of the English Composition Board, University of Michigan* 2.2 (1981): 65–67, 90.

Surveys essential literature on WAC and sets forth the basic theoretical premises for developing a program.

Fulwiler, Toby. "How Well Does Writing Across the Curriculum Work?" *College English* 46 (1984): 113–25.

Describes lessons learned in overseeing a WAC program and conducting faculty workshops for six years. Problems included resistance of some participants to the workshop process, skepticism from teachers of English and philosophy, and difficulties of requiring writing in large classes and in using peer review. Benefits included growth of collegial interactions, a new sense of the importance of writing across the campus, increased confidence of participants in their own writing abilities, changes in teaching methods, and increased publications.

―――. "Journal-Writing Across the Curriculum." *Classroom Practices in Teaching English 1979–1980*. 15–22. Urbana, IL: National Council of Teachers of English, 1979.

Shows how teachers in all curricula can use journal writing to help students increase their writing fluency, facilitate learning, and promote cognitive growth.

―――. "Showing, Not Telling, at a Faculty Workshop." *College English* 43 (1981): 55–63.

Describes a variety of activities that form the basis for WAC workshops held at Michigan Technological University. A practical, inductive approach to faculty workshops, in which discussions of theory follow from various writing and evaluation activities.

―――. "The Politics of Writing Across the Curriculum." National Council of Teachers of English, San Antonio, November 1986. ERIC ED 276 061.

Argues that WAC has become an educational reform movement that questions the nature, purpose, and goals of educational institutions.

―――. "Why We Teach Writing in the First Place." In *Fforum: Essays on Theory and Practice in the Teaching of Writing*, edited by Patricia L. Stock, 273–86. Portsmouth, NH: Boynton/Cook, 1983.

Argues that we should use writing to develop critical, independent thinking, both in the composition classroom and across the curriculum.

―――. "Writing Across the Curriculum at Michigan Tech." *Journal of the Council of Writing Program Administrators* 4.3 (1981): 15–20.

A detailed description of the program at Michigan Tech, especially helpful because it describes in detail the objectives, schedule, and activities of the faculty workshops conducted by Fulwiler and his colleagues.

_____. "Writing Across the Curriculum: Implications for Teaching Literature." *ADE Bulletin* 88 (1987): 35–40.

After briefly describing the beginnings of WAC and its major premises, this article discusses its impact on the classroom, drawing particular examples from literature classes.

_____. "Writing Is Everybody's Business." *National Forum, The Phi Kappa Phi Journal* 65.4 (1985): 21–24.

Argues that "the movement with the most potential to change the mechanistic nature of writing and learning in American classrooms is called 'writing across the curriculum.'"

_____. "Writing Workshops & the Mechanics of Change." *WPA: Writing Program Administration* 12 (1989): 7–20.

Describes how to conduct writing workshops for an interdisciplinary group of college faculty. Comments specifically on leadership qualities, workshop design, writing exercises, and potential problems.

_____. *Teaching with Writing: An Interdisciplinary Workshop Approach*. Portsmouth, NH: Boynton/Cook, 1987.

This book approximates the experience of an interdisciplinary WAC workshop aimed at high school and college teachers in every subject area, setting forth the major premises of WAC and describing a variety of writing practices meant to transform classes from a teacher-centered into a student-centered focus.

_____. ed. *The Journal Book*. Portsmouth, NH: Boynton/Cook, 1987.

In forty-two articles collected in this book, authors such as Ann Berthoff, Peter Elbow, Toby Fulwiler, and Chris Thaiss explore the uses of student journals, describing implications and applications, theory and practice.

Fulwiler, Toby, and Art Young, eds. *Language Connections: Writing and Reading Across the Curriculum*. Urbana, IL: National Council of Teachers of English, 1982.

The earliest collection of articles on WAC, written by teachers in the program at Michigan Technological University and including an article on the premises behind the program by Randall Freisinger, one on the use of journals across the curriculum by Toby Fulwiler, and another on the use of poetic writing by Art Young as well as a select bibliography by Bruce Petersen.

Gates, Rosemary L. "*Aitia* and *Kairos*: Classical Rhetoric in the Writing Across the Curriculum Program." Conference on College Composition and Communication, New Orleans, March 1986. ERIC ED 274 974

Describes three areas of classical rhetoric with important implications for WAC: *aitia*, or cause; *kairos*, or the appropriate use of thought and knowledge in specific situations; and the enthymeme and the example, as thinking processes and proofs in a community. Argues that from classical rhetoric we can derive a systematic framework for students to understand thought, investigation, and writing in other disciplines.

Gere, Anne Ruggles, ed. *Roots in the Sawdust: Writing to Learn Across the Disciplines*. Urbana, IL: National Council of Teachers of English, 1985.

A collection of essays describing how teachers in various disciplines such as art, German, social studies, science, math, philosophy, history, etc., implement writing to learn in their classrooms.

Gordon, Joseph W., and Linda H. Peterson. "Writing at Yale: Past and Present." *ADE Bulletin* 71 (1982): 10–14.

Describes the development of Yale's present writing program, consisting of four components: (1) six sequences of freshman writing; (2) writing-intensive courses supported by teaching fellows; (3) small seminars in writing offered by various departments for juniors and seniors; and (4) tutorials in writing located in the residential colleges.

Gottschalk, Katherine. *Writing in the non-writing class: "I'd Love to Teach Writing But . . .": Strategies for Faculty Members Concerned about Student Writing*. Ithaca: Cornell University, John S. Knight Writing Program, 159 Goldwin Smith Hall, Cornell University, Ithaca, NY 14853–3201.

A practical handbook with sections on motivating students to write, writing as a part of reading, writing as a way of studying, the use of writing in the classroom, etc.

Grattan, Mary C., and Susan P. Robbins, "Content Area Models: A Key to Student Writing Improvement in Writing Center Programs." *Teaching English in the Two-Year College* 9 (1983): 117–21.

Argues that the only kind of model that helps students improve their writing is a "facsimile of the product we want them to produce" and that therefore we can help students improve their writing "by giving them models for content-area writing."

Gregory, Marshall W. "Writing, Literacy, and Liberal Arts." *ADE Bulletin* 82 (1985): 27–32.

Argues that teachers of writing should not limit their goals to "trivial claims about practicality," but should teach writing as a part of the liberal arts (as the ability "to think in more developed, precise, and responsible ways") and as an avenue to political and social power (as the ability to influence "the way people think, talk, and write about important issues").

Griffin, C. W. "Programs for Writing Across the Curriculum: A Report." *College Composition and Communication* 36 (1985): 398–403.

This author surveyed 404 institutions of higher education, asking for descriptions of their WAC programs. Of the 194 who responded, 139 described such programs. This report describes the development of these programs, their funding, and the major elements of which they consist.

———. *Teaching Writing in All Disciplines*. San Francisco: Jossey-Bass, 1982.

An early collection of essays on WAC, including a piece by Barbara Walvoord surveying writing process research, one by Toby Fulwiler explaining how students learn through writing, one by Dean Drenk and others that describes a technique for assigning problem-solving writing in large classes, one by Chris Thaiss describing specific WAC practices at George Mason university, and a selective bibliography by Bruce Petersen.

———. "Using Writing to Teach Many Disciplines." *Improving College & University Teaching* 31 (1983): 121–28.

Presenting writing as a process, this article describes how teachers in any discipline can initiate the process through assignments that facilitate student learning, intervene in the process by coaching students as they write papers, and complete the process by evaluating the resulting papers.

Halpern, Sheldon, et al. "Who Can Evaluate Writing: Staffroom Interchange." *College Composition and Communication* 29 (1978): 396–97.

This report of a study of thirty full-time faculty in different departments at Bowling Green State University suggests that "the general faculty are capable of making valid holistic judgments about the quality of student prose."

Hamilton, David. "Interdisciplinary Writing." *College English* 41 (1980): 780–96.

This author describes a discipline-specific writing course, in this case writing for the sciences, in which students write descriptions of their work neither for specialists in their disciplines nor for generalists. Instead they write "serious parodies" of specialized work, projects that can be done with innocent means and with fairly simple supplies, but that require exacting thought. As a result of such projects, he suggests, students will learn to view writing as a means of thinking and discovery in their disciplines.

Hammond, Eugene. "Freshman Composition–Junior Composition: Does Co-ordination Mean Sub-ordination?" *College Composition and Communication* 35 (1984): 217–21.

Distinguishes between the aims of freshman and junior courses in composition at the University of Maryland and shows how the freshman program prepares students for the junior course.

Hansen, Kristine. "Relationships between Expert and Novice Performance in Disciplinary Writing and Reading." Conference on College Composition and Communication, Atlanta, March 1987. ERIC ED 283 220

Argues that English teachers in a freshman English course can initiate students into academic discourse communities by teaching them general strategies for analyzing and producing the discourse of any discipline.

Haring-Smith, Tori, et al., eds. *A Guide to Writing Programs: Writing Centers, Peer Tutoring Programs, and Writing-Across-the-Curriculum.* Glenview, IL: Scott, Foresman, 1984.

Descriptions of WAC programs at 100 institutions of all types, giving length of time the program has existed, percentage of faculty and students involved, and type of training for instructors. Also contains an introductory essay that briefly discusses the origin of WAC and then describes major approaches, including writing-intensive courses, training seminars, and discipline-specific writing courses taught within an English department. The authors also speculate on some of the future problems as well as rewards for WAC.

Harris, Jeanette, and Christine Hult. "Using a Survey of Writing Assignments to Make Informed Curricular Decisions." *Writing Program Administration* 8.3 (1985): 7–14.

This survey of faculty and students at Texas Tech found that the three most frequent types of writing assignments were research papers, essay exams, and reports. The author describes ways to adapt the freshman curriculum to help students learn to complete such assignments successfully.

Hartman, Joan E. "Writing Across the Curriculum: Ease and Dis-ease in Zion." *ADE Bulletin* 74 (1983): 37–43.

A detailed and realistic description of the problems encountered and successes achieved in a yearlong faculty seminar.

Herrington, Anne J. "Classrooms as Forums for Reasoning and Writing." *College Composition and Communication* 36 (1985): 404–13.

Argues that as we integrate writing into specific courses, we and our colleagues need to create classroom situations in which students use writing not only to learn the intellectual and social conventions of particular disciplines but also to explore and shape their ideas.

———. "Writing to Learn: Writing Across the Disciplines." *College English* 43 (1981): 379–87.

Describes WAC workshops funded by FIPSE held at Johnson State College. Shows how faculty can be helped to develop and sequence effective writing assignments.

Holzman, Michael. "Articulating Composition." *College English* 45 (1983): 288–95.

Describes the evolution of a WAC program at the University of Southern California, in which students coregister in a section of freshman composition and a section of a course such as biology or history required in the general education curriculum.

Irmscher, William F. "Writing as a Way of Learning and Developing." *College Composition and Communication* 30 (1979): 240–44.

An early argument that writing is "an action and a way of thinking" that stimulates us to understand ourselves and our ideas, encourages us to think abstractly and therefore to seek relationships and find meaning, and helps us to control our thinking and expression.

Jolliffe, D., ed. *Advances in Writing Research. Vol. 2, Writing in the Academic Disciplines.* New York: Ablex, 1988.

Contains research articles on writing processes and written texts in various disciplines, including articles that do the following: discuss a model for research on writing in the disciplines, study writers' knowledge in the disciplines, describe a model for investigating the functions of written language in different disciplines, study writing in an undergraduate literature class, contrast two texts in the social sciences, and analyze the composing processes of scientists writing journal articles.

Kelly, Kathleen A. "Writing Across the Curriculum: What the Literature Tells Us." Information Analysis, 1985. ERIC ED 274 975

This review of the literature on WAC programs indicates that most have one or more of these four components: (1) students demonstrate writing competency before graduation, through a timed writing test, departmental endorsement, a writing-intensive course, or a course in professional writing; (2) faculty participate in development workshops that convey the ideas that writing is a staged process and that writing is learning; (3) writing faculty offer in-class seminars to help integrate writing into content courses; (4) trained peer tutors in a writing center help students with their writing assignments.

Kelly, Leonard. "The Evaluation of Writing Across the Curriculum at Gallaudet College during the 1984–85 Academic Year." Evaluation/Research Report, 1985. ERIC ED 283 146

This report surveys the first academic year of the college's WAC program, describing various instructors' projects and personal opinions about the program as well as students' opinions about the projects and the effects of WAC on student writing and learning. The report also includes recommendations for improving the preparation, guidance, and support of faculty who adopt WAC in the future.

Kinneavy, James L. "Restoring the Humanities: The Return of Rhetoric from Exile." In *The Rhetorical Tradition and Modern Writing*, edited by James J. Murphy, 19–28. New York: Modern Language Association, 1982.

This important contribution to WAC theory argues that we must reintroduce into various departments of the curriculum, but especially into the department of English, a concern for rhetoric in all its forms, including persuasive rhetoric, which has been neglected and which will lend the humanities a practical dimension they do not now possess.

_____. "Writing Across the Curriculum." *ADE Bulletin* 76 (1983): 14–21.

Analyzes the strengths and weaknesses of two approaches to writing across the curriculum: (1) content area courses taught by specialists within particular disciplines, and (2) writing courses in a variety of areas taught by members of the English department. Seems to favor the second approach, because "forcing all students of the college to speak about their specialities to the uninformed generalist imposes a common language on the university community. It reunites the fragmented 'pluraversity' of the twentieth century into a linguistic university."

_____. "Writing Across the Curriculum." In *Teaching Composition: 12 Bibliographical Essays*, edited by Gary Tate, 353–77. Fort Worth: Texas Christian University Press, 1987.

A bibliographic survey of materials on WAC, including terminology, bibliographies and collections, textbooks, descriptions of programs, and theoretical foundations.

Knoblauch, C. H., and Lil Brannon. "Writing as Learning through the Curriculum." *College English* 45 (1983): 465–74.

Claims that their "review of high school and college programs offering cross-disciplinary writing shows the greater number of them to be little more than 'grammar across the curriculum' or 'packaging information across the curriculum.'" Says that such programs are based on an erroneous assumption that knowledge is stable and bounded, while they should be based on the notion that "knowing is an activity . . . the process of an individual mind making meaning from the materials of its experience." But see Susan H. McLeod's comment and Knoblauch and Brannon's response in *College English* 46 (1984): 615–17; McLeod claims that her examination of four WAC programs shows that all, contrary to what Knoblauch and Brannon say above, stress writing as learning.

Lamb, Catherine E. "Initiating Change as a Writing Consultant." *College English* 45 (1983): 296–300.

Briefly describes her experiences as a part-time writing consultant for her colleagues at Albion College for a year.

Larson, Richard L. "Writing in the Academic and Professional Disciplines: Bibliography, Theory, Practice, Preparation of Faculty." *College Composition and Communication* 34 (May 1985).

This whole issue is devoted to articles on WAC, including a number annotated elsewhere in this bibliography.

Larson, Richard L., with Eve Zarin and Carol Sicherman. *Writing in the Academic and Professional Disciplines: A Manual for Faculty.* New York: Herbert H. Lehman College, City University of New York, privately printed, 1983.

A valuable short guide for faculty outside of English who wish to encourage student writing. Especially helpful in its specific formulations of the ways in which writing is learning and in its practical suggestions for responding to and evaluating student writing.

Lory, Alice, et al. "We Must All Teach Writing." Conference on College Composition and Communication, Kansas City, March-April 1977. ERIC ED 45 475

This early paper describes summer seminars on teaching writing offered to faculty in various disciplines based on "the conviction that every teacher who assigns papers is, to some degree, teaching writing" and that many of those teachers encounter difficulty determining the best means of helping students learn to write well and of evaluating student writing.

Loux, Ann Kimble. "Third-Party Evaluation in a Cross-Disciplinary Writing Program." Conference on College Composition and Communication, Minneapolis, April 1979. ERIC ED 172 208

Describes a group approach to evaluating student papers established in a cross-disciplinary undergraduate writing program. Faculty who participated sought agreement on competency among writing evaluators, separation of the evaluation of content from the evaluation of writing competency, and extension of the audience for student papers.

MacDonald, Susan Peck. "Problem Definition in English Department and Other Academic Writing." Conference on College Composition and Communication, Minneapolis, March 1985. ERIC ED 261 404

Argues for situating academic writing along a continuum with writing about literature near one end and writing in the sciences near the other. Also argues that academic writing is a problem-solving activity and that future research on composing needs should examine whether the problems of certain kinds of writing alter the nature of the composing process and whether many of our notions of good writing are built upon unrepresentative kinds of writing assignments.

Magistrale, Tony. "Writing Across the Curriculum: From Theory to Implementation." *Journal of Teaching Writing* 5.1 (1986): 151–57.

In a survey of participants in WAC workshops at the University of Vermont, finds that nearly every class requires writing, which is generally informational, does not engage discovery and direct involvement with material, and is expressed in a particular discipline's idiom.

Maimon, Elaine P. "Cinderella to Hercules: Demythologizing Composition Across the Curriculum." *Journal of Basic Writing* 2.4 (1980): 3–11.

Describes the ways in which English teachers who want to establish an institution-wide WAC program might dispel the following myths and misconceptions about the teaching of writing: that writing is defined strictly in terms of surface features, that commitment to writing across the university may expand the English department disproportionately, that people outside of English know little about good writing, and that all writing must be graded.

_____. "Collaborative Learning and Writing Across the Curriculum." *Journal of the Council of Writing Program Administrators* 9.3 (1986): 9–15.

Argues that WPAs can transform the current enthusiasm for WAC into an opportunity to create a community of academics by encouraging collaborative learning among faculty in writing workshops—as a classroom procedure to help handle the paper load, as a way to help students internalize the concept of audience, as a way of creating community through acknowledgment, and as a way of creating partnerships between colleges and school districts.

_____. "Knowledge, Acknowledgment, and Writing Across the Curriculum: Toward an Educated Community." In *The Territory of Language: Linguistics, Stylistics, and the Teaching of Composition*, edited by Donald McQuade, 89–100. Carbondale: Southern Illinois University Press, 1986.

Argues we should use writing as a way of teaching our students to join various interpretative communities, the same kinds of communities to which we their teachers belong and which we acknowledge in our own writing.

_____. "Maps and Genres: Exploring Connections in the Arts and Sciences." In *Composition and Literature: Bridging the Gap*, edited by Winifred Bryant Horner, 110–25. Chicago: Chicago University Press, 1983.

Argues that the training of composition teachers has equipped them to make explicit to students the conventions of the written genres of various disciplines and that the goal of courses in composition should be to help "students enter the larger community of academic and public conversation" by teaching them how to compose in a variety of disciplinary genres.

_____. "Talking to Strangers." *College Composition and Communication* 30 (1979): 364–69.

In order to "help our students overcome their apprehensions about academic discourse and at the same time cope with the exigencies of such discourse," we should make use of collaborative learning and guide them through multiple drafts.

_____. "Writing in All the Arts and Sciences: Getting Started and Gaining Momentum." *Journal of the Council of Writing Program Administrators* 4.3 (1981): 9–13.

Argues that a successful WAC program should have two components—(1) a freshman composition course that emphasizes process and introduces students to a variety of procedures in writing; (2) instructors in every department who make writing an "inevitable part of every teaching and learning day." Concludes with a set of suggestions for engaging faculty in the effort to bring about such a program.

_____. "Writing in the Total Curriculum at Beaver College." *CEA Forum* 9 (1979): 7–10.

Describes the program at Beaver College: a cross-disciplinary course in freshman composition, a writing center, writing required in all college courses, course clusters, and advanced writing courses offered by the English department.

Mallonee, Barbara C. "Charting Institutional Change." Conference on College Composition and Communication, Minneapolis, March 1985. ERIC ED 260 456.

Describes a six-year WAC project at Loyola College funded by NEH, which involves the following: teaming content area and English faculty for one year, the content faculty then becoming departmental writing coordinators; a survey assessing faculty attitudes and practices in connection with writing; and the development of a handbook on writing at Loyola.

Mallonee, Barbara C., and John R. Breihan. "Responding to Students' Drafts: Interdisciplinary Consensus." *College Composition and Communication* 36 (1985): 213–31.

As a result of a series of cross-curricular collaborations that paired composition instructors with members of fourteen other disciplines over a four-year period, these authors have identified four areas of responding to student writing "where consensus across the campus can and should be sought": (1) make some basic decisions about how to deal with mechanical and factual errors; (2) develop a limited common terminology for responding to significant features of student writing; (3) develop a process of response that tailors responses to a specific purpose, marks the texts and margins of first drafts as little as possible, weighs the paper against a checklist that sets priorities for judgment, and contains a summary comment that schedules revising activities; (4) decide that the effort is worth it.

Marsella, Joy, and Roger Whitlock. "An English Department Reexamines Itself: Becoming a Department of Literacy." Conference on College Composition and Communication, New Orleans, March 1986. ERIC ED 276 042.

Describes various changes made within a five-year period in the writing program at the University of Hawaii, including a soon-to-be-implemented requirement of five writing-intensive courses necessary for each student's graduation and the creation of a campuswide writing committee formed to examine university writing requirements and articulate activities across the university's seven campuses.

Martin, Nancy, Pat D'Arcy, Bryon Newton, and Robert Parker. *Writing and Learning Across the Curriculum, 11–16.* London: Ward Lock, Reprint. Portsmouth, NH: Boynton/Cook, 1976.

This book constitutes a report on the work of the Schools Council Writing across the Curriculum Project, which was created to disseminate the findings of the research conducted by James Britton and his team of researchers. (See Britton, et al., *The Development of Writing Abilities (11–18),* cited earlier in this bibliography.) The thesis of the book, that language should play a central role in "learning in all parts of the curriculum," has become the central tenet of WAC, and concepts discussed in the book, including the need for teachers of all subjects to provide a variety of audiences and a range of purposes for student writing, have widely influenced teaching practices.

Martin, Nancy, et al., eds. *Writing Across the Curriculum Pamphlets.* Portsmouth, NH: Boynton/Cook, 1983.

These six pamphlets (first published individually from 1973 to 1975 by the Writing Across the Curriculum Project of the Schools Council/London University Institute Education English Department) describe student use of language to understand new ideas, the place of genuine communication in learning, the importance of a sense of audience to writing, the different kinds of writing according to purpose, the relation of talking to writing, and the need to provide students with a range of writing opportunities.

Marx, Michael Steven. "Joining the Composition Classroom and the Content Course: A Contextualized Approach for Teaching Developmental Writing." Developmental Writing Conference, Norfolk, April 1987. ERIC ED 285 175

Argues that developmental writing courses should be recontextualized into the broader educational experience of college so that developmental writers actively engage in opportunities that invite writing to learn while they are learning to write and demonstrates how this might be accomplished by describing a pilot program at the University of Michigan that integrated the teaching of developmental writing and the teaching of introductory psychology.

Matlak, Richard E., et al. "Components of a Successful Interdisciplinary Composition Program." Modern Language Association, New York, December 1978. ERIC ED 170 750

Describes the general education program in Boston University's College of Basic Studies, in which rhetoric and content area instructors work together to plan writing assignments and help students complete them successfully.

McCarthy, Lucille Parkinson. "A Stranger in Strange Lands: A College Student Writing Across the Curriculum." *Research in the Teaching of English* 21 (1987): 233–65.

This article describes a two-year study of one college student's efforts to write competently in different disciplines and concludes that success was affected by unarticulated social aspects of classroom contexts for writing as well as by explicitly stated requirements and instructions.

McLeod, Susan. "Defining Writing Across the Curriculum." *Journal of the Council of Writing Program Administrators* 11.1–2 (1987): 19–24.

This excellent survey describes the two philosophical approaches that inform WAC programs, the cognitive and the rhetorical, and then the major components of WAC programs, including the freshman WAC course, the adjunct course, upper-division writing intensive courses, faculty seminars, and writing helpers and consultants.

———, ed. *Strengthening Programs for Writing Across the Curriculum*. San Francisco: Jossey Bass, 1988.

A collection of essays focusing on the needs of second-generation writing-across-the-curriculum programs. Chapters include information on funding, research, evaluation at different types of institutions. Chapter authors include Margot Soven, Ellen Strenski, Keith Tandy, Toby Fulwiler, Barbara Walvoord, and Christopher Thaiss, among others.

"Membership Directory of the National Network of Writing Across the Curriculum Programs." Available from Christopher J. Thaiss, Department of English, George Mason University, Fairfax, VA 22030.

Moore, Leslie E., and Linda H. Peterson. "Convention as Connection: Linking the Composition Course to the English and College Curriculum." *College Composition and Communication* 37 (December 1986): 466–77.

Defines one role that English teachers can play in cross-curricular writing programs by arguing that they can teach students how conventions operate within discourses written in a variety of disciplines and describes a cross-curricular writing course in which this theory was applied to the study of discourses in art history, history, biology, literature, anthropology, and philosophy.

Morgan, Lorraine, et al. "Pushing the Write Button: Writing-Across-the-

Curriculum.'' Conference on College Composition and Communication, Atlanta, March 1987. ERIC ED 280 028

Describes a WAC program established in the interdisciplinary human biology program at Stanford University in 1984 to develop students' fluency in writing, to improve the quality of student writing, and to help students learn to use writing in studying and learning course content.

Moss, Andrew, and Carol Holder. *Improving Student Writing: A Guidebook for Faculty in All Disciplines*. Pomona, CA: California State Polytechnic University, 1982. Distributed by Kendall/Hunt Publishers, Dubuque, IA.

This guide helps faculty design effective assignments and essay exams, integrate reading and writing, and evaluate student's papers. Especially helpful are the examples of successful assignments taken from a variety of disciplines, specific suggestions for helping students research, plan, and draft papers, and examples of actual on-the-job writing tasks.

Nakamura, Caroline, Robert Fearrien, and Sheldon Hershinow. "Write to Learn: Writing Across the Curriculum at Kapiolani Community College." Pacific Western Division Conference of the Community College Humanities Association, San Diego, November 1984. ERIC ED 252 252

Three papers, the first discussing the need for and purpose of WAC programs generally; the second describing the development of the WAC program at Kapiolani Community College, which includes a WAC committee and writing labs; the third offering guidelines for WAC development based on the contagion model, whereby faculty commit to teaching writing without formal course requirements.

Nochimson, Martha. "Writing Instruction Across the Curriculum: Two Programs." *Journal of Basic Writing* 2.4 (1980): 22–35.

Describes two programs—one at the College of New Rochelle centered around workshops for faculty and one at Drew University, in which faculty participate in a series of workshops and then teach a freshman seminar that combines writing instruction with instruction in their own discipline.

Nold, Ellen W. "Nuts to Normals: Helping Them to Teach Writing Across the Curriculum." Modern Language Association, San Francisco, December 1979. ERIC ED 185 545

Describes the hypotheses, reasoning, and methods used by one writing program administrator to promote writing in a college engineering department, including a six-hour seminar for faculty appointed to teach writing and the provision of writing tutors for faculty who did not want to teach writing.

North, Steve. "Journal Writing Across the Curriculum: A Reconsideration. *"Freshman English News* 14.2 (1985): 2–9.

Argues that since "the function of any written discourse will be determined by the context in which it is used," we cannot proceed too cautiously in selling colleagues on the utility of journal writing on the basis of what it accomplishes for us in our own classrooms.

O'Dowd, Kathleen, and Ernest Nolan, eds. *Learning to Write—Writing to Learn*. Madonna College Humanities Writing Program Dissemination Booklet, privately printed, 1986.

Contains articles on the philosophy of the WAC program at Madonna, the dean's view of the writing program, writing in the senior seminar, writing to facilitate learning in music theory, prewriting in the composition classroom, writing in the social sciences, tagmemics, etc.

Odell, Lee. "How English Teachers Can Help Their Colleagues Teach Writing." In *Fforum: Essays on Theory and Practice in the Teaching of Writing*, edited by Patricia L. Stock, 269–73. Portsmouth, NH: Boynton/Cook, 1983.

Argues that we in English need to help colleagues categorize error, become aware of the range of assignments they can make, be more sensitive to audiences for student writing, and recognize the intellectual demands of specific assignments.

_____. "The Process of Writing and the Process of Learning." *College Composition and Communication* 31 (1980): 42–50.

A call for collaboration with colleagues in other disciplines and a brief analysis of present work on the composing process.

_____. "Teaching Writing by Teaching the Process of Discovery: An Interdisciplinary Enterprise." In *Cognitive Processes in Writing*, edited by Lee W. Gregg and Erwin R. Steinberg, 139–54. Hillsdale, NJ: Erlbaum, 1980

Proposes that teachers from all disciplines help students learn to write by (1) identifying and teaching some of the basic discovery processes they will need to write about course topics, and (2) using frequent short writing assignments as a means of engaging students in and helping them examine these processes.

Odell, Lee, Dixie Goswami, and Doris Quick. "Writing Outside the English Composition Class: Implications for Teaching and for Learning." In *Literacy for Life*, edited by Richard W. Bailey and Robin Melanie Fosheim, 175–96. New York: Modern Language Association, 1983.

On the basis of differences found in a study of the writing of legislative analysts and undergraduates, these authors suggest that teachers help students identify and use the conceptual strategies useful for writing in particular disciplines, attempt to reverse the usual role of generalist-writing-to-specialist-readers that students are typically in and help students understand how a particular writing assignment fits into the overall scheme of a particular course.

Parker, Robert. "The 'Language Across the Curriculum' Movement: A Brief Overview and Bibliography." *College Composition and Communication* 36 (1985): 173–77.

Offers a comprehensive bibliography for the purpose of shifting the American WAC movement to the principles of the British language-across-the-curriculum movement, which acknowledges the "dynamic, developmental interconnections among uses of language" and puts "the emphasis on the instrumentality of language, on language as a means of thinking and learning."

Parker, Robert, and Vera Goodkin. *The Consequences of Writing: Enhancing Learning in the Disciplines*. Portsmouth, NH: Boynton/Cook, 1987.

Presents the historical and thematic background of WAC, the role of writing in the making of knowledge. The latter half of the book presents case studies of students and teachers using WAC.

Penrose, Ann. "Individual Differences in Composing: Exploring Consequences for Learning through Writing." Conference on College Composition and Communication, New Orleans, March 1986. ERIC ED 270 758

Discusses recent research in an effort to refine the claim that writing is a way of learning. Generally concludes that writing can have an impact on the affective and social dimensions of learning, but says that more research is necessary before we accept the idea that it affects the cognitive dimension.

Raimes, Ann. "Comment." *Journal of the Council of Writing Program Administrators* 4.3 (1981): 21–22.

This comment on WAC articles by Toby Fulwiler and Elaine Maimon in this journal issue suggests that the long-range success of collegewide writing programs rests on the degree of institutional commitment to writing and on the rewards for faculty who participate fully in such programs.

———. "Writing and Learning Across the Curriculum: The Experience of a Faculty Seminar." *College English* 41 (1980): 797–801.

Describes a series of WAC seminars held during the academic year at Hunter College. Especially useful as an alternative to intensive summer seminars held at other universities.

Reiff, John D. "Writing in the Disciplines at the University of Michigan." *Fforum* 2.2 (1981): 75–77, 91–92.

A description of writing-intensive courses created by various departments within this university.

Rose, Mike. "When Faculty Talk about Writing." *College English* 41 (1979): 272–79.

Results of a day-and-a-half writing conference held at UCLA. The conference focused on how writing is evaluated in different disciplines and on how writing instruction should be organized at a large university. Recommends reward for writing research and instruction, development of new writing curricula, and new evaluation schemes.

Russell, D. R. "Writing Across the Curriculum in 1913: James Fleming Hosic on 'Co-operation.'" *English Journal* 75.5 (1986): 34–37.

Describes early WAC efforts and compares them with current WAC programs.

———. "Writing Across the Curriculum and the Communications Movement: Some Lessons from the Past." *College Composition and Communication* 38 (1987): 184–94.

Using the examples of early WAC programs at Colgate and Berkeley, both of which flourished in the 1950s but fell victim in the 1960s to the "compartmentalized structure of academia and the entrenched attitudes in the university both toward writing and toward interdepartmental programs," this author argues that "WAC programs must be woven so tightly into the fabric of the institution as to resist the subtle unraveling effect of academic politics."

Scheffler, J. A. "Composition with Content: An Interdisciplinary Approach." *College Composition and Communication* 31 (1980): 51–57.

Describes the Freshman Interdisciplinary Studies Program at Temple University, including a writing component, in which freshmen join four to six faculty members in an interdisciplinary study of a topic such as "The Environment." Writing instructors assist students in their writing for this program, and students may satisfy the university's composition requirement through the program.

Schwab, Gweneth. "Measuring Density of Details in Composition and Content Courses." Conference on College Composition and Communication, San Francisco, 1982. ERIC ED 214 171

Reports results of a study comparing student essays written in response to the same assignment given in a content course and a composition course. When essays were scored for "density of detail" and "specificity of development," those written for the content course where there was no writing instruction scored higher. Concludes that the constraints of writing for a class or assignment in which composition skills will be evaluated may prevent students from doing their best.

Schwartz, Mimi. "Response to Writing: A College-Wide Perspective." *College English* 46 (1984): 55–62.

As a result of a survey of faculty and student responses to different texts, this writer finds that the rhetorical values of faculty seem to shift with writing context—depending on perceptions of audience, purpose, style, and content—but that students rhetorical values as writers seem to stay the same. She suggests that "we must better articulate our rhetorical values, for ourselves as well as for students and colleagues."

Sipple, Jo-Ann M. "Planning, Proposing, Preparing, and Prototyping: The Last Four P's of Writing Across the Curriculum Programs That Last." Conference on College Composition and Communication, New Orleans, March 1986. ERIC ED 269 779

Argues that those interested in establishing lasting and effective WAC programs need to examine healthy programs. The anchor of such programs is an organized nucleus made up of the following features: planning, proposing, preparing, and prototyping.

————. "Teacher Protocols: A New Evaluation Tool for Writing Across the Curriculum Programs." Conference on College Composition and Communication, Atlanta, March 1987. ERIC ED 285 150

To evaluate the efficacy of faculty seminars in WAC given for instructors at Robert Morris College, this writer compared the verbal protocols of faculty who had participated in the seminars with those who had not and found that instructors who participated in WAC seminars had a larger repertoire of strategies for planning a variety of writing assignments appropriate for their courses. This writer argues that teacher protocols are an effective evaluation tool for WAC programs.

Smith, Barbara Leigh, ed. *Writing across the Curriculum. Current Issues in Higher Education*. No. 3. Washington, D.C.: American Association for Higher Education, 1983–84.

This monograph contains six articles on the WAC movement, including one by Maxine Hairston on the writing-as-process theory behind the movement, an interview with Elaine Maimon on the way WAC developed, and one by Joan Graham on methods of implementation.

Smith, Louise Z. "Why English Departments Should 'House' Writing Across the Curriculum." *College English* 50 (1988): 390–95.

In response to an article by Catherine Blair cited earlier in this bibliography, this author argues that English departments should house WAC programs, because "the distinction between literature and 'non-literature' is becoming obsolete," and "reader-response theory, with its analogue in collaborative composition pedagogies, can be applied to reading and writing all texts."

Stock, Patricia L. "A Comprehensive Literacy Program: The English Composition Board." In *Fforum: Essays on Theory and Practice in the Teaching of Writing*, edited by Patricia Stock, 85–90. Portsmouth, NH: Boynton/Cook, 1983.

Describes the development of the seven-part writing program at the University of Michigan.

———, ed. *Fforum: Essays on Theory and Practice in the Teaching of Writing*. Portsmouth, NH: Boynton/Cook, 1983.

A collection of essays, some expanded, from the newsletter *Fforum*, including articles on literacy, on the relationships between speaking and writing, on reading and writing, on writing as a way of learning, and on writing and rhetoric. In particular pieces Richard Bailey describes the British approach to WAC, Patricia Stock describes the WAC program at the University of Michigan, James Britton, Sheridan Baker, Toby Fulwiler, and Lee Odell talk about writing and learning.

Storlie, Erik F., and Mary Barwise. "Asking Good Questions, Getting Good Writing: A Teacher's Handbook on Writing across the Curriculum at Minneapolis Community College." 1985. ERIC ED 280 019

The result of the WAC project at Minneapolis Community College, this handbook provides teachers with general principles and practical suggestions for crafting good writing assignments in content area classrooms. It also provides a number of writing assignments for various disciplines.

Sutton, Marilyn. "The Writing Adjunct." Report on program prepared at The Small College, California State College, 1976. ERIC ED 151 787

Describes an individualized composition course offered in conjunction with content courses at six campuses of California State University, which provides an alternative to the traditional instruction of advanced composition. In this course, "students write papers assigned in their subject area course and have weekly interviews with their writing adjunct instructor or peer tutor to discuss their work in progress and receive instructions for revision."

Tchudi, Stephen. *Teaching Writing in the Content Areas: College Level*. Washington, D.C.: National Education Association, 1986.

This book, which would be useful for both English faculty and content area colleagues working in WAC programs, describes the forms of "workaday writing" that can facilitate learning, explains how to assign and coach writing, and sets forth methods for evaluating writing. WAC programs at Michigan Tech, the University of North Carolina at Wilmington, the State University College of New York at Fredonia, the University of Michigan, and Montana State University are summarized. In addition, the lesson plans for twelve WAC workshops are given.

Thaiss, Christopher, ed. *Writing to Learn: Essays and Reflections on Writing Across the Curriculum*. Dubuque, IA: Kendall Hunt, 1983.

A collection of sixteen essays by members of the George Mason University WAC program, containing a brief history of the development of WAC in the U.S. by Laurence Peters, a history of George Mason's program as well as a selective bibliography by Chris Thaiss, and essays by members from the faculty in psychology, business law, computer science, nursing, history, and physical education discussing pedagogical applications.

Walpole, Jane R. "Content Writing." *Teaching English in the Two-Year College* 7 (1981): 103–106.

Notes that students often write better in their composition classes than in their other courses. Suggests ways that composition teachers may better prepare students for the writing they do in other classes.

Walter, James. "Comment and Response." *College English* 46 (1984): 403–405.

Describes an experiment linking a humanities course with a freshman composition course.

Walvoord, Barbara E. "Freshmen, 'Focus,' and Writing Across the Curriculum." *Freshman English News*, 14.2 (1985): 13–17.

One of the few discussions of the problem of teaching students to transfer skills to writing outside the composition class. Data collected by this writer and her colleagues from college students writing in biology and business classes offers a "bore hole" sample of the shapes "focus" takes, and the skills needed to achieve it, in courses at various levels and in various disciplines across the curriculum.

_____. *Helping Students Write Well: A Guide for Teachers in All Disciplines*. 2nd ed. New York: Modern Language Association, 1986.

A detailed guide for teachers in all disciplines who want to help their students improve writing. Shows teachers how to incorporate writing in their courses, make effective writing assignments, respond to student writing, and help students with focus, organization, development, and style.

Walvoord, Barbara Fassler, and Hoke L. Smith. "Coaching the Process of Writing." In *Teaching Writing in All Disciplines*, edited by C. Williams Griffin, 3–14. San Francisco: Jossey-Bass, 1982.

A review of writing process research and its implications for higher education. An excellent document for faculty who want a quick overview of recent research.

Weiss, Robert H. "The Humanity of Writing: A Cross-Disciplinary Program." *Improving College and University Teaching* 27 (Fall 1979): 144–147.

Describes the evolution of West Chester State College's WAC program, describing methods for achieving faculty support and offering a writing consultancy as one major successful component of the program.

_____. "Writing in the Total Curriculum: A Program for Cross-Disciplinary Cooperation." In *Eight Approaches to Teaching Composition*, edited by Timothy R. Donovan and Ben W. McClelland, 133–149. Urbana, IL: National Council of Teachers of English, 1980.

This essay focuses first on how English teachers can create cross-disciplinary writing courses and then on how they can serve as advisors on WAC to colleagues in other disciplines.

Weiss, Robert, and Michael Peich. "Faculty Attitude Change in a Cross-Disciplinary Writing Workshop." *College Composition and Communication* 31 (1980): 33–41.

Describes the day-to-day activities of a faculty writing workshop conducted at West Chester State College. In contrast to the experience of Joan Hartman described above, these authors talk about the "conversion experience" of participants.

Weiss, Robert H., and S. A. Walters. "Research on Writing and Learning: Some Effects of Learning-Centered Writing in Five Subject Areas." National Council of Teachers of English, San Francisco, November 1979. ERIC ED 191 073

The earliest, and still one of the few, experimental examinations of the effect of WAC on students, this study of 178 students and five teachers in the areas of history, psychology, physical sciences, reading theory and practice, and statistics was conducted to test four hypotheses: (1) that the more students write in content areas the better they will write; (2) that more writing in content areas will reduce writing apprehension; (3) that as students do more learner-centered writing they will learn more about the subject; (4) that the concepts about which students do learner-centered writing will be clearer to them than the concepts they do not write about. Findings did not bear out hypotheses one and two, but did support three and four.

Williamson, Michael M. "The Function of Writing in Three College Curricula: Modes and Registers." National Council of Teachers of English, Detroit, November 1984. ERIC ED 252 884

This study of six college teachers—two each from biology, English, and sociology—through interviews and course artifacts examines whether teachers in different disciplines assign different functions to student writing. Finds that the teacher's reading of student writing is structured around communication registers. These semantic patterns are conditioned not only by the customary way of speaking but also by the instructor's idea of what the students should be learning.

Young, Art. "Rebuilding Community in the English Department." *ADE Bulletin* 77 (1984): 13–21.

This author describes the effects on the English department at Michigan Technological University of locating the teaching of writing, to both students and colleagues, at the center of the curriculum, including effects on departmental research, environment, and hiring practices.

Young, Art, and Toby Fulwiler, eds. *Writing across the Disciplines: Research into Practice.* Portsmouth, NH: Boynton/Cook, 1986.

The eighteen essays collected in this book describe the development of the WAC program at Michigan Technological University and attempt to measure its effects on both faculty and students. Essays in the first section describe the theoretical basis for the program, the sense of community it fostered, and the research model that was developed in order to evaluate the program. Those in the second section measure the impact of the program on faculty attitudes toward writing, on pedagogical practices, and on students. Essays in the third section, which describe writing in psychology, biology, engineering, and mathematics, attempt to demonstrate in specific ways that assigning certain kinds of writing does help students learn better, while essays in the final section describe the setbacks and surprises encountered during the development of the program.

Contributors

M. LeRoy Badger, Jr., received his B.A. from Weber State and his M.A. from Utah State, and has done graduate study at the University of Maryland. He has taught English at Prince George's Community College for twenty years, chaired the Freshman Composition Department, authored a history of the College, and developed courses in Old and New Testament Literature.

Bruce Barna is Associate Professor of Chemical Engineering at Michigan Technological University, where he is responsible for the chemical engineering plant design sequence of courses. He has worked in industry as a process manager, a plant engineer, and a plant manager.

Stephen BeMiller is professor of mathematics at California State University, Chico, and has taught for thirty years, mostly in mathematics but also in physical education, business management, history, and humanities. BeMiller also is Coordinator of Faculty Professional Development. He has led numerous workshops about principles of learning and teaching and on writing across the disciplines, especially in science, mathematics, and engineering.

William Blanchard received his M.A. from the University of California at Berkeley. He taught at the University of California, Santa Barbara, and was Chairman of the English Department at Lakeland College (WI) before coming to Prince George's Community College in 1965. He has presented several papers at the Wyoming Conference on Freshman and Sophomore English.

John R. Breihan is an Associate Professor of History at Loyola College in Maryland. He earned degrees from Princeton and Cambridge Universities, specializing in British political history in the late eighteenth and early nineteenth centuries. During the period from 1981 to 1987 he served as codirector of the college writing-across-the-curriculum program, Empirical Rhetoric; from 1984 to 1987 he also chaired the Department of History.

Lois Bueler teaches English at California State University, Chico, where she has been Composition Coordinator since 1984. She received her Ph.D. from the University of Colorado in 1976, taught at Winona State University (MN), where she codirected the Great River Writing Project, and has published articles on Renaissance literature and a book on the natural history of the Canidae.

Kathleen Campbell is a professional theater director and designer and Assistant Professor of Theater at George Mason University where she teaches courses in script analysis, theater history, and theatrical design. She has also taught freshman composition and interdisciplinary courses in the arts.

320

Catherine Cant is an Associate Professor of Mathematics at Prince George's Community College. She received her A.B. from Randolph-Macon Women's College and her M.S. from the University of Connecticut. Through participation in the National Capital Area Writing Project, she has become a teacher/consultant in writing across the curriculum, giving lectures and workshops on writing to learn mathematics.

Robert P. Clark is Professor of Government and Politics at George Mason University in Fairfax, Virginia, where he has taught political science since 1977. He is the author of five books, two having to do with Basque politics and two with Third World political development. His doctorate is from Johns Hopkins University School of Advanced International Studies.

Gregory G. Colomb was Associate Professor of English and Director of Writing Programs at the University of Chicago and now holds those posts at the Georgia Institute of Technology. He is the author of *Designs on Truth* a forthcoming study of the poetics of eighteenth-century mock-epic. He has written a series of articles, some with Joseph Williams, on the grammar of professional texts and on teaching academic and professional writing.

Mary Jane Dickerson has been teaching writing and literature courses at the University of Vermont since 1966. She has led workshops for university and high school faculty on teaching writing in all disciplines. With historian Henry Steffens she has published *Writer's Guide: History*, which emphasizes ways of writing to learn history.

H. Fil Dowling, Jr., is Associate Professor of English at Towson State University in Baltimore. Since April 1985, he has edited the *Maryland English Journal*, an NCTE affiliate journal. His publications on composition, journal use, and writing across the curriculum have appeared in *CCC* and other journals. A member of BACWAC since 1981, he was elected BACWAC's Coordinator in the summer of 1987 for a three-year term.

Douglas Eagles has taught at Georgetown since 1972. His publications include research on the bone structure, musculature and nervous system of crustaceans and on the heart functions in mammals. He is the recipient of several fellowships and awards including the National Institutes of Health Post-Doctoral Fellowship and the Biomedical Research Grant Award (1981; 1982).

Clyde Ebenreck received his Ph.D. in Philosophy and additional degrees in theology and psychology. He taught theology, psychology, and education at various colleges before coming to the Philosophy Department at Prince George's Community College in 1971. Current interests include the philosophy of religion, Native American thought patterns, and shamanism.

Elizabeth A. Flynn is Director of the Institute for Research on Language and Learning, and Director of the Writing-Across-the-Curriculum Program at Michigan Tech. She is editor of the journal *Reader* and coeditor of *Gender and Reading: Essays on Readers, Texts, and Contexts* (Johns Hopkins, 1986). She has published articles in *College Composition and Communication, College English, New Orleans Review, The Writing Instructor*, and elsewhere and chapters in *Language Connections* (NCTE, 1982) and *Writing in the Disciplines* (Boynton/Cook, 1986) and elsewhere.

Sylvia Helen Forman is Associate Professor of Anthropology and Chair of the Anthropology Department at the University of Massachusetts. Her special fields are gender roles, applied anthropology, urban technological societies, human ecology, and the cultures of Latin America. She is now working on patterns of fertility, mortality, and marriage in an Indian village in the Ecuadorian Andes.

Keith Fort is Professor of English, Director of Freshman English, and codirector of the Writing Program at Georgetown, where he has taught for almost thirty years. He has published numerous short stories along with *College English* articles on the teaching of composition.

Tom Fox received his Ph.D. from Indiana University in 1986. His dissertation explored how gender, class, and race affect styles of literacy, and he is currently analyzing the relationships between the conversations and the compositions of black students. At California State University, Chico, where he teaches in the English Department, he coordinates the Writing Center and the Basic Reading and Writing Program.

Toby Fulwiler developed the Faculty Writing Project at the University of Vermont, where he also teaches courses in composition and American literature. His books include *Teaching With Writing* (1987), *The Journal Book* (1987), *College Writing* (1988), and *Reading, Writing, and the Study of Literature*, coedited with A.W. Biddle (1989).

Thomas Garrah began teaching in 1969 at Prince George's Community College, where he is currently an Associate Professor. He is a graduate of King's College (PA) and the University of Notre Dame, and has taught at Aquinas College (MI) and Utica College (NY). He specializes in Business Communications and is a genealogical researcher.

Virginia Johnson Gazzam is an Associate Professor of Biology at Towson State University in Baltimore. She received an Ed. D. in Science Education from the University of Maryland. She has published articles in *Journal of College Science Teaching, The Science Teacher*, and *Journal of Research in Science Teaching*. She has spoken about writing across the curriculum at the National Association for Research in Science Teaching (NARST) convention, CCCC, Penn State Conference on Rhetoric and Composition, National Association of Biology Teachers, and over twenty WAC programs on college campuses.

C. W. Griffin is professor of English at Virginia Commonwealth University. He has published essays on teaching writing and on writing across the curriculum, edited a collection of essays on writing across the curriculum, and written a textbook on business writing. He is currently working on a book about teaching Shakespeare through film and performance.

Liz Hamp-Lyons received her Ph.D. in Applied Linguistics from the University of Edinburgh, Scotland. Associate Director for Assessment of the English Composition Board and Assistant Professor of English at the University of Michigan since 1986, her research and publication interests are in language testing and composition. She is coauthor of *Research Matters* (Newbury House, 1984) and *Study Writing* (Cambridge University Press, 1987).

Janice Haney-Peritz has taught courses in literature, critical theory, and composition for eleven years, seven of them at Beaver College. She has published articles in a variety of journals, including *ELH, Studies in Romanticism*, and *Women's Studies*. Currently, she is working on the MLA-sponsored annual annotated bibliography of the Romantic Movement and a study of the discursive deployment of sexuality in eighteenth- and nineteenth-century English literature.

Julia A. Harding was Lecturer in the University of Massachussetts' School of Management from 1984 to 1987. She received her Ph.D. in English from Case Western

Reserve in 1978 and has had a successful and varied career as consultant to business and teacher of writing. In 1987 she won an Exxon award from the American Assembly of Collegiate Schools of Business for the development of a liberal arts curriculum within the School of Management.

Gail W. Hearn, coauthor of *Writing in the Arts and Sciences* and *Readings in the Arts and Sciences*, has for the last fifteen years taught writing-laden courses in comparative anatomy, animal behavior, and ecology. Her research interests range from the behavior of DNA-associated proteins to the structure of mammalian scent glands, to her current research on the behavior of monkeys in captivity.

Carl E. Henderson, who is an Assistant Professor at Harford Community College, has taught English, reading, and computer courses. A Maryland Writing Project Summer Fellow in 1984, he currently serves as Coordinator of HCC's Communication's Skills Center, which uses a computer-based approach to teach writing skills.

Anne J. Herrington is an Associate Professor of English at the University of Massachussetts, and has worked in, studied, and written about Writing-Across-the-Curriculum programs. In 1987 she conducted the CCCC Winter Workshop on that topic. In a less serious moment, she delivered a paper on Dining Across the Curriculum at the Nutrostylistics session of the 1985 CCCC.

Donald C. Holsinger is Associate Professor of History at George Mason University, where he teaches courses on Africa, the Middle East, historical methods, and modern global history. Since 1981 he has been active in the Writing-Across-the-Disciplines movement, and has published and led workshops on writing-to-learn.

Gertrude B. Hopkins is Associate Professor and Coordinator of the English Department at Harford Community College in Maryland. She has been a Teacher Consultant with the Maryland Writing Project, is a published poet, and teaches World Literature as well as a variety of writing courses.

Robert W. Jones is Director of the Center for Teaching Excellence and Director of the Professional Engineering Writing Project at Michigan Tech. He is also an Associate Professor of Rhetoric and Linguistics in the Department of Humanities. He has published articles on writing across the curriculum in *College Composition and Communication* and *Language Connections* and presented papers on the subject at the Lilly Conference on College Teaching and Interface 1987: Humanities and Technology Conference. He is now conducting research on writing in industry.

Malcolm Kiniry is currently Director of Writing at Rutgers-Newark. At UCLA he was Coordinator of the Freshman Preparatory Program, an intensive composition sequence for underprepared writers. He is coeditor with Patricia Chittenden of *Making Connections Across the Curriculum* (Bedford Books), and with Mike Rose he has coauthored the forthcoming *Strategies for Academic Thinking and Writing* (also Bedford Books).

Victor Lams, who received his Ph.D. from Northwestern University in 1965, is a professor in the English Department at California State University, Chico, where he was Composition Coordinator from 1979 to 1984. He has published articles on Keats and on nineteenth-century periodical essays and is now writing a book about Samual Richardson's novel *Clarissa*.

Joel Leonard directs the student education program at California State University, Chico's Meriam Library, and also teaches research methods for the Geography Department. From 1985 to 1987 he helped coordinate Chico's Writing-Across-the-Disciplines program.

Joyce N. Magnotto is an Associate Professor of English Studies and the coordinator of writing across the curriculum at Prince George's Community College. She serves on the Board of Consultants of the National Network of WAC Programs. She and Barbara Stout have recently published the results of national survey on WAC programs in community colleges.

Elaine P. Maimon is Dean of Experimental Programs and Professor of English at Queens College, City University of New York. Formerly, she was Associate Dean of the College at Brown University, where she also taught graduate courses in composition theory and practice. As Associate Vice-President and Professor of English at Beaver College, she initiated and directed one of the nation's first programs in writing across the curriculum. Widely published in professional journals, she is a coauthor of *Writing in the Arts and Sciences* and *Readings in the Arts and Sciences*, and is coeditor of *Thinking, Reasoning, and Writing*.

Barbara C. Mallonee is Assistant Professor and Writing Director of the Honors Program at Loyola College in Maryland. She has published "Responding to Students' Drafts: Interdisciplinary Consensus," with John R. Breihan, *CCC*, May 1985. She and Breihan codirected the writing-across-the-curriculum project, Empirical Rhetoric, that ran from 1982 to 1987, and are in the process of analyzing a series of three surveys of faculty (1983, 1985, 1987) to determine shifts and constants in faculty attitude and practices.

Eleanor McKenna is Coordinator of the Junior/Senior Writing Program at the University of Michigan. Her research and publication interests are in discourse analysis of writing in the disciplines and composition. She has published articles on the analysis of academic discourse, and has just completed a study of longitudinal change in intellectual complexity in the writing of a group of twenty undergraduates at the University of Michigan.

Christine McMahon teaches freshman writing at Prince George's Community College and directs the college's Writing Center, which she developed. She holds an MA from Catholic University and has done further graduate work in teaching writing. A Fellow of the National Capital Area Writing Project, she does private consulting and has published in *Teaching English in the Two-Year College*.

Sally J. McNelis is English Department Chairman and Staff Development Coordinator at Golden Ring Middle School in Baltimore. She received her L.A. from Pennsylvania State University and her M.A. from Loyola College in Maryland. She has published "Improving Writing in the Disciplines" in *Educational Leadership*, April 1986; and coauthored with Gloria Neubert, Towson State University, "The Write Place: A Resource Center for Students and Teachers" in *Refocus*, April 1986 (Maryland Association for Supervision and Curriculum Development).

Charles Moran is Professor of English and Director of the University Writing Program at the University of Massachussetts. As an undergraduate he specialized in English after an extensive bout of Chemistry. He has taught at the University since 1967, moving from the teaching of literature, particularly the modern novel and eighteenth-century British literature, to the teaching of writing.

William J. Mullin is a theoretical physicist who does research on low-temperature quantum systems, especially liquid and solid helium. He received his Ph.D. from Washington University and has been at the University of Massachusetts since 1967. He does his best physics while running (and his best running while seated at his desk). He is coauthor of a textbook, *Introduction to the Structure of Matter*.

Barbara F. Nodine, a coauthor of *Writing in the Arts and Sciences* and *Readings in the Arts and Sciences*, and a coeditor of *Thinking, Reasoning, and Writing*, teaches developmental psychology and special education at Beaver College. A former president of the American Psychological Association Division on Teaching Psychology, she has written numerous research articles and essays on child development, story grammar, and the teaching of writing in psychology.

Anne Nordhus coordinates the Writing Effectiveness Screening Test and Writing Proficiency course program at California State University, Chico. She has taught English at university and high school levels, coordinated the Chico State Writing Center, and supervised student teachers. In the mid-1970s, she started a writing-across-the-curriculum program with an interdisciplinary group of student teachers under her supervision.

Patricia E. O'Connor came to Georgetown as coordinator of the Writing Program in 1983 after many years of high school teaching in urban schools. She directs a training program for teaching assistants as well as the Articulation Program with the D.C. Public Schools. She is currently teaching both in the English department and in a special adult-literacy program at Lorton Prison.

William Peirce has been a college teacher since 1965 and Chair of the Composition Department at Prince George's Community College since 1981. He has published critical articles on Conrad, Ford, and Hopkins, and has presented workshops on teaching literature and composition at national and regional conferences.

Elizabeth Renfro has been teaching English at California State University, Chico, since 1974 and has been coordinator of the Writing-Across-the-Disciplines program since 1985. A published poet, Renfro is also poetry and design editor for Flume Press, publishers of a yearly volume of poetry. Renfro's other writing includes a textbook *Basic Writing: Process and Product* (Holt, 1985), and *The Shastan Indians* (Naturegraph Press, forthcoming).

Mike Rose has taught in and administered a number of preparatory and developmental writing programs and is currently Associate Director of the UCLA Writing Programs. He has written on the cognition of composing, pedagogy, curriculum, development, and policy, and his recent work includes *Perspectives on Literacy* (coedited with Eugen Kintgen and Barry Kroll for Southern Illinois University Press) and, for The Free Press, a book on underpreparation in America entitled *Lives on the Boundary*.

Diane Shoos is Assistant Professor of French at Michigan Technological University with interests in French cinema and visual communication. She recently published an article in *Literature and Psychology*.

Jo-Ann M. Sipple is Professor and Chair, Department of Communications and Director, Writing Across the Curriculum, at Robert Morris College in Pennsylvania. She has taught a variety of language, literature, and writing courses at RMC for twenty years. She has authored two books—*The Writing Tutor: A Guide to Solving Common Writing Problems* (Charles Merrill, 1984), and *Teaching Writing: Making Theory Practice Connections* (Charles Merrill, 1984).

James F. Slevin is currently Chair of the English Department and Director of the Writing Program at Georgetown University, where he has taught since 1975. He has written and lectured widely on the teaching of writing, including the aims of university-wide writing programs.

Rosemary L. Smith has been a member of the Prairie Writing Project staff since 1977. She has given numerous workshops and lecture-demonstrations on the theory and practice of teaching writing. In addition to composition theory, her areas of expertise include the literature of the American frontier and Canadian literature. She currently teaches literature, composition, and Canadian Studies at Moorhead State University, where she is Professor of English. Her Ph.D. is from the University of Washington, in American Literature.

Mary Helen Spear has been a Professor of Psychology at Prince George's Community College since 1972. She received her B.S. from St. Louis University, and her M.A. and Ph.D. from the University of Maryland. She is currently involved in adult-learning and prior-learning assessment and is President of the Experimental Learning Assessment Network (ELAN).

Henry Steffens has been a faculty member of the University of Vermont since 1969. He received his M.A. and Ph.D. degrees from Cornell University. His teaching interests include the history of science, European cultural history, and the philosophy of history. He has published *Science, Technology and Culture* with H.N. Muller, *The Development of Newtonian Optics in England, James Prescott Joule and the Concept of Energy*, and *The History of Science in Western Civilization* with L.P. Williams. He recently completed *The Writer's Guide: History* with M. J. Dickerson.

Chris David Stenberg is Assistant Professor at Robert Morris College, Pittsburgh. His primary teaching responsibilities are in undergraduate cost and management accounting and secondary responsibilities in advanced accounting and auditing. Since WABD implementation, 274 students have taken the redesigned cost-accounting course. He is currently writing a college textbook in cost accounting that integrates WABD concepts.

Ellen Strenski is Assistant Director for Upper Division and Graduate Writing in the UCLA Writing Programs. She is coauthor of *The Research Paper Workbook* (2nd ed., Longman, 1985), *Making Connections Across the Curriculum* (Bedford, 1986), and *A Guide to Writing Sociology Papers* (St. Martin's, 1986). She is a contributor to *Writing Across the Curriculum: The Second Stage* (Jossey-Bass, 1988), and author of *Cross-Disciplinary Conversations About Writing* (St. Martin's, 1989).

Keith A. Tandy is a Professor of English at Moorhead State University, Moorhead, Minnesota, where he teaches remedial English and writing theory courses for teaching-credential candidates. He has a Ph.D. from the University of California, Berkeley. He is the Director of the Prairie Writing Project and the Coordinating Director of the Minnesota Writing Project, North Central Regional Director and a member of the Advisory Board of the National Writing Project.

Christopher J. Thaiss is Director of English Composition and former Director of the Plan for Alternative General Education at George Mason University. Active in the development of school and college writing-across-the-curriculum programs since 1978, he also coordinates a national network of these programs. Since 1978 he has been associate director of the Northern Virginia Writing Project. Thaiss's publications include *Speaking and Writing: Classroom Strategies and the New Research* (coedited with Charles Suhor), *Writing to Learn: Essays and Reflections on Writing Across the Curriculum* and *Language Across the Curriculum in the Elementary Grades*.

James W. Thomasson joined the Georgetown Theology Department in 1967 after receiving his Ph.D. in Religious Studies from Yale. In 1971 he received the Edward B.

Bunn Award for Faculty Excellence. In addition to scholarly books and articles, he has published two volumes of poetry and has spent many years working on an historical novel based on the life and thought of Kierkegaard.

Brooks Thorlaksson, former coordinator of both the Professional Development Program and the Basic Writing Program at California State University, Chico, currently teaches freshman and advanced composition courses and conducts workshops on writing and revision.

Barbara E. Walvoord is Associate Professor of Writing/Media at Loyola College in Maryland, and a founder and former codirector of BACWAC and the Maryland Writing Project. She has led many workshops on writing across the curriculum. She has authored *Helping Students Write Well: A Guide for Teachers in All Disciplines* (1986). Her published textbooks are *Three Steps to Revising Your Writing for Style, Grammar, Punctuation, and Spelling* (Glenview, IL: Scott, Foresman/Little, Brown, 1988) and *Writing: Strategies for All Disciplines* (Englewood Cliffs, NJ: Prentice Hall, 1985).

Timothy Wickham-Crowley has been an Assistant Professor of Sociology at Georgetown University since the fall of 1986. He teaches several undergraduate courses including "Political Sociology," "Social Movements," and "Revolutions and Society." His recent publications include "The Rise 'And Sometimes Fall' of Guerrilla Governments in Latin America" in *Sociological Forum*.

Joseph M. Williams is a professor of English and Linguistics at the University of Chicago. A teacher of writing, linguistics, and stylistics, he also serves as a consultant in these areas to the federal government and private corporations. His books include *Style and Variables in English* and *Style: Ten Lessons in Clarity and Grace*.

Art Young is Campbell Chair in Technical Communication and Professor of English and Professor of Engineering at Clemson University. He and Toby Fulwiler have coedited two other books on writing across the curriculum—*Language Connections: Writing and Reading Across the Curriculum* (NCTE, 1982), and *Writing Across the Disciplines: Research into Practice* (Boynton/Cook, 1986).

Stanley M. Zoltek received his Ph.D. from the State University of New York at Stony Brook and is an Associate Professor of Mathematics at George Mason University. Although he has taught a wide range of courses, he is especially interested in the role mathematics plays in general education. He has used writing both as a tool for teaching mathematics and as a means of helping students deal with their "math anxiety."